Re-Thinking International Relations Theory via Deconstruction

International Relations (IR) theorists have ceaselessly sought to understand, explain, and transform the experienced reality of international politics. Running through all these attempts is a persistent, yet unquestioned, quest by theorists to develop strategies to eliminate or reduce the antinomies, contradictions, paradoxes, dilemmas, and inconsistencies dogging their approaches. A serious critical assessment of the logic behind these strategies is however lacking. This new work addresses this issue by seeking to reformulate IR theory in an original way.

Arfi begins by providing a thorough critique of leading contemporary IR theories, including pragmatism, critical/scientific realism, rationalism, neo-liberal institutionalism and social-constructivism, and then moves on to strengthen and go beyond the valuable contributions of each approach by employing the logic of deconstruction pioneered by Derrida to explicate the consequences of taking into account the dilemmas and inconsistencies of these theories. The book demonstrates that the logic of deconstruction is resourceful and rigorous in its questioning of the presuppositions of prevailing IR approaches, and argues that relying on deconstruction leads to richer and more powerfully insightful pluralist IR theories and is an invaluable resource for taking IR theory beyond currently paralyzing 'wars of paradigms'.

Questioning universally accepted presuppositions in existing theories, this book provides an innovative and exciting contribution to the field, and will be of great interest to scholars of international relations theory, critical theory and international relations.

Badredine Arfi is associate professor of political science at the University of Florida. His research interests include international relations theory and deconstruction. He has published articles in *Millennium*, *International Political Sociology*, and *International Political Theory*.

Interventions
Edited by: Jenny Edkins, Aberystwyth University and
Nick Vaughan-Williams, University of Warwick

'As Michel Foucault has famously stated, "knowledge is not made for understanding; it is made for cutting." In this spirit The Edkins - Vaughan-Williams Interventions series solicits cutting edge, critical works that challenge mainstream understandings in international relations. It is the best place to contribute post disciplinary works that think rather than merely recognize and affirm the world recycled in IR's traditional geopolitical imaginary'
Michael J. Shapiro, University of Hawai'i at Mãnoa, USA

The series aims to advance understanding of the key areas in which scholars working within broad critical post-structural and post-colonial traditions have chosen to make their interventions, and to present innovative analyses of important topics.

Titles in the series engage with critical thinkers in philosophy, sociology, politics and other disciplines and provide situated historical, empirical and textual studies in international politics.

Critical Theorists and International Relations
Edited by Jenny Edkins and Nick Vaughan-Williams

Ethics as Foreign Policy
Britain, the EU and the other
Dan Bulley

Universality, Ethics and International Relations
A grammatical reading
Véronique Pin-Fat

The Time of the City
Politics, philosophy, and genre
Michael J. Shapiro

Governing Sustainable Development
Partnership, protest and power at the world summit
Carl Death

Insuring Security
Biopolitics, security and risk
Luis Lobo-Guerrero

Foucault and International Relations
New critical engagements
Edited by Nicholas J. Kiersey and Doug Stokes

International Relations and Non-Western Thought
Imperialism, colonialism and investigations of
global modernity
Edited by Robbie Shilliam

Autobiographical International Relations
I, IR
Edited by Naeem Inayatullah

War and Rape
Law, memory and justice
Nicola Henry

Madness in International Relations
Psychology, security and the global governance of mental health
Alison Howell

Spatiality, Sovereignty and Carl Schmitt
Geographies of the nomos
Edited by Stephen Legg

Politics of Urbanism
Seeing like a city
Warren Magnusson

Beyond Biopolitics
Theory, violence and horror in world politics
François Debrix and Alexander D. Barder

The Politics of Speed
Capitalism, the state and war in an accelerating world
Simon Glezos

Politics and the Art of Commemoration
Memorials to struggle in Latin America and Spain
Katherine Hite

Indian Foreign Policy
The politics of postcolonial identity
Priya Chacko

Politics of the Event
Time, movement, becoming
Tom Lundborg

Theorising Post-Conflict Reconciliation
Agonism, restitution and repair
Edited by Alexander Keller Hirsch

Europe's Encounter with Islam
The secular and the postsecular
Luca Mavelli

Re-Thinking International Relations Theory via Deconstruction
Badredine Arfi

The New Violent Cartography
Geo-analysis after the aesthetic turn
Edited by Sam Okoth Opondo and Michael J. Shapiro

Insuring War
Sovereignty, security and risk
Luis Lobo-Guerrero

Re-Thinking International Relations Theory via Deconstruction

Badredine Arfi

LONDON AND NEW YORK

First published 2012
by Routledge
2 Park Square, Milton Park, Abingdon, Oxon, OX14 4RN

Simultaneously published in the USA and Canada
by Routledge
711 Third Avenue, New York, NY 10017

Routledge is an imprint of the Taylor & Francis Group, an informa business

First issued in paperback 2013

© 2012 Badredine Arfi

The right of Badredine Arfi to be identified as author of this work has been asserted by him in accordance with the Copyright, Designs and Patent Act 1988.

Designs and Patents Act 1988. All rights reserved. No part of this book may be reprinted or reproduced or utilised in any form or by any electronic, mechanical, or other means, now known or hereafter invented, including photocopying and recording, or in any information storage or retrieval system, without permission in writing from the publishers.

Trademark notice: Product or corporate names may be trademarks or registered trademarks, and are used only for identification and explanation without intent to infringe.

British Library Cataloguing in Publication Data
A catalogue record for this book is available from the British Library

Library of Congress Cataloging in Publication Data
Arfi, Badredine.
Re-thinking international relations theory via deconstruction / Badredine Arfi.
  p. cm. – (Interventions)
Includes bibliographical references.
  1. International relations–Philosophy. 2. Deconstruction. I. Title. II. Title: Rethinking international relations theory via deconstruction.
  JZ1242.A74 2012
  327.101–dc23
           2011036838

ISBN: 978-0-415-78360-6 (hbk)
ISBN: 978-0-203-12736-0 (ebk)
ISBN: 978-0-415-71321-4 (pbk)

Typeset in Times New Roman
by Taylor & Francis Books

To Mariam and Youssef Tayebi

Contents

	Acknowledgments	xi
1	Re-thinking via deconstruction *qua* affirmation	1

Introduction 1
Re-thinking IR via (a reading of) Derrida's thinking 12
Outline of the chapters 20
Promises of Re-thinking IR theory via experiences of deconstruction 24

2	'Testimonial faith' in/about IR philosophy of science: the possibility condition of a pluralist science of world politics	26

Introduction 26
Jackson's plea for a Weber-inspired science in IR 29
Weber's ideal-type and the 'linguistic turn' 31
Jackson's testimonial faith for a wager-based miraculous science 41

3	Khôra as the condition of possibility of the ontological *without* ontology	54

Introduction 54
Critical realist ontology and Bhaskar's dialectic 56
The mode of negative theology and the logic of without 57
Khôra qua receptacle 61
Khôra as the condition of possibility of the ontological 63
Relevance to 'concrete' IR research, and more 64

4	Re-thinking the 'agent-structure' problematique: from ontology to *parergonality*	71

Introduction 71
Structure in IR literature 73
Structure through the work of deconstruction 76
Agency: a re-thinking via deconstruction 81
Re-thinking the agent-structure problematique 95

x Contents

    The parergonality of the 'agency-structure problem' and 'social theory' 98

5 Identity/difference and othering: negotiating the impossible politics of *aporia*   102

    Introduction 102
    Muslims in Western Europe 104
    Tibi: integration despite 'other-ing'? 107
    Tariq Ramadan: post-integration despite 'other-ing'? 109
    Identity, difference and undecidability 112
    Difference and deferral without positivity—différance 114
    Identity—a play 'out of joint' 118
    Othering—originary autoimmunity 124
    Beyond the aporia of othering? 127
    Going beyond the aporiatic politics of identity 132

6 Autoimmunity of trust *without* trust   136

    Introduction 136
    Theories of trust 138
    Undecidability and decision 141
    The as-if *gesture 143*
    Autoimmunity of as-if trust, subject, and responsibility 151
    Aporiatic politics of trust 153

7 Re-thinking international constitutional order: the autoimmune politics of binding *without* binding   157

    Introduction 157
    Binding, performative violence, and antoimmunity 158
    The aporia of binding 166
    Lessons 168

8 The quest for 'illogical' logics of action in IR   170

    The 'logic of action' 170
    Logic of communicative action (argument) 173
    Logics of consequences and appropriation 186
    Logic of practice 190
    Logic of habit 197
    The undecidability and autoimmunity of logics of action 201

9 Concluding *without* a Conclusion   203

    Notes   211
    Bibliography   224
    Index   235

Acknowledgments

I wish to express my deepest thanks and gratitude to many who have helped me in bringing this book to fruition through their feedback, support and encouragement, directly and indirectly, knowingly and unknowingly. I remain especially indebted to Nick Onuf, Maja Zehfuss, and Larry George for their invaluable inputs. I also thank Stefano Guzzini, Benjamin Herborth, Patrick Jackson, Oliver Kessler, Hans-Martin Jaeger, Torsten Michel, Martin Weber, and Colin Wight for very interesting discussions and feedback on the topics of the book on various ISA panels. Oliver Kessler deserves all the credit for organizing these panels and a forum in the Review of International Studies.

Earlier versions of some chapters of this book have been published before or presented at various conferences. Some parts of Chapter 5 were published in "Euro-Islam: Going beyond the Aporiatic Politics of Othering," *Journal of International Political Sociology*, 4 (3) (September 2010): 236–252 (Wiley Blackwell publisher). Chapter 6 is a revised version of "Auto-Immunity of Trust without Trust," *Journal of International Political Theory* 6 (2) (October 2010): 188–216 (Edinburgh University press). Chapter 7 is a revised version of "Rethinking International Constitutional Order: The Auto-immune Politics of Binding without Binding," *Millennium: Journal of International Studies* 39 (2) (December 2010): 299–321 (Sage publisher). A version of Chapter 3 was accepted for publication in the *Review of International Studies* before the book was contracted and is in press under the title of "*Khôra* as the Condition of Possibility of the Ontological without Ontology" as part of a forum organized by Oliver Kessler. I gratefully thank the anonymous reviewers and editors of these journals for their important critiques and feedbacks.

An earlier version of Chapter 5 was presented at the *Workshop for Islam in Europe*, organized by the Center of European Studies, University of Florida, March 6, 2009. An earlier version of Chapter 2 was presented at the *Workshop on Epistemology and Method In International Relations*, March 26–27, 2010, University of Florida. A part of Chapter 3 was presented at the *51st International Studies Association (ISA) Annual Convention* at New Orleans, Louisiana, February 17-20, 2010. Parts of Chapters 1 and 8 were presented at the *52nd International Studies Association (ISA) Annual Convention*, March

16–19, 2011, Montreal, Canada. I am grateful to all participants on the panels where these papers were presented for their valuable feedbacks.

I thank Craig Fowlie, Nicola Parkin, Jennifer Edkins, and Nicholas Vaughan-Williams at Routledge for their supportive feedback on, and speedy processing of, my proposal and the whole manuscript. I also thank Paola Celli, senior production editor, for her excellent work.

Last and not least, my warmest gratitude goes to my family.

1 Re-thinking via deconstruction *qua* affirmation

Introduction

This book is an effort to re-think international relations (IR) theory, or, more accurately, various theories of IR, yet without suggesting a new paradigmatic 'ism', a synthesis of sorts, or any type of grand theorizing. Rather, the book proposes a new conceptual-operational framework for critiquing and re-thinking IR theories.

Why am I using 're-think' with a hyphen and not simply 'rethink' as one word, or 'think' *tout court* since every re-thinking is a thinking anyway? Why am I writing 'theories' and not simply 'theory'?

I take the position that any thinking is inescapably a re-thinking because there always is more or less iteration in it of traces of what preceded it. However, I simultaneously take the position that any re-thinking is also more or less invention, an innovative thinking within which there are traces of expectations of what might come after it. There always is a constitutive concatenation of change, invention and repetition in a process of re-thinking/thinking. Repetition takes the form of traces that shape, or haunt through and through, whatever we think in re-thinking. As the saying goes, we cannot build anything without relying on the shoulders of the previous/existing giants—so-called major works and defining texts and theories. The invention shows up as an unpredicted and un-anticipated coming of new ways of otherwise conceptualizing, arguing, formulating, and critiquing.

This book takes thus the dual position, first, that simultaneous iteration and change is the condition of possibility of thinking, that is, without iteration and change no thinking is possible, and, second, that simultaneous iteration and change is also the condition of impossibility of a thinking *qua* originary thinking. That is, iteration and change always already inscribe traces both of past and future (as expectations of) thinking in any present thinking, including the most innovative ones. Therefore, in thinking we cannot not be re-thinking.

Why 'theories' in the plural and not simply 'theory'? First, it has become widely accepted in the study of IR (and social science or social theory discipline as well as philosophy) that seeking a 'grand theory' of anything is a totalitarian delusion and an utopian illusion that harm and obstruct the process of thinking more than help the understanding of the subject-matter of study. It is no surprise that students of IR of all stripes are divided and continuously so, thereby remaining engaged in a seemingly never ending proliferation and dissemination of 'isms', approaches, etc.; a situation that IR enjoys or suffers from (depending where you stand on the issue of pluralization and diversification). As such we cannot not speak always already of theories as a multitude and in the plural. Second, this is a book about theories of IR, or, more accurately, it is an effort that seeks to read, critique and re-affirm through almost unavoidable displacements a number of theoretical/conceptual works in IR in ways more or less different from what is customarily done in so-called mainstream of IR discipline. In other words, I read a number of IR texts to re-think their 'thinking' of IR. In doing so I neither simply negate nor do I simply re-affirm them; I do both and neither at the same time, more or less. I thus critique to affirm, re-affirm to displace, and displace to open the horizon of thinking to/in unanticipated ways of thinking and conceptualizing. I thus read to re-affirm the possibility of other readings, readings that keep the possibility of futural readings always already open.

In affirming, re-affirming, displacing, and opening the thinking of IR to future possibilities of thinking that simultaneously entail risks and chances, I deploy a 'new language' or 'framework' with which and through which I proceed to explore the various theories. In other words, I suggest a conceptual framework or, more precisely, a framework of conception which makes it possible to affirm, re-affirm and displace as well as keep always open the possibility of future (re-)conceptualizations inherent within the process of conceptual thinking. Yet my reliance on this 'language' does not strictly mean that I rely on so-called 'linguistic turn' in social theory and philosophy, or, more generally put, in various ways of thinking about life (and death). However, I do not deny the importance of the 'linguistic turn'. To the contrary, I find it inescapable, if however in a certain way as I explicate later on in the book. My thinking about IR is unavoidably impregnated with the imperative of a 'linguistic turn'. I thus espouse the 'linguistic turn' through and through and yet this espousal while being an affirmation and re-affirmation of the 'linguistic turn' is also simultaneously a displacement—another turn of the turn, a turn which is both a turn and an un-turn, without being a complete return. It repeats and changes what it means to take a 'linguistic turn' in thinking IR, with the change assuming the form of a work of deconstruction, a disseminative work, a work that disseminates in re-affirming the 'linguistic turn' and its prior 'others'. This dissemination is constitutive (in important ways) of the ways of reading that I engage into. Consequently, the 'language' that I speak of herein is not just a medium within which one can develop one's own thinking/rethinking, a conclusion which of course concords with the spirit and practice of the 'linguistic turn'. Indeed speaking in/from within a language which is understood à la 'linguistic turn' means that there is an 'other' to language that is 'beyond/outside' language but cannot be addressed or thought of 'outside' language, an 'other' that manifests itself and arrives through and within the process of re-thinking the theories of IR à la 'linguistic turn', in a certain way.

My re-thinking of IR theory is in certain ways internal to IR through and through. I cannot begin except by relying on 'original' and 'authoritative' works of IR, that is, originally published and received as IR works. Yet I can neither exclude nor preclude other—so-called not typically IR—works from supplementing these 'originary' IR works, thereby showing the 'originary' debts of so-called authoritative IR works to various 'outsides' of IR. This eventually leads the project towards directions that are non-controllable not only in questioning and enlarging what can be defined as 'IR' as such (if this is possible or meaningful), but also towards 'endpoints' that seem to always remain deferred, suffering an incessant process of differentiation, yet a differentiation that always fails to efface the traces of the spectral haunting of the original IR works which I read and critique in the first place. In other words, my way of reading and re-thinking the IR works that I focus on seeks to 'meet' the 'other' within these works through the textual weaving of these very works when read through the 'conceptual language' that I use, that is, through works of deconstruction that bring forth their own pseudo-conceptual apparatuses, all the while avoiding an appropriation of this 'other' by turning it into a familiar linguistic being (that is, a concept).

On the one hand, one might think of these readings as 'immanent' readings since I rely on the conceptual frameworks deployed in the very texts themselves to read them, if in different ways however. *On the other hand*, the immanent readings are accurately speaking not faithfully immanent as they bring forth *pseudo-concepts* that undermine the 'origin' and context of immanence. In other words, the immanent readings are rendered and exposed as originarily autoimmune, that is, as inherently and constitutively self-perverting their origins and the immanent readings since they disclose an always already spectrally haunted nature of the texts themselves. The immanent readings reveal a constitutive heterogeneity and heteronomy of the IR theoretical texts. The theories are thus found to follow a logic of undecidable aporia, which continuously displaces through deferral and differentiation whatever presuppositions are posited to undergird the theories themselves and the thinking thereof.

Because of this way of reading theories of IR, I am not claiming to present a new theory or theories of IR as such. Nor am I claiming to present an integrated story—a sort of synthesis—about a given set of theories that address a certain issue-area of IR literature. Rather, on the face of it the book might seem to be a collection of a variety of insights and critiques of various topics or issue-areas, some dealing with 'foundational' issues, others dealing with practical and/or policy problems, and others dealing with methodological ways of thinking of IR. While these choices are indeed more or less eclectically and somewhat arbitrarily done, they do nonetheless illustrate, if indirectly perhaps, one of the motives driving any engagement in a work of deconstruction. Whereas I am not presenting a 'coherent' narrative on so-called substantive issues I do believe that there is a good degree of faithfulness to the claim of the project—that is, to present a re-thinking of IR theories. More specifically: I am seeking to re-think IR theories by engaging them into works of deconstruction. Because of this, some might say that this is the overriding theme of the project, a meta-narrative of the book. I agree if with a cautionary 'perhaps', that is, I agree only under the condition of a destabilizing, without being destructive, 'perhaps'.

On the one hand, I do engage into a work of deconstruction in every chapter of the book. I thus critique and supplement to displace all the theories that I focus on, with supplements that not only question but also add something new to the stories being told in the theories. *On the other hand*, my supplements are never conclusive enough (in the common sense of the term conclusion, that is, to come to an end or bring an end) either to jettison what I begin with, or to present what I add as replacements of certain elements of critiqued theories. Yet, the supplements are presented as being necessary and inescapable. Why? Simply because my supplements are not just at the level of theories, they also are at the level of the presuppositions of the theories, by which I mean the conditions of possibility and impossibility of the theories, whether the latter speak of ontology, epistemology, methodology, logic, practice, or anything else. At this point, one might be led to conclude that this book is thus about the conditions of possibility and impossibility of a given set of IR theories, or even perhaps that it is about theorizing IR without claiming a grand theory of theorizing. Neither statement is inaccurate, that is, more or less. Indeed, *on the one hand*, this is in part what I do in the various chapters.

Yet, *on the other hand*, speaking of conditions of possibility and impossibility raises the issue of such a 'speaking and/or writing' in and of itself. In other words, I am not only engaged in critiquing the various theories from 'certain' angles, I am also simultaneously undermining the very process of formulating IR theories by speaking of the conditions of impossibility of these theories. One key marker (if one can put in this way) of a work of deconstruction is to neither destruct/destroy nor stabilize a theory (or a text, to put it more broadly), yet there always is some level of undermining in a certain way. The undermining itself occurs in different ways.

First, the work of deconstruction shows that any theory is always already sustainable only via a conscious deployment of some sort of amnesia about the 'borrowings' from outside IR theories, borrowings that are rhetorically used to legitimate and authoritatively anchor the validity of the theoretical arguments, borrowings that are presupposed to be self-sustaining even when and after they are de-contextualized away from their originary contexts and texts (assuming that this is more or less possible). Yet deconstruction shows that such an amnesia is never complete because the text remains haunted by the traces of the theories, concepts, ideas, and contexts that the amnesia seeks to efface, not only at the level of rhetoric but also at the constitutive and/or conceptual level, and even more so at the level of conditions of possibility and impossibility of the theories themselves, in the language deployed and in the analytics of the arguments presented.

Second, the work of deconstruction shows that the role of the speaker, writer, analyst is inseparable from the framing process that the texts resort to in formulating arguments and the like. Not only do we see this not surprisingly at the level of 'rhetoric' (if by this we mean the usual understanding of rhetoric), but also in the performativity of the text. The text is presented as being constative, and it indeed is. Yet it also is inescapably performative, and it makes what it claims to be making by 'saying it', by saying and implying that it is constative. The constative cannot escape being performative and the performative cannot occur without being constative. Yet because the two are inextricably mutually constituted, they more or less neutralize the claims of the text in the very moment that the text makes its 'claims'. In other words, the text claims to be making an event, that is, to eventually and eventfully introduce some theoretical arguments to the literature, and because of this the text is deconstructible. The work of deconstruction brings forth the aporiatic nature of the text in making the claims that it makes. This *'second hand'* leads to a *'third hand'*.

On a third hand, I show in my practice (of writing) that the claims of the project are also at work within my very text. In other words, my text is (more or less) an instantiation of the pseudo-conceptual framework that I deploy in seeking to immanently critique a number of IR theories through a work of deconstruction. My text deconstructs itself through itself by ineluctably putting into practice the various aporias that inhere not only in the theories that I critique but also in the conceptual, logical, rhetorical strategies and 'pseudo-concepts' that I rely on in trying to make the cases that I claim to be making. Put differently: As the reader might have already noticed I am writing this introduction at this very moment using the pseudo-concepts (such as aporia, dissemination, autoimmunity, supplement, trace, non-originary origin, spectrality, etc.) that I use in the immanent critiques of the following chapters. Yet, were I to succeed in doing so, that is, in introducing my book using the pseudo-conceptual framework of deconstruction in a strict and exclusive way, this would imply that I failed in fact in carrying out the project. Why? Because if I were to succeed in, say, satisfying readers with critical (deconstructive) eyes, this would imply perhaps a certain closure is possible. This would be the Achilles' heel of my project. This leads to the issue of impossible closure that the work of deconstruction always shows to be the case in any text and hence any theory, both in the text being deconstructed and in the work of deconstruction itself, that is, in the text reporting the work of deconstruction.

The issue of closure is of great importance in deconstruction because it seeks and demonstrates the non-closure of any text (theory and otherwise). This however does not fare well with most students of social sciences. Many students of IR do indeed raise questions like: If we were not interested in seeking closure on theorizing IR, even if only at the level of a (Kantian-like) regulative idea, utopia, or telos, what is the purpose of the whole enterprise? What would be the purpose of the 'social scientific' enterprise of the study of IR? What would be the utility of IR theory as a way of impacting on the world or reconstructing it? Not only is it often assumed that accumulation of knowledge is a primarily normative goal (e.g., in statements such as "now we understand better" and the like), it also is the case that many students of IR (and other social sciences) would see their enterprise as futile if they were not driven by a goal of seeking closure, even if only as a norm and even if only as a temporary closure which is potentially liable to ad hoc addenda. Yet closure is the *nemesis* of deconstruction, or, more accurately, deconstruction sees closure as violent totalitarianism. Unfortunately, to many this makes deconstruction nihilistic. This is an issue that I explore in three ways.

First, I show the impossibility of closure through the immanent critiques that I develop. I thus explicate a number of irresolvable aporias that necessarily haunt the various theories that I explore.

Second, I suggest a re-thinking of the process of theorizing which does not seek closure through resolving these aporias but rather structurally makes non-closure as the condition of possibility of theorizing itself.

Third, I endeavor to be as forthcoming as I can be about the conditions of impossible closure in my own exploration of these issues by deploying the very pseudo-concepts of the work of deconstruction. I thus engage in a sort of immanent self-deconstruction to the extent that I can perform it. Of course, were I to believe that I might succeed in this effort, it would mean a closure of my own argument and hence the failure of my very argument on the impossibility of closure. Yet the failure is precisely the success of the whole enterprise. In other words, the project has two simultaneous continuous moments or turns. *On the one hand*, I endeavor to be as accurate, thorough and complete as I can be in developing various works of deconstruction, that is, in immanently critiquing the theories and then re-affirming them in different ways through a deployment of pseudo-concepts of deconstruction and thus explicating the aporias inherent within the theories and extensions thereof. *On the other hand*, the very explications of the aporias and the deployment of deconstruction's pseudo-concepts also inherently prevent/preempt a closure, that is, an erasure, effacement, or lifting of the aporias of the theories.

This makes my conclusions always already deconstructible. This means that attempting to reach any conclusion regarding the success or failure of my works of deconstruction inherently also turns out to be an aporia resulting from two imperative calls both of which are irresistible. *On the one hand*, there is an (institutional, disciplinary, practical, pragmatic, ego-psychological, even, some would say, ethical) urgent call to reach—or, at least, to seek—closure at every turn of the project. *On the other hand*, there is deconstruction's call for resisting closure forever.

Because I show through the very experience of writing about the practice of deconstruction that my conclusions are always already deconstructible, I expect that opponents of deconstruction (and like-minded) approaches to see the project as yet another dangerous attempt that threatens the scientific, or, at least, the scholarly and serious character of IR theory. They would consider the project as inherently wrong and thus a failure, even going as far as describing it to be nihilistic. I also expect sympathizers whom I can envision to be at least of two types (and many more). A first group might see the project as a success in playing the 'game' of deconstruction, without necessarily adhering to any particular or more or less general aspect, or to the conclusions, of the project. A second group might see (the success or failure of) the project as an instantiation of the work of self-deconstruction of the project within itself.

My point is that the possible occurrence—the possibility as such—of all these (and possibly many other) attitudes is what the project is about, that is, as a project that seeks to experience what it argues through a work of deconstruction, in the text and through the readership context of the text. To put it in a summary form: I want to show an 'inherent' work of deconstruction of my book within my book as it unfolds and evolves through my writing. An overall goal of this book is thus to offer a frame of thinking about IR theory through works of deconstruction via a deployment of pseudo-concepts that constitutively evade/prevent/preempt positing any closure, both at the level of the critiques of IR theory and at the level of the context of these critiques, that is, in my writing reporting my experience of deconstructing the texts of IR theory (with the important note that the two levels are always mutually implicated).

Yet such an endeavor is self-contradictory—a performative contradiction—because the project is a book with a finite number of pages and words, thereby suffering from a violently self-imposed (physical and more or less conceptual) closure, if I desire the book to see the light of publication. *On the one hand*, this is inescapable for any human effort—the only book that would not suffer from violent closure of some sort is a book that is not written and remains always to come. *On the other hand*, what this project seeks to do is to avoid, or, more strictly speaking, to explicate what it means to claim not to be abiding by the usual spatial logic of inside/outside. In other words: the project seeks to conceptualize how it (any book) transgresses the very logic that defines it *qua* book through a delineation of boundaries between its 'inside' and the 'outside'.

That this indeed is *de facto* the case for any book is testified to, for example, by what we refer to as bibliography and multitude of citations in the text, footnotes and endnotes, and so on. Without these supplements no book could be thought of as such in today's world of publishing. These previous works amount to a condition of possibility of the book, thereby defending, for example, the belief in the hypothesis of accumulation of knowledge. They also are the condition of impossibility of the book because at the same time they undermine the 'proper' character of the book, the book as standing for a 'proper book' (much like a 'proper name'), as a singular contribution to the

8 *Re-thinking via deconstruction* qua *affirmation*

literature, in one way or another. Of course not adding the supplement is out of question because the book would then be charged, prosecuted and sanctioned for plagiarism, a death sentence for the author's subjectivity *qua* author.

However, despite this normative framework for publishing and writing, which is often but not always enforced through norms of academic or otherwise integrity and laws of copyright and the like, the very theorization process in and of itself as usually thought of and practiced (in IR and elsewhere) is not faithful to this *de facto* constitutive norm of what counts as a book, or, more generally, text. I do not mean to say that authors are dishonest or corrupt; rather, I want to highlight the impossibility of such a task, that is, the task of producing a 'proper' book or 'proper' theory (*qua* text), a singular text, a text which is not haunted by traces of the memories of the past and traces of expectations about the future (of the text and its author). Put differently: A text constitutively and originarily makes a promise that it is a 'singular' contribution which does not violate the norm banning plagiarism. Yet a promise is not a promise as such if it is not pervertible, that is, a promise constitutively carries within it the possibility of being breached.

This can be seen to be instantiated in how for the most part theories are built through concepts and frameworks that obey certain conceptual logics. Yet very few students of social sciences probe into the presuppositions that undergird their logics of thinking, arguing and writing. I am not here speaking of the logic of, say, rationalist or constructivist theories, although these are not excluded. I am more importantly referring to the presupposed constitutive logics that undergird these theoretic-substantive (for a lack of a better term) logics. For example, IR students speak of logics of consequences, appropriateness, practice, and habit, etc., as logics of action. The work of deconstruction shows (in upcoming chapters) that these logics are presupposing certain conditions of possibility which are also conditions of impossibility of these logics. Deconstruction shows that these logics suffer from an undecidable aporia of non-closure, even when claimed to be closed, even if only more or less so. Deconstruction also shows that they cannot escape a constitutive dependence on what can be termed (to use a commonly accepted sense of logic) as 'illogical' and as based, for example, on negations of Aristotelian laws of the excluded middle or non-contradiction. Moreover, deconstruction shows that these negations are not in a Hegelian sense. Rather, these are negations that negate while still affirming, and affirm while still negating, they negate and denegate at the same time—they are negations without negation.

This is illustrated in so-called Weberian notion and technique of 'ideal-type'. It is usually the case that students of IR (and social science/theory) think of the logics of action as ideal-types which are, according to Weber, not to be found in the 'empirical' world as such. Not only does the work of deconstruction show that these Weberian ideal-types are constitutively speaking not as ideal as Weber presents them to be, they are rather 'too' historical and thus inescapably 'too' empirical. It also shows that the thinking that deploys these ideal-types and the like are anchored in conditions of possibility that are also conditions of impossibility of such thinking (and conceptualizing) methodologies (in the sense of Weber). The work of deconstruction shows the non-neatness of the logic of ideal-type methodology in that it is anchored in precisely what it seeks to efface, the irrational and the historical, or more generally, the unessential 'other', an 'other' of what is supposed to be essential to the logic of ideal types. Therefore, the project shows how the 'outside' or 'other' of logic is inherently present in the 'inside' or 'logic' of logic (so to speak) and that the spatiality of inside/outside (of a theory, a logic, etc.) is in itself undecidable and always dependent on conditions of possibility that create the sense of spacing between the inside and outside, a sense of fuzzy spacing that simultaneously undermines the inside/outside opposition.

What the work of deconstruction thus suggests is that theorizing or speaking of logic *cannot not* be a restless process of negotiation between what is conditional and the impossible unconditional which is independent of conditions and contexts. Yet deconstruction does not deny that decisions about theories and logics of action are made, that is, that the process of shuttling negotiations is interrupted, and that it is interrupted because of a sense of urgency that necessarily accompanies the undecidability that mares and constitutes the process of theorizing and, more generally, writing books; books that might become authoritative enough to set standards and even more or less recast thinking on certain issues, and perhaps even the very processes of theorizing, writing, and thinking. This implies that the never resting shuttling negotiation comes to a halt, even if it is not a permanent stop. Put differently: This is the problem of the authoritativeness of a book, a text, and IR theory as theoretical texts.

Decisions are made and as such they determine what goes up and what goes down not only in the realm of publishing, that is, at the level of presses (academic and commercial), Decisions are also made at the level of reviewers and editors and so on; decisions that are done following certain norms and habits, etc. Yet these decisions are never merely decisions on a finite set of options that are evaluated according to a set of criteria, and so on and so forth. In fact at any level of the decision making process there is much undecidability, an undecidability that forces, or more accurately, calls upon a would-be decider to decide while inescapably assuming responsibility for the decision, knowing very well that the knowledge acquired for the sake of making the decision is not, will never be, enough. That is: the decision maker is faced with undecidability but cannot escape the urgency of deciding, thereby assuming the responsibility for the decision, a responsibility that verges on irresponsibility because ultimately made under conditions of non-knowledge or non-relevance/insufficiency of available knowledge, post hoc justifications to the contrary notwithstanding. And yet such decisions produce positions of authority for certain works and not others. This means that such an authority is through and through political, indeed an aporiatic political act that all existing institutional norms and practices as well as personal normative and otherwise commitments and rationalizations can never explain/justify, at least not to the full satisfaction of the 'other' affected by the decision that creates a position of authority for a certain work.

This however does not prevent us from continuing to write 'impossible-to-close' books and seek to publish them, seek an audience of acceptance, or even better, critique, both of which counting as a measure of recognition, if not always accompanied with a fame of authoritativeness. We cannot control the *fate* of our writings and yet we have *faith*, a certain faith even if not acknowledged as such, or not acknowledged at all. Such a faith is the condition of possibility of our belief in a possible future for our writings, that is, that the writings would somehow survive after the authors are done writing them. We see the future to come as promising a chance for our work to be recognized and make a difference. Yet we also know that the future is simultaneously the possibility of a threat of oblivion to our work. We nonetheless do proceed, we keep saying *yes* to a future that we struggle to keep open, a futural future. This is what we do in so-called 'practice' of writing books.

This project seeks to show these (as well as what some might say counterparts of these) aspects of the future at work in a book—this book—about IR theory. The project seeks thus to include in its pseudo-conceptual framework the notion and practice of letting the future be always a future so as to keep the future always open to new possibilities and, of course, impossibilities, to new chances and threats. Put differently: this book seeks to deconstruct a number of IR theories as well as the context of these works of deconstruction, a context which is nothing but this very text. Moreover, this text (book) has a context, that is, all previous texts that this book explicitly or implicitly relies on and draws from. This book thus seeks to show that, as Derrida said it, '*il n' y a pas de hors texte*' (there is no outside text), which, as Derrida explained many times, means that there is nothing outside the context.[1] This implies that this book (text) does not possess a demarcated self-identity even if it would have a physical existence—it is a text, within layers upon layers of texts; a book is never identical to itself at any point in time, is never present as a self-identical book. What does this mean?

This issue is one illustration of the larger issue of how identity is re-thought through the work of deconstructing the notion of time, or, more accurately, in the context of this book, time *qua* conceptual time that undergirds every conceptual framework and its concepts as deployed in IR theory and social theories in general. That deconstructing time is an important issue in IR theory has to do with the fact that rarely is the question of time raised at the level of presuppositions whenever, wherever and under whatever form time is brought forth into a conceptual framework. That there are many explicitly time-dependent theories in IR and social theory is not the issue here. What this project does is to raise the question of the presuppositions of the notion of time, a concept which is usually taken as self-evident in these theories. In other words: what are the conditions of possibility and impossibility of the notion of time as deployed, for example, in IR? Deconstructing the notion of time is a *sine qua non* act of the work of deconstruction; it is one of the key markers of deconstruction, if deconstruction can mark.

Briefly: The fact that any notion of 'now' is inherently constituted through a demarcation between a present 'now', a past 'now', and a future 'now', and that this demarcation cannot be pinned down, that is, before the moment we intend to seek to pin down a present 'now' it is a future 'now' and the moment we think that we pinned it down or are pinning it down, it has already receded into a past 'now' after having been a future 'now', and so on and so forth. This implies that all what we are dealing with are traces of past 'now' and future 'now'. It means that every instant of time is nothing but a movement of traces and that therefore the very identity of any moment or instant is constitutively made up of traces, their past and future movements.

This implies that because time is nothing but what remains or comes as traces, every identity is never identical to itself at any moment; the self is constitutively divided, always already. Deconstructing the notion of identity of 'anything' in this way, as the consequence of the deconstructed notion of time due to the movement of trace, implies that any concept has no identity; it means that any concept always already constitutively differs from itself and is deferred through a spacing of its identity due to a movement of traces. Therefore, the final, ultimate or unique meaning of any concept can *never* be pinned down (a fact which is widely recognized) despite incessant and tremendous efforts to better conceptualizations and refinements of methodologies. Deconstruction shows that this is so because the condition of possibility of any concept is at the same time the condition of its impossibility, that is, a concept cannot be identical to itself; a concept cannot 'be'; it is never 'is'; its 'is' never is. As Ferdinand de Saussure argued many decades ago this has to do with the fact that a language (and any system of signification) is made up of differences without any positivities that differ, and that these differences are always a movement of differentiation which implies that the meaning of any sign is always deferred, always to come and never arrested anywhere in language. Eventually this Sausserian insight led to the 'linguistic turn' mentioned earlier.

This is the movement that this project *qua* book seeks to show in its own text, in its signifying dynamic weaving, a weaving which takes expression in pseudo-concepts that are constituted through the movement of traces, pseudo-concepts that emerge through a work of deconstructing theories of IR and that are then put to work in the very text reporting on the work of deconstruction. This project by deploying these pseudo-concepts shows its own deconstructibility and thus both the chance of its non-teleological perfectibility and the risk of its pervertibility, a chance and a risk which are heterogeneous to one another, yet indissociable from one another, showing up always together.

Interrupting this restless shuttling of negotiating the purpose and strategy of the book, I move on in the next section of this introduction to discuss briefly as a warm-up exercise some elements of Derrida's work on deconstruction that I call upon in writing this book. The last section of the chapter then points very briefly to key points of the subsequent chapters.

Rethinking IR via (a reading of) Derrida's thinking

Drawing on Jacques Derrida's *œuvre* in re-thinking IR theory is not something new. Yet it is never an easy task for a number of reasons. First, Derrida's work is very large, very complex and not easily explicable, to say the least. Not only Derrida is a philosopher; he also is his 'own' brand of philosophy that does not abide by many norms of 'academic' philosophy. His work is at the same time philosophical and literary, more or less, and more rather than less, and sometimes beyond both. His style of writing is at times 'authentically' philosophical, at other times 'genuinely' literary, and in most cases both at the same time, while at still other times it is neither and in fact destabilizes both while re-affirming both and more—Derrida's genre, if he has one and I am almost sure that he would not accept this claim, is not uniformly discernible; it is (would I dare to say) undecidable. Derrida's writings/ lectures/interviews in most cases illustrate or put to work what he writes/ speaks in them. His interventions through speeches, writings, and acts are simultaneously constative and performative of the work of deconstruction.[2]

Second, Derrida's work is by and large not recognized in IR theory. Although there are forays (and increasingly more so I should emphasize), he remains as far as so-called mainstream is concerned more of a stranger in IR theory, if not perceived as simply a nihilistic way of thinking about politics or anything else for that matter. Usually when mentioned Derrida often than not gets incorporated into the so-called trends of 'post-modernism' and/or 'post-structuralism', characterizations that of course not only he never accepted, nor do they reflect the vastness and richness of his thought, let alone his writing style which is a marker of his thought. There is however a good number of students of IR who have sought to draw on Derrida's thinking in their efforts to address various issues and aspects of the study of IR.

The following works thus illustrate the richness and novelty of drawing on Derrida's work to conceptualize and re-think IR theory: David Campbell's *National Deconstruction: Violence, Identity, and Justice in Bosnia*, Maja Zehfuss' *Constructivism in International Relations: The Politics of Reality*, Jenny Edkins' *Poststructuralism and International Relations: Bringing the Political Back In*, and Dan Bulley's *Ethics as Foreign Policy: Britain, the EU and the Other*.[3] Whereas Campbell[4] and Bulley draw on Derrida to analyze the possibility and practice (or lack thereof) of ethics in IR, Edkins and Zehfuss draw on Derrida to critique/rethink IR theory.

In her effort to 'bring the political back in' IR theory, Edkins (1999: 65) presents "a reading of Derrida that sees his work as addressing 'the political' from the first." She (Edkins 1999: 65) thus argues that Derrida's "work on the undecidable is central to the argument concerning repoliticization" of IR that she calls for. Zehfuss draws on Derrida's deconstruction to submit constructivist thinking of IR, more specifically, the thinking of three key figures—Nicholas Onuf, Friedrich Kratochwil, and Alexander Wendt—to a rigorous critique to disclose how the 'politics of reality' is played out within IR theory. Through a "Derridean commitment," Zehfuss (2002: 10) is able "to reveal not what the constructivists in question *intend* to do, but what their theories do do, that is, how their own assumptions undermine their stated purpose and make their theories unravel." Zehfuss' strategy consists in deconstructing simultaneously what we usually call theoretical arguments (in this case, constructivism) and empirical materials (German military involvement abroad) based on her "interpretation of Derrida's claim that 'there is nothing outside of the text'," (Zehfuss 2002: 10). She concludes that "although constructivism is about construction [of the reality of international politics], it takes reality as in many ways given" (Zehfuss 2002: 35). Zehfuss (2002: 36) then makes the general point that "the challenge is to overcome the boundaries of our thinking which make us believe that we are constrained by reality, rather than by our vocabulary, by our inability to think beyond what we construe as reality." Zehfuss does not seek to resolve this issue with any certainty. Rather, she seeks to take up "the issue of why such a politics is necessary and why it is impossible unless we question the idea of reality as a limit" (Zehfuss 2002: 37). She states at the end of the book that "precisely because 'reality' appears to lock us in, appears to be an insurmountable boundary, inventing new gestures which might enable us to respond to the demands of responsibility towards others, however imperceptibly, requires all our creative energy. Making problematic what appears to us as real is only the first step, but it is a necessary one" (Zehfuss 2002: 263). Isn't Zehfuss, even if seemingly only through a 'mere' rhetorical gesture, effectively and actually ending her book by powerfully widely re-opening the horizon of future thinking of IR theory? I think so.

Starting from a deep 'empirical' analysis of the tragedy of the 'national deconstruction' of Bosnia, Campbell calls for "a substantial rethinking of the categories and relationships that constitute the political imaginary of international society," that is, a "deconstructive thought" which is a "necessary prerequisite for historical and political progress" (Campbell 1998: 13–14). Campbell thus draws on Jacques Derrida and Emmanuel Levinas to re-think ethics, politics, and subjectivity. Campbell proposes that "only the ethos of deconstructive thought can appreciate the contradictions, paradoxes, and silences of political problems in a complex world" (Campbell 1998: 242). Despite, or rather because of, the urgency of solving the world's problems, such as the Bosnian tragedy, "deconstructive thought," states Campbell at the end of the book, "calls for an ongoing political process of critique and invention that is never satisfied that a lasting solution can or has been reached" (Campbell 1998: 242). Much like Zehfuss, Campbell seeks—after all has been done and said—to keep open the future of new possibilities, to let the future always already have a future, how? They both offer a deconstructive way of re-thinking politics that lets politics be politics and not simply a pre-determined/calculated program of action.

Bulley focuses on the issue of ethics in foreign policy. Using a deconstructive analysis, he argues that "all criteria for judging ethics, both in policy *and* academic circles, destabilize themselves in such a way that no firm foundation for moral judgment is allowed. The concepts and ideas ... are marked by irresolvable but *necessary* contradictions" (Bulley 2010: 442). Bulley (2010: 456) argues for "the existence of a necessary and fundamental politics of ethical foreign policy that cannot be effaced by claims to knowledge or a set of 'criteria' for judging humanitarian interventions and ranking responsibilities." Much like Zehfuss and Campbell, Bulley is led (through a work of deconstruction) to conclude that "seeking to retain the politics of ethics, the idea that one *does not know* the right thing to do, leaves us open to the possibility that an ethical relation to the other can occur, perhaps, in an individual situation beyond replication. ... This hope, even if a hope without firm content, remains key to retaining the politics of ethical foreign policy" (Bulley 2010: 457). Following the footsteps of these authors who have relied on Derrida's deconstruction as a means of re-thinking ethics in IR and as a way of 'reading' IR theory and practice, I show in this book that Derrida's work is so rich and so versatile that we can learn from it in re-thinking almost any aspect of IR theory/ practice.[5]

Third, Derrida has addressed during his long career a number of issues that are usually considered to be part of what counts as IR scope (without implying that there is any sort of consensus on what is this scope). He spoke for example of cosmopolitanism, the problems of Europe, immigration, the Cold War, Globalization (or mondialization—worldwidelization as he termed it), a new 'International' when he reconsidered Marx's legacy, terrorism, democracy around the world, nuclear weapons, war, justice, law, international law, etc. Yet as a philosopher he did not (necessarily) speak of and analyze these issues as IR scholars usually speak or think about them (as if such a strict IR way exists or can be imagined anyway). Whereas his insights have guided or helped many IR scholars, Derrida is not an IR scholar in the institutional or disciplinary sense of the term. This poses a problem of 'translation' into so-called IR discipline. This book seeks to contribute to this ongoing effort of drawing on and translating Derrida's deconstruction as explained in the first section of the chapter.

Fourth, much like any other discipline in social sciences and social theory, IR has a politics of its own discipline manifested in long debates (or even absence thereof) and conflicts on what counts as mainstream IR and what counts as being on the fringe, as well as what counts as threats to the sense of having a discipline of knowledge about 'international/world/global' politics as such. Whereas compared to other fields of social sciences, IR is perhaps one of the most diverse disciplines (as testified for by its self-produced sociology of its history and incessant proliferation of 'isms'), novelties about thinking IR are almost always met with stiff resistance. Whereas so-called post-modernist and so-called post-structuralist approaches[6] have more or less become part of the IR discourse on itself and its realm of study (which does not imply that resistance to these has subsided), Derrida's thinking is by and large in the minority group (so to speak) when it comes to drawing on/translating/learning from various great philosophical oeuvres, which (would I dare to say?) is a trademark of IR scholarship (with economic theory and sociology coming to mind first for most IR students). Indeed, despite the serious efforts of approaches such as IR feminist, post-structural or post-colonial (and others) theorists' contributions who have been drawing on various non-conventional (by IR so-called standardized practice) philosophies and social theories, Derrida's thinking is still by and large 'alien' to IR (as compared for example to Foucault's thinking).

For these reasons and perhaps others that I may have missed, writing a book that seeks to re-think IR theory by drawing on Derrida's thinking is a very difficult challenge. Not only one needs to understand well such a very complex and large oeuvre to be able to draw on it in a persuasive and *not too violent* way. It is also the case that one needs to introduce it to the IR discipline keeping in mind the 'alien' character of this oeuvre to the great majority of IR scholars. One cannot for example simply more or less summarize the general contours of certain specific aspects of Derrida's thinking and then show how they apply to the subject-matter at hand by explicating the insights that one gets from such an exercise. Many have done this and it is one way of drawing on Derrida. In fact this is what students of IR usually do in borrowing from other areas of knowledge whether it is, for example, microeconomics, sociology, or social psychology. Yet I do believe that such an approach is somewhat shortsighted for it takes for granted two assumptions (to say the least).

First, it is presupposed that such a borrowing makes sense. Even if one were to take these presuppositions as working assumptions, it does not make them less determinative of one's thinking.[7] Needless to remind oneself of interminable debates and critiques of, for example, the rational unitary actor assumptions in rationalist approach or the black box 'working assumption' in Waltz' neo-realism. In other words, the borrowing is based either on a logic of analogy or a rationalized possible decontextualization, not to mention a belief in the 'objectivity' of the arguments sustaining the assumptions.

Second is an even more serious, if largely unnoticed, issue. We often assume that it is possible to borrow or, more specifically, *translate* from one realm of knowledge which possesses its own conceptual 'language' and practice into another realm of knowledge with a different conceptual 'language' and practice. To do this we assume either that the borrowed conceptual language is 'objective' enough so that it can be excised from its original context or that we can faithfully *translate* it into an equivalent language while preserving the 'essential' elements of the original conceptual framework. Not only do students of translation tell us that this cannot be achieved at the level of 'certainty' or 'purity' which is often assumed to be the case in IR. It is also the case that the very act of translation is more often than not justified through channeling 'empirical evidence' from the original field and through hypothesis testing (broadly conceived, that is, statistically speaking and otherwise) in IR. While this is a more or less accepted practice in IR (especially, for students of IR who believe in the possibility of a science of IR), it still presupposes a more or less unity of science (or if you prefer knowledge). It is rare that today's scholars of IR mention or adhere to logical positivism (as a philosophy of science in IR), yet its specter is still very much looming large over much of IR students' practice of borrowings from other disciplines.

These two issues are even more crucial when it comes to drawing on Derrida's oeuvre. Not only does Derrida have his own genre of thinking about all the issues that he addressed. It is also because Derrida has questioned (without however dismissing) the very basis of what we usually call knowledge in social sciences, namely, the metaphysics of presence[8] as the ground for knowledge. Derrida questioned the notion that there is a transcendental signified (or signifier for that matter) which can transcend the play of signification.[9] This led Derrida to develop what he terms as pseudo-concepts which are not concepts in the usual sense of the term; that is, these are terms that destabilize the metaphysics of presence. This means that Derrida's 'conceptual language' is not as we usually think of it. It also implies that any approach that seeks to draw on Derrida's thinking cannot simply borrow or translate some more or less 'transcendental' signified into another conceptual language without at the same time falling in precisely what Derrida sought to deconstruct—the metaphysics of presence (or logocentrism) and the impossibility of a transcendental signified. This however is no easy task.

Not only is it the case that any language including 'conceptual language' is collective, which means there has to be some sort of a 'language community' for it to exist. More importantly, as clearly shown by Derrida, one cannot completely escape the metaphysics of presence. Derrida even stated that we can only possibly seek to deconstruct the metaphysics of presence from within the metaphysics of presence. In other words: we cannot go beyond it, even when we deconstruct it. And yet we cannot just submit to it and not question it; we *must*[10] seek to go beyond it by redefining the very notion of border and cloture, or, more accurately, by disclosing through a work of deconstruction the undecidable character of such a 'going beyond' and closure, thereby keeping the horizon always already open for future goings beyond the metaphysics of presence. To this end Derrida invented a number of undecidable motifs to think, write and speak *within* the metaphysics of presence *while* deconstructing it and *going beyond* it in a certain way. Deconstruction therefore seeks through tedious work to recognize, speak, and respect the radical alterity of an 'other' of the metaphysics of presence from within the metaphysics of presence. Derrida used the French language to destabilize and deconstruct many of its motifs and thus came up with 'new' motifs which both carry within them traces of the 'usual' French language while at the same incurring a displacement towards 'new' meanings that make the 'new' motifs undecidable such as trace, différance, autoimmunity, supplementarity, iterability, dissemination, etc. These are still meaningful in certain ways; yet they inescapably oscillate between different meanings and as such escape the Aristotelian binary logic of oppositions which commonly dominates our thinking, concepts and theories.

This implies that any attempt to draw on Derrida in re-thinking IR theory can be done, and only so, through two heterogeneous yet indissociable movements. *On the one hand*, one must necessarily use a common language, including of course the conceptual language of IR. *On the other hand*, one must bring forth the undecidability of such a conceptual language, thereby re-inscribing it into a pseudo-conceptual language that destabilizes the original conceptual language and turns it into traces that would still vibrate within the undecidable pseudo-concepts. In brief, the work of deconstruction, as explained by Derrida (Kearney 1984: 123–24),

> is always deeply concerned with the 'other' of language ... The critique of logocentrism is above all else the search for the 'other' and the 'other of language.'. ... The other, which is beyond language and which summons language, is perhaps not a 'referent' in the normal sense which linguists have attached to this term. But to distance oneself thus from the habitual structure, to challenge or complicate our common assumptions about it, does not amount to saying that there is nothing beyond language.

Deconstruction is thus not a *tabula rasa*;[11] it does not destroy existing (linguistic, conceptual, theoretical, and otherwise) structures and institutions from the outside. Deconstruction would neither be possible nor effective without inhabiting these structures and institutions (Derrida 1974: 24). The first task of deconstruction is

> a systematic elucidation of contradictions, paradoxes, inconsistencies, and aporias constitutive of conceptuality, argumentation, and the discursiveness of philosophy. Yet these discrepancies are not logical contradictions ... Nor are these necessary inconsistencies the result of inequality between form and content.
>
> (Gasché 1986: 135)

The contradictions, aporias, and inconsistencies that deconstruction operates on are not always logical contradictions in the Aristotelian sense of the term. They are fissures in the discourse which a regulated (conceptual) economy seeks to avoid for the sake of preserving the consistency that seems to orient the discourse (Gasché 1986: 136). Derrida (1978: 158) thus defines contradiction as "nothing other than the relation-to-self of diction as it opposes itself to scription, as it *chases* itself (away) in hunting down what is properly its *trap*."[12] This means that this contradiction is inherent and constitutive rather than being contingent. Aporia, in the sense of Derrida (1993: 15–16), is "an experience of not knowing what path to follow or coming to the point where no path can be found" (Norris 1982: 49). More specifically, aporia is much more than antinomy because

> the contradiction of equally valid and necessary propositions found in an antinomy is solved by showing how it is "apparent or illusory," by dialecticizing the contradiction in a Hegelian or Marxist manner, or by rendering it as a "transcendental illusion in a dialectic of the Kantian type" ... the deconstructive articulation of the aporia shows it to be irreducible and constitutive to the degree that it cannot be overcome. While a Hegelian or Marxist thought, for example, would exploit the constitutive and necessary nature of the aporia in order to engender a dialectical progression, for Derrida the irreducible and interminable nature of the aporia will always disrupt this progress by showing how thought and action remain caught in the movement of the 'double bind'. Instead of being sublated or overcome, the aporia for deconstruction becomes the very ordeal of all experience. The aporia must be endured as interminable in order for experience to take place ... the deconstructive aporia is perhaps best formulated by showing how the conditions for the possibility of something also prove to be the conditions for its impossibility.
> (Horwitz 2002: 158–59)

Therefore, for Derrida the politics of aporia is the possibility condition for (re-)invention, change and transformation.

What the operation of deconstruction attempts to do therefore is to provide an account for these contradictions and aporias by 'grounding' them in *ungrounded*, undecidable pseudo-concepts, also termed as 'infrastructures' (Gasché 1986: 142). This process of grounding without a ground (in the usual sense of the term) is neither a process of essentialization nor one of neutralization. Deconstruction, according to Derrida (1982: 329), "does not consist in passing from one concept to another, but in overturning and displacing a conceptual order, as well as the non-conceptual order with which the conceptual order is articulated." The overturning and displacing of a *conceptual* order unfolds simultaneously with an overturning and displacing of the *non-conceptual* order within which, or against which, the conceptual order is itself formulated. Derrida terms this logic of deconstructive operation wherein a concept or notion is put to work through overturning and displacing as the logic of *paleonymics*. Derrida (1981a: 71) describes it as follows:

> What, then, is the 'strategic' necessity that requires the occasional maintenance of an *old name* in order to launch a new concept? With all the reservations imposed by this classical distinction between the name and the concept, one might begin to describe this operation. Taking into account the fact that a name does not name the punctual simplicity of a concept, but rather a system of predicates defining a concept, a conceptual

structure *centered* on a given predicate, we proceed: (1) to the extraction of a reduced predicate trait that is held in reserve, limited in a given conceptual structure (limited for motivations and relations of force to be analyzed), *named* X; (2) to the delimitation, the grafting and regulated extension of the extracted predicate, the name X being maintained as a kind of *lever of intervention*, in order to maintain a grasp on the previous organization, which is to be transformed effectively. Therefore, extraction, graft, extension.

Therefore, writing a book that proposes a re-thinking of IR theory by drawing on Derrida's philosophy not only requires that one deploys his ideas and insights in an 'adequate' way, but also that the *style* of writing and arguing must in itself be more or less a deconstruction 'at work'. In other words: not only do I seek to deconstruct a given set of IR theories. I also *must* write in such a way that my writing itself is a practice of deconstruction. This means that one cannot simply follow some standard ways of 'scientific' or 'standard' writing, and that's it. This could be done but only as one of three steps that the work of deconstruction requires. This is what I tried *to explain and practice* in the first section of this introduction, without alerting the reader that I was doing so (of course, the initiated reader has by now detected and recognized this strategy).

At this juncture, I am faced with a dilemma:[13] Should I try to summarize Derrida's thinking at this point so as to initiate, even if briefly only, the uninitiated reader or should I follow another strategy? Because it is extremely hard to summarize Derrida's thinking (for reasons explained earlier) and because one would require a large number of examples and illustrations as well as quotes from Derrida's texts to do so, I decided that perhaps a strategically effective way to proceed is to continually introduce Derrida as I move on within the chapters. That is: I introduce from Derrida's thinking whatever is needed to carry out the task of each chapter, with of course some inescapable overlap and repetition. However, I believe that the overlap is justified for the sake of more clarification in different contexts, especially for the uninitiated reader.

I thus move on to introduce in the next section each of the chapters, highlighting the general contours of the specific IR theory (or argument) which is deconstructed in the chapter. Before doing so I clarify one more issue. It is customary that a 'good' book on re-thinking IR begins by a constructive critique of extant literature and then builds on it to achieve its task (Alexander Wendt's critique of neorealism comes to mind). *On the one hand*, this book does not strictly speaking follow this norm. Instead, I focus (more or less) on a limited number of important books/works which I use as entry points for the work of deconstruction. The lessons of the latter are however far from being limited by these various works as they speak to many large bodies of literature in IR theory and beyond, even if not specifically critiqued or even mentioned. *On the other hand*, and, as already pointed out, I begin by contextualizing my work of deconstruction somewhere within some 'texts' of extant literature. Extant IR theory literature thus plays the role of a 'metaphysics of presence' that I seek to deconstruct and displace in another way so as to disclose the aporiatic undecidability within it and think its conditions of possibility and impossibility.

Outline of the chapters

Although I have organized the chapters in a certain way, putting at the beginning issues about the possibility of knowledge and then ontology and ending with the logics of action and ethics in IR, the chapters can be organized in any another way. This has to do with the fact that there is much overlap between the various issues even if discussed in separate chapters and even if I do not always make it transparent that it indeed is the case. Moreover, if there is a strong legacy that we have inherited from Derrida it is his career-long pursued goal to show in various fields of knowledge and in a variety of writing genres (philosophical, literary, and otherwise) that boundaries are always already widely porous and that any so-called 'outside' is always already spectrally haunting any so-called 'inside'. As it will become clearer with the introduction of Derrida's motifs, such as the *trace*, *différance*, *autoimmunity*, *supplementarity*, *iterability*, *dissemination*, etc., these very motifs show at work (so to speak) the aporiatic nature of boundaries, closures, origins, self-presence, and so on. Perhaps to the disappointment of readers who believe in some sort of linear accumulation of knowledge, following the 'logic' of a work of deconstruction in re-thinking IR and endeavoring to manifest it in the writing itself necessarily preempt any 'true' origin to the 'argument' of the book, or any 'true' conclusion for that matter. Therefore, the book can simultaneously be read as a 'whole' and as 'parts' of a 'whole'. To paraphrase the difficulty, one can perhaps venture to say: the 'whole is in the parts and the parts are greater than the whole'.

This means that I am raising the key question of the notions of 'less' and 'greater', a question that emerges as soon as one realizes that a work of deconstruction does neither obey the Aristotelian logic of 'either/or; neither/nor' nor the Hegelian law of sublation of the negation of negation. As I am writing this book I realize that it obeys an 'illogical logic' of 'either-or and both-and-neither'. Put differently: I am realizing that to realize this project I cannot simply finish it or present it *as if* it were a restricted economy of writing, because of all the vibrations and oscillations that this seemingly benign *as-if* implies (as explained later in the book). Rather, in *realizing* this project I realize that it is what Bataille and Derrida call a general economy of writing (a book). Yet in order for it to be a book as we usually speak of it and deal with when we go, say, to a bookstore, it has to be presented *as if* it were a restricted economy—that is, a well delimited and delineated book with a well-defined introduction, subsequent chapters, and a conclusion chapter, and moreover a preface which is always written in an *après coup* way. The preface necessarily opens up a chance for the book to be read and survive. It however simultaneously poses a threat that the book might very well be thrown into the dustbin of history, or even more to the black-hole of oblivion and complete erasure before publication, immediately after the preface is quickly read. Simply put: a preface always written in après coup is both the condition of possibility and impossibility of an actually written book to be a read-book. And yet, yet another yet, I cannot escape in writing this book what can be termed as the metaphysics of the 'published book'. In order to show that a book is never just a 'book' in the usual sense of a book, I cannot not write the 'book' as we usually think of it. Hence, I *must* introduce the different chapters of the book.

Chapter 2 presents a re-thinking of the philosophy of social science of IR. It does so by considering the restless debates on the methodology of conducting inquiry in IR. I specifically develop the work of deconstruction by considering one recently published book, Patrick Jackson's 2010 book, *The Conduct of Inquiry in International Relations: Philosophy of Science and Its Implications for the Study of World Politics*. Jackson's suggestion for settling the continuous debates on the philosophy of science is to make whatever provisional commitments—*wagers*—we cannot but make about matters of ontological philosophy and to be as clear as we can be on such commitments, even while knowing very well that these matters and issues can never be settled definitively. Ultimately, Jackson testifies that 'leaps of faith' are the justification of these wagers. I agree with the implications of Jackson's text more than what Jackson allows his discourse to do. I suggest that we must/cannot not *testify* with a 'Yes' to leaps of *faith*, if with a *faith* which is a *faith* without *faith*, which is more than knowledge and turns into non-knowledge, a *faith* through which we *testify* on/for the possibility condition of knowledge and non-knowledge for/about/in IR.

Chapter 3 continues to probe into the conditions of possibility of knowledge in IR by zooming in on ontology. The chapter raises the questions: *Is it possible to speak of the ontological without ontology?* The answer is a qualified yes; a yes based on a logic which neither negates nor affirms the ontological, all the while rejecting ontologism. I propose that we instead forego ontologism which means that we need to re-think ontology *qua* ontological discourse without positing ontologism. We thus need a *logic* of thinking about the ontological *without* ontologism, without the 'essence' of ontology. Drawing on Derrida, I call this logic the logic of *without [sans]* which negates without completely negating, that is, negates and denegates at the same time. I explicitly propose to think of the ontological as *khôra*, a pseudo-notion which does not possess any determination of its own except by assuming the role of a 'receptacle' (of sorts) to determinations and which operates through the logic of without. I end the chapter by arguing that thinking of IR theory in this way implies a re-thinking of the work of IR theory as *ergon* and any philosophical enframing thereof (Critical Realism or otherwise) as *parergon*. This entails a logic of *parergonality* unfolding within a movement of *différance*—difference, deferral, and temporization—between IR work and any philosophical enframing thereof.

Chapter 4 considers the so-called problem of agent-structure. Many students of IR (and social theory) argue that we must consider the problem at the level of ontology first. I call instead for exploring *the presuppositions* of such an ontological positing itself as a way of thinking *the conditions of possibility* of the agent-structure problematique and *the conditions of impossibility* that make it an *undecidable* problematique. To this end I engage into a work of deconstruction which affirms a thinking of 'structure' *as* an *undecidable structurality* and a thinking of agency *as* an i*mpossible yet necessary restless negotiation* between an *unconditional event of agency* and a *conditional agency qua originary performativity of inaugural interpretation*. The chapter ends by proposing that in thinking about the agent-structure problematique we need to think within a logic of *parergonality* where the agent–structure problem is thought of as a *parergon* and social theory as an *ergon*.

Chapter 5 considers the concept of identity, which IR social constructivism has turned into one of its defining concepts. Speaking of identity is, according to conventional wisdom, tantamount to speaking also of difference and otherness. The pair identity/difference has in fact more or less become one of the signatures of political theory today and most debates about identity and difference in politics end up more or less crystallized around binary oppositions. The chapter raises the following questions: What if one were to problematize both identity and difference? The chapter presents a deconstruction of the concepts of 'identity', 'difference' and 'other'. The deconstruction highlights the impossible aporia of othering and suggests a new way of thinking about such an aporiatic politics. The work of deconstruction leads to the proposal that the undecidable duo *identity/difference is an iterable play of dissemination which obeys the law of supplementarity, and différance is its condition of possibility.* This makes identity out of joint with its 'self', not identical to its 'self', an identity *without* identity. The work of deconstruction shows that autoimmunity accounts for this originary self-destruction which is originarily constitutive of identity. Autoimmunity is thus an originary movement that imprints non-closure in identity as the latter seeks to reach closure by securing self-certainty through othering. The work of deconstruction then shows that going beyond the politics of aporia of othering means a never-resting, continuous shuttling negotiation between a structural promise of going beyond the aporia of 'identity *without* identity' and momentarily interrupted and halted, yet always already disrupted, senses of identity.

Chapter 6 engages into a work of deconstructing the concept of trust in social theory and IR literature. A common thread of these and other approaches is that trust is thought of as the result of suspending judgment on uncertainty and fear of betrayal and exploitation and deciding to act on a *leap of faith* of sorts after having exhausted all possible knowledge on actors and their environment. Although this *as-if* element seems to be an essential part of the process of trust, it has surprisingly remained under-theorized. I propose, following Derrida, that the 'as-if' rhetorical gesture is an event in the sense of 'saying as-if' and as such the 'as-if' gesture is a pervertible promise (in the sense of Derrida). I then propose that trust based on 'as-if' rhetorical gesture is autoimmune. Because trust *qua as-if* leap is autoimmune this makes the politics of building trust an aporia which obeys the logic of without which simultaneously negates and denegates. The chapter then discusses the ensuing impossible politics of aporia to conclude that building trust within the terrain of structural undecidability is a going beyond the aporiatic politics of undecidability to a 'trust *without* trust'.

Chapter 7 proposes a re-thinking of international constitutional order by using as entry point G. John Ikenberry's theory of constitutional order via binding institutions. The work of deconstruction reveals a number of aporias within Ikenberry's theory. I propose to think of these aporias as a *chance* to extend his theory to unexplored possibilities. Pursuing this *chance*, I reconsider the role of 'arbitrary exercise of power' in the theory to argue that the binding institutions are founded and conserved through 'an arbitrary exercise of power' which assumes the form of, what Derrida calls, *an originary performative violence*. The binding become (more or less) legitimate as a result of retroactively (more or less) effacing this originary violence. The 'arbitrary exercise of power' is thus essential to Ikenberry's argument and is both its conditions of possibility and impossibility. I then argue that what Ikenberry characterizes as opportunism reflects the fact that the binding institutions are inherently *autoimmune* to their own logic and rules, and this condition makes the institutional binding a binding *without* binding. Therefore, I argue that *autoimmunity* with its law of *without* (that is, an undecidable *denegated* negation) haunts the constitutional order through and through. The chapter ends with a suggestion that we need to re-think both the very notion of 'binding' as well as the logic of founding and conserving international order through binding institutions. To this end, our thinking and analysis should be one of restlessly riding a 'negotiating' shuttle between possible theoretical formulations of world order and the impossibility of closing the theorizing process.

Chapter 8 proposes a deconstruction of the logic of action as a key explanatory notion. I specifically engage into a work of deconstruction of a number of illustrative texts (Pierre Bourdieu on the logic of practice, James G. March and Johan P. Olsen on the logic of consequences and the logic of appropriation, Ted Hopf on the logic of habit, and Thomas Risse on the logic of communicative action) to explore the presuppositions underpinning these logics of action. The work of deconstruction shows that each logic is marred with undecidability and that 'trace' is their condition of possibility and impossibility, thereby making them 'out-of-joint' with their supposed logic of action. The work of deconstruction does not however negate these logics of action; rather, it laterally displaces them to show their undecidability. It thereby generalizes the logic of consequences into a logic of responsibility which always already verges on and is thus contaminated by irresponsibility; the logic of appropriateness into a logic autoimmunity which always already while affirming propriety threatens it with impropriety; the logic of habit into a logic of iterability which always already implies at the same time both repetition and transformation, thereby making habit never identical to itself; the logic of practice always already haunted by an originary faith which both ensures a simultaneous 'practicality' and its perversion into 'ideality'; and the logic of communicative argumentation into an autoimmune logic with performative contradiction as its condition of possibility and impossibility.

Promises of re-thinking IR theory via experiences of deconstruction

Having introduced, if very briefly only, the various works of deconstruction that I develop in the various chapters of the book, I still owe it to the reader to explain why I am writing this specific book on the issues that I summarized in the previous section. In other words: What am I proposing? What am I implying? What promises am I seeking to honor in writing this book? And what am I promising to 'harvest' at the 'end' of this book?

A key question driving my motivation to write this book is that IR theorists have ceaselessly sought to understand, explain, and transform the experienced reality of international politics. This challenge is no less true today than in the past, notably in the work of contemporary IR theories, including pragmatism, critical realism, rationalism, neo-liberal institutionalism, social-constructivism, and classical realism. What is puzzling about these diverse efforts is a persistent, yet unquestioned, quest by theorists to develop strategies to eliminate or reduce the antinomies, contradictions, paradoxes, dilemmas, and inconsistencies dogging their approaches. A serious critical assessment of the logic driving this unquestioned quest is however lacking. The book promises to address this issue via works of deconstruction.

Specifically, the book promises to achieve three aims. First, the book promises to provide a thorough critique of leading contemporary IR theories, including pragmatism, critical realism, rationalism, neo-liberal institutionalism, and social-constructivism through reading a number of texts on a number of substantive issues. However, my approach is not to summarize what some might call a 'core' of each approach and then deal with it. These and other approaches to IR theory are in fact spectra of approaches themselves and thus speaking of cores is, I think, committing injustice to these approaches in the first place. Moreover, deploying deconstruction as a strategy of reading these theories makes it impossible to think about approaches in terms of cores. What I do in the book is thus to read (as explained earlier) a given set of texts without seeking to address what some might see as 'cores' (or paradigms, or schools, etc.). Yet, my readings do speak to many aspects of these approaches in a variety of ways. Second, these approaches are all valuable but none on its own terms is able to explain the logic driving their shared quest to eliminate antinomies, contradictions, paradoxes, dilemmas, and inconsistencies from their theories. The book seeks through works of deconstruction to strengthen and go beyond the valuable contributions of these approaches by explicating the consequences of taking into account the antinomies, contradictions, paradoxes, dilemmas, and inconsistencies of these theories. Third, the book through the experience of deconstructing the various texts that I consider makes, I think, a case for a pluralist IR theory which, counter-intuitively, affirms antinomies, contradictions, paradoxes, dilemmas, and inconsistencies as an invaluable resource for taking IR theory beyond currently paralyzing 'wars of paradigms'.

More broadly, the book promises to demonstrate through the works of deconstruction that questioning many taken-for-granted presuppositions of IR theory is far-reaching for IR theory and its relation with the experienced political reality. These presuppositions include, *inter alia*, the delineation between the philosophy of ontology and philosophy of science, the demarcation between faith and social science, the Aristotelian logic based on the laws of non-contradiction and identity, and the linear notion of time. As such, this volume promises to show that deconstruction is an indispensable thinking framework, essential to addressing the self-limitations, self-contradictions, antinomies, dilemmas, and inconsistencies of IR theories and their disconcerted and frustrating relations with experienced reality. By the same token, the book seeks to demonstrate that the work of deconstruction is resourceful and rigorous in its questioning of the presuppositions of prevailing IR theories and, more generally, of theorizing in the social sciences.

The book is thus written in such a way that its approach to re-thinking IR theory integrates theory within a larger discursive context of social theory and philosophy and within the context of writing a book à la deconstruction. The book thus promises to be innovative in three important ways. First, the book allows for immanent critical assessments of important texts of IR theory and their unexplored presuppositions. Second, the book offers extensions to these texts that take them beyond their self-imposed limitations while avoiding the trap of closure or even foreclosure. Third, the book seeks to fulfill its promise of remaining faithful to deconstruction by proposing a re-thinking of what a 'conclusion' of a book is and can be; that is, the conclusion of a book written through works od deconstruction, a conclusion which can only be a concluding *without* a conclusion, a concluding which continues the work of deconstruction to the very (physical) end of the book.

2 'Testimonial faith' in/about IR philosophy of science

The possibility condition of a pluralist science of world politics

Debates on the methodology of conducting inquiry in IR are restless. In an effort to move the debates forward, beyond 'passions and dogmatisms', Patrick T. Jackson has recently proposed a Weberian inspired notion of science that he anchors and grounds through the methodology of ideal-types. Jackson's suggestion for settling the continuous debates on the philosophy of science is to make whatever provisional commitments—wagers—we cannot but make about matters of ontological philosophy and to be as clear as we can on such commitments, even while knowing very well that these matters and issues can never be settled definitively. Ultimately, Jackson testifies that 'leaps of faith' are the justification of these wagers. I propose to reconsider the notion of Weber's ideal-type through a work of deconstruction. This then opens up a deconstruction of Jackson's key notions of wager and faith. I thus seek to affirm (in a certain way) Jackson's conclusions by taking them to where he refuses to/could not go.

Introduction

Debates on the methodology of conducting inquiry in International Relations (hereafter IR) are restless with new 'isms' emerging at increasing rates.[1] Many, if not most, students of IR prefer more or less closure on these debates, at least at the level of the philosophy of science.[2] One of the latest attempts in IR scholarship at defining some broad guidelines and contours for closure on IR philosophy of science is Patrick Jackson's book *The Conduct of Inquiry in International Relations: Philosophy of Science and Its Implications for the Study of World Politics*. This is a serious effort not only at comprehensively summarizing the general contours of the issue but also at branding a few important signposts and guidelines on what the problems are and what solutions thereto might look like.

In this chapter, I discuss three aspects of Jackson's book that are of paramount importance to its proclaimed value-added. These are: a Weber-inspired three-criteria definition of social science, a reliance on Weber's notion of ideal-type to summarize, critique and amend extant IR literature on the relationship between the philosophy of ontology and the philosophy of science, and a wager-based justification of a pluralist science of world politics.

Jackson argues that for a research to be counted as science, the work has, first, to be systematic in relating its presuppositions to its conclusions. Second, the work has to be publicly criticizable at least within the community of relevant scholarship. Third, the work has to produce or at least should seek to produce 'worldly knowledge' about the world which is taken to exist given the presuppositions of the work. Jackson then endeavors to suggest a typology of 'isms' defined through two dimensions or *wagers*: a first *wager* dealing with what he terms as an ideal-typical choice between *mind-world dualism* and its opposite *mind-world monism*, and a second *wager* dealing with what he terms as *transfactualism* and *phenomenalism*. These two *wagers* constitute "two of the most important commitments of philosophical ontology made by IR scholars, and suitably abstracted they provide a useful way of clarifying debates about the philosophy of science in the field," writes Jackson (2010: 35). Jackson's (2010: 34) goal is to offer

> a methodological principle ... that we should regard positions on the character and conduct of science to rest on provisional commitments—*wagers*—about matters of philosophical ontology that can really never be settled definitively.

Jackson's suggestion for more or less settling the continuous debates and infightings that seem to be plaguing IR debates on philosophy of science is to make whatever provisional commitments or wagers we *must*, or *cannot but*, make about matters of ontological philosophy and to be as clear as we can on such commitments, even while knowing very well that these matters and issues can never be settled definitively. Instead of leading-nowhere debates, wagers are, says Jackson (2010: 34), what "constitute worlds, in that they quite literally set the stage for the kinds of empirical and theoretical puzzles and challenges that a scholar takes to be meaningful and important." Jackson explains that "At a minimum, a wager locates and specifies three things: the researcher, the world to be researched, and the character of the relationship between them" (2010: 35). In the final analysis, Jackson testifies that these wagers "require of their practitioners a commitment that is like nothing else so much as an existential leap of faith" (Jackson 2010: 197). That is, a 'leap of faith' is the ultimate justification of Jackson's wagers-based approach to settling the issue of never ending fighting on the conduct of inquiry in IR.[3]

I agree with much of Jackson's critique and assessment of the debates on the philosophy of science in IR. Much of his analysis drives home many of the intricacies of the debates as well as highlights a great number of nuanced differences across a wide spectrum (or spectra) of approaches in IR. Jackson's analysis is sharp, more often than not very perceptive, sometimes breathtaking, and almost always to the point. His reliance on Weber's methodology of ideal-type is exemplary in its conceptualization. One is easily tempted to stop right here and adopt Jackson's text as a landmark and an arresting work. Yet, this is precisely where Jackson's text begins to deconstruct itself from within itself.

Having spent a large number of pages in critiquing the limitations of extant approaches to philosophy of science/methodology in IR, having made a strong case for how we should rely on *wagers* and ultimately *leaps of faith* in doing IR research, having recognized the unsuitability of disciplining the IR field, having embraced a non-foundationalist pluralist science of world politics, Jackson (2010: 195–96) solemnly declares:

> I wanted to articulate a definition broad enough that most of our scholarly ways of 'doing IR' would fit underneath it. Only in that way can the 'science question' *be put to rest once and for all*: *by articulating a big enough tent that the overwhelming majority of what takes place in IR scholarship can fit underneath it.* This does not mean that every conclusion reached by every IR scholar should somehow be accepted, or that every procedure that ever IR scholar engages in is equally valid—but *it does mean that for most claims advanced by most IR scholars, their scientific status should not be in question.* (emphasis added)

In other words, Jackson has arrived or at least wants to arrive and close in on an almost total solution, *once for all*, on what science is/should be in IR, and which work would count as 'scientific'. However, before jumping to a conclusion for or against Jackson, we need to pause and ask: How are we to understand the *'be put to rest once and for all'* and *'big enough tent'*? Are these *mere benignly* rhetorical turns (as if such things existed)? Or, perhaps, is it more a conclusion warranted by Jackson's very Weberian conceptual framework? Are this *'to be put to rest once for all'* and this *'big enough tent'* to be understood in the sense of Weberian ideal types of sorts? This would most likely be in tune with Jackson's ideal-typification of the various approaches to the philosophy of science in IR. His 'total' and 'final' solution to the conduct of inquiry in IR *qua* science would then not be a 'realistic' solution (both understood in the sense of Weber) to the social reality of the IR field. Perhaps yes. Perhaps no since Jackson (2010: 211–12) ends the book with a profession of hope:

> I sincerely hope that my lexicon is not the last word on these issues, and I just as sincerely hope that it will need to be replaced at some time in the not-too-distant future … Like any lexicon—indeed, like any methodology, or any argument—mine is a means rather than an end in itself, and the basis on which it should be judged can be nothing other than its practical effect in generating a wide variety of systematic, worldly knowledge about world politics.

Therefore, his *'to be put to rest once and for all'* is without really putting to rest once and for all, after all is said and done. Jackson indeed seeks to remain faithful to his definition of science as systematic and criticizable effort to produce worldly knowledge about world politics. What is happening in

Jackson's text? I think that the text is deconstructing itself in various ways, a work of deconstruction the weaving and intricacies of which I seek to follow in this chapter.

I organize the discussion as follows. First, I summarize Jackson's approach to Weber's inspired notion of science which is anchored and grounded in the methodology of ideal-types. This paves the way for reconsidering the notion of Weber's ideal-type through a work of deconstruction. This then opens up the discussion for Jackson's key notions of 'wager' and 'faith' which play decisive roles in 'grounding' Jackson's framework. In this endeavor, I do not seek to, nor can I, negate Jackson's praiseworthy efforts. Rather, the goal is to affirm (in a certain way) his conclusions by taking them to where he refuses to/could not go. In doing so, I follow Derrida to suggest a pseudo-notion of 'faith' and 'testimony' which are the conditions of possibility of knowledge (in IR and otherwise) and without which we cannot speak of science as such. I thus agree with the implications of Jackson's text more than what Jackson allows his discourse to do. I suggest that we must/cannot not *testify* with a 'Yes' to leaps of *faith*, if with a *faith* which is a *faith* without *faith*, a *faith* which is more like *a desert in the desert*, which is more than knowledge and turns into non-knowledge, a *faith* which always already lets the future have a non-determinable future, a *faith* through which we *testify* on/for the possibility condition of knowledge and non-knowledge for/about/in IR.

Jackson's plea for a Weber-inspired science in IR

The debates on the philosophy of science in IR seem to be interminable. Rather than seeking to opt for this or that philosophy, for this or that foundation, or even for jettisoning foundations, or being anti-foundationalist altogether, Jackson's book promises to remain open; it opts for a pluralist science of world politics. Such a call seems indeed to be vindicated from the very heart of the practices of 'doing' IR. The very proliferation of debates upon debates (and non-debates) leading to bifurcation upon bifurcations into '*-isms*' and '*-isms about-isms*' evidence much pluralism in doing IR. Jackson's goal is to make sense of all of this while at the same time rescuing the—or, more precisely, a certain—idea and practice of science, without falling into dogmatism or a vertigo of passions. Jackson wants to be as clear as possible, as rigorous as possible, and as unambiguous as possible. What a better choice than to call upon the specter of Weber to his help. Jackson (2010: 193) thus announces that:

> I have followed Max Weber in defining science in very broad terms: the careful and rigorous application of a set of theories and concepts so as to produce a 'thoughtful ordering of empirical actuality'.

The upshot of this allegiance to Weber's methodology entails a certain way of thinking of science. Jackson (2010: 193) explains that his definition of science yields three constituent components of a scientific knowledge-claim: it must be systematically related to its presuppositions; it must be capable of public criticism within the scientific community—and in particular, public criticism designed to improve the knowledge being claimed; and it must be intended to produce worldly knowledge, whatever one takes 'the world' to include.

Many students of IR research would most likely agree that this is a fair, representative, and comprehensive description and expectation of what science is/should be. Very few would disagree with Jackson's (2010: 193) statement that "we *have* to insist ... that IR scholars make a real effort to systematically connect their conclusions with their premises." Jackson (2010: 193) recognizes that such a position "is likely uncontroversial for *substantive* premises." Yet he goes much further, stating that such a position "applies even more directly to *methodological* premises and presuppositions in the realm of philosophical ontology." It is only by doing so that we might be able to avoid unnecessary "mismatches and misunderstandings," argues Jackson (2010: 193). Systematic connection between premises and presuppositions is in fact the condition of possibility not only of agreements but also of the possibility of "meaningful scientific controversy about a claim." (2010: 194). Moreover, "if such systematicity is to meaningfully exist in the first place it cannot, by definition, be part of a 'private language' comprehensible only to the researcher," explains Jackson (2010: 194). All systematic, scientific claims ought always to be publicly criticizable at any given moment within (at least) relevant scientific communities (2010: 194), with the proviso that such public criticisms are "coupled with an appropriately broad account of the diverse bases on which scientifically valid knowledge can be produced," so much so that "public criticism is a healthy aspect of any scientific community" (2010: 194). The intended product—knowledge claims—would be "worldly knowledge," that is, "the realm of facts," where the latter "are accessible to anyone employing the proper procedures for disclosing them, and depend not on revelation or intuitive insight but on systematic demonstration and public, if technical, argumentation" (2010: 195). Jackson explains that "by 'world' I mean simply that realm of actuality that a methodology takes to exist" (2010: 195).

Jackson rationalizes his approach by reminding us that "no compelling detailed consensus about science in general exists, whether among scientists or among philosophers of science" (2010: 195). This implies that even the skeptics about his line of argumentation should at least recognize the possibility that it is not far-fetched to *wager* (perhaps *à la Blaise Pascal*) on the possibility of science in IR as well as on the possibility of perhaps going beyond the seeming stalemates that plague IR debates on the philosophy of science. All in all, Jackson's Weber's inspired definition of science is neat and quite appealing to common sense (of course, if we can speak of such a thing as common sense given the state of affairs in IR debates that Jackson deplores so much). Moreover, his deployment of Weber's methodology of ideal-types in assessing, critiquing, and amending the spectra of approaches to philosophy of science in IR is highly commendable (and I would add quite coherently and cohesively developed throughout the various chapters). Jackson's approach is Weberian through and through.

What if one were to question the unambiguity and purity of Weber's ideal-type methodology? What would be the implications for Jackson's passionate and faithful plea for a pluralist science of world politics? Would Jackson remain committed to his Weberian approach? Apparently not completely since he testifies that in the final analysis Weber's ideal type methodology does not settle the issue of how to ground (or not ground) or rather how to put to rest the proliferation of new approaches in the philosophy of science, or in Jackson's terms, how to justify the presupposition-ing of one's wagers. In fact, *testifies Jackson, this can only be done through leaps of faith*. To what extent is Jackson justified in making such a proposition? Is Jackson still a Weberian? Can we re-think the methodology of ideal types and the 'leap of faith' proposition in another way so as to find perhaps that the two are more connected than what Jackson's discourse shows, or at least does not show enough? My response is yes, if in a certain way. I am thus not suggesting that Jackson is wrong in advocating a sort of 'originary' role for 'leaps of faith' in grounding one's wagers. Rather, I want to *testify* with Jackson but beyond Jackson about a certain *necessary* role of 'faith' in grounding one's wagers and, more generally, any knowledge. I develop this line of thinking in two steps. I first present a necessarily brief deconstruction of the 'ideal-type' by taking Weber into a 'linguistic turn', yet developed enough to serve the purposes of this chapter. I then engage a re-thinking of 'faith' through a work of deconstruction, a 'faith' that turns out to be playing an originary role in the grounding of knowledge in IR (and elsewhere).

Weber's ideal-type and the 'linguistic turn'

The so-called *linguistic turn* of the twentieth century has led to many upheavals in philosophy, social theory and social sciences.[4] Weber's methodology of ideal-type was for the most part developed independently of, if more or less contemporaneously with, the linguistic turn. Because Weber's methodology of the 'ideal-type' is about concept formation this suggests that we inquire about the possibility and implications of submitting the 'ideal-type' to a 'linguistic turn'. I do this through a work of deconstruction *à la Derrida*,[5] taking guidance from Derrida's (1978: 292–93) statement that:

> There are thus two interpretations of interpretation ... The one seeks to decipher, dreams of deciphering a truth or an origin which escapes play ... The other, which is no longer turned toward the origin, affirms play ... these two interpretations of interpretation ... are absolutely irreconcilable even if we live them simultaneously and reconcile them in an obscure economy.

In other words, in reading a text one can follow either an interpretation based on a principle or ideal of legitimation for the sake of deciphering meaning or an interpretation based on an absence of such a principle or ideal of legitimation that would legitimize the interpretation. The second interpretation thus consists of a play that does not require any ideal of interpretation; it is an 'illegitimate' interpretation of sorts. The work of deconstruction is to probe into the possibility conditions of such a differentiation between 'legitimate' and 'illegitimate' interpretation. As Derrida (1978: 293) puts it,

> although these two interpretations must acknowledge and accentuate their differences and define their irreducibility, I do not believe that today there is any question of choosing ... we must first try to conceive ... of this irreducible difference.

Therefore, following Derrida, my interpretation of Weber is not to negate this or that interpretation of the 'ideal-type'. I am much more interested in the conditions of possibility as well as the inherent tensions and contradictions that both define and undermine the concept of 'ideal-type' and perhaps by extension any methodology based on it.

I only focus on a limited number of key texts from Weber's corpus wherein he introduces and discusses the notion of ideal-type.[6] Weber defines the ideal type as being

> formed by the one-sided *accentuation* of one or more points of view and by the synthesis of a great many diffuse, discrete, more or less present and occasionally absent *concrete individual* phenomena, which are arranged according to those one-sidedly emphasized viewpoints into a unified *analytical* construct [*Gedankenbild*]. In its conceptual purity, this mental construct [*Gedankenbild*] cannot be found empirically anywhere in reality. It is a *utopia*.
>
> (Weber 1949: 90, *his emphasis*)

Weber (1949: 43) explains that the ideal-type "has only one function in an empirical investigation" and this "function is the comparison with empirical reality in order to establish its divergences or similarities, to describe them with the *most unambiguously intelligible concepts*, and to understand and explain them causally." Weber thus seeks to get rid of the ambiguity that exists in the empirical reality. That is, for Weber 'reality' is irrational and as such cannot be conceptualized but rather needs to be approached with the help of the *most unambiguously intelligible concepts*, such as the ideal-type. Even the historian seeking to make sense of 'reality' cannot avoid doing what Weber suggests, since as he (Weber 1949: 92) put it,

> every conscientious examination of the conceptual elements of historical exposition shows however that the historian as soon as he attempts to go

beyond the bare establishment of concrete relationships and to determine the *cultural* significance of even the simplest individual event in order to 'characterize' it, *must* use concepts which are precisely and unambiguously definable only in the form of ideal types.

He (Weber 1949: 94) also notes that

> if the historian (in the widest sense of the word) rejects an attempt to construct such ideal types as a 'theoretical construction,' i.e., as useless or dispensable for his concrete heuristic purposes, the inevitable consequence is either that he consciously or unconsciously uses other similar concepts without formulating them verbally and elaborating them logically or that he remains stuck in the realm of the vaguely 'felt'.

Three points are worthwhile highlighting at this juncture. First, the ideal-type is clearly an imaginary construct of the mind, an ideal in the strictly logical sense of the term, a purely ideal limiting concept which is fitted to serve as a way for describing 'reality'. It is a construct that only our "imagination accepts as plausibly motivated and hence as 'objectively possible' and which appear as adequate from the nomological standpoint" (Weber 1949: 91–92). Second, the ideal type provides a genetic definition for more historically/empirically fitted categories. Third, the resort to ideal types is unavoidable even for historians who are seeking to describe and understand historical situations, whether they admit it or not.

Having asserted these defining properties of the ideal-type concept, Weber then confesses that the issue is not as unambiguous as he would like it to be. He discovers that there are some unavoidable relationships "between the 'idea' in the sense of a tendency of practical or theoretical thought and the 'idea' in the sense of the ideal-*typical* portrayal of an epoch constructed as a heuristic device" (Weber 1949: 95). Not only this, but Weber also admits that:

> an ideal type of certain situations, which can be abstracted from certain characteristic social phenomena of an epoch, might—and this is indeed quite often the case—have also been present in the minds of the persons living in that epoch as an ideal to be striven for in practical life or as a maxim for the regulation of certain social relationships.
> (Weber 1949: 95)

That is, certain ideal-types are not as originally imaginative constructs *qua* heuristic devices in the minds of analysts as Weber posits them to be by definition. These ideal-types *qua* 'ideals' may preexist in the minds of people living in a certain epoch. Moreover, Weber cannot escape recognizing that

> those 'ideas' which govern the behavior of the population of a certain epoch, i.e., which are concretely influential in determining their conduct,

can, if a somewhat complicated construct is involved, be formulated precisely only in the form of an ideal type, since empirically it exists in the minds of an indefinite and constantly changing mass of individuals and assumes in their minds the most multifarious nuances of form and content, clarity and meaning.

(Weber 1949: 95–96)

Weber is, one the one hand, deploring the messiness of 'multifarious nuances' of the historical categories or ideas while, on the other hand, at the same time, implicitly reintroducing the same 'messiness' into the ideal types by recognizing that there often is much more overlap between the former and the latter than what the 'neat' definition of Weber would allow for. Therefore, despite Weber's struggle to 'purify' the ideal-types as imaginary constructs there always is a hard-to-escape *possibility* that they remain contaminated with traces of historical 'ideas' of certain epochs. Despite his best analytical efforts Weber cannot completely jettison history's imposed ambiguity from the constructed ideal-types, which are posited by definition to be the *most unambiguously intelligible concepts*.

Moreover, even if we were to assume with Weber that it is possible to come up with purely imagined ideal-types as such, they are always already contaminated by whatever aspect they are posited to accentuate by definition. The very aspects that are accentuated are in themselves always already contaminated by history in the sense that they are in themselves historical aspects to begin with, which means that they are always already ambiguous. Yet Weber (1949: 95–96) insists that

> the causal relationship between the historically determinable idea which governs the conduct of men and those components of historical reality from which their corresponding *ideal-type* may be abstracted, can naturally take on a considerable number of different forms. The main point to be observed is that *in principle* they are both fundamentally different things.

What is this *'principle'* that Weber is calling upon to anchor his argument for a clear demarcation between historically determined ideas and ideal-types? Is it a mere rhetorical pretention that there is/might be such a principle of legitimation of the demarcation between historically determined ideas and the ideal-types?

Drawing on Bhabha's post-colonial theory (1997), I propose that the ideal-type concept is but a *hybrid* concept, a concept which follows the *spectral* logic of *hybridity*, which shows how the ideal-type is simultaneously, on the one hand, much less than a unified, pure concept, thereby threatening the very notion of 'pure ideality' of the ideal-type, and, on the other hand, more than just an inherently self-divided, more than just doubled concept wherein both the resilient historical contaminations and the forces of the imaginative construction are in a continuous play of mutual constitution and destitution. As such the very notion of the ideal-type errs in reaching its destination, missing its destiny as a methodological tool in the form of a pure logical imaginary construct, and thereby falling into perpetual *destinerrance*, that is, a hybridity of *destiny, inheritance, and errancy*.[7]

Destinerrance is the source of meaning dissemination which blows up the possibility of a fusion of horizons of meaning of the ideal-type. That concepts are prone to be attributed different meanings through different 'readings' is a known fact. Human language and communication are prone to polysemy, that is, prone to multiplicity of meanings and plurivocity through various tropological movements. A situation of polysemy is one where we have an organized semantic movement within an implicit horizon, a horizon which is built on the assumption of a unitary assumption and/or resumption of meaning, at least potentially. In contrast, the dissemination within distinerrance disrupts and explodes the semantic horizon. Dissemination, according to Derrida (1981b: 26),

> endlessly opens up a *snag* ... a spot where neither meaning, however plural, nor *any form of presence* can pin/pen down [*agrapher*] the trace," and as such dissemination is a constant threat to "that *point* where the movement of signification would regularly come to *tie down* the play of the trace, thus producing (a) history.

Is this not what happens to the 'ideal-type' as a play of ambiguous traces of so-called 'historical' ideas despite Weber's best efforts to rigor and *logical* formulation and cleansing? In addition to the continuous movements of change and repetition that occur in the ideal-type within the very Weberian text, in addition to the impossibility of stopping the play of differences and deferral of traces of 'history', the ideal-type keeps disseminating. There is thus a 'play', "a field of infinite substitutions only because it is finite;" a play which "because instead of being an inexhaustible field, ... , instead of being too large, there is something missing from it: a center which arrests and grounds the play of substitutions" (Derrida 1978: 289). The 'ideal-type' thus does not possess a pure, imaginatively constructed 'ideal' center as Weber wants it to be, and as such it remains subject to the disseminating 'play' of meaning. It suffers from a snag that cannot be mended, a spot where meaning cannot be pinned down. Nor can any meaning pin down the snag opened by the trace in the so-called identity of the ideal-type. The security—ontological security of the ideal-type—is blown up due to a continuous opening of uncontrollable snags and spots under the forces of hybridity and the play of dissemination.

This does not however imply that there is no notion of ideal-type; there is 'ideal-type' but it is an 'ideal type' the meaning of which is continually blown up, more or less. No ideal-type can be in a relation of identity with itself without being immediately blown up—the 'self' of the ideal-type is necessarily disseminated the moment it is formulated and sought to be cleansed from a messy 'earthly reality'. Yet the law of iterability,[8] that is, iterated repetitions with simultaneous changes in the meaning of the ideal-type from context to context, works to preserve this autodivided identity of the ideal-type.

Moreover, the ideal-type is a signifying concept. As put by Weber (1949: 98–99), "an 'ideal type' ... has no connection at all with value-judgments, and it has nothing to do with any type of perfection other than a purely logical one." Nevertheless it is a sign to something, toward something, that is, "the unique individual character of cultural phenomena" which it makes clearly explicit (Weber 1949: 101). Yet as a sign, just like any other sign, it is incomplete, even if we 'experience' and usually think of a sign as if it were complete. What comes in to complete a sign's plenitude has thus to be more primordial than the sign; it is an operation of primordial supplementation.[9] Derrida (1973: 88) explains that

> this concept of primordial supplementation not only implies nonplenitude of presence ... it designates this function of substitutive supplementation [*suppléance*] in general, the 'in place of' (*für etwas*) structure which belongs to every sign in general.

Every sign in general suffers a non-plenitude which does not stay as such but becomes supplemented with a supplement for the sign to be meaningful. This means that supplementarity is the structure that allows us to engage in signification processes. However, this does not/should not imply that the supplement represents an absent signified. Rather, what the supplement does is to be "substituted for another signifier, for another type of signifier that maintains another relation with the deficient presence, one more highly valued by virtue of the play of difference" (Derrida 1973: 89). In other words, meaning differentiation, which creates differences without positive elements, is made possible through supplementarity. The supplement thus comes to supplement and add something to another 'thing'. This is done in a very peculiar way because this addition is one that replaces, more or less. It is an addition through which the supplement "intervenes or insinuates itself *in-the-place-of*," says Derrida (1974: 145). The supplement is thus what comes to take place in the structure of the sign right where the sign is marked by emptiness, yet without adding any positivity to the sign since the latter is thought of as full presence. So, what does the supplement add? It adds nothing; it adds neither a presence nor an absence, because it is neither one. Yet the supplement adds by taking place in the structure which is marked by emptiness.

Doesn't this operation of supplementarity account for the mutual constitution and destitution between, *on the one hand*, the ideal-type as defined by Weber (quoted up above), that is, as a notion formed

> by the one-sided *accentuation* of one or more points of view and by the synthesis of a great many diffuse, discrete, more or less present and occasionally absent *concrete individual* phenomena, which are arranged

according to those one-sidedly emphasized viewpoints into a unified *analytical* construct

and, *on the other hand*, the historical contamination and dissemination inherent within these very accentuated points of view? I think so.

Therefore, dissemination prohibits *telos* while supplementarity prohibits *arche* in the formation of ideal-types. Yet Weber insists in resisting and prohibiting this prohibition of *arche* and *telos* which are none but the inherent and inescapable conditions of possibility and therewith impossibility of his formulation of the ideal-type. He indeed persists in excluding that which his very edifice of ideal-types calls for and enables, that is, the *accentuation* from concrete materials drawn from history and not some *noumenal* framework of certain viewpoints. He (Weber 1949: 102–3) states that

> the logical classification of analytical concepts on the one hand and the empirical arrangements of the events thus conceptualized in space, time, and causal relationship, on the other, appear to be so bound up together that there is an almost irresistible temptation to do violence to reality in order to prove the real validity of the construct.

Weber warns us from the irresistible temptation of doing violence to reality, while violence is the very condition of possibility of his concept of ideal-type. *Weber performatively deploys a violent coup de force to expel violence against reality by committing violence against the supplement of reality* qua *historical contamination, a contamination that inheres deep within his notion of the ideal-type.* Weber *names* the ideal-type through a performative act of violence against the very reality that he seeks to methodologically study and explain.

In sum, the 'ideal-type' *qua* sign is inescapably haunted with traces of 'historical' ideas, is constantly disseminated, and cannot escape the operation of supplementarity in acquiring meaning. Using the 'ideal-type' implies iterating it, which means a simultaneous repetition and change of the meaning of the ideal-type from context to context. The ideal-type is neither a 'pure' logical utopia as Weber wants it to be. Nor is it an unambiguous concept that escapes the messiness of 'multifarious nuances' as wished for by Weber. The ideal type is an undecidable concept. How detrimental is this undecidability to the key function of the ideal-type that Weber sought for it? I ask this question because, as explained later on, it is more or less a similar condition of undecidability that makes it possible for Jackson to advocate a pluralist science of world politics.

As well clarified by Weber and many of his interpreters, Weber formulates the ideal-type as a *tool* through which he addresses the problem of 'objectivity' in social sciences. This transpires, for example, from Weber's efforts "to trace the course of the hair-line which separates science from faith."[10] Weber (1949: 110) declares that the *objective* validity of all empirical knowledge rests exclusively upon the ordering of the given reality according to categories which are *subjective* in a specific sense, namely, in that they present the *presuppositions* of our knowledge and are based on the presupposition of the *value* of those *truths* which empirical knowledge alone is able to give us.

Weber (1949: 111) also states that

the 'objectivity' of the social sciences depends rather on the fact that the empirical data are always related to those evaluative ideas which alone make them worth knowing and the significance of the empirical data is derived from these evaluative ideas. ... The concrete form in which value-relevance occurs remains perpetually in flux, ever subject to change in the dimly seen future of human culture.

The doctrine of *value relevance* is for Weber the "decisive feature of the perspective that is distinctive to the cultural sciences" (Weber cited by Oakes (1988: 145)) and as such undergirds Weber's sense of an objective social science. Weber (1949: 111) explains that:

The concept of culture is a *value concept*. Empirical reality is 'culture' because and insofar as we relate it to value ideas. It includes those segments and *only* those segments of reality that become *significant* to us by virtue of that relation.

This, according to Oakes (1988: 33), constitutes one of the two premises of Weber's axiological polytheism, namely, "the irreducible variability of values and the irresolvability of radical value conflicts." In other words, for Weber, "reality is constituted as culture only on the basis of cultural meanings that are defined in terms of variable and incommensurable criteria for value relevance" (Oakes 1988: 36). As summarized by Oakes, the problematique of Weber's methodology is defined by the following elements:

the doctrine of the irrationality of reality; the conception of culture as constituted by meanings that are defined in terms of their relevance to values; and the variability and the irreducible plurality of values, which entail the variability and irreducible plurality of value relevancies.
(Oakes 1988: 145)

Taken together these three premises produce *the problem of value relevance*, that is, how to decide among possible value relevancies. Weber does not advocate any principle for choosing between competing value-relevancies; rather, he leaves it to individual conscience and personal faith and standpoints—an irreconcilable, eternal conflict (Weber in his *Science as a Vocation*). However, Weber rejects any purely relativist position since he states that ultimately "the investigator is obviously bound by the norms of our thought here just as much as elsewhere" (cited by Oakes 1988: 147). Is Weber contradicting himself? Let us not jump to conclusion. Indeed, as pointed out by Oakes (1988: 149), given Weber's position that any principle of explanation in the social sciences always depends on values, it is not clear what Weber means by *the norms of our thought*. This implies that this is not a call for any universal or transcendental norms of thought. On the face of it, it appears that Weber does reject his friend's, Heinrich Rickert (1986), solution to the problem of value relevancies which consists in positing the existence of an unconditional criterion even if we cannot know now what it is. Oakes (1988: 151) argues however that Weber has fallen into the trap of decisionism that Rickert had fell into before him. Although I find Oakes' position somewhat persuasive, I think that Weber's text allows for more than what Oakes let Weber's text do. Put differently, I am calling for resisting a closure of the Weberian text. I am calling for recognizing the *chance* that inheres in the seemingly aporiatic doctrine of the value relevancies, a *chance* that suggests that the process of interpreting Weber's sense of the doctrine of value-relevance falls under the law of undecidability.

Undecidability is "a determinate oscillation between possibilities" which are "themselves highly determined in strictly defined situations," says Derrida (1988: 148). A good example of undecidability can be grasped through the famous Russell Paradox, which runs as follows. There is a barber living in a town where all men either shave themselves or are shaved by the barber. The barber only shaves those men who do not shave themselves. What about the barber himself? *Does he shave himself?* Let's assume that he does shave himself. This however contradicts the assumption of the story since by assumption he shaves only the men in town who do not shave themselves. Let's thus say: *he does not shave himself*. But the basic assumption is that every man in town either shaves himself or the barber shaves him. So the barber does shave himself. In conclusion: *the barber shaves himself if he does not shave himself, and, conversely, the barber does not shave himself if he shaves himself!* It is undecidable whether the barber shaves himself or not.

Undecidability does not necessarily mean indeterminacy of options or choices. It occurs exactly when we are faced with a well determined and defined structure of options that are competing with one another and we are not able to decide either way. Undecidability indicates the impossibility of a definitive separation between binary oppositions.[11] On the one hand, undecidability enables and activates binary oppositions. On the other hand, undecidability escapes the logic of binary oppositions. Undecidability thus resists and disorganizes binary oppositions without ever constituting third terms and without ever leaving room for a solution in the form of Hegelian sublation. The play of undecidability goes to a point at which a certain displacement of the series of oppositions takes/should take place. This play is such that "we cannot qualify it, name it, comprehend it under a simple concept without immediately being off the mark," says Derrida (1981b: 104). Yet undecidability functions within certain oppositions that are essential for argumentation, if only to undermine these oppositions at the same time by enacting the play of their multiple meanings. That is: undecidability functions by grafting one meaning onto another, thereby simultaneously bringing together and separating possible meanings. This implies that the logic of the play of meanings in undecidability cannot be presented as 'this *and* that' or 'this *or* that.' Derrida (1988: 117) instead argues that the logic of undecidability consists of "'and' and 'or' combinations at the same time; it is a non-binary logic of neither/nor and simultaneously either/or." The logic of undecidability is, according to Derrida, one of spectrality (1994a: 6).

From Derrida's perspective, undecidability is not a cause of paralysis but rather the condition of possibility of decision. Actors decide to act not in spite of, but rather because of, undecidability. Actors decide precisely because situations of undecidability demand decision and prior knowledge is insufficient to make possible programmatic or algorithmic decision. The decision thus takes the form of an act of invention which cannot be grounded in what precedes it (Derrida 1989: 955). The instant of decision is heterogeneous to all (preceding) knowledge. We can thus speak of an aporia that consists of a sense of urgency and that obstructs the horizon of knowledge.

What does this imply for the issue at hand—that is, the problematic doctrine of value-relevance? This means that constructing the 'ideal-type' as a tool through which to address the problem of 'objectivity' in social sciences, which means addressing the problem of the 'doctrine of value-relevance,' is not as problematic as it seems to be at first sight. Weber could not adopt a 'first' principle with which he would have decided on value-relevance. He instead 'invented' the methodology of the 'ideal-type' through which one can think of an 'objective' social science. I argue that Weber 'can do this because the ideal-type is, as discussed earlier, inherently haunted by undecidability. In other words, the undecidability of the value-relevance is 'passed' on into a specter of undecidability haunting the ideal-type.

This way of re-thinking both the tensions within the 'ideal-type' and the problematique of value-relevance is possible only if one follows the 'logic', or, more accurately, the play of a work of deconstruction. The latter brings forth the inescapable spectral law of undecidability as a possibility condition for the deployment of the methodology of ideal-type as a tool for addressing the lack of a 'first' principle adjudication of the problem of value-relevance in social sciences. That is: With a (certain) Weber and contra both Oakes and Rickert, it is possible to simultaneously think an 'objective' social science and a non-adjudicated problem of value-relevance through the undecidable notion of 'ideal-type'.

Put differently, a simultaneous rendering of the ideal-type and the doctrine of value-relevance is possible by affirming a position for the work of deconstruction at the place of other conventional ways of thinking and interpreting such as the Aristotelian, dialectic, or dialogical logics. This allows us to incorporate into a displaced notion of 'ideal-type' both a 'rationality' that Weber's discussion of ideal-type focuses on and an (historical) 'irrationality' of 'reality' that Weber seeks to silence, an 'irrationality' that has survived and haunted the Weberian text under the form of traces (of historical-concepts), despite Weber's best efforts to the contrary, as discussed earlier. This ethos of deconstructing the ideal-type is followed by deploying pseudo-concepts that have been 'affirmed' through the work of deconstruction, or as termed by Gasché (1986), a general infrastructural space of thinking and analyzing, a space populated by chains of undecidable pseudo-concepts such as *iterability*, *supplementarity*, *dissemination*, *spectrality*, *hybridity*, *trace*, and so on. As a result the displaced notion of 'ideal-type' is a quasi-concept which constitutively includes the 'oscillations' of the undecidable pseudo-concepts, and as such would display deconstruction at work within the very re-thinking of the ideal-type and applications thereof. As put by Derrida (1988: 136), the goal is "to take this limitless context into account, to pay the sharpest and broadest attention possible to context, and thus to an incessant movement of recontextualization."

What are some implications of this deconstructive affirmation of a displaced 'ideal-type' for Jackson's approach? Does Jackson address the undecidability that inheres within the methodology of ideal-type? Clearly, Jackson did highlight the undecidability (if without naming it as such) of thinking about the philosophy of science in terms of Weber's notion of ideal-type. Jackson unambiguously decides that the issues are irresolvable and that we ought to opt for a pluralist science of world politics. He justifies such a position as unavoidably based on leaps of faith, an unthought faith which is beyond or outside knowledge, or at least outside the realm of science as he defines it.

Therefore, *on the one hand*, I want to agree, if in a certain way, with Jackson's call for a pluralist science given the undecidability that inheres in the methodology of ideal-types that he deploys to 'read' extant IR approaches to philosophy of science. *On the other hand*, however, I cannot not resist Jackson's dualistic thinking about 'science' and 'faith'. That this is an issue worthwhile exploring comes from Jackson's recognition in the final analysis that faith is necessary for pluralist science (via commitments to wagers) to be as such. Is Jackson losing his sharply probing analytical saw? I do not think so. Yet I think that his text is begging him to go where he refuses to venture. I thus offer to take Jackson's text and line of analysis to where he passionately refuses to go; I thus want to think and explore this 'faith' and its relation with 'science' and 'knowledge' as well as with 'passion' (which Jackson seems to want to silence if without however being able to escape being passionate about his own theoretical gestures and advocacies). I thus hope to present the following as a faithful reading of Jackson's text to think his testimonial faith for a wager-based *miraculous* pluralist science of world politics, yet realizing that this *might* go against Jackson's pragmatic will to believe in faith, *perhaps*.

Jackson's *testimonial* faith for a wager-based *miraculous* science

In adopting Weber's methodology of ideal-types to summarize/analyze extant IR literature on the philosophy of science, Jackson unsurprisingly ends up being faced with the issue of value-relevance, that is, how to adjudicate among the various 'ideal-types' (of philosophy of science in IR) that he proposes. Jackson's (2010: 34) solution is that "we should regard positions on the character and conduct of science to rest on provisional commitments—*wagers*—about matters of philosophical ontology that can really never be settled definitively."

Jackson suggests two wagers: The first wager concerns "the relationship or connection between the researcher and the researched world" and as such "presents an ideal-typical choice between *mind-world dualism* and … *mind-world monism*" (Jackson 2010: 35). The second wager is defined by *transfactualism* and *phenomenalism*. *Transfactualism*, espoused by Critical Realists, refers to "the position that maintains the possibility of knowing things about in-principle unobservables" by holding out "the possibility of going beyond the facts to grasp the deeper processes and factors that generate those facts" (Jackson 2010: 36–37). *Phenomenalism*, espoused for example by Dewey's inspired pragmatists, maintains that "it is neither necessary nor possible for researchers to 'transcend experience by some organ of unique character that carries [them] into the super-empirical' … knowledge, to the contrary, is a matter of organizing past experiences so as to forge useful tools for the investigation of future, as-yet-unknown situations" (Jackson 2010: 37). These two wagers constitute "two of the most important commitments of philosophical ontology made by IR scholars, and suitably abstracted they provide a useful way of clarifying debates about the philosophy of science in the field" (Jackson 2010: 35). Jackson proposes a 2 æ 2 table within which he is able to fit most of the current 'isms' of IR and even make a bid for his analyticism. He emphasizes that his wagers-based approach

> requires a vocabulary that is precise enough to permit significant differences and similarities between scientific methodologies to come to the forefront. This vocabulary is not a framework for evaluation; it is, rather, an instrument of clarification, helping to make explicit what is ordinarily tacit.
>
> (Jackson 2010: 197)

In other words, as clarified by Jackson (2010: 207), "neopositivism, critical realism, analyticism, and reflexivity name four different ways in which scientific research can unfold, not four different self-conscious research traditions or schools of thought within the IR field." Rather, these are Weberian *ideal-types* of IR methodologies. As such, this work of precise clarification and serious disclosure of "philosophical-ontological typology of methodologies," argues Jackson (2010: 39), "has the merit of placing commitments in a common conceptual space, so that when we disagree we are at least disagreeing about the same or similar things. Having a commonplace about which to disagree fosters conversation, not isolation." Give and take the fact that "No philosophical-ontological wager is self-evident, and none is exhaustive of all of the others" (Jackson 2010: 223, ft.5). Jackson's approach thus "calls for dialogical *encounters* between arguments inhabiting different parts of the logical space formed by the combination of basic wagers of philosophical ontology," (Jackson 2010: 210). We do this by taking wagers or bets which, as clearly argued by Jackson (Jackson 2010: 196), are "formally ungrounded." Are they?

That raising this question is legitimate is prompted by Jackson's resolution that these wagers "require of their practitioners a commitment that is like nothing else so much as an existential leap of faith" (2010: 197). For Jackson anything that cannot be resolved empirically or rationally is a matter of faith, examples of which are questions on "the nature of Being" and "the purpose of human existence" (Jackson 2010: 34). Does this imply that faith is not rational and not empirical, that it is idealist and irrationalist? Wouldn't this pose a detrimental problem for Jackson's wager-based approach to his ideal-typical classifying scheme of IR methodologies? Indeed, his book is a sustained effort to *rationally* argue that such an ideal-typology is very useful and to call for methodological pluralism in IR. *Are these calls therefore justified through irrationality and idealism*? The answer is ambiguous since, as expected, Jackson argues that "scientific methodologies are not exactly articles of faith, and methodological diversity and theological diversity are not precisely the same things despite the almost religious tone of many doctrinaire methodological pronouncements;" never mind the fact that Jackson confesses that "there are more than a few similarities between the two" (Jackson 2010: 188–89).

Yet scientific methodologies which are "not exactly articles of faith" are crucially and inescapably, according to Jackson, anchored and only justified in the final analysis through leaps or articles of faith! Is there thus any difference between, say, theology based on articles of faith and Jackson's approach? He seems to more or less think so; he, for example, writes that "unlike theology, methodology is always a *means* toward another end" (2010: 191). Yet, this does not address the issue of whether methodology and theology are really that different given the fact that both are, according to Jackson, anchored and justified through articles and leaps of faith, even if these leaps of faith are presumably different from one another. They seem to have at least some elements of 'faith' in common.

Perhaps, Jackson's call for (philosophy-of-ontology) wagers is reminiscent of Pascal's deployment of the wager to convince the religiously skeptic about the rationality of believing in God.[12] That this might indeed be the case is suggested by Rescher's (1985: 19–21) interpretation of Pascal stating that:

> the [Pascal's] Wager argument's task is to show that belief is rationally warranted—in the specifically prudential (not evidential!) mode of rational warrant ... the Wager argument is aimed at *motivating* belief rather than at *demonstrating* its validity—at inaugurating faith where it is lacking rather than consolidating it where it exists.

Isn't this exactly what Jackson seeks to do? Jackson seems to be using the wager as a rhetorical and persuasive tool much like Pascal who, as argued by Velchik (2009: 5), "appears to be rather interested in persuasion, eloquence, and rhetoric," especially when Pascal explains that "when people are generally better persuaded by the reasons which they have themselves discovered than by those which have come into the mind of others." Moreover, again as explained by Velchik,

> Pascal presented the Wager as an argument to address the doubter in such a way that neutralizes the passions that interfere with conversion. ... The visibly pragmatic argument of the Wager is in fact part of a greater epistemic argument.
>
> (2009: 6–7)

Isn't this also part of Jackson's agenda when he seeks to go beyond the passions which sometimes drive (or rather hold back) IR debates on the philosophy of science?[13]

Jackson's plea is a testimony that we take wagers on a leap of faith. This however raises the question: Is such a leap of faith a *means* to an end, that is, we take the leap of faith to be able 'to do IR'? I think that this transpires throughout Jackson's book. Yet how are we to think of this 'faith'? Doesn't thinking of 'faith' as a means to an end annul 'faith' as we usually think of it? Doing so would call for an inquiry into/about the 'rationality' of this means to an end, which would make Jackson's advocacy a sort of rational path to pluralist science but anchored in leaps of faith. Jackson does not raise these issues, or any other issue about 'faith'. He in fact mentions the word faith only three times in this text without exploring it. Yet, because it is what anchors his thoughtfully rationalized approach to IR philosophy of science through the notion of Weber's ideal-type, this is not only a very pertinent question. It also is an important exploration into the possibility (and perhaps even impossibility) conditions of Jackson's whole edifice.

I speak of faith and passion conjointly because, *on the one hand*, Jackson ends up calling on/for faith as the final anchor of his whole enterprise, while, *on the other hand*, he deplores the passions that, he argues, sometimes drive IR debates (or lack thereof) on matters of philosophy of science. Is Jackson contradicting himself since one usually thinks of faith in terms of passion, or at least together? Jackson seems, for example, to be going against William James who defends in his work on *The Will to Believe* the thesis that:[14]

> Our passionate nature not only lawfully may, but must, decide an option between propositions, whenever it is a genuine option that cannot by its nature be decided on intellectual ground; for to say, under such circumstances, 'Do not decide, but leave the question open', is itself a passional decision—just like deciding yes or no—and is attended with the same risk of losing the truth.

Isn't Jackson's analyticism but a "passion for parsimony, for economy of means in thought" and a "philosophic passion *par excellence*" as James would have put it (1979: 58)? And alongside this passion, again quoting James (1979: 59), "there exists a sister passion ... for distinguishing; it is the impulse to be *acquainted* with the parts rather than to comprehend the whole," in other words, Jackson's analyticism. Perhaps it would not be too far-fetched to say that Jackson's wager-based approach is a passionate testimony for a faith-based/grounded pluralism.[15]

This discussion suggests that we need to take Jackson's text beyond Jackson's too hasty closure. I thus pose the following questions while remaining as faithful as possible to Jackson's faith-grounded approach: Is Jackson's text relying on a notion/practice of faith which is more general than faith in the sense of the religious? Yet, does it make sense to speak of faith in terms other than religious or theological ones? Can we ever escape such connotations? How would such a faith work (or not work) in grounding whatever we call upon it to ground? Is it some sort of a promise that is inherent in the very language and discourse about wagers? Is Jackson telling us something like 'I hereby promise to you pluralism' which would go beyond dogmatism and currently paralyzing passions? Does this faith delineate itself from knowledge? How sustainable is such faith/knowledge delineation if faith is the final grounding of the whole edifice of knowledge that Jackson advocates? Conversely, Jackson's text is a book about knowledge of IR; he is presenting a certain way of systematically thinking about the conduct of inquiry in IR. To this end, he draws extensively on many bodies of literature to make the case for his way of thinking, which eventually leads him to conclude that the final grounding is a leap of faith. Doesn't this make this faith contextually dependent on a huge body of knowledge that he deploys in order to make his case? How and why does Jackson stop his plea and decide that he has reached a threshold beyond which we can't go without falling into the passions and dogmatisms that he deplores? Put differently: How does this 'final' faith reveal itself to Jackson so that he can testify for 'leaps of faith' grounding of the wagers? What is the condition of possibility—that is, revealability—of such a revelation of an ostensibly non-religious faith?

In order to help answer these questions let us explore how one of the fathers of pragmatism—William James—addresses the notion of faith, with whom Jackson shares many elements of pragmatism. According to James, "Faith means belief in something concerning which doubt is still theoretically possible" and "faith is the readiness to act in a cause the prosperous issue of which is not certified to us in advance" (James 1979: 76). Faith thus occurs and is resorted to in the absence of knowledge about the future and even sometimes the present (or the past for that matter). Because our knowledge is always limited, "we cannot live or think at all without some degree of faith. Faith is synonymous with working hypothesis. The only difference is that while some hypotheses can be refuted in five minutes, others defy ages," says James (1979: 79). Faith and knowledge are usually opposed or at least believed to occur as mutually opposites if not contradictory. Yet, argues James,

> No philosophy will permanently be deemed rational by all men which (in addition to meeting logical demands) does not to some degree pretend to determine expectancy, and in a still greater degree make a direct appeal to all those powers of our nature which we hold in highest esteem. Faith, being one of these powers, will always remain a factor not to be banished from philosophic constructions, the more so since in many ways it brings forth its own verification.

What is this faith *qua* power of our nature that James is referring to?[16] It is not religious faith *per se* as we usually speak of it in the sense of theology, a delineation that Jackson would also make. Yet, can we really speak of faith while avoiding the religious as such, if only at the level of connotations due to the historical legacy that is inherited and iterated through and the use of language and cultures? Is a non-religious faith part of non-religious knowledge or any knowledge *tout court*? For Derrida contra Kant, argues Minister,

> even knowledge cannot become 'knowledge' in the Kantian sense, since it is conditioned by an 'originary' faith that is both non-religious and pre-religious. Derrida argues that this faith, which constitutes an originary fiduciary link with others, is the source of both knowledge and religious faith, that is, particular, determinate religious beliefs and practices.
>
> (James 1979: 89)

Let us now continue reading James in conjunction with Derrida's deconstruction of the faith/knowledge distinction, a deconstruction that begins with the question on the meaning of believing and religion. Derrida states that

> We believe we can pretend to believe—fiduciary act—that we share in some pre-understanding. We act as though we had some common sense of what 'religion' means through the languages that we believe ... we know how to speak. We believe in the minimal trustworthiness of this word. ... we believe (or believe that it is obligatory that) we pre-understand the meaning of this word, if only to be able to question and in order to interrogate ourselves on this subject. Well nothing is less pre-assured than such Faktum and the entire question of religion comes down, perhaps, to this lack of assurance.
>
> (Derrida 2002c: 44)

Derrida also raises the question of whether faith is always only related to religion and the religious. His position is that it has not always been the case (Derrida 2002c: 48). Derrida (2002c: 68) then questions the posited distinction (since Kant) between faith and knowledge, stating that

The temptation of knowing, the temptation of knowledge, is to believe not only that one knows what one knows (which wouldn't be too serious), but also that one knows what knowledge is, that is, free, structurally, of belief or of **faith**—of the fiduciary or of trustworthiness.

Yet, according to Derrida (2002c: 66), religion/faith and knowledge/reason have some key resource in common on which they draw in tandem, that is, "the testimonial pledge of every performative, committing it to respond as much *before* the other." More precisely, Derrida asserts that critique (*à la Kant* and otherwise) and reason

> are obliged to put into play an irreducible 'faith,' that of a 'social bond' or of a 'sworn faith,' of testimony ('I promise to tell you the truth beyond all proof and all theoretical demonstration, believe me, etc.'), that is, of performative of promising at work even in lying or perjury and without which no address to the other would be possible. Without the performative experience of this elementary act of faith, there would neither be 'social bond' nor address of the other, nor any performative in general ... nor above all, here, that structural performativity of the productive performance that binds from its very inception the knowledge of the scientific community to doing, and science to technics.
> (Derrida 2002c: 80–81)

Not only does religion but also the very inception of knowledge *qua* performativity require such an irreducible faith as the possibility condition of its structural performativity. "We now know," says Derrida (2002c: 80–81), "that the scientific act is, through and through, a practical intervention and a technical performativity in the very energy of its essence." And this ineluctably performative nature of knowledge "brings into play and confirms the fiduciary credit of an elementary faith which is, at least in its essence or calling, religious" in the sense of "the elementary condition, the milieu of the religious if not religion itself." As such the elementary condition of the religious (without any determinate religion) or, equivalently, this irreducible faith, says Derrida (2002c: 79), "accompanies and even precedes the critical and tele-technoscientific reason, it watches over it as its shadow." Derrida (2002c: 93–94) thus concludes that

> it seems impossible to deny the *possibility* in whose name—thanks to which—the derived *necessity* (the authority or determinate belief) would be put in question, suspended, rejected or criticized, even deconstructed. ... Such would be the place where, before and after all the Enlightenments in the world, reason, critique, science, tele-technoscience, philosophy, thought in general, retain the *same* resource as religion in general.

How does this irreducible 'faith', which does not possess any determinate content, and hence which is different from historical or even messianic religions, appear to us, reveal itself to us? Derrida addresses this issue in terms of the duo of revelation and revealability by asking whether revealability is more originary than revelation which would make revealability independent of all religions, or conversely, whether it is the events of revelation that reveal the possibility of revealability itself (Derrida 2002c: 54–55). That is, is the originary and irreducible faith a revelation or is it the condition of revelation of faith and knowledge as we know them?

This question can be phrased in the context of Jackson's text as: Is the faith that Jackson calls upon to ground a pluralist science a revelation which is revealed to us after going through the tedious process of accumulating and assessing IR knowledge about the philosophy of science? This makes the latter knowledge the condition of possibility of 'faith' to appear to us as such, as necessary for grounding a pluralist science of world politics. Or perhaps it is the other way around. Perhaps it is faith which is the condition of possibility of a pluralist science, an interpretation which would not contradict Jackson's text. In other words, which among 'faith' and 'IR knowledge' is 'revealability' and which is 'revelation'? Or perhaps, we need not choose between the two. Perhaps both are revelation and revealability. Are we facing an aporia?

Derrida argues that there always is a revelation/revealability aporia. According to Ware (2006: 239), Derrida asks "whether revelation and revealability exhaust the possibilities of thinking through the sources of religion" and "whether we can think an event or experience that relates to neither of the *two veils* of revelation and revealability." In other word, if we were to posit revealability as more originary and prior to revelation, "can we think something older than revealability … ?" (Ware 2006: 239). Instead of jettisoning or prioritizing either revelation or revealability, Derrida preserves both and displaces the opposition/hierarchy by suggesting that we need to think of the aporia in terms of its conditions of possibility and impossibility. Derrida retorts that the oscillation between revelation and revealability must be respected for its own sake since "respect for this singular indecision or for this hyperbolic outbidding between two originarities, the order of the 'revealed' and the order of the 'revealable,'" is indeed "at once the chance of every responsible decision and of another 'reflecting faith,' of a new 'tolerance'," (Derrida 2002c: 59). Therefore, Derrida sees the aporia, which is "an experience of not knowing what path to follow or coming to the point where no path can be found," (Norris 1982: 4) not as a problem, not as an obstacle, but rather as a *chance* for another thinking of 'faith', an irreducible faith. Derrida suggests that we can think of the revelation/revealability aporia in terms of three pseudo-notions: *khôra, messianicity,* and *testimony*.[17]

Derrida begins his discussion of *khôra* with Plato's *Timaeus* who presents *khôra* as the place wherein "the demiurge[18] impresses or cuts images of the intelligible paradigms, the place which was already there, which, while radically heterogeneous with the forms, seems to be as old as the forms" (Caputo 1997a: 35). *Khôra*, termed as a place of a third kind, belongs, according to

Derrida (1992b: 105), "neither to becoming, nor to non-being (the *khôra* is never described as a void), nor to Being." *Khôra* is quite unique in its singularity for it defies our common sense of thinking and speaking of 'things' in this world, as either ideal or material. "This nonbeing cannot but be *declared*, that is, be caught or conceived, via the anthropomorphic schemas of the verb *to receive* and the verb *to give*," says Derrida (1995b: 95). *Khôra* is not "a support or a subject which would *give* place by receiving or by conceiving, or indeed by letting itself be conceived," states Derrida (1995b: 95). Nor is *khôra* a sort of super-sensible that can be referred to through a play of metaphors. *Khôra* is a *receptacle*, but one which is radically different from the usual sense of the term. Having no meaning in itself, no essence, and no identity, it nonetheless "receives all without becoming anything" (Caputo 1997a: 35–36). That *khôra* "must remain without form and without proper determination" is required for the *khôra* to be able "to receive all and allow itself to be marked or affected by what is inscribed in it" (Derrida 1992b: 107).

Moreover, *khôra* cannot be spoken of within an Aristotelian logic of 'either this or that', 'yes or no'. All attempts to describe it or understand it can only be done using the phrase 'neither this ... nor that'. "*Khôra*," says Derrida (1995b: 89), defies the logic of non-contradiction, "that logic of 'binarity, of the yes or no'." The *khôra* follows a logic that might, for example, accept as a principle or axiom the invalidation of the principle of non-contradiction as well as the principle of contradiction. Derrida (1995b: 89) explains that "at times the *khôra* appears to be neither this nor that, at times both this and that, but this alternation between the logic of exclusion and that of participation," this impossible situation from the perspective of an Aristotelian logic, looks as impossible "only from a provisional appearance and from the constraints of rhetoric." The logic of *khôra* is the logic of without.

The logic of without is best represented in the simultaneously negative and affirmative meaning that the term *without* is given in the following statements on God by St. Augustine: "God is wise without wisdom;" God is "good without goodness;" God is "powerful without power." The logic of without "does not only avoid the abstraction tied to every noun and to the being implied in every essential generality" (Derrida 2008: 148). What also happens is that "in the same word and in the same syntax," the without acts so that "it transmutes into affirmation its purely phenomenal negativity" (Derrida 2008: 178–79). In the logic of without there seems to be "a principle of demultiplication of voices and discourse, of disappropriation and reappropriation of utterances, with the most distant appearing closest, and vice versa" (Derrida 2008: 178–79). The logic of without has not only "the negative force of depriving or denying words of their old meanings but also the positive force of repeating or re-inscribing their old meanings in new ones" (Bradley 2001: 136).

What does this thinking of the revelation/revealability aporia in terms of *khôra* within the logic of without imply for the notion (or rather pseudo-notion) of 'faith' which is more originary than faith *qua* religion and knowledge *qua* non-religious? How does *khôra* help in thinking the revelation/

revealability aporia? As put by Ware (2006: 251), the spacing of *khôra* is the spacing "between the event of revelation as a determinate set of beliefs, prayers, and hopes, and revealability as the formal possibility and opening of belief, prayer, and hope." The spacing of *khôra* is thus the condition of possibility of both revelation and revealability, of religion and knowledge.

If *khôra* is the spacing that makes possible the aporiatic couple of revelation and revealability, *messianicity* is what creates the *possibility* of expectation, without any determinate expectation though. This messianicity does not await a messiah or anyone/anything else. Derrida (2002c: 56) explains that the messianic "would be the opening to the future or to the coming of the other as the advent of justice, but without horizon of expectation and without prophetic prefiguration." He adds that "the messianic exposes itself to absolute surprise," and as such the messianic ought to "be prepared (waiting without awaiting itself) for the best as for the worst, the one never coming without opening the possibility of the other" (Derrida 2002c: 56). In messianicity we therefore encounter "a general structure of experience" which also obeys the logic of without—a *messianic without messianism* (Derrida 2002c: 56). Derrida (2002c: 56) explains that this general structure of experience is an expectation (or the possibility of expectation) which "is not and ought not to be certain of anything, either through knowledge, consciousness, conscience, foreseeability or any kind of programme as such." These defining features of messianicity are what makes it belong "from the very beginning to the experience of faith, of believing, of a credit that is irreducible to knowledge and of a trust that 'founds' all relation to the other in testimony," and thus makes it inscribe "itself in advance in the promise, in the act of faith or in the appeal to faith that inhabits every act of language and every address to the other," says Derrida (2002c: 56). Derrida (2002c: 57) compares this messianic without messianism to *a desert in the desert* without which "there would be neither act of faith, nor promise, nor future."

Therefore, if *khôra* is the spacing *qua* condition of possibility of the pairs revelation/revealability and faith/reason, and if the *messianic* is the condition of possibility of a general structure of experiential expectation without any determinate expectation of any sort, thereby letting the future always be a future to come, how do these dimensions of the irreducible faith manifest themselves in any discourse? In the spirit of Derrida's thinking on testimony (and attestation) I suggest that the manifestation of this irreducible faith assumes the form of a testimony and attestation of faith.

As discussed earlier, Jackson spends much of the book assessing extant IR literature and presenting his Weberian typology based on thinking the various 'isms' as ideal types based on wagers. Yet when all is done and said Jackson resorts to the 'leaps of faith' as the ultimate justification for the wagers-based typology. Jackson implicitly (or perhaps not) means 'you have to believe me' that this is it, short of which we would continue falling into dogmatism and passionate debates that never resolve anything. How should/can we understand this 'you have to believe me'? Jackson does not, or perhaps he thinks that he cannot, give any epistemic evidence for this 'you have to believe me'. And this is precisely his point: we resort to a leap of faith because we cannot muster any more epistemic or otherwise argument in favor of this or that wager and hence 'ism'. This 'you have to believe me', according to Derrida,

> does not have the meaning of theoretico-epistemological necessity. It is not presented as a probative demonstration to which one has no choice but to subscribe to the conclusion of a syllogism, in the course of an argumentation, or indeed to the display of a thing present. Here, 'you have to believe me' means 'believe me because I tell you to, because I ask you to' or as well 'I promise you that I will tell the truth and be faithful to my promise, and I undertake to be faithful'.
> (Derrida 2005a: 76–77)

Derrida explains that the necessity of this 'believe me' "is not theoretical but performative-pragmatic" and "it is perhaps the only rigorous introduction to the thinking of what 'believe' can mean to say" (Derrida 2005a: 76–77). He also adds that this 'believe me', which is not providing or based on any evidence, is an act of testimony. Derrida explains that

> Testimony, in the strict sense of the term, is advanced in the first person by someone who says, 'I swear,' who pledges to tell the truth, gives his word, and asks to be taken at his word in a situation where nothing has been proven—where nothing will ever be proven, for structural reasons, for reasons that are essential and not contingent.
> (Derrida and Stiegler 2002: 93–94)

Testimony is heterogeneous to the process of evidence; it instead "implies faith, belief, sworn faith, the pledge to tell the truth, the 'I swear to tell the truth, the whole truth and nothing but the truth'" (Derrida and Stiegler 2002: 93–94).

What makes any utterance a testimony? Is it the content of the testimony? If that were the case, then Jackson's profession on the role of leaps of faith in grounding the wagers will be vacuous since he does not say much about this leap of faith. Jackson's profession is still as a testimony as anyone can be since, as put by Morin (2007: 174), "what is essential to the testimony is the relation of the singular witness to the event," and "a testimony is always about the 'secret' regardless of whether it testifies to a worldly event—in principle accessible to all—or to an 'internal' event—in principle inaccessible to any."

Does this mean that Jackson is promising us a 'secret', a secret which is a secret as such, without any content, which is a secret even to itself? That is, a secret which is not a secret in the usual sense of the term; otherwise, it would be tantamount to falling back into some sort of foundationalism, a step that Jackson is careful in not taking. Jackson does not explicitly promise a secret as such. But doesn't he actually, rhetorically, implicitly? I would argue that he does, in a certain way.

The 'secret' of this 'secrecy' is thus that the 'secret' is not a matter of knowing and does not belong anywhere, anytime, in any form or shape to knowledge, to anyone (Derrida 1992b; Derrida and Ferraris 2001). The 'secret' does not exist as such and because of this we cannot see it or know it. This secret is such that *it cannot not continue to denegate*—that is, negate negating itself without reaching a full restitution of—itself.[19] Although there is no 'secret' as such, the 'secret' serves as that which Jackson discursively deploys much like a simulacrum, a copy without an originary original. The simulacrum of a secret points to what exceeds the simulacrum without really pointing to it, to what seems to anchor it, that is, a presumed hidden secret. The simulacrum points to a *possibility* which exceeds it. However, because we are dealing with a simulacrum, the *possibility* that the simulacrum points to is the remainder after the simulacrum is considered as such, that is, after we realize that there is no hidden 'thing' or 'secret' as an original of this simulacrum. *The possibility* of this 'secret' is *the condition of possibility* of the origination of the simulacrum. 'Secret' is thus the remainder of something that is not there to start with but is rather a simulacrum of a non-originary copy (Caputo 1997a: 106–7). The 'true' secret of this 'secret' is that there neither is a positive nor a negative secret behind it, no secret knowledge, no secret knowing. Yet, as such this secret is *the condition of possibility* of the thematizable, objectifiable, and sharable, all the while being without both knowledge and non-knowledge, and therefore cannot be shared, not even as a non-knowledge. The 'secret' is not only factually unknowable but also, and most importantly, structurally unknowable—a structural unknowability (Caputo 1997a: 101).

This 'secret' *qua very possibility of secret* (without any actual or potential content whatsoever) is what impassions Jackson to continue believing in the wagers and testifying without any possibility of epistemic or otherwise evidence for the wagers. Jackson does not say so explicitly in his performative plea, yet his testimony for faith in the wagers implies it for him. However, whether Jackson means it or not, intends it or not, is irrelevant because of the very fact that he is testifying to it by making a plea for it. His act of performative testimony as such is promising, as put by Derrida, a truth "beyond all proof, all perception, all intuitive demonstration" and this "act of faith demanded in bearing witness exceeds, through its structure, all intuition and all proof, all knowledge" (Derrida 2002c: 98).

In the end what Jackson is saying goes something like 'Believe what I say as one believes in a miracle.' This, of course, is not peculiar to Jackson's text by any means. In fact, according to Derrida (2002c: 98), "even the slightest testimony concerning the most plausible, ordinary or everyday thing cannot do otherwise: it must still appeal to faith as would a miracle." It is a "'miraculous' experience;" it is "testimonially miraculous." Therefore, Jackson's plea for believing in the wagers-based typology is a sort of pure attestation which, as put by Derrida, "pertains to the experience of faith and of the miracle." It is an experience of faith, says Derrida, which is "implied in every 'social bond,' however ordinary," rendering "itself indispensable to Science no less than to Philosophy and to Religion" (Derrida 2002c: 99).

Jackson's plea for faith is therefore not for a faith in anything, it is not a faith with a content; rather, it is a call for a faith without faith in any dogmatism or anything else. It is, as put by Caputo, "to believe without quite knowing in what it is believed'," (Caputo 1997a: 61).Yet, this faith without faith is not faithlessness either since it is indeed presumed to anchor our wagers-based 'isms' that we deploy to do IR research. Jackson's plea for faith is a faith without a faith, which is, as put by Caputo (1997a: 63),

> "a decision inscribed in undecidability where undecidability is structurally ingredient in faith, not the opposite of faith but the element, the space in which faith makes its leap, the horizon in terms of which faith understands its limits, understands that it is faith."

Therefore, although it might appear that Jackson's plea for leaps of faith as ultimate justification for the wagers is some sort of hand-waving or anything-goes type of argument, it is the contrary. And my goal in this work of deconstructing Jackson' approach is thus not a call against the book. Rather, my deconstruction of Jackson's ultimate plea for leaps of faith has, as put by Caputo (1997a: 63–64),

> *nothing* to do with its simple destruction—*au contraire*! ... deconstruction's undecidability goes hand in hand with a certain faith, *sans savoir, sans avoir, sans voir* and a certain passion of not knowing ... Deconstruction takes the form of a general or non-determinable faith in the impossible, of ... 'the essence of faith *par excellence*, which can only ever believe in the unbelievable' ... Deconstruction comes down to an affirmation or hope or invocation which is a certain *faith* in *the* impossible, in something that pushes us beyond the sphere of the same, of the believable, into the unbelievable, that which exceeds the horizon of our pedestrian beliefs and probabilities, driving us with the passion of *the* impossible, *the* unbelievable.

This, I think, is what more or less Jackson's text more or less does or allows us to do. I thus want to offer to Jackson a friendly call and walk with him the walk of the aporia that the book has put *en marche* but stopped short of espousing it. *This faith in a chance of walking the aporia is what I wager on!*

3 *Khôra* as the condition of possibility of the ontological *without* ontology

The chapter seeks to reject the dogma of positive ontology (termed as *ontologism*) by raising the question: Is it possible to formulate social (IR) theory without ontology? The answer is a qualified yes; a yes based on a logic which neither negates nor affirms ontology, all the while rejecting ontologism. The chapter specifically proposes that we forego ontologism which means that we need to re-think ontology *qua* ontological discourse without positing ontology *qua* ontologism. To this end, the chapter explicitly proposes to think of the ontological as *khôra* in the sense of Derrida, a pseudo-notion which does not possess any determination of its own except by assuming the role of a 'receptacle' (of sorts) to determinations and which operates through the logic of without. The chapter argues that thinking of IR theory in this way implies a re-thinking of the work of IR theory as *ergon* and any philosophical enframing thereof (Critical Realism or otherwise) as *parergon*. This entails a logic of *parergonality* unfolding within a movement of *différance* between IR work and any philosophical enframing thereof.

Introduction

Is IR theory (and social theory) possible without a positive ontology? Do we need ontology as the very first step toward/of theorization? Is or isn't ontology a consequence of the theorization process? Is a meta-theoretical/theoretical delineation nothing more than a rhetorical/discursive artifice? If that were the case, why should we give priority to one assumption/consequence (e.g., ontology) over others? What are the conditions of possibility and/or limitations for giving priority to any ontological assumption?

It is almost unthinkable among social scientists nowadays to envision a formulation of social theory that does not posit an ontological beginning point, that is, by making explicit/implicit assumptions on the most basic ontological entities—subjects, objects, agents, structures, and/or processes—that one takes to be the foundations of the (world-) view being explored or posited. This is usually considered a theoretical necessity of, as much as a desire for, soundness driven by our conception of what theorizing means, or should mean. The issue is even put at the heart of what politics is, or is about.

"Politics is the terrain of competing ontologies," says Wight (2006: 2). He, and, well before him, Walker (1993: 82), and Wendt (1999: 6), as well as most of today's social scientists/theorists, all assert that theories necessarily presuppose a basic positive ontology upon which all other considerations are built and that there is *no social theory without ontology.*

This chapter recognizes that we need to speak of the *ontological* for social theory to be possible. Yet the chapter rejects the dogma of positive ontology (termed as *ontologism*) and raises the question: *Is it possible to speak of the ontological without ontology?* Is it possible to formulate social theory without ontology? The answer is a qualified yes; a yes based on a logic which neither negates nor affirms ontology, all the while rejecting ontologism. As strange as this position might sound I think that although ontology is *always* a discursive *construction* it is not possible to formulate a social theory *without* a notion of the *ontological*. The issue then is not that we jettison ontology altogether, once for all. I propose that we instead forego ontologism which means that we need to re-think ontology *qua* ontological discourse without positing ontology *qua* ontologism. We thus need a *logic* of thinking about the ontological which retains ontology *without* ontologism, a sort of ontological without the 'essence' of ontology. This is the logic the logic of *without (sans)* introduced in the previous chapters. I am thus calling for a re-thinking of the logic underpinning our thinking about the ontological through a logic of the ontological *without* ontology.[1] Yet, if there is no ontologism, what framework then defines the ontological? I suggest that we need to replace what the critical realists (and others) take as ontological entities and processes with something which is neither an ontology nor non-ontology and is a little bit of both at the same time (in a certain sense to be explicated later). To this end, I suggest that we focus on the presuppositions in terms of which it is possible to speak (or not speak) of ontology as a grounding discourse. I explicitly propose to think of the ontological as *khôra*, already briefly introduced in the previous chapter, a pseudo-notion which does not possess any determination of its own except by assuming the role of a 'receptacle' (of sorts) to determinations and which operates through the logic of without (*sans*).

In order to carry out this work of deconstructing 'ontology' I use as an entry point Colin Wight's 2006 book. The first section of the chapter thus provides a brief summary on the issue of ontology as presented by Wight (2006). The section also briefly discusses the position that Bhaskar takes on ontology in his 1993 book *Dialectic* (1993). Bhaskar rejects ontologism— termed as the dogma of ontological monovalence—and makes absenting absence (real negativity) the ground of any ontological foundation.[2] The next section of the chapter goes beyond Bhaskar's suggestion via a questioning of the very logic of the possibility (or non-possibility) of ontological foundation either as negativity or positivity. I argue that Bhaskar's focus on real negativity is a thinking of ontology based on a mode which is reminiscent of negative theology.[3] The following section discusses the mode of negative theology and its deconstruction which, instead of completely rejecting negative theology, generalizes it using the logic of without and the notion of *khôra*. Building on this I suggest a new way of thinking the *ontological* in social theory as *khôra*-logical, which allows us to go beyond the 'via negativity' and 'via ontologism' modes of theorizing.[4] I end the chapter by addressing the issue of relevance to IR research of this way of re-thinking the *ontological* via a deconstruction of a taken for granted delineation of philosophical ontology from scientific/social ontology.

Critical realist ontology and Bhaskar's dialectic

Critical realists (following Bhaskar (1979)) argue that IR theorists have for the most part either followed a positivist approach in theorizing or fallen into the trap of an *epistemic fallacy* by conflating ontology with epistemology in the sense that 'only that which can be known can exist.' Instead, critical realists argue that there is a reality 'out there,' even if humanity did not know it. In Bhaskar's terms, we have "intransitive" objects that are independent of, and transcend, human knowledge of them.[5] Thus, reality is made up of transitive and intransitive objects, with only the former contextually dependent on human knowledge. Critical realists seek to reinstate to intransitive objects— that is, ontological entities—their due role in IR theory. However, this might lead us to an *ontological fallacy* which fails to recognize "the constructional role of discursive elements in relation to ontology, (and thus the discursive relativity of social ontologies and ontological features)," and which insists "on the search for ontological features independent of discursive knowledge" (Layder 1985: 273).

Is it possible to avoid simultaneously both the epistemic and ontological fallacies? Yet, why do we feel obligated to avoid these fallacies in the first place? Perhaps, we can also ask: Is it possible to sustain both 'fallacies' and that instead of having an 'either-or' situation we might have a 'both-and' situation? Is it possible to fall neither in the ontological fallacy nor the epistemic fallacy *and* yet accept bits of both at the same time, that is, a situation of *'neither-nor' and 'both-and'*? This line of questioning is definitely *not* logical if one adheres to the logic of inquiry that rejects contradictions as unacceptable, as *illogical*.

The 'logic' behind rejecting something as being a 'fallacy' is at stake here. Perhaps what usually counts as fallacy is instead a source of great insight that, if adequately re-thought, might help us better conceptualize social theory *qua* discourse. This indeed is the task, or at least motivation, of this chapter (and the book). Instead of rejecting this or that 'fallacy', I argue that we need to deconstruct the usual *either-or* logic underpinning the notion of fallacy by showing how under a more generalized logic of *'neither-nor' and 'both-and'*—*a logic that combines both mutual exclusion and participation*—we would not have to and cannot prioritize ontology over epistemology, or vice versa for that matter. We need a different logic, a logic that does not from the outset reject contradictions and where, more generally, *aporias* do have a role to play. In such a logic, contradictions, paradoxes, inconsistencies, and *aporias* could be thought of as constitutive of conceptuality, argumentation, and discourse. Bhaskar's thinking on the possibility of naturalism in social theory, which has since 1993 radically changed, seems to provide a step toward such a generalization of the logic behind our thinking on ontology.

Rejecting what he termed as dogmatic ontological monovalence,[6] that is, taking positive ontological entities as foundations, Bhaskar asserts that "negativity is constitutively essential to positivity ... Non-being is a condition of possibility of being" (1993: 46). He argues that "non-being exists" and that "non-being has ontological *priority* over being" (Bhaskar 1993: 39; his emphasis). Bhaskar (1993: 4–5) therefore considers real determinate absence, or, as he also terms it, *absenting absence* and negativity, as a foundational property of the ontological status of reality itself. This makes reality one where "negativity is a condition of positive being" (Bhaskar 1993: 47).

Although *Dialectic Critical Realism* is to some extent the state of the art in Bhaskar's approach, it has yet to find its way into the discourse of IR critical realists, give and take very casual references here and there.[7] Yet Bhaskar has intended to generalize and deepen his approach to social science—the 1979 possibility of naturalism—with his dialectical critical naturalism (Bhaskar 1993: 152), which makes *negativity or the absenting absence as the ground for everything else*. This raises a serious problem for critical realists who still advocate (positive) ontology. It indeed would mean that what comes first (that is, a positive ontology) is not first after all. It is missing something, which, because it is missing, is not ontological, since we are talking about ontology as a first ground. Ontology in the 1993 sense of Bhaskar, as origin, is thus not originary enough for it needs something else—a non-being—to be as such. According to Bhaskar, non-being is constitutive of being and is its ground of ontological existence as such.

Yet Bhaskar, I argue, is still falling prey to a serious problem—that of resorting to the thinking mode of negative theology (of sorts). While Dialectic Critical Realism is not a negative theology *per se*, it however shares some of the dangers and weaknesses that negative theology falls prey to. I develop this line of thinking by following Derrida through a brief excursion into discussing some tensions of negative theology (which negates any naming of God for the sake of preserving the name of God). Of course, this is not to imply that one must go through 'negative theology' to grasp the importance of this critique of Bhaskar.[8] I begin next by summarizing the general contours of negative theology and then present Derrida's deconstruction of it.

The mode of negative theology and the logic of without

Negative theology is a mode of thinking and speaking—or, more appropriately, of how to avoid thinking and speaking—about God, without falling into the error of "naming something one actually brings into existence, something which has nothing to do with the Unnameable" (Almond 1999: 152). Negative theology seeks to deny "every analogy between God and ordinary beings" (Milem 2007: 193). In doing so, it ends up always rejecting any linguistic or otherwise description of God as being inadequate such as opposing the naming of God, all in the name of God. The only path which is left as a way of speaking and thinking of God is negation. Critics charge that negative theology is nihilistic and empty speech, that it defeats the purpose of speech, and that "the pushing of negations to their hyperbolic limit, the compounding of the negations of negations ends up, in Hegelian style, at God or some kind of asymptote, as the guarantor of negativity leading to truth" (Ryba 1997: 112).

Negative theology is however one example of a general mode of thinking and speaking wherein we speak of what the 'thing' cannot be or is not. The thing in itself is thus a pure transcendental, extra-linguistic, and cannot be appropriated through any discourse or language. The claims that this mode makes—by negating them—are everything that the thing in itself cannot be. This leads to major conceptual, logical, and linguistic difficulties since "every claim to the 'things themselves' is a claim within and by means of the resources of certain semi-systems, linguistic and otherwise, situated within the framework of a complex set of contextual presuppositions which can never be saturated" (Caputo 1997: 17). Negative theology has as a result become "a reserve of language, almost inexhaustible in so few words" (Derrida 1995b: 85).The literature of negative theology thus "holds desire in suspense, and always saying too much or too little, each time it leaves you without ever going away from you" (Derrida 1995b: 85). Much of the controversy on/in negative theology revolves around the issue of whether by stating that God is a *Being* that is beyond *beings* negative theology ends up jeopardizing the very 'negativeness' that it deploys in defining its own discourse. This is the issue that Derrida sought to address in his deconstruction of negative theology, and, more generally, *via negativae* in any discourse.

Derrida's purpose in deconstructing negative theology is neither to negate it, nor to jettison it. Nor is it to affirm it either. The goal is to probe into the presuppositions and conditions of possibility and impossibility of the discourse of negative theology. Derrida's line of attack addresses the core question of 'how to avoid speaking?' Because speaking, writing, and thinking are all expressed in a language and because language always precedes us, this leads Derrida (1992a: 97) to conclude that "at the moment when the question 'how to avoid speaking?' is raised and articulates itself in all its modalities—whether in rhetorical or logical forms of saying, or in the simple fact of speaking—it is already, so to speak, *too late*." One has already spoken, if only to affirm that one is not speaking. Derrida (1992a: 103) makes it clear that "there cannot be an absolutely negative discourse: a *logos* necessarily speaks about something; it cannot avoid speaking of something; it is impossible for it to refer to nothing."

How can negative theology then pretend to be speaking of 'not speaking of God and of the beyond of being' even if it portrays these as unspeakable? Negative theology seeks to negate and instead ends up *denegating* its negative discourse, thereby affirming its discourse. When negative theology engages in a "sweet rage against language," when it shows a "jealous anger of language within itself and against itself," when it demonstrates a "passion that leaves the mark of a scar in that place where the impossible takes place," (Derrida 1995b: 59–60) this amounts to a "wounded, breached, auto-deconstructing" discourse which is nothing but an affirmative end, an end that is affirmed and not negated (Caputo 1997b: 43). This makes negative theology fall prey to the logic of the double bind of *negation/denegation*. *On the one hand*, negating the name of God, and, *on the other hand*, simultaneously negating everything else except the name God. Not surprisingly, negative theology is thus a positive onto-theology—it refuses to positively attribute determinations to God but only as a way of affirming a super-essentiality of God (Bradley 2002: 59). Negative theology seeks to negate *without* negating and to affirm without affirming. There are thus, says Derrida (1995b: 68), two movements within the discourse of negative theology:

> *On the one hand* ... the principle of negative theology, in a movement of internal rebellion, radically contests the tradition from which it seems to come ... Negative theology uproots itself from there after the fact [*après coup*], in the torsion or conversion of a second movement of uprooting ... But *on the other hand*, and in that very way, nothing is more faithful than this hyperbole to the originary ontotheological injunction ... when one says: 'God is not,' 'God is neither this nor that, neither that nor its contrary' or 'being is not,' etc., even then it is still a matter of saying the entity [*étant*] such as it is, in its truth, even were it meta-metaphysical, meta-ontological.

This logic of without is what makes it possible for negative theology to always say "too much or too little" and to leave "you without ever going away from you" (Derrida 1995b: 85). What is the effect of this logic of without that seems to empty out the meaning of terms all the while affirming them, but yet without completely turning them into empty signifiers?

Derrida (2008: 148) argues that the without in St. Augustine's statements[9] "does not merely dissociate the singular attribution from the essential generality: wisdom as being-wise in general, goodness as being-good in general, power as being-powerful in general." The strange logic of without "does not only avoid the abstraction tied to every noun and to the being implied in every essential generality" (Derrida 2008: 148). What also happens is that "in the same word and in the same syntax," the without acts so that "it transmutes into affirmation its purely phenomenal negativity" (Derrida 2008: 148). The logic of without seeks to account for what "the principle of the good" which not only is beyond being, but also simultaneously "transcends the good." We thus get a notion of God as "the good that transcends the good and the being that transcends being" (Derrida 2008: 178–79). In the logic of without there seems to be "a principle of demultiplication of voices and discourse, of disappropriation and reappropriation of utterances, with the most distant appearing closest, and vice versa" (Derrida 2008: 178–79). The logic of without has not only "the negative force of depriving or denying words of their old meanings but also the positive force of repeating or re-inscribing their old meanings in new ones" (Bradley 2001: 136). Derrida (1986b: 90) explains that:

> If I write, for example: the water without [*sans*] water, what has happened? Or again, a reply without reply? The same word and the same thing seem removed from themselves, taken away from their reference and their identity, while continuing to be left to traverse, in their old body towards an entirely other [*tout autre*], dissimulated in them. But not [*pas*] more than in *pas*; this operation does not consist simply in depriving or denying, it is necessary in itself. It forms the trace or the step [*pas*] of the entirely other about which it is concerned, the retreat [*re-trait*] of the *pas*, and of the *pas* without *pas*.

The logic of without is characterized by three main features. First, although there is no repetition of meaning without change, it is also true that no change could completely eradiate the trace of previous meanings. There is always a process of simultaneous iteration and change. As put by Bradley (2001: 136–37), "every word or thing ... is *without* itself, that is, in a process of play between its old body and an entirely new other." Second, Derrida (2008: 158) explains that the *without* "marks neither a privation, a lack nor an absence ... it has the double and ambiguous meaning of what is above in a hierarchy, thus both beyond and more. God (is) beyond Being but as such is more (being) than Being: *no more being* and *being more than Being*: being more." This is expressed in French as '*plus d'être*'. Third, the logic of without is neither one of reversing a meaning to its opposite, nor one of double negation which takes us back to the original term. Nor is it one of Hegelian dialectic sublation that progresses towards a higher notion. The logic of without is a sort of a tripartite negation of 'without without without', 'step without step', 'not without not', ('*pas sans pas*') (Derrida 1987a: 401); it is "a negativity without negativity [*pas sans pas*]" (Derrida 1987b: 129); it is a "conjunction-disjunction" (Derrida 1995b: 76).

Negative theology tries to escape the logic of without, which always breaches and ruptures its discourse, by attempting to eject the 'transcendental' from the front door but only to bring it /let it come from the back door in an even more 'purified' or 'essentialized' version, in the form of a super-essentiality, thereby practicing *a logic of contraband* against its own discourse. Deconstruction seeks to save negative theology from seeking such a closure (Caputo 1997b: 6), that is, saving negative theology from the ultimate goal of negative theology. The solution consists in moving negative theology from the logic of contraband to a grammatology that would inscribe it and exceed it without return (Caputo 1997b: 11). This is what Derrida suggests through a reading

Khôra *as the condition of possibility of ontology* 61

of Plato's *Timaeus* from which he takes the notion of *khôra* (receptacle), but as expected, by displacing it into a sort of generalized *khôra*.

Khôra qua receptacle

Derrida draws on Plato's *Timaeus* who presents *khôra* as neither being a form nor a sensible thing. Rather, it is the place wherein "the demiurge impresses or cuts images of the intelligible paradigms, the place which was already there, which, while radically heterogeneous with the forms, seems to be as old as the forms" (Caputo 1997b: 35). As already discussed in the previous chapter,[10] *khôra* belongs "neither to becoming, nor to non-being" (Derrida 1992a: 105).The *khôra* defies our usual sense of thinking and speaking of 'things' in this world, as either ideal or material. The discourse of/about *khôra* is neither a metaphor nor does it deploy metaphors as logical or rhetorical tools. *Khôra* is a Greek word. Yet *khôra*, as used in Plato's *Timaeus*, does not have a meaning (at least not in the usual sense of the term meaning). *Khôra* is a *receptacle*. Having no meaning in itself, no essence, and no identity, it nonetheless "receives all without becoming anything" (Caputo 1997a: 35–36).

If *khôra* is a receptacle, does this make *khôra* a location, a place? Are we speaking of 'a place of a place'? Derrida (1995b: 56) argues that "*khôra* is over there but more 'here' than any 'here'." In arguing so, Derrida (1992a: 105) is in fact displacing the meaning of 'place' as we are accustomed to using the word in a positive (or even negative) sense. Derrida (1995b:57) explains that this 'place' "is not *that in which* is found a subject or an object. It is found in us." However, *khôra* "will always already be occupied, invested, even as a general place, and even when it is distinguished from everything that takes place in it" (Derrida 1995b: 109). *Khôra*, not a place, "marks a place apart, the spacing which keeps a dissymmetric relation to all that which, 'in herself,' beside or in addition to herself, seems to make a couple with her" (Derrida 1995b: 124–25). If *khôra* is always occupied, can we temporally 'distinguish' *khôra* from what occupies it? Derrida (1995b: 126) proposes that "in order to think *khôra*, it is necessary to go back to a beginning that is older than the beginning, namely, the birth of the cosmos, just as the origin of the Athenians must be recalled to them from beyond their own memory." This implies that *khôra* is neither historical nor temporal. Although there is *khôra*, "nothing happens through it and nothing happens to it" in time, in history, which makes it completely absent from historical change and not an agent of historical change; it is ahistorical and atemporal (Derrida 1993: 107).

Does the *khôra* have any determination at all? According to Plato "*khôra* is 'amorphous'" at the level of its 'beingness' (Caputo 1997a: 94), since the very 'beingness' of *khôra* is neither being nor non-being, let alone any other determination that the *khôra* might be thought to have. That the *khôra* "must remain without form and without proper determination" is required for the *khôra* to be able "to receive all and allow itself to be marked or affected by what is inscribed in it," (Derrida 1992a: 107). Yet, *khôra* does have what can be termed as pseudo-determinations. *Khôra is self-less, escapes the realm of metaphors,* and *follows the logic of without.*

First, a pseudo-determination of the *khôra* is that it 'receives' determinations without possessing or appropriating them. It gives place to determinations without turning them or experiencing them as its own properties, hence the name of *receptacle* (Derrida 1995b: 99–100). However, although *khôra* receives *qua* receptacle it does not become, nor could it be likened to, "its sensible imprints, which vanish from it without a trace" in it (Caputo 1997a: 94).The *khôra* is a working receptacle that receives without having a receiving self, a self as receptacle.

A second pseudo-determination of the *khôra* is that metaphors cannot be used to determine it, the reason being that it would mean attributing some borrowing from the 'sensible' or 'intelligible' forms. This would not work because these borrowings are themselves inscribed in the *khôra*, which is neither sensible nor intelligible. Derrida (1995b: 113) explains that the reason has to do with the fact that "the discourse on *khôra* is no longer a discourse on being, it is neither true nor probable and appears thus to be heterogeneous to myth." Derrida (1995b: 117) also explains that "if *khôra* is a receptacle, if it/she gives place to all the stories, ontologic or mythic, that can be recounted on the subject of what she receives and even of what she resembles but which in fact takes place in her, *khôra* herself, so to speak, does not become the object of any *tale*, whether true or fabled." As discussed in the previous chapter, a third pseudo-determination of the *khôra* is that it its logic is the logic of without.

Because *khôra* does not possess anything proper to it, in order to 'work (in French: *travail*)'as receptacle it has to borrow 'tools'—concepts, ideas, discourse, etc.—from whatever is being received in the *khôra*. The *khôra* is deployed as infrastructure in a discourse and "the discourse on *khôra* thus plays for philosophy a role analogous to the role which *khôra* 'herself' plays for that which philosophy speaks of, namely, the cosmos," in Plato's *Timaeus* (Derrida 1995b: 126). Hence, to be deployed, for example, in negative theology, the *khôra* would have to use 'tools' from negative theology itself. The *khôra*, which is a desert of sorts, becomes "the site where 'negative theology' and its 'analogates' happen" (Caputo 1997b: 54).

Note that although the discourse on the *khôra* seems to be forming an inversion of the Platonist discourse on the Good as beyond Being and Christian Neoplatonist discourse of God as beyond Being, it is not strictly speaking an inversion. Although it seems that we have, on the one hand, in the Platonist and Christian Neoplatonist discourses, "a hyper-essential sur-reality for which words fail us, of which words fall short" and, on the other hand, in the discourse on the *khôra*, "a hypo-essential sub-reality, an almost unreal, indeterminable indeterminacy which seems rather to fail words, to fall short of word or meaning" (Caputo 1997a: 96), this opposition is however misleading. The *khôra* is the 'place' that makes possible the *discourse* on the Good and God, on the hyper-essentiality and the hypo-essentiality, receiving all without making any as its own. Likewise, I argue, the *khôra* is the receptacle and the 'place' for Bhaskar's real negativity and for the positive ontology of the critical realists.[11]

Khôra as the condition of possibility of the ontological

How are we to think that *khôra* is the receptacle for Bhaskar's discourse on real negativity (or non-being as the foundation of being) and for the critical realists' discourse on the intransitives of positive ontology? First, the logic of without blurs, on the one hand, the delineation between non-being and being, and, on the other hand, the delineation between intransitives and transitives. Bhaskar can speak of non-being only by using speech, which is a being. This means that we have a non-being *without* non-beingness since it is within a being (a speaking), a part of a being. Likewise, critical realists' intransitives are intransitives *without* intransitivity (at their core if we can term it in this way) since they can only be spoken of within transitive discourses.

Second, is it possible to generalize Bhaskar's discourse about non-being so as to displace the hierarchy that he creates between non-being and being? He states that "if there was a *unique* beginning to everything, it could only be from nothing by an act of radical autogenesis" (1993: 46; his emphasis). Yet he does not address the seeming contradiction between speaking of the possibility of a unique beginning to everything and speaking of an act of radical autogenesis. Is the latter part of 'the everything' what uniquely begins through autogenesis? Isn't he positing a beginning, or a condition, that 'is' before the unique beginning to everything? Or perhaps, more accurately, isn't he saying that the possibility of an act of autogenesis has to precede the possibility of a unique beginning to everything? For the possibility of an act of autogenesis to be before the possibility of everything, the possibility of such an act 'emerges' in a 'place', a 'receptacle' which does not 'exist', in a receptacle which 'is' without being a being. Isn't this precisely how *khôra* works in a discourse about beginning, just like in *Timaeus'* discourse on the evolution of the cosmos? *Khôra* is thus the condition of possibility that is presupposed in Bhaskar's discourse on real negativity (or non-being) as the condition of possibility of being and non-being.

Bhaskar (1993: 46) further clarifies that "*if* there was an originating Absolute, nothing would be its schema or form, constituted at the moment of initiation by the spontaneous disposition to become something other than itself." The italicized '*if*' is probably meant to emphasize that Bhaskar is speaking of a potentiality not actually affirming that this is what happens. However, this reading cannot be accurate since real negativity will not be the unique beginning. Yet if we were to assume that Bhaskar thinks that this is a plausible scenario then he runs into trouble because in the very same statement he is speaking of 'disposition to become'. Doesn't this imply that the Absolute is not absolutely the beginning? Where does the disposition come from, or perhaps, where is it 'located'? One solution to this difficulty is again to resort to *khôra*. As noted by Derrida (1995b: 124–25), *khôra* "marks a place apart, the spacing which keeps a dissymmetric relation to all that which, 'in herself,' beside or in addition to herself, seems to make a couple with her." This means that within a discourse on real negativity, *khôra* will be a receptacle wherein there is a dissymmetry between the real negativity and the discourse that speaks of it in terms of Absolute and disposition to become. The *khôra* works within such a discourse as the deployment of a discourse of originary performativity, that is, a discourse which speaks of a retroactively-positing of an autogenesis of the Absolute and its spontaneous disposition to become something. There is no Absolute or disposition to become *qua* discourse prior to or outside this double discourse about real negativity—an originary performative discourse which deploys a discourse of '*as-if* the Absolute emerges through autogenesis'. Therefore, *khôra* works through the event of 'saying the non-being'. And 'saying the non-being' is all there 'is'; all what there 'is' is a discourse of/on the non-being. The key feature of the event is discursively equipped with a *khôral* quality in the sense that the event occurs in a receptacle which does not possess any determinations of its own. The receptacle or *khôra* is the mode of 'saying' which is constitutive of the event of 'saying real negativity' and which does not exist apart from 'saying real negativity'.[12]

In sum: I propose that we think of the ontological as neither positive nor negative but as one which is both at the same time without assuming a sublation that would generate a Hegelian unity of higher order. How? I propose to re-think the ontological in terms of its *ontologicality*, that is, the presuppositions that form the conditions of possibility of the discourse on the ontological. I suggest that these can be thought of in terms of *khôra*.

We would hence think of the ontologicality of 'the ontological *without* ontologism' within the logic of without, the logic of '*neither–nor*' and '*both–and*'—a *logic that combines both mutual exclusion and participation*. There is a sort of partial emptying and erasure of the property 'ontology' from the 'ontological', with the result that it is neither a real negativity in the 1993 sense of Bhaskar, nor a positive intransitive in the sense of the critical realists; rather, it is the condition of possibility to real negativity and positive intransitives.

Relevance to 'concrete' IR research, and more

What is, some might argue, the relevance of this way of thinking for 'concrete' research in IR? This is an important issue. Yet I think that there is another question that needs to be addressed first. Indeed, raising the issue of 'concrete' research seems to be taking for granted the possibility of delineation between philosophical ontology and (scientific or) social ontology with the usual (and Critical Realist) understanding that "a philosophical ontology" is "an inquiry into which is logically prior to the development of any scientific or social ontology" (Patomäki and Wight 2000: 215). This view is in fact almost a 'given' in IR literature (and most of social theory). The argument goes something like that instead of concentrating on pursuing 'self-reflexively critical dead-end' we must decide on a certain frame/framing; that is, we must enframe IR research (using CR or any other philosophical system/frame).

One purpose of this chapter is to suggest new ways of thinking how to go beyond this dualistic framing of theory.[13] Thus, I support more or less Patomäki's (2010: 85) insightful view that:

> Philosophy can no longer claim the role of a general regulator of conceptual work that is part of all scientific research. Although philosophical reflection and criticism have their legitimate moments in the dialectics of science, the capacity of these philosophical moments to enlighten and guide practices and understandings is limited. Moreover, philosophy has no monopoly over the deepest questions, and often seems unable to pose them. ... It is best to conceive philosophy not as a separate academic field but as part of all scientific activities.[14]

Likewise, in an effort to go beyond dead ends that seemingly plague IR theory on this issue, Jackson (2010), as already discussed in the previous chapter, provides an elaborated and thorough discussion of this issue. Agreeing with how Patomäki and Wight approach the issue of delineation, Jackson (2010: 196–97) explains that:

> I have termed the basic philosophical components of a specific scientific methodology 'wagers' or 'commitments' ... although they are foundational to particular modes of knowledge-production, they are themselves incapable of being definitively justified ... and thus require of their practitioners a commitment that is like nothing else so much as an existential leap of faith ... Talking about such wagers of philosophical ontology requires a vocabulary that is precise enough to permit significant differences and similarities between scientific methodologies to come to the forefront. This vocabulary is not a framework for evaluation; it is, rather, an instrument of clarification, helping to make explicit what is ordinarily tacit.[15]

Is the underlying philosophical/social ontology demarcation sustainable when thought in terms of ontological *qua khôra*-logical? This is a question about the issue of 'framing', or more precisely, framing via philosophical ontology—wagers in Jackson's term—of the process of theorizing. Critical Realism and Jackson's pragmatism/analyticism (or any other enframing) would want to settle down (even if only in principle or, as some might put it, methodologically) the issue of what constitutes the frame for concrete IR theory. Yet this way of thinking ignores the role of 'enframing' in the formulation of theories. I thus not only heed Patomäki's (2010: 62) call that "recent developments in cosmology, physics and biology, including astrobiology, as well as theories of emergence and complexity, have made CR out-of-date in some important regards." I also call for a re-thinking of the relations of both 'philosophy of ontology' (à la CR, Jackson, or otherwise) and whatever insights we learn from contemporary sciences as a frame or *parergon* of the process of theorizing social theory without ontologism. The delineation between philosophical ontology and social (scientific) ontology is, I argue, unsustainable due to the logic of *parergonality*, which can only be ignored through an act of violent silencing of one or the other side of the parergon/ergon. In this endeavor I draw insights from Derrida's statement on art when he (Derrida 1987b: 45) writes that

> this permanent requirement—to distinguish between the internal or proper sense and the circumstance of the object being talked about—organizes all philosophical discourses on art, the meaning of art and meaning as such, from Plato to Hegel, Husserl and Heidegger. This requirement presupposes a discourse on the limit between the inside and outside of the art object, here a discourse on the frame.

And when he (Derrida 1987b: 54) also states that

> philosophical discourse has always been against the parergon. But what about this *against*. A parergon comes against, beside, and in addition to the ergon, the work done [*fait*], the fact [*le fait*], the work, but it does not fall to one side, it touches and cooperates within the operation, from a certain outside. Neither simply outside nor simply inside. Like an accessory that one is obliged to welcome on the border, on board [*au bord, à bord*].

Before explicating my argument, let me briefly discuss Derrida's notion of *parergon* and the logic of *parergonality*. As put by Derrida (1987b: 9), the parergon is

> neither work [*ergon*] nor outside the work [*hors d'oeuvre*], neither inside nor outside, neither above nor below, it disconcerts any opposition but does not remain indeterminate and it *gives rise* to the work. It is no longer merely around the work. That which it puts in place—the instances of the frame, the title, the signature, the legend, etc.—does not stop disturbing the *internal* order of discourse on painting, its works, its commerce, its evaluations, its surplus-values, its speculation, its law, and its hierarchies.

We can paraphrase this text and apply it to CR's or Jackson's enframing of IR almost verbatim, that is: *the enframing is neither inside IR theory nor outside it, neither above nor below; the enframing disconcerts any opposition but does not remain indeterminate and it gives rise to the work of IR theory. The enframing is not merely around IR work. That which the enframing puts in place does not stop disturbing the internal order of IR discourses.* Derrida (1987b: 56) also explains that:

> The *parergon* inscribes something which comes as an extra, *exterior* to the proper field ... but whose transcendent exteriority comes to play, abut onto, brush against, rub, press against the limit itself and intervene in the inside only to the extent that the inside is lacking. It is lacking *in* something and it is lacking *from itself*.

This can be translated onto IR as: CR (or any other approach) *qua* the *parergon* or enframing of IR inscribes something which comes as an extra, exterior to the proper IR field. Yet the transcendent exteriority comes to play, and press against the limit of IR itself and intervenes in the inside only to the extent that the inside (IR theory) is lacking in something. Moreover, the frame, according to Derrida (1987b: 61), has

> a surface which separates [it] ... not only ... from the integral inside, from the body proper of the [work], but also from the outside, from the wall on which the painting is hung ... from the whole field of historical, political inscription.

Translated in terms of IR theory, we would say that CR (and other philosophical approaches) is a discourse which separates itself not only from the integral inside, that is, IR theory, but also from the outside of IR theory (all other fields of social theory, etc.) and from the whole field of historical, political inscription in IR and elsewhere. The *paregonal* frame thus does not obey the logic of 'either this or that' and does not respect any border delineations. As Derrida (1987b: 61) put it:

> The parergonal frame stands out against two grounds [*fonds*], but with respect to each of these two grounds, it merges [*se fond*] into the other. With respect to the work which can serve as a ground for it, it merges into the wall, and then gradually, into the general text. With respect to the background which the general text is, it merges into the work, which stands out against the general background.

This means that in the case of IR theory, *on the one hand*, CR (and any other enframing) serves as a 'ground' for IR theory and as such merges in what constitutes the philosophical context of IR theory and then gradually into theories of knowledge. *On the other hand*, CR (and other enframings) merge into IR theory and are constitutively impossible to demarcate from IR theory when contrasted against the general background of knowledge beyond IR. As such, according to Derrida (1987b: 61), "the *parergon* ... disappears, buries itself, effaces itself, melts away at the moment it deploys its greatest energy." This means that any enframing of IR theory disappears, buries itself, effaces itself, and melts away at the moment it is deployed. Yet the *ergon* or IR theory cannot be as such without an enframing (CR or anything else). What makes enframing and the enframed work essentially enmeshed and inseparable is what is lacking in both the *parergon* (enframing) and the *ergon* (IR work), or more precisely, as put by Derrida (1987b: 80–81),

> against what is *lacking* in it; not against the lack as a posable or opposable negative, a substantial emptiness, a determinable and bordered absence (still verifiable essence and presence) but against the impossibility of *arresting différance* in its contour, of arraigning the heterogeneous [*différance*] in a pose, of localizing, even in a meta-empirical way, what metaphysics calls ... *lack*, of making it come back, equal or similar to itself ... to its proper place.

That is, what is lacking in both the enframing (of IR) and the work (IR) is the impossibility of arresting the play of *différance* in its contour, the supposed contour between the frame and the framed, a contour which never stops *différantially* disappearing and appearing into both the outside and the inside of IR work. *Différance*, explains Derrida (1973: 142–43),

> is what makes the movement of signification possible only if each element that is said to be 'present', appearing on the stage of presence, is related to something other than itself but retains the mark of a past element and already lets itself be hollowed out by the mark of its relation to a future element.[16]

Therefore, as nicely put by Harvey (1989: 71–72),

> The *parergon/ergon* distinction is one which floats, oscillates and ultimately can be shown to be a mirroring yet distancing relation of *différance*. It is a relation of doubling which belies the linear temporality of an origin/copy relation. The *ergon* is not simply prior (temporally or historically) to the *parergon*. Rather, they 'come into existence,' or are 'given' simultaneously. It is this simultaneity, however, that within the structure of parergonality presents itself as a temporal contingency of before and after which thus entails a certain attachability and in turn a detachability of parergon to an ergon already fully formed.

I think that this undecidability of the *parergon/ergon* distinction is what prompts Jackson (2010: 34) to declare:

> let me now offer a methodological principle and a provisional set of distinctions that, when combined, form what I believe is a useful typology for the discussion of the philosophy of science in IR. The methodological principle is that we should regard positions on the character

and conduct of science to rest on provisional commitments—*wagers*—about matters of philosophical ontology that can really never be settled definitively.

Wagers which are, as quoted up above and as discussed in the previous chapter, grounded on an 'existential leap of faith', nothing more and nothing less. This undecidable relation "between *ergon* and *parergon*, between the frame and the enframed" is what "deconstruction problematizes ... in order to reveal that which grounds both *ergon* and *parergon* and makes the relation possible, which is evidently neither term, but rather parergonality. What parergonality entails includes the parasitic contamination of inside and outside, internal and external, interior and exterior distinctions" (Harvey 1989: 65). The relation between the enframing (of IR theory) and the work (IR theory) is one of *parergonality*, which is not, again as explained by Harvey (1989: 71),

> simply the law of the relation between *parergon* and the *ergon*, but it opens out onto the lack that inhabits the *ergon* in order to make the *parergon* possible and makes its appearance as essential effaceable. That is, the lack in the *ergon* (the work) cannot as lack be recognized, cannot as such be named ... Rather, it is in evidence only by effect: the effect of the parergon which 'fills it,' albeit inadequately, incompletely and inappropriately, and this 'in' is of necessity. The *ergon* as *ergon* offers itself as complete, as not lacking, and hence the status of the *parergon* can be reduced to an extrinsic appendage, detachable and inessential. It is the hiddeness and the clandestine operation of filling the hidden lack which organizes the relation of *ergon* to *parergon* which will be analyzed here as the 'central' issue of parergonality.

Paraphrasing Harvey, the relation between IR work and its enframings is a double one. IR work is never fully complete, never fully finished, never fully independent, but rather entails an inner lack which calls forth the enframing to complete it. The work or IR theory is never without a frame. The relation between the enframing (of IR) and the work (IR theory), which is one of *parergonality* "is always of necessity double; appearing as externality, in fact internally connecting" (Harvey 1989: 74).

To conclude without seeking to impose closure on a necessarily open discourse on IR theory: thinking of the ontological *qua khôra*-logical is necessarily part and parcel of doing 'concrete' IR research since any enframing of IR is always already played out according to a logic of *parergonality* within a movement of *différance* between the inside (of IR work or *ergon*) and the outside (enframing or *parergon*); all within the 'receptacle' *qua khôra*. This implies that the customary practice of seeking a more 'concrete' IR theory/research is not only not possible, which is unsurprisingly seen in the continuous proliferation of new ways of approaching IR without any rest or respite. It also means that any cut or interruption is but a temporary one which is necessarily doomed to be replaced by more movement. We can interrupt and cut but this is only a deferral and a temporization toward more difference to come, which ineluctably remains haunted with traces of past theorization and pushed forward through the promise for more.

4 Re-thinking the 'agent-structure' problematique
From ontology to *parergonality*

Seeking to formulate a solution to the so-called agent-structure problem is still an open question today. Many students of IR (and social theory) argue that we must consider the problem at the level of ontology first. I argue that taking such a position is already eschewing the question and to a large extent pre-ordaining our theorizing process to keep revolving toward and within the same problems and difficulties that the issue has been marred with for quite some time now. I call instead for exploring *the presuppositions* of such an ontological positing itself as a way of thinking *the conditions of possibility* of the agent-structure problematique and *the conditions of impossibility* that make it an *undecidable* problematique. To this end I engage into a work of deconstruction through which I propose that in thinking about the agent-structure problematique we need to think within a logic of *parergonality* where the agent-structure problem (qua *parergon*) and social theory (qua *ergon*) distinction is a mirroring yet distancing relation of *différance*.

Introduction

More than two decades ago now, Alexander Wendt (1987) (re-)raised the agent-structure problem in IR theory while David Dessler (1989) pondered: "What is at stake in the agent-structure debate?" These and many other efforts have indeed put this debate at the heart of IR theory as the latter became the theater of a most fruitful era of IR theorizing.[1] One of the recent episodes was enacted by Colin Wight in his 2006 book *Agents, Structures and International Relations: Politics as Ontology*. More generally, a quick perusal of many widely cited works shows a strong tendency towards rephrasing the question as being not so much one of epistemology or methodology, but rather as one that needs to be first addressed as a question of ontology. Wight's overall project in effect seeks to bring ontology back at the heart of IR theory through a reconsideration of the agent-structure problematique.

In this chapter I argue that taking such a position is already eschewing the question and to a large extent pre-ordaining our theorizing process to keep revolving toward and within the same problems and difficulties that the issue has been marred with for quite some time now. Put differently: this is a call for escaping the strait jacket of (Aristotelian/metaphysical mode of) ontological thinking on the agent-structure problematique in IR. More accurately: this is a call for going all the way down to *the presuppositions of ontology* itself so as to theorize *the conditions of possibility* of the agent-structure problematique and *the conditions of impossibility* that make it an *undecidable* problematique.

I thus suggest that a satisfactory thinking of the agent-structure problematique, which does not necessarily entail (or not entail) a resolution of the problematique, can/should be achieved or at least attempted before we begin to think about/with ontological entities such as agents, structures, processes, etc. ... This way of thinking of the agent-structure problem falls within the purview of the call for an ontological *without* ontologism of the previous chapter and hence goes against the widespread belief that the theorization process needs always to start from some choice of originary ontology. Currently widespread conception of sciences, including social sciences and IR, is indeed based on a *regime of truth* which stipulates that we need to begin with ontological entities whether, for example, in physics, biology, IR, social theory, or any other discipline seeking to be and/or remain a science.

Instead of positing an ontological beginning with agents, structures, or both as co-constituted (via structuration, morphogenesis, or otherwise), or even process, I anchor my theoretic-discourse in *undecidability* or *infrastructural space* of *différance, trace, iterability, autoimmunity, spectrality, etc*. Thinking about the agent-structure problematique using such a *hauntology* (instead of ontology) allows us to think about the *aporias* and contradictions as well as other conceptually difficult-to-resolve theoretical issues, without however falling into the trap of seeking totalizing resolutions or (Kant-like regulative) idealizations. This leads to a re-thinking of the agency-structure problematique in terms of a *conditional/unconditional aporia* as the condition of possibility and impossibility of the discourse on the agency-structure problematique.

The chapter develops this argument in several steps. The 'Structure in IR literature' section provides a critique of the notion of structure in the IR literature via a focus on Wight's (2006) summary of the literature on the issue as an entry point. This paves the way for a critique of the social-theoretic bases of these IR theories on the agent-structure problem. The 'structure through the work of deconstruction' section presents Derrida's deconstruction of the notion of structure, or, more accurately, a deconstruction of the notion of *structurality* (of structure) as commonly used to displace it into undecidable infrastructures which follow a law of hauntology. This is followed in 'Agency: a re-thinking via deconstruction' by a deconstruction of the notion of agency. This section begins with a discussion of Wight's theorization of the notion of agency, a discussion which highlights the role of undecidability in thinking about agency. The section then advances the argument for thinking of agency *as an impossible yet necessary negotiation* between an *unconditional event of agency* and a *conditional agency as originary performativity of inaugural interpretation*. 'Re-thinking the agent-structure problematique' then suggests a re-thinking of the agent-structure problematique. I end the chapter by proposing that in thinking about the agent-structure problematique we need to think (much like in the previous two chapters) within a logic of *parergonality* where the agent-structure problem is thought of as a *parergon* and social theory as an *ergon*.

Structure in IR literature

In this section I discuss the notion of structure in IR and social theory literature by building on Wight's (2006) summary and critique. Wight critiques different models of structures by analyzing many inconsistencies that lie within Giddens' conceptualization of structures as rules and resources, by probing this notion as used by Onuf, Dessler, and Wendt in IR literature, and, especially, by showing how Wendt is quite equivocal in seeking to stick to Bhaskar's version of scientific realism while at the same time advocating Giddens' theory of structuration as a resolution of the agent-structure problem. Wight (2006: 145) counters this with a Bhaskarean approach where "the notion of a layered reality and the concept of emergence are crucial aspects of the general ontology." He adopts Bhaskar's argument that "there is an ontological hiatus between society and people" and that this hiatus requires a sharp distinction between "the genesis of human actions, lying in the reasons, intentions and plans of people, on the one hand, and the structures governing the reproduction and transformation of social activities, on the other" (Bhaskar 1979: 46, 44–46). Put differently: the notion of hiatus implies an originary ontological dualism of agents and structures. Bhaskar argues that human agency and society "cannot be reduced to or reconstructed from one another" (Bhaskar 1986: 124). Wight argues that in the literature we either have a disappearance of both agent and structure, which are then replaced with "praxis" as he claims is the case in structuration, or we have an originary ontological dualism.[2]

This dualistic way of analyzing ontology is also put at work in Wight's (2006: 165) critique of what he terms as the linguistic model of structures which, according to him, views all relations as internal. To this end Wight relies on Bhaskar's position that it is "essential to recognize that some relations are internal and some are not" (Bhaskar 1979: 54) and that "for Bhaskar, although the elements are constituted (in part) by relations, they also have a set of properties not constituted by these relations," yet the elements are co-constitutive (Wight 2006: 165). Wight's reading of what he calls the linguistic model of structure is based on assuming a pure Saussurean model of language which, for example, fails to emphasize the non-closure of a structure. Indeed, if we instead adhere to a notion of open structure, we would not be able to speak of an internal versus an external.[3] Wight, following Bhaskar, thus defines an external relation between A and B "such that either A or B can exist without the other." An external relation is a contingent one and "is neither necessary nor impossible," which does not prevent it from having "significant social effects." An internal relation between A and B is one in which "if and only if A would not be what it essentially is unless B is related to it in the way that it is" (Bhaskar 1979: 54; Wight 2006: 169–70). As innocuous as these definitions might appear, they in fact carry within them a heavy baggage of unacknowledged presumptions. What does Wight mean by "contingency," "necessary," "essentially," "is"? Wight does not raise these questions, which most likely means that he takes them as self-evident, irrelevant, or at least that they can in principle be settled. This is not surprising since this is consistent for his belief in the possibility that social structure, including language *qua* social structure, can have an objective ontological existence, independent of the human users/subjects.

Wight claims that his new conceptualization of structure should not only be able to build on the strengths of extant approaches, but also pave the way for a meta-theory of the agent-structure problem. The latter is then expected to offer a better handle on the co-constitution feature that many authors have advanced as a goal but, according to Wight, failed to effectively theorize without falling into epistemology or methodology traps or fallacies. In a nutshell, Wight's approach consists in espousing Bhaskar's argument that "social life occurs on a terrain constituted by four interdependent dimensions or planes of activity," otherwise termed as the social cube; these are: "1. Material transactions with nature (resources, physical attributes, etc.); 2. Inter-intra-subjective actions (rules, norms, beliefs, institutions, etc.); 3. Social relations (class, identity, production, etc.); 4. Subjectivity of the agent (subjectivity, identity, etc.)" (Wight 2006: 174). These planes are thought of as intersecting with one another and are multiply determined, each obeying its own logic. Wight uses this as a basis for defining *his notion of social structure as relations linking together these various planes of social life.* Ironically, Wight's social structures are not ontologically primordial entities—the social structures are relating together ontologically more primordial entities, *the planes of social activity.* This is much like the process-based approach where one has to assume the pre-existence of certain entities—relata—before one is able to talk about processes of relations, and which Wight condemns as being self-contradictory. Moreover, the planes of social activity (e.g., plane 4) contain what most other theorists and approaches would define as agency, or at least, elements/aspects of agency such as subjectivity. One way out for Wight could be to argue that he is defining structural relations or structurality rather than structures *per se*. However, this would not solve the problem of lack of ontological primacy, a primacy that he ought to advocate to remain self-consistent (which he wants to be). Likewise, his (and others') critique that Giddens' notion of structure is ill-defined since it encompasses both resources and rules is also coming back to haunt him. In fact, the planes of social activity that he adopts from Bhaskar not only include Giddens' sense of structure but also much more.

Throughout, there is a tension marring Wight's critiques of other works; he is too self-referential, if most of the time rather subtly so. Wight's critique implicitly takes his notion of planes of social life and structure as a self-evident Archimedean standpoint and in comparison to which he levels his critique. This self-referentiality is clearly shown in his critique of those who rely "too much" on analogies between structures in general and linguistic structures. Not surprisingly, Wight attributes a subservient (and perhaps subversive) role to language. This is ironic though. On the one hand, he clearly admits that all planes of social activity "are mediated by language" (Wight 2006: 174). While, on the other hand, he fails to ask questions such as: Can the planes of social activity be 'as such' without language? Can 'social activity' be social without a language or a system of signification without which it would be impossible to have a 'social' and which determines all meanings of this 'social'? What is placed at a secondary position—a tool, that is, language and its signification processes—is in fact constitutively essential for the very existence of the planes of social activity. This shortsightedness on the role of 'language' is symptomatic of a lack of thorough exploration of the conditions of possibility and impossibility of the planes of social activity and the consequent relational structures that Wight argues constitute a totality.[4] I argue that these and similar issues are the first stepping stones of a (re-)thinking of the agent-structure *problematique*.

In sum: Wight does a (more or less) thorough job in summarizing and critiquing extant IR literature on the notion of structure. His verdict is that not only this literature lacks consistent and useful notions of structure, but also this state of affairs has become an obstacle on the path of addressing the agent-structure problem. In developing this position Wight has managed to disclose a number of *undecidable* features of this literature. Yet in explicating his proposal Wight ends up also showing much *undecidability* in his various definitions of structure. For example, contra his own claim, Wight finds it very difficult to unequivocally delineate the defining features of agency from those of structure, and vice versa.

Why is it so? And why does Wight, in following Bhaskar, think he must and can delineate the properties of agency from those of structure? Is Wight falling prey to the very pitfalls that he identified in extant IR literature? Are these pitfalls inescapable? These and similar questions in fact constitute a strategic entry point for a deconstruction approach to the problem of social structures (and agency). As explained by Derrida (1978: 19), the strategy is not "to counter the simple choice of one of the terms or one of the series against the other," a position which is taken by Wight. Yet, contra Wight and Bhaskar, the point for Derrida (1978: 19; his emphasis) is to "maintain that it is necessary to seek new concepts and new models, an *economy* escaping the system of metaphysical oppositions;" oppositions that Wight heavily relies on in critiquing others and in building his critical realist edifice.

In the next section, I summarize a deconstruction and reconfiguration of the notion of structure using a number of Derrida's undecidable motifs. I think it helpful to repeat at this point of the discussion how a work of deconstruction proceeds. Formally speaking, the deconstruction of a given concept first discloses the conventional meanings and uses of this concept as a way of highlighting the sources of the difficulties encountered by extant literature on this concept. The work of deconstruction then displaces the meanings of the given concept so as to keep 'old' meanings while at the same time redeploying them to graft 'new' meanings that not only partially overlap with the old ones but also encompass a more general movement of signification that highlights inescapable *aporias* associated with the given concept. Therefore, the work of deconstruction at once discloses, displaces and affirms the play of meanings. I apply this strategy to Wight's notion of structure. The purpose is to highlight the aporias within Wight's notion of structure and then to re-affirm the *structurality* of structures in another way which neither seeks to silence or resolve the aporias nor to stop the process of thinking on these aporias and consequences thereof.

Structure through the work of deconstruction

De Saussure's theory of language and Lévi-Strauss' applications thereof to social structures were the foundations of what came to be known as (linguistic) structuralism which then later on evolved to become the structural approach to social theory and social sciences in general—structuralism.

Saussure's approach to language is based on a number of key observations and insights (Saussure 1974). First, the basic unit of language is the sign which unites a sound-image or a signifier, with a concept or a signified. Second, the sign has an arbitrary nature in the sense that there is no natural or pre-given relationship between the signifier and the signified parts of a sign. Any seemingly obvious relationship is only a function of convention in any given language. Third, meaning and signification emerge from within the system of language itself. Using these insights Saussure formulates his approach to language in two parts. The first one consists in advancing the thesis that there are only differences without 'positive' terms in language (Saussure 1974: 12). The second insight, which qualifies the first one, is that a pure system of differences holds only if we keep a strict separation between signified and signifier (Saussure 1974: 121). Therefore, as summarized by Howarth (2000: 22; his emphasis), in Saussure's theory of language, "the *identity* of any element is a product of the *differences* and *oppositions* established by the elements of the linguistic system."

Claude Lévi-Strauss extended Saussure's analysis of linguistic structures to the study of social structures and society. His contribution consists of (1) shifting attention from the study of conscious linguistic phenomena to their underlying unconscious structures, (2) focusing on the relations between terms instead of treating them as independent, (3) introducing the concept of a system of elements, and (4) seeking general laws either through induction or logical deduction (Lévi-Strauss 1968; Howarth 2000: 23). Lévi-Strauss' approach is anchored in two premises. First, he posits the existence (at least in principle) of deep structures underpinning the various activities and practices of a society. These deep structures can be disclosed and studied as they manifest themselves in language, myths, and systems of cultural signification such as totemism, cooking, dress codes, and other social activities (Lévi-Strauss 1968: 87). Second, all societies share a common underlying structure (Howarth 2000: 23). This approach is illustrated in Lévi-Strauss' analysis of totemic representations and myths as systems of differences and oppositions that exist between their constituent elements (Lévi-Strauss 1968: 208–11).

Despite the importance of these breakthroughs, one cannot fail to notice that both Saussure and Lévi-Strauss ended up undermining part of their revolutionary potentials in dislodging then prevailing understandings of language and social structure. Saussure's insights, that language is made up of relations of differences without positivities and that language is form and not substance, are undermined in his rigid separation between the signifier and signified and his positing of a one-to-one correspondence between the two. This is problematic since it implies the possibility of finding pure signifiers and pure signifieds whereas the other side of Saussure's theory implies that "if one tries to find a pure signifier one only finds other signifiers" (Howarth 2000: 29). In addition, Saussure falls into essentialism (of a structuralist type) in fixing the meaning of signs in a necessary fashion when he argues that the identity of the sign is produced by the *overall system* of linguistic values. He thus thinks of language as a closed totality, a system of differential elements which is a fully constituted object (Howarth 2000: 30–31). Saussure's structuralist theory of language is thus equivocated. This problem of totalization of the structure likewise persists in Lévi-Strauss' analysis of social structures, as he admitted late in his career (Lévi-Strauss 1994: 10). On his own recognition, his task before then had been to uncover the relationships between pre-existing and pre-formed objects as explicated in his methodology (Lévi-Strauss 1968: 84).

The closure or totalization of language as system of signification and the rigid fixity of the signifier and signified within the sign are two entry points through which Derrida initiated his deconstruction of Saussure's inspired structuralism. Derrida partially espoused Saussure's theory of the sign that meaning and signification presuppose the existence of language as a system of differences. He, however, rejected Saussure's move to divide the sign into the signifier or material form (sound-image) and signified or ideal form (concept). Derrida argues instead that there is 'something' in the sign that allows it to be repeated from context to context, if in an altered 'something'. He calls this 'something', which is not a positive linguistic being, a *mark*. The latter has the property of subsisting independently of the speaker, writer, hearer, or reader (Howarth 2000: 38–39). Yet the mark is not a 'substance' because it is not present in itself. Rather, its signification depends on the effects of other traces and differences between them.

Moreover, the *trace* includes both the materiality of the signifier and the ideality of the signified. As Derrida (1982: 315) put it, "the possibility of repeating, and therefore of identifying, marks is implied in every code, making of it a communicable, transmittable, decipherable grid that is iterable for third party, and thus for any user in general." Therefore, the trace is a pure play of differences, that is, differences from the effects of other traces, and it is this play of differences which actively constitutes any given trace and meaning (Derrida 1981a: 26). As such traces are not traces of any positive element of language or sign. Rather, *traces* precede the emergence and existence of signs and it is only through their plays that language is possible.

Because any sign can break away from anyone context and acquire (more or less) new meanings in other contexts, Derrida argues that any sign can always be grafted and re-grafted on various chains of signification and can always be inserted and re-inserted in new contexts. Derrida assigns this property of sign *re-grafting* to what he calls a 'minimal remainder' of meaning which enables the sign to be used as almost the 'same' sign in various contexts and chains of signification (Howarth 2000: 39). This is the result of two movements. First, there is the interplay of different *traces* of meanings which precedes the appearance of the sign. Second, there is "the necessary deferment of some possibilities not actualized or signified by the play of traces" (Howarth 2000: 40). Derrida introduces the pseudo-notion of *différance* as a way for capturing how meanings are produced through a combination of the play of signifiers in these two movements—difference and deferral. This play of traces is not a play of presence against presence, or even against absence (Derrida 1978: 292). As such the play of traces undermines any attempt to totalization of the field of meaning, and makes the latter "a field of infinite substitutions" (Derrida 1978: 289). How does this affect the notion of structure? Derrida (1978: 15–16) explains that

> *strictu sensu*, the notion of structure refers only to space, geometric or morphological space, the order of forms and sites. Structure is first the structure of an organic or artificial work, the internal unity of an assemblage, a *construction*; a work is governed by a unifying principle, the *architecture* that is built and made visible in a location ... Only metaphorically was this *topographical* literality displaced in the direction of its Aristotelian and *topographical* signification.

Derrida (1978: 16) argues that the metaphorical sense should be "interrogated and even destroyed as concerns its figurative quality." Why should we do this? The answer is two-pronged. First, "so that the nonspatiality or original spatiality designated by it may be revived." Failing to do so "runs the risk, through a kind of sliding as unnoticed as it is *efficacious*, of confusing meaning with its geometric, morphological, or, in the best of cases, cinematic model. One risks being interested in the figure itself to the detriment of the play going on within it metaphorically." Second, "metaphor is never innocent. It orients research and fixes results. When the spatial model is hit upon, when it functions, critical reflection rests within it. In fact, and even if criticism does not admit this to be so" (Derrida 1978: 17).

The topographical metaphor is built on the idea that there is a center (e.g., principle of organization in Kenneth Waltz' definition of the structure of anarchy) that grounds and defines the structure. The center plays the role of arresting and hence grounding the play of substitutions (Derrida 1978: 289). However, this is precisely what the movement of play (of traces) is against. First, the play is "permitted by the lack or absence of a center or origin" (Derrida 1978: 289 Derrida 1978: 289). The existence of a rigid center would stop the play of differences and thus the play of signification, or signification *tout court*. Should this occur, it would mean that the center has exhausted signification and therefore made totality possible. This is not possible though "because the sign which replaces the center, which supplements it, taking the center's place in its absence ... is added, occurs as a surplus, as a *supplement*" (Derrida 1978: 289; original emphasis). That it is not possible to achieve totalization in the process of signification is due to the fact that "the movement of signification adds something, which results in the fact that there is always more, but this addition is a floating one because it comes to perform a vicarious function, to supplement a lack on the part of the signified" (Derrida 1978: 289). All in all, Saussure's principle that language consists of differences allowed Derrida to think of the signifier as possessing a property of overabundance, which is manifested in "its supplementary character," which in turn is "the result of a finitude, that is to say, the result of a lack which must be supplemented" (Derrida 1978: 290).

Structuralism, according to Derrida (1978: 26), "prohibits the consideration of that which is incomplete or missing, everything that would make the configuration appear to be a blind anticipation of, or mysterious deviation from, an orthogenesis whose own conceptual basis would to be a *telos* or an ideal norm." To be a structuralist then means "first to concentrate on the organization of meaning, on the autonomy and idiosyncratic balance, the completion of each moment, of each form; and it is to refuse to relegate everything that is not comprehensible as an ideal type to the status of aberrational accident" (Derrida 1978: 26). Even that which is not structured, that is, the so-called pathological/deviant, is not recaptured as the absence of structure. Rather, the pathological "is organized" and "cannot be understood as the deficiency, defect, or decomposition of a beautiful, ideal totality" (Derrida 1978: 26). Therefore, there is a structuralist urge that seeks to achieve "the comprehensive description of a totality, of a form of a function organized according to an internal legality in which elements have meaning only in the solidarity of their correlation or their opposition" (Derrida 1978: 157). Contra this, the genetic urge is about "the search for the origin of foundation of the structure" (Derrida 1978: 157). However, according to Derrida, this focus on the notion of a center of the structure ends up undoing the very structurality of structure (Gasché 1986: 146). Indeed structurality has been

> neutralized or reduced, and this by a process of giving it a center or referring it to a point of presence, a fixed origin. The function of this

center was not only to orient, balance, and organize the structure—one cannot in fact conceive of an unorganized structure—but above all to make sure that the organizing principle of the structure would limit what we might call the play of the structure.

(Derrida 1978: 278–79)

Here we face a contradiction, or as Derrida terms it, a contradictory coherence. People always think that

The center also closes off the play which it opens up and makes possible. As center, it is the point at which the substitution of contents, elements, or terms is no longer possible. At the center, the permutation or the transformation of elements ... is forbidden. ... the center, which is by definition unique, constituted that very thing which is a structure which while governing the structure, escapes structurality. ... The center is at the center of the totality, and yet, since the center does not belong to the totality (is not part of the totality), the totality has its center *elsewhere*. The center is not the center. The concept of centered structure—although it represents coherence itself ... – is contradictorily coherent.

(Derrida 1978: 279)

In sum, what Derrida (1978: 279) rejects is the concept of centered structure wherein the concept of a play would be "based on a fundamental ground, a play constituted on the basis of a fundamental immobility and reassuring certitude which itself is beyond the reach of play."

How can one begin to regraft the notion of structure—or rather structurality—while avoiding the pitfall of positing a center that determines the structure and hence negates the very *structurality* of structure and the play of traces? Derrida (1978: 280) argues that this happens at the moment we recognize "the absence of the transcendental signified" which then "extends the domain and the play of signification infinitely." Therefore, we can understand or interpret structure in two different ways. First, the usual sense seeks to "describe what is peculiar to the structural organization only by not taking into account, in the very moment of this description, its past conditions: by omitting to posit the problem of the transition from one structure to another, by putting history between brackets. In this 'structuralist' moment, the concepts of chance and discontinuity are indispensable," (Derrida 1978: 291). It also "seeks to decipher, dreams of deciphering a truth or an origin which escapes play and the other of the sign, and which lives the necessity of interpretation as an exile." Second, the other sense or interpretation is not "turned toward the origin;" it rather "affirms play and tries to pass beyond man" who "throughout the entire history—has dreamed of full presence, the reassuring foundation, the origin and the end of play" (Derrida 1978: 292). Therefore, instead of thinking about structure in terms of structuring effects as commonly done in the literature, Derrida proposes to think of structurality in terms of *traces* (and traces of traces) and *the play of traces*, with the latter always being a movement of *différance*, that is, difference, deferral and temporalizing delay of meaning. In short, For Derrida, structure is a *différantial play of traces (of traces)*.[5]

What does this re-thinking of structure imply for the agency-structure problematique? For starters, it suggests that deconstructing the agency-structure problematique should not/will not lead to a jettisoning of structures. Rather, it suggests a *focus on the structurality of structure* and a displacement of structure into infrastructures of *différantial play of traces*. Moreover, thought of in this way structure not only does not have a center or an origin, but it also is not a totality and remains constitutively open through the play of *différance*. There is no line of demarcation of what counts as structure and what counts as not structure anymore. Does this imply that we cannot anymore delineate agency from structure?

Agency: a re-thinking via deconstruction

This section presents a deconstruction of agency for which I use Wight's proposal of a tripartite notion of agency as an entry point. This paves the way for an argument that the 'agentic' property of actors is better thought of as sovereignty. Doing so opens up a space of thinking about agency where one does not need to oppose agency to structure as usually done in the literature. That is: I engage a work of deconstruction of *agency qua sovereignty*. This deconstruction then leads to a re-thinking of agency as being two heterogeneous but indissociable notions: first, as *unconditional event of agency* and, second, as *conditional event qua originary performativity of inaugural interpretation* with the unconditional event of agency being the condition of possibility and impossibility of the conditional agency. Following Derrida, I call the conditional form a 'saying agency'. The unconditional event of agency is strictly speaking not a property of the subject; rather, it is an un-anticipatable event that can only befall on the subject. The conditional agency *qua* 'saying agency' is always registered *après coup*, after the event of agency has happened.

Wight's notion of agency

Agency is an old problem of philosophy and social theory which has commonly been thought of in opposition with structure (Loyal and Barnes 2001: 507). It is along this 'commonest way' of thinking agency that Wight (2006: 11), heeding Bhaskar's advice that human agents and structures have different properties, presents an ontological theory of agency which is claimed to be clearly demarcated from structure. Wight (2006: 206) first adopts Spivak's insight that it is in the "freedom of subjectivity" that agency is located. He then complements this with Bhaskar's idea that "agents are particulars which are the centres of powers" and that an agent is "simply anything which is capable of bringing about a change in something (including itself)" (Bhaskar 1978: 109; Wight 2006: 211). Wight summarizes Bhaskar's notion of agency in the social world as "referring to embodied, intentional causality, or praxis" (Bhaskar 1994: 100; Wight 2006: 212).

In an effort to avoid falling into the trap of thinking of agential power as residing in a "thing", Wight draws on Margaret Archer to complement Bhaskar's notion of agency, thereby making agency "layered and differentiated and inextricably linked to social contexts through the relations in which it is embedded" (Wight 2006: 212–13). He ends up with a tripartite concept of agency—agency$_1$, agency$_2$, agency$_3$—with all three parts necessarily involved in any invocation of agency. *Agency$_1$* relates to "the freedom of subjectivity;" *agency$_2$* "refers to the way in which agency$_1$ becomes an agent of something and this something refers to the socio-cultural system into which persons are born and develop;" *agency$_3$* "refers to those positioned-practice places which agents$_1$ inhabit," as social actors (Wight 2006: 213). Wight (2006: 214) further explains that "the positioned-practices are structural properties that endure irrespective of the agents that occupy them, and as such cannot be reduced to the properties of the agents$_1$ that occupy them."

Wight's conceptualization is innovative and shows a high degree of complexity. Yet his efforts end up being plagued with a number of problems. First, in suggesting a three-layered agency, is he talking about agency or a structure that has some agentic powers (assuming that we grant him for the time being the benefit of the doubt that these agents are to be thought of as "endowed with the capacity to bring a change" which seemingly can only occur through agency$_1$)? The indeterminacy is detrimental since he sets out, heeding Bhaskar's advice, to characterize the properties that *differentiate* agency from structure—yet his notion of agency is at its core defined as a structure with three basic elements. The demarcation seems undecidable. Is this really a problem? Isn't this rather symptomatic of un-theorized aspects of Wight's meta-theory? I propose (and explain later) that it indeed is the case and that it has to do with the conditions of possibility and impossibility of the notions of agency and structures.

Second, Wight relies on social theory to explicate what he means by agency$_2$ when he uses the notions of "socio-cultural system," "born," and "develop" (terms that he takes as self-evident). He claims to be working at the level of *meta-theory* but then draws on elements from *social theory* (which is based on a choice of ontology in the first place) to explicate his so-called meta-theoretical concepts and ideas. Is social theory the condition of possibility of his meta-theory, which is supposed to be the basis of social theory? This means that his meta-theory is but an additional layer of social theory, thereby facing him with circularity and *perhaps* completely undermining his claim to begin from ontology.

Third, there is no unambiguous (or no undecidable) sense of agency (in the sense of Wight following Bhaskar) at any of the levels. The problem of agency₁ is that using the notion of subjectivity does not unequivocally imply agency as "capable to bring change in something including itself," except if one assumes a Cartesian/Newtonian subject, which Wight does not do. After a brief discussion of some literature on the problematique of the subject and the so-called 'death' of the subject, an issue that he discounts somewhat too hastily, Wight (2006: 209–10) anchors his notion of the fragmented subject and agency in a sense of 'self', which thinks and reflects and possesses intentionality and autonomy to a certain extent from the 'social' out there.[6] What if this 'self' is always already different from itself, that is, always already not only divided within itself but also *autoimmune* to itself, that is, the auto of the 'self' is immune to the 'self', the 'self' is self-immune to 'self'? How can we then speak of intentionality, autonomy or reflection of an autoimmune, always already internally, divided 'self'? Pursuing this line of questioning, which deconstruction opens up, threatens the very foundation of Wight's edifice—the scientific realist positing of ontological foundations.

The problem with agency₂ is that it is a "way," another term for process, which then suggests that Wight's approach perhaps belongs to the camp of the process-based approaches to ontology. However, he characterizes these approaches as self-defeating since, according to him, the approaches end up positing positive originary ontological entities among which supposedly ontologically-primary processes unfold. The question is: Is he or is he not rejecting process-based theorizing? The response seems to be an undecidable 'yes and no'. The problem with agency₃ is that it is a position, that is, a position within a structure which does not possess any of the agentic properties that Wight is presumably hunting for.

I propose that these seeming problems of undecidability have to do with many unspoken presuppositions on the primacy of ontology in theorizing agency. I begin by considering an issue which is rarely discussed, let alone theorized and critiqued, in the literature on the agency-structure problematique—that is, thinking of agent as sovereign subject. I suggest that not deconstructing/problematizing the sovereign subject in thinking about the agency-structure problematique is a major gap. One can venture to say that most, but by no means all, discussions of agency in social theory presume either implicitly or explicitly an intentional, autonomous, sovereign subject. As mentioned earlier, although Wight does pay some attention to the problematique of the 'subject', he ends up reinforcing his scientific-realist dispositions by positing a kind of a minimal 'self' as a necessary starting point for agency to be. As discussed down below, a deconstruction of the sovereign subject provides an entry point from where we can see the sources of many difficulties that many social-theoretic approaches have encountered in trying to go beyond positing agent and structure as ontologically primordial, even when describing them as being co-constituted à la Giddens, Archer, or otherwise. The sovereign (as, for example, defined by Carl Schmitt, Hobbes, Rousseau and others) is the one who enacts the exceptional, the one who is outside the structural constraints of the law, and, more generally, outside 'normality'. Isn't this what the 'commonest way' (to use Loyal and Barnes' expression) of thinking agency means by the opposition of agency and structure? This implies that to deconstruct agency is thus tantamount to deconstructing sovereignty in terms of Derrida's undecidable infrastructures (such as *différance, trace, iterability, autoimmunity,* etc.).[7] This thus implies that both 'structure' and 'agency' are thought of in terms of infrastructures, which are not necessarily the same, but yet are connected in what Gasché terms as the general system of infrastructures.[8]

Agency qua *sovereignty*

For Bhaskar and Wight an agent is "simply anything which is capable of bringing about a change in something (including itself)" (Bhaskar 1978: 109; Wight 2006: 211). Coole (2005: 135) argues that political agents "emerge as provisional concentrations of agentic capacities that acquire more or less coherence and duration, depending upon their context." For Loyal and Barnes (2001: 507), "'agency' stands for the freedom of the contingently acting subject over and against the constraints that are thought to derive from enduring social structures." For Giddens (1976, 75), a person has agency to the extent that this "person (i.e. an agent) 'could have acted otherwise'." For Butler (1995: 134), "to the extent that a performative appears to 'express' a prior intention, a doer *behind* the deed, that prior agency is only legible as *the effect* of that utterance." As these quotes (and in fact much of the literature on agency) show, agency is usually thought of in terms of an element of provisional, contingent freedom to act (or not act, or act otherwise) against, through or outside social structural constraints. As such the agent (*qua* agent) *contingently* acts.[9] How to think of this *contingency* of acting (or not acting, or acting otherwise)? The difficulty in this question has to do with the fact any agent finds itself always already immersed in preexisting structures. Yet thinking of agency as 'contingent' implies that we cannot know that it would occur before it effectively does, otherwise it will part of a structure of knowledge in a certain way.

I suggest that we think of this 'contingency' as an event in the sense of Derrida, an event which cannot be predicted but can only surprise us. Agency would thus be un-anticipatable, something which remains un-appropriable.[10] However, thinking of agency as such an event makes it seem as if agency is extra-structural, or, in other words, as if it is a non-structural residual which resists structural determination. This is a problem because it seems that thinking of agency *qua* event solidifies the ontological demarcation of structure and agency even more. This is an issue that must be addressed.

Another difficulty that emerges from thinking of agency as 'contingency' has to do with the process of registering the occurrence of agency. Indeed, should we think of agency in the sense of event, this would mean that 'knowing' this event, 'knowing' that agency has been exercised, would cancel the event which is un-anticipatable as such. This suggests that perhaps when agency does occur it can only be registered *après coup*, after the event has been transformed into a non-event (in the sense of Derrida which is to be explained), that is, into a memory trace. Yet the process of 'registration' effectively occurs through an act of registering agency *after* witnessing its occurrence, after it has ceased to be an event. How to think of this 'act' of registration of agency? Is the process of 'registration' of agency a retroactive performativity? I argue that it indeed is the case, as explained later.

Yet, even if we were to think of registered agency in terms of retroactive performativity, it remains short of fully being *agentic* in the sense of the event because performativity cannot escape the law of iterability, that is, of transformative repetition, of simultaneous repetition and change. This means that registered agency *qua* retroactive performativity remains context-bound and limited in many ways—it is simultaneously change and conservation, invention and repetition. Perhaps, we are facing an *originary* performativity which effects an *inaugural interpretation*, that is, an interpretation which produces a registration of agency, of course *après coup*.

I am thus proposing two different ways of thinking about agency—agency *qua* un-anticipatable event and agency *qua* originary performativity of inaugural interpretation. The first type of agency is of the order of the *unconditional*, whereas the second type of agency is of the order of the *conditional*. Unconditional agency is what eludes all attempts at theorizing agency, whereas conditional agency is what has usually been termed as agency in extant literature on the agency-structure problematique (and elsewhere).

Unconditional event

This section introduces the notion of unconditional event in the sense of Derrida. This paves the way to a discussion of conditionality as contaminating the unconditional event. It also paves the way for discussing the aporiatic relation of spectrality between conditional and unconditional, that is, a relation through which the unconditional spectrally haunts the conditional. I then consider how we can performatively think unconditionality *qua* impossibility without fatally contaminating it *too much* with the possible conditional, that is, without performativity appropriating the *eventness* of event by turning it into a calculable mastery over the event, thereby annulling the unconditional un-anticipatable event as such. This can be done through dissociating unconditionality from sovereignty. This is possible because sovereignty is deconstructible. A work of deconstructing sovereignty then shows that sovereignty is autoimmune and opens up the possibility of a thinking of conditional event in the sense of 'saying event', which is always already spectrally haunted by the unconditional event as its condition of possibility and impossibility.

The notion of event for Derrida is very different from what we usually take as being an event. For Derrida, an event is not just something that happens or occurs, although this is also true. An event, argues Derrida (2007b: 443), "is that which goes very quickly; there can be an event only when it's not expected, when one can no longer wait for it, when the coming of what happens interrupts the waiting." Derrida (2002b: 233–34) explains that the event "must not only surprise the constative and propositional mode of the language of knowledge (*S* is *P*), but also no longer let itself be commanded by the performative speech act of a subject," otherwise "what takes place, arrives, happens, or happens *to me* remains still controllable and programmable within a horizon of anticipation or precomprehension, within a *horizon*, period. It is of the order of the masterable possible, it is the unfolding of what is already possible." Moreover according to Derrida (2002b: 234), "the pure singular eventness of *what* arrives or of *who* arrives and arrives *to me* ... would suppose an *irruption* that punctures the horizon, *interrupting* any performative organization, any convention, or any context that can be dominated by a conventionality." The event arrives only where it cannot be subjugated by the speech act, either constative or performative. For an event to arrive *qua* event, it must be impossible, or as put by Derrida (2002b: 234), "only the impossible *can* arrive" *qua* event. The force of the event overruns, exceeds, and exposes all performative force. Derrida (2002b: 234–35) explains that the force of the event is "irreducible to the force or the power of a performative, even if it gives to the performative itself, to what is called the *force* of the performative, its chance and its effectiveness." In order to go beyond the possible as a limit and, hence, consider the event *qua* impossible we need to go beyond the performative (and, of course, the constative) so that we can see the arrival of the event since, as put by Derrida (2003b: 43), "the performative cannot avoid neutralizing, indeed annulling, the eventfulness of the event" because of "the power that an ipseity gives itself to produce the event of which it speaks" and thus "appropriates for itself a calculable mastery over it." What we thus need to do is to avoid appropriation by the performative, an appropriation which occurs through a calculable mastery over the event, since for an event to occur as event it should be beyond all mastery and must affect passivity (Derrida 2003b: 43).

However, the event *qua* unconditional is not pure; it is contaminated by a certain complicity with the conditional (Derrida 2002b: 235). First, because our thinking/discourse is conditional and we are trying to think the unconditional, the contamination of the unconditional by our conditionality is inherently inescapable. Second, unconditionality and conditionality are not simply opposite to one another; rather, the relationship between the two is, as Derrida states (2001: 45), shifty enough to escape the logic of binarism. Although the unconditional and conditional are absolutely forever heterogeneous to one another, they are also non-dissociable from one another, and yet incommensurable with one another. Derrida explicates this relationship through the example of hospitality; he (Derrida 2003a: 128–30) argues that unconditional hospitality

> is in advance open to someone who is neither expected nor invited, to whomever arrives as an absolutely foreign *visitor*, as a new *arrival*,

nonidentifiable and unforeseeable, in short, wholly other. ... The visit might actually be very dangerous, and we must not ignore this fact, but would a hospitality without risk, a hospitality backed by certain assurances, a hospitality protected by an immune system against the wholly other, be true hospitality? ... An unconditional hospitality is, to be sure, practically impossible to live; one cannot in any case, and by definition, organize it. ... But without at least the thought of this pure and unconditional hospitality, of hospitality *itself*, we would have no concept of hospitality in general and would not even be able to determine any rules for conditional hospitality ... these two hospitalities are at once heterogeneous and indissociable. Heterogeneous because we can move from one to the other only by means of an absolute leap, a leap beyond knowledge and power, beyond norms and rules. ... But—and here is the indissociability—I cannot open the door, I cannot expose myself to the coming of the other and offer him or her anything whatsoever without making this hospitality effective, without, in some concrete way, giving *something determinate*. This determination will thus have to re-inscribe the unconditional into certain conditions. Otherwise, it gives nothing.

Third, the relationship between the conditional and the unconditional is one of hauntology and spectrality. Caputo (2003: 15) explains that the unconditional "is perfectly capable of being described as a ghost, as a shade or a specter, a demi-being, not real enough to do anything but able only to haunt us with uncanny possibilities, above all, the haunting possibility of the impossible." The unconditional is an impossibility that haunts the conditional, that is, "the possibility of failure must continue to mark the event, even when it succeeds, as the trace of an impossibility, at times its memory and always its haunting" (Derrida 2002: 362).

Fourth, the unconditional is independent of sovereign mastery. According to Derrida (2003b: 43), an event occurs in passivity and is a freedom that is no longer tantamount to the power of a subject; this freedom is without autonomy and is heteronomy without servitude; a freedom that resembles a passive decision. Because of this feature Derrida (2002b: 235) states that "it would be necessary to dissociate a certain *unconditional* independence of thought ... from any phantasm of *indivisible sovereignty* and of sovereign mastery."

Therefore, to be able to think the unconditional event we need to deconstruct the notion of indivisible sovereignty. Why? Because sovereignty is "the concentration, into a single point of indivisible singularity (God, the monarch, the people, the state or the nation-state), of absolute force and the absolute exception ... the sovereign is the one who decides exceptionally and performatively about the exception, the one who keeps or grants himself the right to suspend rights or law" (Naas 2006: 39). Therefore, on the one hand, sovereignty is "indivisible, unshareable, and unspeakable *or it is not at all*;" yet, on the other hand, sovereignty is autoimmune, immune to itself (Naas

2006: 39; his emphasis). Before continuing further, we need to discuss what autoimmunity is.

Autoimmunity stands for the biological process through which an organism turns against its own self-protection (Cohen 2004). The immune system, which is supposed to protect the body from outside threats, turns against the healthy cells of the body 'sensing' them as threats and thus attacks them. This transaction is without prior rules given in advance. Nor does it possess any absolute assurance since "there is no absolutely reliable prophylaxis against the auto-immunitary" (Derrida 2003b: 41–42).

First, autoimmunity compromises the immune system, that is, the very selfhood of the self. Derrida (2005c: 45) explains that "the autoimmune ... consists not only in committing suicide but in compromising *sui-* or *self-*referentiality, the *self* or *sui-*of suicide itself." Rather than being opposed to immunity, autoimmunity, argues Naas (2006: 34), "is a self-destructive 'force'" which emerges from the very gesture of immunization itself. Every entity that seeks to immunize itself ends up, and, more accurately put, begins simultaneously, also generating autoimmunity, immunity of itself to itself. This means that we do not have a self, an ipseity that then compromises itself through some sort of post-hoc injury or even suicide. Autoimmunity is constitutive of the selfhood of the self, of ipseity. Ipseity is originarily auto-immune to its own ipseity. Ipseity cannot be, cannot be spoken of or be thought about without autoimmunity always already compromising it. Autoimmunity is always already originary.

Second, autoimmunity is more originary than ontology; it turns ontology into a *hauntology* where a specter haunts the self originarily. This means that we are pre-ontologically autoimmune. "'I am' would mean 'I am haunted'," says Derrida (1994a: 133). This implies that "the I cannot do without the specter; life cannot do without non-life; identity without difference; or the uniqueness of a living *autos* without repetition, iteration, and, thus, death" (Naas 2006: 23). We can say that autoimmunity is originary spectrality that divides any ipseity within itself. There is thus an originary *automaticity* in autoimmunity (Naas 2006: 34). Autoimmunity originarily inhabits ipseity which means that autoimmunity originarily undermines the indivisibility of the 'I', the 'self' and ipseity. Autoimmunity thus is an "implacable law of the self-destructive conservation of the 'subject' or of egological ipseity" (Derrida 2005c: 55). According to Derrida and Naas (Derrida and Naas 2006: 18), "'autoimmunity' appears to name a process that is inevitably and irreducibly at work more or less everywhere, at the heart of every sovereign identity."

Third, autoimmunity is a radicalized, non-closed, non-teleological maximization of *aporia* and *double bind*. Aporia, double-bind and similarly acting notions not only function to show internal contradiction and undecidability. They also and more importantly show "an internal-external, nondialectizable antinomy," which risks creating paralysis, which "thus calls for the event of the interruptive decision" (Derrida 2003a: 35). Autoimmunity is thus more maximal in the sense that it calls for the irruptive event *qua* impossible and unpredictable, the event of the decision within the terrain of undecidability where many logics (such as spectrality) are operative. Yet, autoimmunity is the condition of possibility of the decision in the terrain of undecidability, continuous negotiation and "invention of new ways of calculating or reasoning" between the calculable and the incalculable.

As such, autoimmunity creates a rupture in the notion of sovereignty. One immediate implication of autoimmunity is that it allows sovereignty "to be perpetually re-thought and reinscribed" (Naas 2006: 18). This implies that sovereignty has within itself 'itself' and it produces what undermines it within itself (Naas 2006: 18). Autoimmunity is therefore always already constitutive (and de-constitutive) of sovereignty. Derrida (2005b: 101) explains:

> To confer sense or meaning on sovereignty, to justify it, to find a reason for it, is already to compromise its deciding exceptionality, to subject it to rules, to a code of law, to some general law, to concepts ... to compromise its immunity. This happens as soon as one speaks of it in order to give it or find it some sense or meaning. But since this happens all the time, pure sovereignty does not exist; it is always in the process of positing itself by refuting itself, by denying or disavowing itself; it is always in the process of autoimmunizing itself, of betraying itself.

How does this autoimmunity relate to and affect the unconditional? Naas explains that "autoimmunity at once destroys or compromises the integrity and identity of sovereign forms and opens them up to their future—that is, to the unconditionality of the event" (Naas 2006: 18). Autoimmunity is what allows us to think the unconditionality of the event, that is, a possibilization of the unconditional event. The double bind of autoimmunity is therefore what makes the impossible possible.

How can we think this 'impossible possible' so as to make it into a 'possible' in a certain way? The impossible here is in the sense of the "more-than-possible, the transgression, the chance, the aleatory, the breach, the rupture, the passage to the limits, the *ébranler* and the *solicitation* of the same" (Caputo 1997a: 51). The impossible possibility is a very peculiar one since "even when something comes to pass as possible, when an event occurs as possible, the fact that it will have been impossible, that the possible invention will have been impossible, this impossibility continues to haunt the possibility ... It remains impossible; it may have taken place but it's still impossible" (Derrida 2007b: 452–53).

In order to think the impossible we need to 'possibilize' it. How to do it? How does this mutual contamination of the possible and the impossible work? For Derrida (2002b: 349–50), thinking the possible as the impossible is thinking that "the 'condition of possibility' is a 'condition of impossibility'." Yet Derrida (1997b: 29) cautions us that "the possibilization of the impossible possible must remain at one and the same time as undecidable" and should remain uncertain and plagued with the "inassurance of the 'perhaps'." Instead "possibilization," in the sense of Derrida (2002b: 359), "allows itself to be haunted by the specter of its impossibility, by its mourning for itself: a self-mourning carried within itself that also gives it its life or its survival, its very possibility."

How does the mutual contamination of the possible and the impossible work? How does impossibility open its possibility? It does it by leaving "a trace," which is a chance and a threat, a right "*within* that which it makes possible." Thus trace is what enables a possibilization of the impossible, which is, lest we forget, a possibilization *without* possibilization, that is, without turning the impossible into a possible. This can also be rephrased as: The impossible is the trace of its impossibility obeying the logic of *without* (introduced in previous chapters). It is as if one is partially removing some 'part' of impossibility from the impossible *qua* trace and turning it into a 'part' of possibility without full possibilization. The condition of possibility of this kind of possible is such that it "gives the possible a chance but by depriving it of its purity" (Derrida 2002b: 362). Derrida (2002b: 362) illustrates how this purity deprivation works in the performative (such as in making a promise):

> the possibility of failure is not only inscribed as a preliminary risk in the condition of the possibility of the success of a performative ... The possibility of failure must continue to mark the event, even when it succeeds, as the trace of an impossibility, at times its memory and always its haunting.

Therefore, rather than opposing impossibility to the possible, although impossibility seems to be opposed to the possible, impossibility "gives itself over to possibility," that is, impossibility "runs through possibility and leaves in it the trace of its withdrawal" (Derrida 2002b: 362). Impossibility penetrates possibility under the form of a trace, as a trace that remains after impossibility withdraws from possibility, if we can term it in this way. However, this withdrawal is a withdrawal *without* withdrawal since impossibility was not there (in the possibility) to start with, but was rather always already there as a trace; that is, the impossibility was never a fully present one, was always already fading as a trace. This means that the possible is a possible impossible within which the trace (of the impossible which always already was a trace) runs through and through. The possible "is always bound to an irreducible divisibility that affects the very essence of the possible," as impossibility (Derrida 2002b: 358). Impossibility is always already a specter that haunts the possible.

In sum: Autoimmunity makes sovereignty a possible conditional which is always already haunted with impossibility. This implies that agency *qua* sovereignty is also autoimmune to itself and as such it is a haunted conditional. This also means that the unconditional event (of agency) spectrally haunts conditional agency *qua* sovereignty through and through, thereby making it possible, keeping in mind that unconditional event of agency and conditional agency are mutually indissociable and heterogeneous.

Yet, how to 'speak' of this conditional agency? I propose that such a conditional agency is always spoken of *après coup*—conditional agency is agency *qua* 'saying agency', which is an originary performativity of inaugural interpretation, as explained down below.

Conditional agency qua *originary performativity of inaugural interpretation*

How to think of this conditional agency which is always spoken of, theorized, *après coup*, that is, registered and known only after it has been exercised and deployed and has ceased to be as such? Put differently: how to think of this discourse, or saying, of conditional agency? Is it just a performative act that retroactively constitutes this *après coup* conditional agency? However, the act of performativity is not—should not, could not—be sufficient for this task because, as discussed earlier, the unconditional event haunts the conditional agency and the unconditional blurs the performative/constative distinction and escapes both. This means that we need to re-think such a performative act since 'registering' agency *après coup* does involve performativity, in a certain way.

Performativity allows us *to do things with words* and thus can be seen as *founding, engendering, being at the origin'* of something new, or a *transformation* of something already in the world. A key feature of Derrida's approach to performative is a blurring of the dichotomy of constative/performative. This goes against the conventional understanding which assumes that the constative is used to describe, unveil, point to the 'what is' and that the performative is used to institute, produce, transform.[11] The blurring comes from the fact that "the only way to claim that language functions performatively to shape the world is to do so through a constative, such as 'Language shapes the world'; but on the other hand, there is no way to claim the constative transparency of language except by a speech act" (Culler 2000: 511–12). That is, whenever we are *constatively* describing or pointing to 'something', we are simultaneously *performatively* acting in bringing about this 'something', and vice versa.

The context, or more accurately, change in the context, is a crucial determining aspect of the performative/constative tension. The latter is more or less made possible by what Derrida terms as *iterability*. Derrida argues that no performative act can succeed as such without being subject to iterability as its condition of possibility since iterability is the possibility of repeatability when the context changes. Iterability is thus the power that "the inscription has, once it is inscribed, to continue working in the complete absence of the intentional structure that originally inhabited it" (Miller 2001: 106). In fact, there is "a general iterability—without which there would not even be a 'successful' performative" (Derrida 1988: 17). As such, iterability inherently makes any performative act an impure one since it creates the possibility of iterating the same performative but in very different, and sometimes mutually exclusive, contexts.

Iterability is also the possibility condition for alteration and change. According to Derrida (1988: 62), "iterability alters, contaminating parasitically what it identifies and enables to repeat 'itself'." Yet, arguing that there is change in the context does not necessarily imply a *tabula rasa* because "a context never creates itself *ex-nihilo*; no mark can create or engender a context on its own, much less dominate it" (Derrida 1988: 79). What we have is that it is always possible to have a contextual transformation and iterability is the condition of possibility of such a transformation. There is no communication through performative acts or otherwise without iterability, that is, without simultaneous repeatability and alterability.

That iterability is a necessary feature of performativity makes the latter not just a source of engendering or transforming something but also originary (Derrida 1989: 1007–9). First, iterability requires that the origin repeats itself. However, this repetition is not meant in the usual sense of the term. It is originarily repetitive in the sense that it alters itself to give itself the value of origin, and thus to conserve itself. Second, iterability is such that it "inscribes conservation in the essential structure of foundation" (Derrida 1989: 1007–9). Third, "iterability precludes the possibility of pure and great founders," (Derrida 1989: 1007–9). This means that inauguration is not a pure foundation but rather a foundation impregnated with conservation—something is created which carries in it something that is conserved (Culler 2000: 509–10). This implies that because iterability is originary and because iterability breaches the performative act, performativity is in fact *originary* performativity. This *originary* performativity produces an *inaugural interpretation* which is, as put by Derrida (1994: 51), "an interpretation that transforms the very thing it interprets."

Put differently, performativity begins from a pre-existing context; however this context is not thought of as an external condition of possibility. Rather, the context becomes the context of the performative "only when the speech act intervenes within it, however weakly and without power to saturate it" (Miller 2001: 111). The performative act acts on "the context it enters, even though in retrospect that context seems to have been there already as the ground of the speech act's efficacy" (Miller 2001: 111). The performative act transforms the context wherein it acts instead of presupposing it (Miller 2001: 112). Therefore, iterability turns the performative act into one that brings into existence, *while being performed*, its own condition of possibility. The performative act transforms the context into a co-emerging/transformed experience through which and because of which the performative is efficacious (Barton 2003: 244). An originary performative is thus one that acts in narrating itself and as such transforms/engenders the very context of its narration, thereby making the narration and the act one and the same thing.

This notion of performativity differs in important ways from the notion used in conventional (that is, Austin's and Searle's) speech-act theory. First, whereas in speech-act theory there is a clear demarcation between the constative and the performative, in Derrida's sense such a demarcation is undecidable as the two always already contaminate and implicate one another.

Second, whereas the context of the performative can be the condition of felicity (or infelicity) of the performative in speech-act theory, *the performative in the sense of Derrida conterminously engenders its context with it*. This means that, because the performative is more than just a speech act (à la Austin), what we might think of as an extra-performative element needed for the creation of institutions, in the sense of speech-act theory, is also part of the context, and the latter cannot be demarcated from the performative as the two are always co-implicated with one another.

Third, *acting through narrating itself simultaneously engenders self-legitimation of the performative act while creating a sense of inauguration* or, more precisely, an inaugural interpretation of the very conditions of self-legitimation. Inaugural interpretation acts by lifting "itself by its own bootstraps" (Miller 2001: 124). For example, speaking of the act of founding law, Derrida (1989: 941–43) states that the operation of inauguration "would consist of a *coup de force*, of a performative and therefore interpretative violence." Why 'violence'? Because a silencing and suppressing wall is often put up as a limit; the latter appears "at the supposed origin of said conditions, rules or conventions, and at the origin of their dominant interpretation" (Derrida 1989: 943). The discourse reaches its own imposed limit, and this self-limiting of the discourse creates a suspension "by a pure performative act that would not have to answer to or before anyone" (Derrida 1989: 991–93). The imposition of such limits would have succeeded in the act of founding what in retrospect is posited as its presuppositions, an *après coup* production. The *après coup* act produces 'interpretative models' which retrospectively legitimates the 'success', with the proviso that this 'retrospective' act is simultaneous with the performative act; it is part of the performative act (Derrida 1989: 993).

What these interpretative models therefore do is to retrospectively "give sense, necessity and above all legitimacy to the violence that has produced, among others, the interpretative model in question, that is, the discourse of its self-legitimation" (Derrida 1989: 993). The interpretative model justifies the violence that leads to its appearance in the first place, a perfect tautology at work (Derrida 1989: 987). We can thus say that originary performativity is neither a purely productive nor a purely destructive or transformative act in the sense that originary performativity transforms what pre-existed it into its *own* condition of possibility; all the while making sure that the act is self-legitimating. Although it appears that we have a founding violence and a legitimating/ conserving violence, Derrida (1989: 997) argues that "the very violence of the foundation ... must envelop the violence of conservation ... and cannot break with it." That there cannot be two types of violence is due to the fact that iterability

> inscribes the possibility of repetition at the heart of the originary ... there is no more ... a pure founding violence, than there is a purely conservative violence. Position is already iterability, a call for self-conserving

repetition. Conservation in its turn refounds, so that it can conserve what it claims to found.

(Derrida 1989: 997)

We are thus dealing with an inaugural interpretation which "may pretend simply to state, show, and inform, but it actually produces," argues Derrida (2007b: 447). Such an interpretation is performative through and through, despite being "naturally unsaid, unavowed, and undeclared" as such. Yet this does not change the fact that this kind of 'saying the event' does indeed make 'the event', even if it looks only as a simple saying of the event (Derrida 2007b: 447).[12] Derrida (2007b: 447–48) explains the difference by calling our attention to the fact that "event-making is covertly being substituted for event-saying." That we can only see this as "saying the event" is what "overtly presents itself as performative: the modes of speaking that consist not in informing, reporting, relating, describing, or noting" while at the same time effectively "making something happen through speech" (Derrida 2007b: 447–48). Yet the event in 'saying the event' is pervertible since the performative which says it also neutralizes it, and as such it is a conditional event. This means that the unconditional event haunts the 'saying the event' *qua* conditional event and is at the heart of the possibility of the event in 'saying the event', as discussed earlier, but 'saying the event' is not unconditional since it is a performative which falls under the law of iterability (as discussed earlier).

Applied to the case of agency, we thus have: the unconditional event of agency haunts the 'saying agency' *qua* conditional event—that is, registering *après coup* the occurrence of agency in the realm of knowledge is haunted by the unconditional event of agency. We cannot register a 'saying agency' without its condition of possibility, which is inscribed in it by an unconditional event of agency, with the latter being unanticipatable, *untheorizable*, that is, beyond knowledge and expectations.

To recap: I propose to re-think agency as 'unconditional event of agency' with the latter being unanticipatable and untheorizable but nonetheless being the condition of possibility of an originary performativity of inaugural interpretation occurring *après coup* and creating its own presuppositions and self-legitimation, that is, conditional agency *qua* 'a saying agency' in the sense of Derrida. As such, conditional (or *après coup*) agency falls under the law of autoimmunity in the sense that agency *qua* unconditional event of agency originarily haunts the possibility of *après coup* conditional agency *qua* 'saying agency'. Because the unconditional event of agency and the conditional 'saying agency' are at the same time mutually indissociable and heterogeneous, *agency qua sovereign act* emerges as a *negotiation* (in the sense of Derrida) between the un-anticipatable *unconditional event* of agency and the *après coup* conditional registering of agency through a 'saying agency'. To fully grasp the meaning of this statement, we need to discuss *negotiation* in the sense of Derrida.

For Derrida (2002b: 296), *negotiation* involves undecidability between an urgency to interrupt and an imperative to continue the negotiation. This *urgency* is however different from "the empirical briefness of a lapse of time," since "even if one had at one's disposal a virtually unlimited amount of time, the structure of urgency, that is, the *interruption* of reflection, of reflection according to a determinate mode, would be irreducible," even after "a thousand years of reflection" (Derrida 2002b: 298–99). This means that "one negotiates by engaging the nonnegotiable in negotiation." Moreover, this negotiation is a "without-rest", "the impossibility of stopping," which implies that there is "no thesis, no position, no theme, no station, no substance, no stability, a perpetual suspension, a suspension without rest" (Derrida 2002b: 13). Therefore, in engaging in negotiation of this sort, we must realize that "negotiation is different at every moment, from one context to the next. ... It must be adjusted to each case, to each moment without, however, the conclusion being a relativism or empiricism" (Derrida 2002b: 17). Negotiation thus can be thought of as "the shuttle ... between two positions, two places" (Derrida 2002b: 12). Yet this sense of negotiating "does not prevent us from cutting. One must cut. But one is never sure of the right time, there is always a risk" (Derrida 2002: 31). In short, one negotiates with the non-negotiable (the unconditional event of agency) "to let the future have a future, to let or make it come, or, in any case, to leave the possibility of the future open" (Derrida and Stiegler 2002: 85), and thus to preempt a shutting down of the possibility of sovereign agency, the event-ness of which being threatened to be eradicated by the *après coup* 'saying agency'.

Agency is therefore autoimmune to itself, never being able to gather itself, or show itself *qua* self; it remains *out of joint* with itself, never self-present to itself, registered only through a 'saying agency' which cannot escape being haunted by the un-anticipatable unconditional event of agency as its condition of possibility. Agency is thus an infinite negotiation between an unconditional event of agency and an *après coup* registered play of conditional 'saying agency', a play of differing, deferred and temporized traces of registered agency, a *différantial play of traces* of (conditional) agency through traces of registered 'saying agency'.

Re-thinking the agent-structure problematique

Based on the work of deconstruction of the previous sections I now propose a reconfiguration of the agent-structure *problematique* in terms of Derrida's infrastructures. I begin with a brief summary of the issue via Wight's book.

The agent-structure problematique—a summary

Wight's 2006 book has more or less summarized current IR literature on the agent-structure problem. Efforts to go beyond the dichotomy of individualist versus structural theories of IR, argues Wight, led IR theorists to draw for the most part on three theoretical approaches, namely, Roy Bhaskar, Anthony Giddens, and Margaret Archer. These efforts sought a resolution of the dichotomy of individualism versus structuralism, which became known as the agent-structure problem.

Wight's line of critique is driven by his own Bhaskarian mode of analyzing ontology and theory. His verdict is that "all adequate resolutions of the agent-structure problem will require a metatheoretical perspective that can elaborate the properties of agents and structures and their interrelationships at the level of social ontology" (Wight 2006: 88–89). Wight henceforth hunts for authors who agree with him in formulating the agent-structure problem as essentially being an ontological problem. Not surprisingly, Wight rebukes, for example, Doty for not thinking about the issue from an ontology-first perspective and instead looking at the agent-structure problem from the perspective of undecidability, thereby anchoring the problem into what Doty terms as the indeterminacy of practice (Doty 1997). Wight (2006: 82–83) asks: "what in Doty's account enables practices? What are the conditions of possibility for practices? What are the causal powers and processes that produce practices?" While these are important questions, they once more disclose the underpinning framework of Wight's thinking, namely, scientific realism *à la* Bhaskar. Likewise, Wight (2006: 83) raises a few concerns about Jackson and Nexon's relational ontology, in fact returning their approach back to ontology *à la* scientific realism.

Wight's critique of Hollis and Smith's rejection of all resolutions of the agent-structure problem is most revealing of what is not explicated in Wight's own discourse. Wight essentially rebukes them for using a discursive approach that establishes how the discourse of scholars is embedded in the very 'social facts' that they study. Wight (2006: 86), deploying his critical-realist way of thinking, states that "they are guilty of conflating the 'reality of the model' (which is an analytical construct) with the 'model of reality' (which is rooted in the social reality under study)." Drawing on Bourdieu, Wight (2006: 88) declares then that "the distortion of social reality is an inescapable fact for all of us ... Underpinning this belief, however, and what makes it possible, is the notion that our representations are indeed that (distortions) and not mere constitutive performative utterances in the process of creating worlds." This is simply a re-affirmation of the scientific realist belief that there is a world 'out there' whether we know it or not and irrespective of any shortcomings and distortions of our representations of it. Yet, isn't Wight's scientific realist perspective in itself and which is already being presupposed in critiquing Hollis and Smith (and Doty and others) one type of distortion that Bourdieu speaks of? Isn't there a hidden assumption of a ground that stabilizes—or, more accurately, assumed by Wight to stabilize—Wight's identification of what is a distortion and what is not? Isn't his declaration a performative utterance *par excellence* seeking to create 'a fact on the ground' of social theoretical inquiry? Isn't it an inaugural interpretation *par excellence* to create the very ground of a self-legitimating discourse? As such, Wight 'succeeds' in showing that the agent-structure problem has indeed been an important ontology-first problem for many scholars, irrespective of their assumed theoretical framework (à la Giddens or Archer, for example). Those who fail to qualify as members of this cohort are discounted as either being unclear (e.g., Doty, and Jackson and Nexon) or as pessimistic (e.g., Hollis and Smith).

Wight's summary and critique of the agent-structure problematique (as it developed in IR literature) manages, if perhaps inadvertently, to formulate a number of crucial questions of 'meta-theory',[13] that is, raising questions about the taken for granted presupposition that we need to begin with ontology in theorizing about politics. While Wight's book is not wrong in raising the question of politics as ontology, it however stops short of dealing with the most important questions of 'meta-theory', namely, the presuppositions of ontology and social theory. Therefore, Wight is right to argue that the agent-structure problem is not solvable in the sense of formulating a final solution to it. *Yet, this only calls upon us to think about the conditions that make thinking about solutions possible—an indeed possible thinking because a huge amount of effort has been spent toward that goal—but at the same time make it impossible to formulate a solution.* In the following I explore the conditions of possibility and impossibility of not only a solution to the agent-structure problem but also of *the very positing of a problem in the first place*, that is, by *problematizing* the agency-structure *problematique*.

Problematizing the problematique

Drawing on the above deconstruction of structure and agency, I propose to re-think what is usually considered as 'structural' with the help of undecidable pseudo-concepts such as *trace, différance, iterability, spectrality*, and *auto-immunity*, etc. I also propose to re-think at the same time what is usually thought of as non-structural aspects of the problematique along two dimensions—on the dimension of the unconditional using '*the unconditional event of agency*' and along the dimension of the conditional using the notion of '*saying agency*'. This implies that what we have is the space of infrastructures and the unconditional event, or unconditional *tout court* as the conditions of possibility and impossibility of the problematique, keeping in mind that the conditional and the unconditional are at the same time heterogeneous to one another and indissociable from one another. Therefore, speaking of an agency-structure problematique means speaking of an aporiatic relationship of simultaneous heterogeneity and indissociability of the conditional and the unconditional. This means that what we are used to call the 'structural' corresponds to the conditional and what Barkin (2010) calls the non-theorizable agency is the unconditional. This means then that the co-constitution is always already inescapable and is not only one of simultaneous indissociability but also at the same time one of heterogeneity—the 'co-constitution'[14] is aporiatic.

In other words, each side of the agency-structure problematique as commonly understood in the literature has a conditional and an unconditional aspect, that is, the conditional being an inscription of the unconditional into certain conditions and the unconditional always already haunting the conditional *qua* its condition of possibility, with the two being simultaneously heterogeneous to and indissociable from each other. Thus, the conditional of this problematique would correspond to the conventional sense of structure and its unconditional would be thought of in terms of infrastructures. Likewise, the conditional of agency would correspond to an always *après coup* 'saying agency' and the unconditional would be the unconditional event of agency. Yet what I term the unconditional of structure and the unconditional event are not separate types of unconditional but rather a singular unconditional, which at the same time haunts both the conditional structure and the conditional *après coup* 'saying agency'. And this spectral haunting obeys the logic of the undecidable infrastructures of trace, mark, différance, iterability, auto-immunity, etc ... In sum, the problematique is nothing but the unconditional/conditional aporia. As shown by Derrida, this aporia can neither be lifted nor resolved, as explicated in the next section.

The parergonality of the 'agency-structure problem' and 'social theory'

What sorts of conclusion can one draw from such a re-thinking of the agency-structure problematique? Agreeing with Wendt (1987), Wight (2006: 4) argues that "all theories presuppose a solution to the agent-structure problem, whether explicitly acknowledged or not." A satisfactory understanding, critique and evaluation of IR theories need thus to have a thorough look at the assumed solutions of the agent-structure problem that subtend the theories. "The agent–structure problem is essentially an ontological problem," says Wight (2006: 3), and as such provides a good way of exploring his thesis on the primacy of ontology over epistemology. What makes this choice a suitable one for critiquing IR theory is that

> understood as an ontological problem the agent–structure problem is best understood as a series of attempts at constructing social ontologies. Given that all theories have their own preferred solution, this means that the agent–structure problem is a problem with no overarching and definitive solution.
>
> (Wight 2006: 4)

This means that the IR literature on the agent-structure problem provides a "fertile" laboratory for testing Wight's thesis. Furthermore,

> the agent–structure problem cannot be solved in the sense of a puzzle with an answer, but rather represents competing visions of what the social world is and what it might become. As such all theories, practical discourses, ethical injunctions and political practices contain a solution to

the agent–structure problem. Perhaps this means that we have too many solutions.

(Wight 2006: 4)

Based on the discussion of the previous sections, I propose that we do not have 'too many solutions', not even one solution as such. First, *there is no solution because there is no problem*. And there is no problem because *there is no 'structure' as such and no 'agency' as such*. What we have is an infra-structural space of undecidables (*différance, trace, autoimmunity*, etc.) and a *différantial* play of an impossible *negotiation* between the *unconditional* event of agency and the *conditional* agency of 'saying agency' *qua* originary performativity of inaugural interpretation. Second, what we have is urgency-driven interruptions of the impossible negotiation between the unconditional and conditional, interruptions which are necessarily temporary, autoimmune and aporiatic.

Here is the aporia:

> There are no solutions, because, *on the one hand*, any such declared solution is always already haunted by the condition of its impossibility—the impossibility of being an unconditional solution. *On the other hand*, social theory cannot not seek solutions to what it posits as problematic. The aporia consists of *two simultaneous movements—one movement* seeks to settle the problematique on a certain solution, even if it is an impossible task to realize; *another movement* blows up any chance for such a solution because it constantly displaces the terms of the negotiation so as to prevent any finalizing interruption. And the two movements are indissociable while being completely heterogeneous to one another.

Yet this aporia is precisely the *chance* that social theory remains always already open to new inventions and new re-thinking. This does not mean that the aporia is without risks or even dangers such as totalization and foreclosure of thinking via (originary/ontological, teleological/ regulative-idealist, or otherwise) dogmatism. The two sides are inseparable—no chance of invention without a risk of rigidity and dogmatism, and every dogmatism is haunted by a chance for opening and invention. The process of theorization is an autoimmune one.

Having said this, I do not imply that 'agency', 'structure' or the so-called 'agency-structure problem' are red herrings. *On the one hand*, these are concepts that shape our thinking in social theory (and elsewhere) and as such they are effectively 'socially real'. The large repertoire of social theories and their *disciplining* disciplines can neither be ignored nor can they be completely overcome or overpowered. Concepts are not simply neutral 'tools' that we deploy to understand some sort of a 'reality' out there, critical and scientific realism to the contrary notwithstanding. Rather, concepts are constitutive of that 'reality', through and through. *On the other hand*, these concepts are deconstructible and conditional, thereby always already creating the possibility of not deploying them, or deploying them differently, under different conditions. Yet not deploying them or deploying them differently cannot escape the traces of these concepts in our thinking about social theory and social reality; traces that haunt the conditions of possibility of new inventions in thinking and social reality. In fact, these concepts have become part of the disciplining power of social theory disciplines and as such they are part of the *parergon* that frames contemporary social theory (*qua ergon*).

Yet (another yet), I argue that the *demarcation* of an agency-structure problem is unsustainable, not simply because of co-constitution, but rather due to the logic of *parergonality*, which can only be ignored through an act of violent silencing of one or the other side of the parergon/ergon, that is, 'agency-structure problem'/'social theory'. In making this claim I (again) draw insights from Derrida's statement on art when he (Derrida 1987a: 45) writes that

> this permanent requirement—to distinguish between the internal or proper sense and the circumstance of the object being talked about—organizes all philosophical discourses on art, the meaning of art and meaning as such, from Plato to Hegel, Husserl and Heidegger. This requirement presupposes a discourse on the limit between the inside and outside of the art object, here a discourse on the frame.

And when he (Derrida 1987a: 54) also states that

> philosophical discourse has always been against the parergon. But what about this *against*. A parergon comes against, beside, and in addition to the ergon, the work done [*fait*], the fact [*le fait*], the work, but it does not fall to one side, it touches and cooperates within the operation, from a certain outside. Neither simply outside nor simply inside. Like an accessory that one is obliged to welcome on the border, on board [*au bord, à bord*].

We can, in a certain way, make sense of the impossible logic of the 'agency-structure problem', its disciplining effects and its dangers in social theory through the work of deconstruction within which there is both undecidability and affirmation through the play of the various undecidable infrastructures and the aporia of conditional/unconditional event of agency. More specifically: we must displace the discourse on the problematique of 'agency-structure' into a logic of *parergonality* as the condition both of possibility and impossibility of a 'social theory' anchored in 'agency' and 'structure' as two of its key concepts and their presupposed problematic relationship. Yet the logic of *parergonality* makes the relationship between the 'agency-structure problem' as *parergon* and 'social theory' as *ergon* as one where, as (once again) nicely put by Harvey (1989: 71–72), the *parergon/ergon* distinction is one which floats, oscillates and ultimately can be shown to be a mirroring yet distancing relation of *différance*. It is a relation of doubling which belies the linear temporality of an origin/copy relation. The *ergon* is not simply prior (temporally or historically) to the *parergon*. Rather, they 'come into existence,' or are 'given' simultaneously. It is this simultaneity, however, that within the structure of parergonality presents itself as a temporal contingency of before and after which thus entails a certain attachability and in turn a detachability of parergon to an ergon already fully formed.

Isn't this what Wight does so skillfully (if at times perhaps despite his intent not to do so) in drawing on 'social theory' to expound his 'meta-theory' of the 'agent-structure problematique'? Therefore, that Wight resorts to such a theorizing strategy is not an oversight or lack of consistency or sensitivity to the occurrence of self-contradictions. Rather, it shows the *logic of parergonality* at work in Wight's and most attempts to theorize the 'agent-structure problem' by relying on 'meta-theory'.

5 Identity/difference and othering
Negotiating the impossible politics of *aporia*

How would different ways of thinking, speaking, conceptualizing and understanding key notions such as 'identity', 'difference', and 'other' impact on the issue of 'identity/difference' as we think, write, speak, and address it? This chapter proposes a re-thinking of 'identity/difference' through a deconstruction of the concepts of 'identity', 'difference' and 'other'. The deconstruction highlights the impossible aporias of othering and suggests a way of thinking beyond such an impossible politics of aporia. Whereas in the previous chapters I used IR theory as an entry point to the work of deconstruction here I frame the re-thinking of identity/difference within the issue of Islam in Europe, or 'Euro-Islam', as an illustrative 'empirical' case.[1] Whether at the level of theory, practice or policy, very few scholars and practitioners pay enough sustained attention to the fact that how we think/not-think, speak/silence, inscribe/erase, and address/ignore various aspects of the 'Islam in Western Europe' issue has much to do with the concepts of 'identity' and 'other'. Whereas policy-makers, activists, peace-advocates, and fear-mongers continuously deploy these concepts for or against certain strategies, agendas and purposes, it is incumbent to deconstruct these concepts so as to open up a horizon for re-thinking the possibility of a 'Euro-Islam'. The chapter argues that re-thinking 'Euro-Islam' is more or less an aporiatic politics of 'Othering' and that it is possible to go beyond this aporia in a certain way using a non-Aristotelian logic of without, the pair of undecidable concepts immunity/autoimmunity, and Derrida's notion of 'negotiation'.

Introduction

The notion of identity is undoubtedly a core concept in social sciences and humanities. Speaking of identity is usually tantamount to speaking also of difference and otherness. As summarized by Connolly (1991: 64), "identity requires difference in order to be, and it converts difference into otherness in order to secure its own self-certainty." The pair identity/difference has in fact more or less become a signature of political and social theory today and most debates about identity (and difference) politics end up more or less crystallized around binary oppositions. Even among those who raise doubts and skepticism about binary oppositions such as in what is often termed as 'postmodern' discourses and narratives more often than not many end up using reified and fixed oppositions such as otherness/sameness, contingency/necessity, and singularity/universality, with the first term usually valorized and the second term marginalized. Identity is thus usually more or less thoroughly conceptualized whereas difference is taken as self-evidently meaning difference between identities; that is, difference is defined through the notion of identity. Difference *qua* notion is therefore not problematized, or at least not problematized as much as identity is (Brubaker and Cooper 2000: 6–8). Moreover, identity stands simultaneously for a fundamental and consequential sameness, as something deep, basic, abiding, or foundational, as highlighting the processual, interactive development which conditions collective action, and as highlighting the unstable, fluctuating, and fragmented nature of the self. A common immediate reaction is to condemn this versatility in conceptualizing identity, never mind that difference is not theorized, or almost.

What if however one is to espouse this versatility and the lack of coherence, cohesiveness and crispness? What if the notion of identity is not a notion in the usual sense of the term 'notion' but is perhaps a pseudo-notion which escapes the Aristotelian logic of 'either this or the anti-thesis'? What if the notion of identity violated the Aristotelian law of 'identity' (P = P)? That is, what if the notion of identity, which is commonly used with the connotation of being unitary and more or less stable to be meaningful, is originarily and structurally internally heterogeneous and that self-heterogeneity is a structurally originary feature of identity? Wouldn't the literature using the concept of identity be faced with a sort of *undecidability* on what identity is and/or is not? What if we need to theorize difference before identity?

In this chapter I propose to address some of these questions through a deconstruction of the concepts of 'identity', 'difference' and 'othering'. The work of deconstruction suggests a logic that would enable us to re-think 'identity *without* identity' which while affirming identity seeks to displace its meaning at the same time and re-think difference *qua* difference as more originary that identity, if in a certain sense that needs to be clarified. This re-thinking highlights the *aporiatic* character of the politics of identity and suggests how to address this aporiatic politics.

In the previous chapters I considered various 'theoretical IR works' as entry points to the work of deconstruction. In this one I proceed differently. 'Muslims in Western Europe' begins with a discussion of an 'empirical' situation, that is, so-called Euro-Islam or the role of Islam in Europe. This however, I must confess, is a misnomer since I am using as entry points texts anyway, the only difference thus being that these are not texts of IR theory as such. Yet they do speak in more or less theoretical ways to core issues of IR theory such as, for instance, the issue of identity. This should not be a concern at all if one remembers that deconstruction does not differentiate between texts, that is, all texts are deconstructible (as testified by Derrida's works of deconstruction of texts from many disciplines: from poetry, to religious texts, to novels, to philosophical texts, to documents such as the Declaration of Independence, etc.). A text is a text to be deconstructed (in fact Derrida would say that a text always already deconstructs itself) irrespective of where it belongs and what it does or claims to do or not to do. I find this particular entry point into the work of deconstruction helpful in illustrating the contradictions and aporias that we encounter in deploying the concepts of identity, difference, and other/othering in seeking to understand 'empirical' problems. Having done so, I then move to a deconstruction of the concepts of identity, difference, and othering. I present then some suggestions on the issue of Euro-Islam as re-thought through the work of deconstruction.

Muslims in Western Europe

Defining a 'Euro-Islam' is at stake for/about Muslims in Western Europe. More often than not discourses and attitudes on 'Euro-Islam' are addressed either as issues of preserving and maintaining an Islamic identity (identities), or reconstructing an identity (identities) for Muslims in accordance, if not in complete harmony, with so-called European values and identity (identities). Moreover, the framing of 'the problem of Muslims in Western Europe' unfolds within larger discourses about European identity wherein the Muslim populations are still thought of as an 'other'. It seems that Euro-Islam is an 'other' of Europe from within Europe.

The issue of Islam and Muslims in Western Europe is often referred to as a 'the problem of Islam in Europe', as an ideological battlefield within Western Europe that more or less exposes "the boundaries and limits of multiculturalism" (Zemni 2002: 1). Speaking of multiculturalism in Western Europe is tantamount of speaking of identity concerns and problems of identification (Grillo 2007). This is then more often than not phrased using various sets of binary oppositions based on identity versus other. The debates on Islam in Europe are as much an issue of integrating and/or assimilating Muslims in Western Europe through a redefinition and/or reconstruction of their identities as an issue of discerning an 'identity' of Europe that might be receptive enough to the idea of incorporating some 20 million Muslims as fully-fledged citizens with their heterogeneity, diversity and multitude of views, aspirations, and frustrations.

Many Muslims in Western Europe find themselves living between the need, if sometimes the necessity, of preserving their religious and cultural practices and sense of belonging, the need to adjust to living within very different societies, and the need to navigate within a transnational environment characterized by increasingly globalized public spaces of religion, culture, politics and economy. They are thus faced, on the one hand, with the imperative to preserve or redefine who they are and what they stand for in terms of their religiosity and the doctrines of Islam and, on the other hand, with the necessity of making common demands in the face of pressures to integrate and/or assimilate in the host societies and systems of governance (Kastoryano 2003; Korteweg and Yurdakul 2009; Koopmans *et al.* 2005).

In addition, Muslims debate among themselves and with others the issues of their entry into public life and their potential or actual involvement in politics, the extent of which, under what format, and toward what ends and goals, as well as through what means and at what levels—local, national, and/or European Union. These in turn generate challenges of participation and representation of Muslims in democratic institutions. All these issues and many others—such as education, religious institutions, and issues of food—are also shaped and influenced as well made more acute by how Muslims are, and/or feel being, portrayed in the news media (Poole 2002; Carlbom 2006; Bowen 2004; Soysal 1997; Brown 2006). The situation of Muslims in Western Europe is thus a highly complex one, increasingly becoming more challenging as Muslims and their diverse types of leaderships and informal and formal institutions and the host countries and governments seek to address some of these issues, either unilaterally or in coordination or cooperation with others.

However, if one were to summarize, one of the key issues that both unites and divides Muslims in Western Europe is the challenge that westernization/Europeanization poses to their so-called Muslim identity (or identities). The slogan of an 'authentic' and 'pure' Islam and Islamic identity (identities) portrayed as some sort of an antidote or cure for the Westernization 'threat' is an element shared by the Muslims' socio-political realities across the world and Western Europe. Of course, this is not to argue that the majority of Muslims believe or do not believe in this and similar slogans. Yet it is a discursive reality that has its adherents/subjects and opponents/resistors. What makes such a discursive reality even more prominent is that many non-Muslims—either in academia, the news media, the policy world, or elsewhere—seem to promote it in one way or another (Otterbeck 2005; Saint-Blancat and di Friedberg 2005).

In dealing with Islam and Muslims, West European governments have resorted to policies that seem to indicate a break between the pre-9/11 and post-9/11 eras (Allen 2004). Whereas in the former era, most governments were interested and more or less effectively engaged in searching and implementing quick-fix types of policies (such as cracking down on what is perceived as threatening Islamic militants and tightening the process of immigration) in addressing the religious and more generally cultural and ethnic as well as socio-political issues pertaining to Muslims, in post-9/11 the trend among West European governments has been gravitating toward one of two policy poles (Haddad and Golson 2007: 487–89). On the one hand, many governments sought to create and institutionalize some sort of representative bodies of Muslims, bodies that would be some sort of interlocutors between the government and the Muslim constituents. On the other hand, West European governments sought also to initiate and/or facilitate the construction/reconstruction as well as promote and maintain what can be termed as Islamic spaces. This effectively amounts to the governments pro-actively playing the roles of "arbiter and chief architect of a 'moderate' European Islam" (Haddad and Golson 2007: 487–89).[2]

Whereas in pre-9/11 the policies were geared toward integration and assimilation in the host societies, in the post-9/11 environment the issue has become how to construct the 'right' kind of Muslim that deserves and can live in the midst of West European societies. For example, whereas in the past West European governments were interested and actively engaged in more or less passively or proactively outsourcing "Muslim spiritual leadership so as to maintain allegiance to their native lands," they now seek to find ways and mechanisms through which they can domestically build "loyal Muslim" leaderships (Haddad and Golson 2007: 487–89). Therefore, we now have more or less two mutually supportive ways of governmental interaction with the Muslim population at various levels. The goal is more or less, as put by Haddad and Golson (2007: 499), "to recreate Islam as a Westernized, liberal, manageable religion" and to construct "obedient Muslim Europeans." Muslims thus end up being engulfed at the center of multiple debates on integration and adaptation with most of these debates revolving on the issue of security, either when the governments and other actors emphasize that their efforts are not against Islam or when so-called 'Islamo-fascism' is condemned.

Muslims have responded differently to these efforts and rhetoric. Quite often Muslims publically condemn the states as seeking to implement policies the goal of which is to change, and even destroy, the Islamic identity of Muslims living in Western Europe (Haddad and Golson 2007: 513). Efforts by governments to address the issue end up (more often than not) deepening a sense of marginalization, especially when the states call upon Muslims to "police themselves." Many Muslims would feel pressured to either condone or condemn this or that position, which usually turns out to be perceived as a threat against the Islamic identity (Volpi 2007: 452–53).

What transpires from this very brief discussion is that the stakes for/about Muslims in Western Europe are defined in terms of identity, either as an issue of preserving and maintaining an Islamic identity (or identities), or reconstructing an identity (identities) for Muslims in accordance, if not complete harmony, with so-called West European values and identity. None of these two sides of the stakes is uniform or homogenous, and much less consensual. Each of these two sides is a wide spectrum of views, opinions and attitudes as well as perceptions, or, more broadly, a variety of discourses. Yet most of these discourses are explicitly framed through the trope of identity, deployed by positing a certain identity (or identities), or deployed for the sake of protecting, or denying a certain identity (or identities). This issue is vividly transparent in the discourse on so-called 'Euro-Islam' (Karic 2002: 435).

Moreover, these discourses unfold within larger discourses about/for the daunting issue of European identity (Delanty 2002: 352–53). Not only is Europe home to a very large number of 'indigenous' European languages, ethnicities, nationalities, religious denominations and communities, as well as states. Western Europe is also today home to millions of peoples whose lineage comes from outside of what is defined to be geographical Western

Europe. This makes Europe "as much a site of longings rooted in tradition—regional, national and European—as it is a site of transnational and trans-European attachments" (Amin 2004: 1–2). In seeking to define or construct its identity, Europe finds itself immersed in murky waters, which are nicely described by Derrida as follows (Derrida 1992d: 12–13):

> What we find difficult to do and think today, for Europe, for a Europe torn away from self-identification as repetition of itself, is precisely the unicity of the 'today', a certain event, a singular advent of Europe, here and now. Is there a completely new 'today' of Europe, a 'today' whose novelty would not resemble—especially not—what was called by another well-known program, and one of the most sinister, a 'New Europe'? ... Is there then a completely new 'today' of Europe beyond all the exhausted programs of *Eurocentrism* and *anti-Eurocentrism*, these exhausting yet unforgettable programs? ... Am I taking advantage of the 'we' when I begin saying that, in knowing them now by heart, and to the point of exhaustion ... we *today* no longer want either Eurocentrism or anti-Eurocentrism? Beyond these all too well-known programs, for what 'cultural identity' must we be responsible?"

That is, seeking a European identity makes the latter both an imperative goal and an elusive one. Europe thereby finds itself torn away from its self-identification precisely as it seeks to repeat itself, to identify itself. Europe can neither forget its past nor can it abandon itself to that memory. Europe in short wants neither the specter of Eurocentrism nor its opposite, anti-Eurocentrism. However, such a story of European identity does not stop at, nor did it start with, Eurocentrism. Nor would it stop with anti-Eurocentrism either—it is still unfolding today.

In sum, some may say there is nothing unique or peculiar to 'Euro-Islam' thought of as an identity problem in Western Europe. I do not disagree. And this is why I would like to argue that what eludes one in thinking of Euro-Islam has more to do with the notion of identity as such, and not 'Euro-Islam' in particular. In the next section, I attempt to emphasize this problematique even more by briefly examining the cases of two individuals—Bassam Tibi and Tariq Ramadan—who more or less epitomize the dilemmas of the Muslims' 'identity' in Western Europe.

Tibi: integration despite 'other-ing'?

Bassam Tibi was born in Syria, grew up there to become an Arab leftist, became dismayed with pan-Arabism, and then immigrated to Germany in the late 1960s after the defeat of the Arab left. In Germany he studied at the Frankfurt school of critical theory under the guidance of Horkheimer and then became a professor of international relations with an endowed chair. He extensively travelled around the world, wrote and lectured on the role of

Islam in Western Europe as a religion, culture, and political force. He is an energetic activist in Germany, Europe, and the world at large, with access not only to German leading political and cultural figures but also worldwide.

Tibi argues for the critical importance of developing a 'Euro-Islam' that will peacefully accommodate religious beliefs within an inclusive democratic European culture of citizenship. He advocates a re-thinking and reforming of Islam in Western Europe which would require abandoning Islamic shari'a as a whole (Tibi 2008: xiii-xiv). He proposes "the religion- and race-blind civilizational idea of Europe" that will be "combined with a reformed Islam" as a bridge (Tibi 2008: 157). Not only his idea of Euro-Islam will purportedly "embrace a multiple identity" (Tibi 2008: 157), it will also aim "at the incorporation of the European values of democracy, laïcité, civil society, pluralism, secular tolerance and individual human rights into Islamic thought" (Tibi 2008: 157). Tibi argues that this is possible because there are many Islams, and not an essential Islam anywhere in the world (Tibi 2008: 165). This goal can be achieved through "a compromise between the competing assertions of a European identity and of an Islamic identity" which will be possible only if "inspired by the idea of Europe and the historical experience of the Hellenization of Islam in the better days of Islamic civilization" (Tibi 2008: 198–99). In short, "Euro-Islam is based on a Europeanization and on embracing pluralism" (Tibi 2008: xiii-xiv). To achieve this "not only Muslims need to become European citizens of the heart," but "also Europeans themselves are challenged to deliver what the 'idea of Europe' promises" (Tibi 2008: 36).

Thus, for some forty years Tibi has continuously argued that a Euro-Islam (Tibi 2008: 165). Yet, despite his best efforts and broad achievements, Tibi still suffers from a lack of 'sense of belonging'. He declares: "I acknowledge with all clarity that I have failed to become a European in Germany ... European societies continue to be ethnically exclusive entities unable to integrate non-European immigrants" (Tibi 2008: 36). Europeans are still "other-ing" and marginalizing Muslims (Tibi 2008: 1). Tibi is dismayingly "concerned about including Muslims living in Europe" (Tibi 2008: 172), why? Because the existing polity is not one that seeks or can overcome "an 'other-ing' of Islam and of its believers;" Tibi's solution is a "culturally healthy Europe, i.e. one with stable identity" (Tibi 2008: 172).

One can perhaps argue that Tibi is a peculiar and unique case and is in no way representative of the large population of Muslims living in Western Europe. However, the case of Tibi is not meant to be exemplary of the Muslims, nor of non-Muslim Europeans either. Yet it is not far-fetched to see in him more or less epitomized the dilemmas of BOTH the Muslims (if at large, that is, excluding both the rejectionists of integration and the callers for complete dissolution of any sense of being Muslim) in Western Europe AND the drive for a European identity. On the one hand, Tibi is integrated within Europe; how can he not be so since he is someone who holds the only Islamic studies chair in Germany and who has signed an official declaration with the president of Germany? On the other hand though, he himself declares his sense of non-belongingness. Tibi is thus resiliently seeking integration within Europe despite a still persisting drive for 'othering' Muslims and Islam in Western Europe. Much of the same dilemma seems to also face Tariq Ramadan, if in different ways.

Tariq Ramadan: post-integration despite 'other-ing'?

Tariq Ramadan, who was born in Switzerland, is the (maternal) grandson of Hassan al-Banna, founder of the Muslim Brotherhood in Egypt in the early twentieth century and the son of Said Ramadan, a Muslim Brotherhood leader who was expelled from Egypt. Ramadan received his training in philosophy and French literature at Geneva University with two doctorates, in philosophy and Arabic and Islamic studies. Ramadan was also trained in Islamic sciences at al-Azhar University in Cairo. He has held various academic positions in Islamic studies in Europe. In 2004 he made it to the Time's list of 100 most influential people in the world. Ramadan is a well-known scholar activist and public intellectual who has extensively travelled in Western Europe and around the world. He has held debates on Islamic issues with a variety of academic, non-academic and political figures (such as a televised debate with then French interior minister Nicholas Sarkozy). He has for the last two decades or so been promoting in a large number of books, articles, editorials, public lectures and various outlets, such as conferences and the like, a project of a 'European Islam' which presents Europe as a 'home' for Islam and as 'house of testimony' for Muslims (Ramadan 2004: 76). He defines "the European environment as an *area of responsibility*" and "an *area of testimony*" for Muslims (Ramadan 2004: 77; his emphasis).

Ramadan's positions have won him a large constituency of followers among the Muslim populations, especially the youth, in Europe, as well as many non-Muslim sympathizers. At the same time, the circle of those who see him either as a threat or simply as a deceiver is very large. There seems to be no consensus on his work (Berman 2007). R. Scott Appleby (quoted in Buruma 2007) describes Ramadan as someone who is

> doing something extraordinarily difficult if not impossible, but it needs to be done. He is accused of being Janus-faced. Well, of course he presents different faces to different audiences. He is trying to bridge a divide and bring together people of diverse backgrounds and worldviews. He considers the opening he finds in his audience. Ramadan is in that sense a politician. He cultivates various publics in the Muslim world on a variety of issues; he wants to provide leadership and inspiration.

Ramadan characterizes himself as "a Salafi reformist," which means that his "aim is to protect the Muslim identity and religious practice, to recognize the Western constitutional structure, to become involved as a citizen at the social level and to live with true loyalty to the country to which one belongs"

(Buruma 2007). 'Muslim identity' is of the essence for Ramadan. He explains that "hardly a Western society has been spared its own searing questions of 'identity' or its 'integration'-related tensions" (Ramadan 2006: 14). His activism and scholarly work aim at contributing to the formation in Europe of a new 'We', that is, "a 'We' that would bring together men and women (of all religions and those without religion) who would undertake to resolve the contradictions of their society. Such a 'We' would henceforth represent this coming together of citizens who seek to struggle together for their future" (Ramadan 2006: 15).

Ramadan and Tibi seem to more or less agree on a number of issues. Ramadan, much like Tibi, thinks that Europe needs to engage in a process of reevaluating its identity so as to become more inclusive of Muslims and escape the trap of ethnocentrism. Much like Tibi's dismay with the thorny issue of identity, Ramadan has remained constantly concerned with "the central question of identity," perceiving it as "a vital one for Muslim living in the West" and speaking of it as a "malaise that can result from not knowing very well how the outlines of that identity are drawn ... the old immigrants are not very clear about whether they wanted to be 'Muslims' in the West or rather 'Pakistani, Turkish and Arab Muslims' in the West" (Ramadan 2004: 77–78). Likewise, both Ramadan and Tibi highlight the importance of culture in understanding and practicing Islam. However, whereas Tibi argues that there is no 'Islam' but only many 'Islams', Ramadan maintains that "there is only 'one' Islam, as defined by the unity of its Credo (*al-'aqida*, the six pillars of faith), and by the unity of its practice (*al-'ibadat*, the five pillars of Islam)" (Ramadan 2007: 23). This is not to say that Tibi would completely disagree with this but rather that he would reject the implications that Ramadan draws from this in terms of Muslim identity and the role of Islam in public (political) life. Whereas Ramadan seeks to keep Islam and the Muslim identity as an important aspect of public and private life and would go even to deny the delineation between the two spheres as far as the role of Islam is concerned, Tibi in contrast seeks to keep Islam outside the public sphere and rather restrict it to the realm of the private.

Another major difference between Tibi and Ramadan concerns the role of 'Sharia' in defining the identity and life of Muslims as citizens of European countries. Whereas Tibi calls for a jettisoning of Sharia and sees it as a threat to a stable Europe, Ramadan argues that it is an essential component of Muslims' sense of identity and life as citizens of Europe. However, Ramadan's call is nuanced since his sense of Sharia is a reformed one built on a combination of a reinterpretation of the 'authentic texts' of Islam and through understandings of the contexts of today's world (Ramadan 2004; 2009). He thus states that "to apply the *Sharia* for Muslim citizens or residents in the West means explicitly to respect the legal and constitutional framework of the country of which they are citizens" (Ramadan 2004: 95).

Another important difference between Tibi and Ramadan is that the former calls for an integration of Muslims as 'citizens of the heart' whereas the latter calls for post-integration which does not "equate socioeconomic issues with problems of uneasy or failed religious or cultural integration" (Ramadan 2009: 268). Ramadan believes that Muslims in the West are already American, Canadian, and European, and still Muslims. The issue is not whether to integrate into these respective societies but rather 'post-integrated' Muslims should contribute more. However, for that to happen, Ramadan agrees with Tibi that non-Muslim fellow citizens should "integrate the fact that Muslims are their fellow equal citizens" (Ramadan, quoted in Chu 2009). He also agrees with Tibi that Muslims "are still 'the others'" in many European societies. The post-integrated European Muslim, for Ramadan, is at a middle position between being a *"Muslim without Islam,"* that is, a Muslim who lives his/her life without actually living it according to the principles of Islam, and a *"Muslim in Europe out of Europe,"* who secludes him/herself from the European environment. A post-integrated Muslim in Europe is one who is aware of his/her multi-dimensional identity and who is ready to be involved in his/her society and play the role which is his or her, as a Muslim and a citizen (Ramadan 1999: 196).

In sum, for Ramadan, there "should be a European-Islam just as there is an African-Islam or an Asian-Islam" (Ramadan 1999: 198). And, as if responding to Tibi, he adds that "while some scholars wanted, in terms of allegiance, to set the reference to the Islamic way (*Shari'a*) against that of a country's constitution, we now realise that it is in the name of the teachings of *Shari'a* that Muslims must respect the legal framework of the country they live in" (Ramadan 1999: 213). Because of this Tibi perceives Ramadan as a disturbing rival from whom he dissociates himself, even characterizing Ramadan's project as an offense to the idea and stability of Europe (Tibi 2008: 156; 176; 186; 190; 210).

What is at stake? That Tibi and Ramadan are more or less unique cases or perhaps examples of the dilemmas that Muslims face in Western Europe is arguably without much doubt. Yet, aren't they precisely cases of a much deeper, much stronger 'phenomenon'? Aren't they experiencing at personal, cultural, ideological, intellectual, and religious levels in thinking about and seeking to change or build a Muslim identity (or identities) in tandem with a transformation of European identity what Derrida described for Europe as being neither for Eurocentrism nor for anti-Eurocentrism? Put more vividly: Are Tibi and Ramadan—*qua* Muslims who declare themselves proud of being Muslims and Europeans—saying that *today we do not want this or that identity but rather a middle point which keeps eluding them*? Or, perhaps, their respective quests are structurally elusive and cannot be otherwise. Tibi and Ramadan are seeking to construct different versions of 'Euro-Islam' and 'Europe' which are expected to overcome an 'othering' of Islam and of its believers. Aren't Tibi's and Ramadan's tasks seemingly impossible? Why and to what extent?

The remaining part of the chapter raises this issue into a set of theoretical questions: Do we need to think about these issues in terms of identity? Isn't this a self-imposed limitation on our thinking? Can't we, mustn't we, instead more or less give up the concept of identity in thinking about these thorny issues of a sense of belongingness? When stating that "we *today* no longer want either Eurocentrism or anti-Eurocentrism?" Derrida seems to be rejecting both Eurocentrism and anti-Eurocentrism. He seems to be arguing for an identity that no longer wants to be 'either this or its anti-this'. Is he seeking an identity *without* identity? Ramadan rejects the position of a *Muslim without Islam* whereas Tibi seems to call for it. Yet Tibi clearly recognizes his failure. Likewise, Ramadan rejects the position of *being a Muslim European without actually living as a European;* he rejects some sort of *being a European without being European*. Tibi seeks an *integrated Euro-Islam* as one of *many possible Islams*. Ramadan seeks a *post-integrated European Islam* as one concretization of *one universal Islam* and yet cannot think of Islam as universal without framing it through a concrete Islam. Moreover, both Tibi and Ramadan seem to agree for the necessity of going beyond the situation where Muslims are subjected to a process of 'othering' within *their* European countries. What is this logic of thinking about identity which while affirming identity seeks to displace its meaning at the same time? In the rest of the chapter, I argue for such a position—that is, I seek to displace the meaning of identity and turn it into an identity *without* identity; a thinking that highlights the aporiatic character of the politics of identity under the unusual logic of without which was introduced in the previous chapters.

Identity, difference and undecidability

The notion of identity is such a core concept in social sciences and humanities to a point where identity ends up meaning too much or almost nothing (Brubaker and Cooper 2000: 1). Brubaker and Cooper argue that identity stands simultaneously for a fundamental and consequential sameness, as something deep, basic, abiding, or foundational, as highlighting the processual, interactive development which conditions collective action, and as highlighting the unstable, fluctuating, and fragmented nature of the self (Brubaker and Cooper 2000: 6–8). A commonly held reaction, much like that of Brubaker and Cooper, is to condemn this versatility of the notion of identity as creating too much vagueness and fuzziness.

What if however one is to espouse such a versatility and lack of coherence? Isn't this what Michel Foucault seems perhaps to be implying when he states that "if genealogy in its own right gives rise to questions concerning our native land, native language, or the laws that govern us, its intention is to reveal the heterogeneous systems which, masked by the self, inhibit the formation of any form of identity"? (Foucault 1977: 162) Perhaps, the very fact of defining identity or its 'border' is the *problem* for, as put by Derrida (Derrida 1993: 11),

> the identity to oneself and therefore the possible identification of an intangible edge—the crossing of the line—becomes a *problem*. There is a

problem as soon as this intrinsic division divides the relation to itself of the border and therefore divides the being-one-self of anything.

Isn't this also a key characteristic of Europe's identity and culture today and always? (Amin 2004: 1–2) It appears difficult to define Europe's identity beyond providing a long and always expanding and non-closeable list of what might be counted as part of Europe. It is also the case that many among these elements are mutually undermining or contradicting, without any sign that any of them might be overcome by the other, no matter how much knowledge we acquire or calculation we engage into; something will also escape us or emerge from somewhere (Derrida 1992d: 12–13). Can we decide what Europe's identity is? Are we perhaps instead faced with a situation of undecidability? Likewise, aren't Tibi and Ramadan faced with some sort of undecidability concerning a Muslim's sense of belongingness? Aren't the Muslims of Western Europe also facing a sort of undecidability as being Europeans to some extent without being Europeans in many ways? Therefore, the literature using the concept of identity is faced with is a sort of undecidability on what identity is or is not.

Speaking of identity is usually tantamount to speaking also of difference and otherness. As summarized by Connolly (1991: 64), "identity requires difference in order to be, and it converts difference into otherness in order to secure its own self-certainty." However, if identity requires difference, doesn't this imply that we need to have a notion of difference to begin with? Isn't it only after we have a notion of difference that we can say that 'identity requires difference'? Perhaps, it would make more sense to posit simultaneously both a notion of 'identity' and a notion of 'difference'. This means that Connolly's statement would need to be rephrased as something like 'identity requires difference and difference requires identity'. Alternatively, we can also begin with 'identity' and 'otherness' which would allow us to arrive to 'difference', that is, difference is difference between 'identity' and 'otherness'. However, this does not square well with Connolly's statement for he seems to imply that 'difference' and 'otherness' are one and the same 'thing'; that is, 'identity' creates 'otherness' as 'difference' and then makes it into 'otherness'. This would mean that identity is not truly or, more precisely, originarily, 'unitary'. 'Identity' originally possesses a notion of 'difference', that is, within itself, before it projects it outside itself into 'otherness'. Isn't this what Derrida (1992d: 75) is saying about Europe's identity when he states that Europe "is related to itself not only in gathering itself in the difference with itself and with the other heading ... but in opening itself without being able any longer to gather itself"? It would seem that a statement about identity as 'conventional' as that of Connolly already raises fundamental questions about our commonsensical thinking of 'identity' and 'difference'. The conventional notion of identity presupposes a notion of difference and the conventional, and often un-problematized, notion of difference presupposes a notion of identity. Therefore, the couple of notions identity/difference seems to be marred with much undecidability in the sense that whenever we use the notion of identity we are always faced with a sort of impossible choice between identity and difference.

Identity obeys the law of undecidability in the sense that whenever we use the notion of identity we are always faced with a sort of impossible choice between at least two options which usually take the form of a binary opposition. Tibi's 'ordeal' in his quest for a 'Euro-Islam' is a good case in point. Tibi is both a Muslim who adheres to Islam and at the same time adheres to what he believes Europe is, or should be. Yet by his own recognition he lacks a feeling of belongingness to Europe, and Euro-Islam that he advocates is yet to become a social-reality. Although he does not say it so but it appears from his strongly worded descriptions of Muslim groups in Western Europe that he does not really feel as being one of them either. He even rejects people like Tariq Ramadan who, much like Tibi, also calls for a European Islam and argues that Europe is a land of Islam. In other words, Tibi belongs to both Europe and 'Islam' and is alienated from both at the same time. Yet he cannot decide to leave either one. This is not to say that he is in a sort of 'no-man land', in an in-between space. To the contrary: Tibi is quite assertive on his sense of being both a Muslim and a European. Isn't this what he means by his continuous call for a Euro-Islam? Perhaps, this is the reason why, by his own recognition, he has failed to achieve this goal. That is: Euro-Islam is an undecidable. Does this mean that Tibi's dream would remain an impossible one? Isn't Ramadan also seeking an impossible European Islam through what he terms as radical reformation, which he never seems to be able to radicalize enough as shown in his series of books from 1999 to 2009? According to Derrida, it is quite the contrary! Undecidability is the possibility condition of decision—there is no decision as such without going through the ordeal of undecidability. This would mean that undecidability is the condition of possibility of both Tibi's project and Ramadan's project on identity. How can we understand the meaning of such 'impossible' possible projects? Is identity so difficult to conceptualize because it is 'out of joint'?

I suggest that to understand the meaning of the undecidable identity/difference duo we need to re-think the notion of difference and identity simultaneously. My goal is not to reject the usual thinking of identity and difference as mutually constitutive. Rather, I seek to displace the meanings of identity and difference without however falling back into the trap of essentialism, oppositions, and hierarchical orderings.

Difference and deferral without positivity—*différance*

We usually think of difference as difference between two (or more) 'things' in the sense that these 'things' are more primordial than their difference. This position is, as discussed in the previous paragraph, not sustainable under closer scrutiny. Conversely, thinking of difference first is not easily accepted in the usual way of thinking about identity. Part of this difficulty comes from the

The aporia of Identity/difference and othering 115

way we think of difference itself, that is, as a 'finite' process of differentiation. Therefore, in re-thinking difference we need to be careful so as to keep the process of differentiation non-finite in the sense of being non-closed.

We could, for example, think of a differentiation that begins from an origin and then leads to a new 'different' thing. Keeping the momentum we can think of an infinite chain of differentiation that would lead to a never-ending, a never-stopping process of creating 'new' things. The notion of non-closure can thus be thought of as not arresting the process of differentiation once it has begun. Even if this looks like an improvement on thinking of difference as the difference between 'two' things, we still end up with an originary 'thing' and a process of differentiation. For this originary 'thing' to be an origin as such it has to have a notion of difference or differentiation embedded into it to start with (*per* our assumption to think difference as first). This would lead us back to the first problem, that is, the difficulty of discerning identity and difference from one another as the one seems to require a notion of the other as its condition of possibility. This means that what is usually thought to be an 'originary' thing, and from where the process of differentiation begins, is not fully originary as one would like it to be. This implies that as we need to have a non-closed process of differentiation we also need to have a process of 'non-originarity'. In other words, the differentiation extends after the 'other' thing which differs from the origin and precedes the 'origin', making the latter a non-originary origin itself. What we are left with then is a continuous process of differentiation that constitutes differences and differences of differences, *ad infinitum*. Isn't this what de Saussure's theory of language and more generally of semiotic systems, is about? We saw in the previous chapter that two key aspects of Saussure's linguistics are, first, the fact that language is made up of differences only, and, second, that these differences are pure differences in the sense of not being differences between *positive terms* (Saussure 1986: 117–18). A Saussurean recasting would make identity as a non-positive term and the system of identity/difference a system of pure differences. Yet identity, despite all its conceptual difficulties, has been a useful notion, even if it is abused, misused, overused, etc. How can we then re-think identity so as not to completely jettison it as a useful notion but without falling into the trap of reifying it into a positive entity? I suggest that we adopt a Saussurean approach, if however modified in far-reaching ways by following Derrida's deconstructive approach which suggests that 'difference' should be re-thought as *différance*.

First, we begin with the condition of possibility of difference. What makes difference possible if we assume that we do not have positive entities that can be differentiated? Derrida (1982: 11) puts the emphasis on the systematic *play* of differences without assuming positive entities. He calls this play *différance*, that is, a systematic play of differences without positive elements that 'differ', as the condition of possibility for the formation of concepts, conceptuality, and conceptual systems in general, and as the movement by which "any system of reference in general, becomes 'historically' constituted as a fabric of differences" (Derrida 1973: 141). He explains that *différance* is "the playing movement that 'produces'—by means of something that is not simply an activity—these differences, these effects of differences" (Derrida 1982: 11). However, this is not a call for essentializing difference at the expense of identity. Derrida states that "this does not mean that the *différance* that produces differences is somehow before them, in a simple and unmodified—in-different—present. *Différance* is the non-full, non-simple, structured and differentiating origin of differences," (Derrida 1982: 11). Différance *qua* movement is necessarily "understood beyond the metaphysical language," says Derrida (1982: 12). In sum, *différance* is neither an origin of the differences, nor does it precede them, nor does it have an essence, nor is it positive or negative. *Différance* is a play of differentiation leading to difference plus a simultaneous, ineluctable process of deferral, a temporizing delay. This deferral maintains the non-closure and always delays any outcome of the process of differentiation. Derrida refers to this 'ever escaping' outcome of differentiation a certain alterity; he specially states that "*différance* maintains our relationship with that which we necessarily misconstrue, and which exceeds the alternative of presence and absence" (Derrida 1982: 20).

Différance does not negate oppositions, nor does it sublate them in some sort of a Hegelian way or otherwise. Rather, *différance* maintains both terms in a relationship, not only of difference, but also in a systematic play of differences, in a relationship of deferral. Pairs of opposites which suffuse and sustain our discourses—e.g., identity/difference—are reconsidered, not to be erased, but rather to be kept so that "each of the terms must appear as the *différance* of the other, as the other different and deferred in the economy of the same" (Derrida 1982: 17). A relation of *différance* between the two terms implies a "displaced and equivocal passage of one different thing to another, from one term of an opposition of the other" (Derrida 1982: 17).

In the systematic play of differences 'something' seems to remain throughout the play of difference and deferral; what is this 'something'? This 'something' cannot be a present 'thing', nor can it be an absent 'thing' either. Presence and absence are a pair of opposites which are related as such, that is, in a relationship of opposition, thanks to *différance* as their condition of possibility. Presence and absence are in a relationship of *différance* with one another. "Différance", explains Derrida (1973: 142–43), "is what makes the movement of signification possible only if each element that is said to be 'present', appearing on the stage of presence, is related to something other than itself but retains the mark of a past element and already lets itself be hollowed out by the mark of its relation to a future element." This means that *différance* is a differing and a deferring relationship between 'terms' which turns these 'terms' into a concatenation of presence and absence. Each term contains within itself both the *mark of a past* element and the *mark of the relation with a future* element. This is the effect of the *trace*, which, according to Derrida (1973: 142–43), "relates no less to what is called the future than to what is called the past, and it constitutes what is called the present by this very relation to what it is not, to what it absolutely is not; that is, not even to a past or future considered as a modified present."

However, we are so much accustomed to thinking about the trace in terms of an origin that we usually, often without hesitation, relate the trace to *what it is a trace of*—a non-trace. We are thus forced to "wrench the concept of the trace from the classical scheme, which would derive it from an originary nontrace and which would make of it an empirical mark, one must indeed speak of an originary trace," says Derrida (1974: 61). *Trace* in Derrida's sense is the origin of origin; *trace is the condition of possibility of any origin*. The *trace appears* ('within' what would-look-like positive elements) *by erasing itself, it appears by disappearing*. Derrida (1974: 61) explains that

> the trace is not only the disappearance of origin—within the discourse that we sustain and according to the path that we follow it means that the origin did not even disappear, that is was never constituted except reciprocally by a nonorigin, the trace, which thus becomes the origin of the origin.

However, the disappearance is also a movement of appearance since were the trace to disappear completely we will be left with an essentialized absence. The trace appears and disappears at the same time—it appears by appearing to disappear and disappears by appearing. The trace is *neither* positive *nor* negative and is *both* and *neither* at the same time. This means that we have traces and traces of traces which are differences of traces and differences of differences (of traces). *A trace is always a trace of a trace*.

What does this imply for the pair identity/difference? First, we need to speak of *différance* and not simply of difference. Second, instead of speaking of identity we need to speak of traces and traces of traces which are in a relationship of *différance*, that is, in relations of difference, deferral and temporizing play. Does this explain, even if partially only at this stage, the elusive character of identity and the constant concatenation of change and stability that we encounter in thinking about or in trying to conceptualize identity? To think of identity as a trace means that identity is not originary in any meaningful sense of the term. There is always 'something', that is, a trace, which precedes identity when thought of in this way. Third, identity as a trace (of a trace) is also affected through *différance* by the *mark of its relation to a future trace. Identity is thus a play of traces*, or more precisely, a *never stopping play of traces of traces*. Yet this does not reverse the opposition or hierarchy identity/difference into difference first then identity second. We still have 'differences' between 'identities' (*qua* play of traces of traces) and all are intimately and inextricably engaged in a relation of *différance*, which is their condition of possibility without however preceding either one. Thinking of identity in these terms implies, as I explain next, that identity is a play, a play which is not ordinary but is rather a play 'out of joint'.

118 *The aporia of Identity/difference and othering*

Identity—a play 'out of joint'

We can grasp a certain sense of 'out-of-joint-ness' through the expression 'time is out of joint'. The notion of time as we usually think of it is a 'conjoined time' which we take to be linear, homogeneous, and teleological (Ware 2004: 106). This notion of time is built on a notion of presence which is linearly and progressively divided into past-present, present-present, and future-present. This means that each instant, event, and moment has a determinate content and meaning. In contrast, the notion of "disjointed time, by disrupting linearity and our notion of chronological order, opens up the possibility of conceiving of an a-temporal event, an event that remains always already outside the flow of history" (Ware 2004: 106).

A notion of 'conjoined' identity would in comparison mean that, if it changes, it involves a—continuous or discreet—series of changes from one form to another, with each of these forms understood in the sense of presence. We would thus have a past identity, a present identity and a future identity. In contrast, identity would be 'out of joint' when such delineations are not possible anymore. Not only is it not possible to speak of change from one identity stage to the next, but it is also not possible to speak of a *stage* of identity *tout court*. Saying that identity is out of joint means that, as explained by Derrida (1992d: 9) in his analysis of culture, "what is proper to a culture is to not be identical to itself," which can be paraphrased as 'what is proper to an identity is not to be identical to itself'. Identity thus does not close in upon itself, always escaping itself.

Laclau (1990: 39) explains that "every identity is dislocated insofar as it depends on an outside which both denies that identity and provides its condition of possibility at the same time." Likewise, Mouffe (1994: 109–10) states that "not only are there no 'natural' or 'original' identities, since every identity is the result of a continuing process, but that this process itself must be seen as one of permanent hybridization and nomadization," and then concludes that "identity is, in effect, the result of a multitude of interactions that take place inside a space whose outlines are not clearly defined." Identity is structurally exposed to an outside that prevents its closure, an outside that prevents identity to be identical in/with itself. This is no surprise given the discussion at the end of the previous section that identity is to be thought of in terms of the *play* of traces of traces and relations of différance among these traces. What is this notion of *play*?

The notion of play is usually construed as referring always to *a subject* of the play or the playing subject, an *object* of the play, a *place* and *context* of the play, a *finality* and *end* of the play, and of course a (positive and/or even negative) *meaning* of a play. All these italicized notions are displaced by the movement of *différance*. To consider all these displacements is beyond the limited scope of this chapter. Instead, I discuss a few characteristics of the play which are relevant for the purpose at hand. Suffice it to emphasize that in the sense of Derrida (1978: 292), play is, first, "the disruption of presence;" second, play "is always play of absence and presence, but if it is to be thought radically, play must be conceived of before the alternative of presence and absence;" and, third, play forces us to re-think our notion of being such that "Being must be conceived as presence or absence on the basis of the possibility of play and not the other way around." In the following I discuss identity as play of *iterability*, *dissemination*, and *supplementarity*.

Identity as play of iterability

One feature of identity, however conceptualized, is that identity changes. Yet no identity changes so radically as to begin from a blank sheet. There is always 'something' that is more or less changed in the seemingly most stable and fixed of identities, and there is always 'something' that is more or less preserved or repeated in the most radically changed identities. Change and repetition are key features of identity however we may think of it. To combine ineluctable change with ineluctable repetition is however not easily conceptualizable, especially using conventional frameworks of thinking in terms of 'either this or that', that is, Aristotelian logic. Nor would a Hegelian type of sublation work either; such a sublation would result in a stable higher form of identity, a sort of self-identity (*à la* self-consciousness). The question thus is how to think of identity *qua* play (out of joint) such that we can account simultaneously for both change and repetition.

Thinking of identity as a play of traces (of traces) already opens up the way for both change and repetition. Trace is something that is more or less preserved. However, trace, in the sense of Derrida, is neither present nor absent, neither appearing nor disappearing, and both at the same time. The sense of preservation that we get is therefore a very peculiar one—it is a sort of change that occurs through preservation; it changes through preservation and is preserved through changing. Moreover, a play in the sense of Derrida is a play of *différance*, that is, of difference and deferral of traces. This movement is what Derrida terms as *iterability*.

Iterability is what makes it possible for any (linguistic, semiotic or otherwise) mark or sign "to be repeated and still to function as a meaningful mark in new contexts that are cut off entirely from the original context, the 'intention to communicate' of the original marker of the mark" (Miller 2001: 78). However, iterability is much more than just the possibility condition for repetition or repeatability. Iterability is also the possibility condition for alteration and change. Derrida (1988: 62) explains that "iterability alters, contaminating parasitically what it identifies and enables to repeat 'itself'." He also states that iterability "leaves us no choice but to mean (to say) something that is (already, always, also) other than what we mean (to say), to say something other than what we say *and* would have wanted to say, to understand something other than" (Derrida 1988: 62). Yet, arguing that there is change in the context and lack of control on what we say and mean does not imply a *tabula rasa* for every new context. The fact is that, says Derrida

(1988: 79), "a context never creates itself *ex-nihilo*; no mark can create or engender a context on its own, much less dominate it." What we have is that "contextual transformation remains an always open possibility," and iterability is the condition of possibility of such a transformation. Therefore, no act of sustaining or changing an identity can succeed as such without being subject to iterability as the condition of its possibility.

That identities are dependent on the context of communicative interaction has of late been widely accepted in social theory. Iterability redefines the concept of communication. When we communicate with others we assume that our communications are repeatable, even when the context within which we first communicated has changed. We usually expect our communication through writing, for example, to be and remain readable in different contexts. Iterability is this possibility of repeatability when the context changes and/or when the author and/or the interlocutor are absent, or change. Derrida (1988: 7) argues that this iterability is a feature that "structures the mark of writing itself no matter what particular type of writing is involved." Not only is iterability a general feature of communication. It also is a necessary one. Derrida (1988: 7) states that "a writing that is not structurally readable—iterable—beyond the death of the addressee would not be writing." There is no writing and no communication without iterability, that is, without simultaneous repeatability and alteration as well as loss of control over meaning. This has fundamental implications for the notion of identity. Identity cannot escape the law of iterability.

More specifically, what does the law of iterability entail for identity? Iterability implies that identity is never something stable, self-transparent or self-certain. Identity is traces that are the results of other traces coming under the law of iterability. There is never ending change and repetition, with the two not only simultaneously unfolding, but also mutually contaminating one another, simultaneously undermining and reinforcing one another. Moreover, the process of iteration and change creates differences that are deferred and deferrals that are differentiated. The processes of differentiation and deferral never stop. Yet this does not imply *tabula rasa*—there is always a remnant of traces within traces that are both transmitted as well as changed. Iterability reinforces the law of *différance* that runs within identity as a play, and *différance* is—*qua* condition of possibility—what sustains the iterability of identity. The result is that one does not have a 'one' identity, or even 'multiple' identities. Rather, *one has an identity and does not have an identity at the same time*, at any point in time. One's identity is in constant simultaneous change and repetition, and is not. One's *identity is out of joint*.

Yet the out-of-joint-ness of identity does not make it less useful, if however as a pseudo-concept that violates Aristotelian logic. As soon as one seeks to assert an identity, the identity is changed and in order to change an identity one needs to repeat it. Repetition occurs through change and change occurs through repetition. One can therefore speak at any point in time neither of a singular identity nor of a multiplicity of identities. As soon as one tries to 'catch' one's identity it escapes, it disseminates, not because one misses it, but because it was there to 'live' with/through, without being there to be 'grasped'. The play of iterability forces identity to remain in a flux of *dissemination*; it is never able to gather itself for itself, in itself.

Identity as play of dissemination

That identity is prone to be attributed different meanings through different 'readings' is not much in dispute in the literature. The readings and interpretations are of course mediated through language and, more generally, various semiotic and communication systems. Human language and communication are prone to polysemy, that is, prone to multiplicity of meanings through various tropological movements. A situation of polysemia is one where we have an organized semantic movement within an implicit horizon, a horizon which is built on the assumption of a unitary assumption and/or resumption of meaning. In contrast, *dissemination* disrupts and explodes the semantic horizon. Derrida (1981b: 26) explains that

> dissemination endlessly opens up a *snag* ... a spot where neither meaning, however plural, nor *any form of presence* can pin/pen down [*agrapher*] the trace. Dissemination treats—doctors—that *point* where the movement of signification would regularly come to *tie down* the play of the trace, thus producing (a) history. The security of each point arrested in the name of the law is hence blown up.

This is what happens to identity as a play of traces (of traces) under the law of *iterability* and the condition of possibility of *différance*. And this is also what occurs in the *out-of-joint-ness* of identity. There is more however. In addition to the continuous movements of change and repetition that occur in identity, in addition to the impossibility of stopping the play of differences and deferral of traces (of traces), identity is always disseminating. Identity contains, to paraphrase Derrida, a snag that cannot be mended, a spot, a trace where meaning cannot be pinned down. Nor can any meaning pin down the snag opened by the trace in identity for that matter. The security—ontological security of identity so to speak—is blown up due to the constant opening of uncontrollable snags and spots in any identity. This does not however imply that there is no identity; there is 'identity' but it is an 'identity' that is constantly blown up, more or less. No identity can be an identity without being immediately blown up. Identity is always already un-identical to its 'self'; its 'self' is always differing and deferred from itself. Yet the law of iterability works to preserve this appearing-disappearing and disappearing-appearing identity, that is, as traces. An important question remains buried in this argument though.

Speaking of traces seems to create the impression of a 'forward' momentum or movement in the play of *différance* and hence identity. The out-of-joint-ness of identity implies not only that we do not have a linear—*qua* linearity of time—unfolding of various movements. There also is a 'backward' momentum, a movement that ties together the non-originary character of trace to what is seemingly unfolding 'afterwards'.[3] A movement that works so as to make the non-originarity of a trace more transparent by adding to it what supplements it, an addendum that replaces the non-originary trace. This is the law of *supplementarity* through which the supplement is added to the origin from the 'outside' to replace the origin at the place of the origin, without the supplement being a positive element in itself.

Identity as a play of supplementarity

If the sign is not a positive element (in the sense of de Saussure), what is it? How do we get the impression that it indeed acts much like a positive element? This means that there is a sign but this sign is incomplete; it lacks something, it is not plenitude. Yet we 'experience' and usually think of a sign as if it were complete. The operation that comes in to complete the sign's plenitude has to be more primordial than the sign. This is what Derrida calls primordial supplementation. Derrida (1973: 88) explains that "this concept of primordial supplementation not only implies nonplenitude of presence ... it designates this function of substitutive supplementation [*suppléance*] in general, the 'in place of' (*für etwas*) structure which belongs to every sign in general." Every sign in general thus suffers a non-plenitude which does not stay as such but becomes supplemented with a supplement.

The supplementation is a substitution that supplements, rather than fully replacing what it supplements. The addition comes to be essential for the sign to be as such. "The concept of the supplement," says Derrida (1974: 145), "harbors within itself two significations whose cohabitation is as strange as it is necessary. The supplement adds itself, it is a surplus, a less-than plenitude enriching another plenitude, the *fullest measure* of presence. It cumulates and accumulates presence." Therefore, the supplement is an exterior 'other' which is added to a seeming plenitude to make the latter what it is, a seeming plenitude. The two aspects or significations of the supplement are in a strange relationship with one another. As explained by Derrida (1974: 145),

> each of the two significations is by turns effaced or becomes discretely vague by the presence of the other. But their common function is shown in this: whether it adds or substitutes itself, the supplement is *exterior*, outside of the positivity to which it is superadded, alien to that which, in order to be replaced by it, must be other than it.

The supplement is a strange thing since "it cannot even be called presence" (Derrida 1974: 154). As such the supplement play is under constraint while at the same time exceeds all conventional languages (Derrida 1974: 154). The supplement is neither full presence nor full absence. It rather "occupies the middle point between total absence and total presence" (Derrida 1974: 157).

The supplement is still, if to a certain extent only, under the rule of presence since the latter considers the supplement as "a non-presence," thereby "excluding" it, and determining it "as *simple exteriority*, pure addition or pure absence" (Derrida 1974: 167). However, this operation of exclusion is appropriated within the supplement since, as put by Derrida, "the work of exclusion operates within the structure of supplementarity" (1974: 167). The supplement is a 'nothing' that comes to supplement a 'full presence'. To sum up: According to Derrida (1974: 303–4), the supplement is such that

> There is no present before it, it is not preceding by anything but itself, that is to say by another supplement. The supplement is always the supplement of a supplement. One wishes to go back *from the supplement to the source*: one must recognize that there is *a supplement at the source*.

What does the supplement do? First, supplementarity is the operation that allows us to engage in signification processes. However, this does not/should not imply that the supplement represents an absent signified. Rather, what the supplement does is to be "substituted for another signifier, for another type of signifier that maintains another relation with the deficient presence, one more highly valued by virtue of the play of difference" (Derrida 1973: 89). In other words, differentiation, which creates differences without positive elements, is made possible through supplementarity.

Second, the supplement comes to supplement and add 'something' to another 'thing'. This is done in a very peculiar way because this addition is one that replaces. It is an addition through which the supplement "intervenes or insinuates itself *in-the-place-of*" (Derrida 1974: 145). If the supplement "fills, it is as if one fills a void." If the supplement "represents and makes an image, it is by the anterior default of presence" (Derrida 1974: 145). The supplement supplements as a vicarious compensation which is both adjunct and subaltern. Because the supplement "is not simply added to the positivity of a presence, it produces no relief, its place is assigned in the structure by the mark of an emptiness" (Derrida 1974: 145). The supplement is thus what comes to take place in the structure of the sign right where the sign is marked by an emptiness, yet without adding any positivity to the sign since the latter is thought of as full presence. So, what does the supplement add? It adds nothing; it adds neither a presence nor an absence, because it is neither one. Yet the supplement adds by taking place in the structure which is marked by emptiness.

Third, the supplement defies Aristotelian logic which takes as a valid axiom the principle of non-contradiction since the supplement is neither presence nor absence and is thus beyond binary oppositions. Likewise, that the supplement does not obey any (Hegelian) dialectic is transparent in the fact it cannot be sublated in a higher totality or abstract concept (Derrida 1974: 246). The logic of the supplement is such that it transgresses against holding a boundary between the inside and the outside; it blurs the negative and the positive, the same and the other.

Supplementarity thus helps us understand in what sense différance can be prior to differing and deferring. Supplementarity shows how the 'origin' is not originary enough to precede différance since there is a primordial division in it that supplementarity brings forth. Supplementarity shows that there is "supplementary difference" which "vicariously stands in for presence due to its primordial self-deficiency" (Derrida 1973: 88). Supplementarity radically recasts the notion of origin from its usual meaning as being the first, the source, the cause, etc. As put by Gasché (1986: 209), due to the operation of supplementarity, "an origin, subsequently, is an effect brought about *ex post* by an originary substitution of an origin that had fallen short of itself from the start ... an origin ... *must* call upon them [supplements] and repel them at once. Only as a supplement for another origin already impaired can an origin itself require a substitute."

How does this apply to identity? How does the law of *supplementarity* work in the case of identity *qua* play? For identity to be a play of *différance* of traces, and because the trace is neither absent nor present while being always the trace of a trace, we already have a movement of supplementarity acting on the trace. For a trace to be the trace of a trace, it means that the trace acts as a supplement to become the trace of a trace. One can perhaps very pictorially say the trace 'inside' the trace is what the trace of trace is. Therefore, what is also important is that the movement of supplementarity allows the 'backward' movement of the trace that takes the place of the origin 'inside' the trace. Again very pictorially, one can perhaps venture to say that différance pushes a 'forward' movement of differentiation and deferral, and supplementarity pushes a 'backward' movement that denies the originary character of whatever might be thought of as an origin. The supplement acts 'backwardly' to ensure that the origin remains dependent on an external supplementary element without which the origin cannot be an origin, which thus makes the origin a non-originary origin. Therefore, if différance prohibits *telos* then supplementarity prohibits *arche*. Moreover, iterability prohibits any radical discontinuity, cut or gap between non-originary origin and the non-teleological yet-to-come, at any one moment in the play of identity. This ensures that the supplement is not as external/outside as it appears to be, and the origin is not as prior to the external/posterior as it might appear to be.

Bringing together the discussions of this section, we can say the undecidable duo *identity/difference is an iterable play of dissemination which obeys the law of supplementarity, and différance is its condition of possibility*. This makes identity out of joint with its 'self', not identical to its 'self', that is, always already depending on an 'other', a topic I consider next.

Othering—originary autoimmunity

A key aspect of the usual discourse on identity/difference that I have not yet thoroughly considered is the notion of othering. As an entry point to discussing this issue let us once again reconsider Connolly's (1991: 64) statement that "identity requires difference in order to be, and it converts difference into otherness in order to secure its own self-certainty." What to make of this process of otherness which is usually thought to emerge through difference and differentiation? How does the proposed re-thinking of the undecidable pair *identity/difference* help us re-think the process of othering? As pointed out by Connolly, difference is usually converted into otherness for the sake of self-certainty of identity. Put differently: identity seeks to immunize itself by drawing, so to speak, a defensive wall around itself, which is nothing else but difference converted into otherness. Does identity succeed in doing so, in immunizing itself? As discussed in the previous section, we do not have identity and difference but rather an undecidable duo *identity/difference*, which is an *iterable play* of *dissemination* under the law of *supplementarity*, and *différance* as its condition of possibility. What does immunization mean and entail in this situation? I suggest that under the combined effects of *différance, iterability, dissemination* and *supplementarity*, the process of identity immunization is radically changed into a process of identity's *autoimmunity*.

As discussed in Chapter 4, under the condition of autoimmunity individual autonomy is originally immune to itself, to ipseity, and thus cannot immunize itself to its others, even if these others threaten to destroy the autonomy of the self through this originary autoimmunity (Naas 2006: 28). As put by Derrida (2005c: 150–51), "an always perilous transaction must thus invent, each time, in a singular situation, its own law and norm, that is, a maxim that welcomes each time the event to come." Therefore, autoimmunity "enables an exposure to the other, to *what* and to *who* comes—which means that it must remain incalculable" (Derrida 2005c: 152). What makes autoimmunity work is any desire for immunity against the other. Whenever we seek to immunize ourselves against the wholly other, we succumb to the process of autoimmunity, which provides the condition of possibility for the event to happen, the event of the *tout-autre* (wholly other). Put differently: an originary desire for an immunized ipseity always already triggers autoimmunity which will have been always already undermining ipseity itself.

How does this operation of autoimmunity impact on identity *qua* play? According to Connolly (1991: 64), a self-certain identity is reached through two processes: first, identity requires difference in order to be as such, as identity, and, second, identity converts such difference into otherness to secure self-certainty, to immunize itself. We already saw that the first part of the process is an undecidable play of 'identity/difference', and that this play is an iterable play of dissemination obeying the law of supplementarity with différance as its condition of possibility. The second process—securing self-certainty or immunization—comes ineluctably and originarily with and fosters an operation of autoimmunity. The latter makes the identity/difference duo always already liable to the arrival of the wholly other, which will have always already been within the duo identity/difference. What is this 'always have-been-there liability' to the arrival of the wholly other, the other that cannot be appropriated or domesticated by identity, by the self? Isn't this what othering is all about, if

126 *The aporia of Identity/difference and othering*

in a much more radical way? Conventional thinking about identity and difference has it that othering is an ineluctable effect of the formation of identity through difference. However, when thinking of identity as a play in the above sense then we can see that othering is not an effect of difference but rather an originary liability to an originary arrival of the completely other.

Thus, in seeking to secure self-certainty, in desiring a secured self-certainty, identity attempts to immunize itself to the other through difference. However, this very process of immunization inherently and ineluctably possesses its nemesis with or within it—auto-immunization. In seeking to immunize itself to the other, in seeking to launch a process of othering, identity faces simultaneously autoimmunity, an immunity to its self or auto. An identity (at least understood in the usual sense) cannot not seek to immunize itself, but in doing so it cannot at the same time avoid facing autoimmunity, which is but an expression of the identity's liability to an always already arriving wholly other. *This is an aporia. On the one hand*, identity cannot not seek to secure self-certainty, while, *on the other hand*, it cannot not enact at the same time what precisely undermines self-certainty. That which identity seeks to achieve on the one hand, it seeks to destroy it on the other hand, doing both at the same time, no one preceding the other. Can identity escape this aporia? Can identity not engage in a process of othering, an inexorably aporiatic othering? Can identity not engage in a process of othering, the inexorably aporiatic othering? This would mean that identity would have to be re-thought in terms other than the pair identity/difference.

But haven't I already suggested re-thinking the identity/difference pair in terms of an iterable play of dissemination which is subject to the law of supplementarity with différance as its condition of possibility? Does this re-thinking of the identity/difference provide us with a way to go beyond the aporia of immunization/auto-immunization? We can say that, in addition to thinking of identity/difference as an iterable play of dissemination subject to the law of supplementarity with différance as its condition of possibility, identity/difference is also subject to autoimmunity. Is this really something 'new'? In other words, how does autoimmunity differ from, relate to or correlate with différance, supplementarity, iterability, and dissemination? We saw earlier that we can, more or less, think of différance as a 'forward' movement of differentiation and deferral, supplementarity as a 'backward' movement of originary addition and replacement, iterability as movement of simultaneous change and repetition of traces of traces, and dissemination as a blowing up of the horizon of meaning. These and other undecidable infrastructures are, as put by Gasché (1986: 147), "irremediably plural, represent the relation—connection, *ratio, rapport*—that organizes and thus accounts for the differences, contradictions, aporias, or inconsistencies between concepts, levels, argumentative and textual arrangements, and so on that characterize the discourse." One can add to this list that autoimmunity accounts for an originary self-destruction which is originarily constitutive of the self itself, of identity. We can perhaps think of autoimmunity as an originary movement of self-destruction

The aporia of Identity/difference and othering 127

that originarily haunts the self, which ensures that the self is never in full closure with itself. As the play of dissemination prohibits an arresting of the movement of identity signification by blowing up any possibility of a horizon of meaning, autoimmunity is thus an originary movement that imprints non-closure in identity as the latter seeks to reach closure by securing self-certainty through othering.

Does thinking of these infrastructures and their mutually related dynamics and movements mean that we can go beyond them, that there is a beyond of the infrastructures? The work of deconstruction tells us that these are the conditions of possibility of the discourse on the aporia of othering. The question is: Is it possible to go beyond the aporia of othering, in a certain way, and what would that mean?

Beyond the aporia of othering?

We have seen that 'othering' is the undecidable pair of immunization/auto-immunization that originarily haunts identity. This means that we are faced here with the issue of passing through an aporia of undecidability of immunity/autoimmunity. Can one go through this aporia, beyond undecidability? What is the meaning, or how should we think, of this 'going' and this 'beyond'? "How can a path pass through aporias? What would a path be without aporia? Would there be a way, without what clears the way, there, where the way is not opened, whether it is blocked or still buried in the nonway?" asks Derrida (1995b: 83). His response is: "I cannot think the notion of the way without the necessity of deciding there where the decision seems impossible. Nor can I think the decision and thus the responsibility there where the decision is already possible and programmable." Derrida describes this as the impossible politics of aporia.

Impossible politics of aporia and the logic of without

Beyond the aporia of othering: Is this a meaningful statement? An aporia is the impossibility to decide between equal poles of decisions, the condition of undecidability. Can one go beyond the undecidability of aporia? How should we think of this 'going' and this 'beyond'? These are important questions because we have seen that 'othering' is not the simple process of othering that we usually speak of when thinking of identity and the other. The 'othering' is autoimmunity, or, more accurately, it is the undecidable pair of immunization/auto-immunization that originarily haunts identity. We are faced here with the issue of passing through an aporia of immunity/autoimmunity. Derrida (1995b: 83) describes this as the politics of aporia, an impossible politics, a double politics of the impossible. What is a politics that would take us beyond this aporia—a politics of aporia?

The politics of aporia, of passing through a path of aporia, is an impossible politics. However, this is an impossible by definition. As discussed in the previous chapter, in order to think the impossible we need to 'possibilize' it in a certain way. As also discussed earlier, the impossible is the trace of its impossibility obeying the logic of *without*. Impossibility penetrates possibility under the form of a trace, as a trace that remains after impossibility withdraws from possibility. This means that the possible is a possible impossible within which the trace (of the impossible which always already was a trace) runs through and through. Impossibility is always already a specter that haunts the possible. The impossible politics of aporia is thus a politics that obeys the logic of *without*. That is: the impossible politics is impossibility *without* impossibility.

Yet, isn't the logic of *without* tantamount to, or, perhaps more accurately, operative within the laws of *autoimmunity, supplementarity, iterability, dissemination*, and *différance*? Indeed, *autoimmunity* works to immunize the self against itself *without* becoming fatal—we are left with undecidability between immunity and autoimmunity. *Supplementarity* adds but also replaces but *without* being a full plenitude. *Iterability* repeats and changes *without* either operation becoming fully developed. *Dissemination* works to blow up the horizon of meaning *without* completely eradicating meaning or its possibility. *Différance* differentiates and defers *without* reserve, *without* allowing a telos to exist. Since thinking of identity is indeed thinking of the identity/difference duo as an *iterable play* of *dissemination* subject to the law of *supplementarity* with *différance* as its condition of possibility, we can thus say that identity is 'identity *without* identity'. This makes 'identity politics' an impossible politics of identity *without* identity.

There is however one more facet of the politics of aporia that should be addressed. Derrida argues that the politics of aporia is the enabling condition for the emergence of genuine responsibility. This, as I explain later, opens up the way for thinking of a beyond of the politics of aporia in terms of a subject always already responsible before the wholly other, where the wholly other, as explained by Caputo (1997a: 51–52), "is any singularity whatever, whoever" which we "cannot generalize, cannot universalize, cannot formalize."

Responsibility through the politics of aporia

Undecidability is the condition of possibility of decision, a decision which in itself is the condition of responsibility. Not knowing how to decide and what to do is the possibility condition of decision, despite the fact that it looks like a negative condition of decision (Derrida 1999a: 66). Responsibility in the sense of Derrida emerges when the subject is faced with decision, a decision which is to be made within the politics of aporia. Derrida (1999a: 66) argues that

> there would be no decision, in the strong sense of the word, in ethics, in politics, no decision, and thus no responsibility, without the experience of some undecidability ... a decision has to go through some impossibility in order for it to be a decision.

Should a decision come into being through a calculable program, this would destroy all sense of responsibility. The decision would have been transformed into a programmable effect of determinate causes for which there can be no ethical or political responsibility. As he (Derrida 1992a: 41) put it,

> the condition of possibility of this thing called responsibility is a certain *experience and experiment of the possibility of the impossible: the testing of the aporia* from which one may invent the only *possible invention*, the *impossible invention*.

Situations of undecidability thus demand decision. The latter takes the form of an act of invention which cannot be grounded in what precedes it. The act of invention involves an "anxiety-ridden moment of suspense" (Derrida 1989: 955). Derrida (1989: 963) puts it in even stronger terms, stating that

> the undecidable is ... the experience of that which, though heterogeneous, foreign to the order of the calculable and the rule, is still obliged ... to give itself up to the impossible decision, while taking account of law and rules. A decision that didn't go through the ordeal of the undecidable would not be a free decision.

However, if undecidability is not a call for undecision, it is not a recipe for decisionism either. Derrida (1988: 116) explains that "even if a decision seems to take only a second and not to be preceded by any deliberation, it is structured by this *experience and experiment of the undecidable*." Clarifying the meaning of undecidability, Laclau argues that "to think of undecidability as a bottomless abyss that underlies any self-sufficient 'presence' would still maintain too much of the imagery of the 'ground'. The duality undecidability/decision is something that belongs to the logic of any structural arrangement" (1995: 93–94). Nor does undecidability disappear after the decision is made. Rather, the ordeal of the undecidable "is not a surmounted or sublated ... moment in the decision. The undecidable remains caught, lodged, at least as a ghost— but an essential ghost—in every decision, in every event of decision" (Derrida 1989: 965). This haunting of the decision has two consequences.

First, faced with undecidability and hence an urgency to decide with precipitation the subject has to take, cannot not assume, responsibility for the decision; a responsibility which is thus heterogeneous to knowledge since the decision is heterogeneous to knowledge (Derrida 1999a: 66). This responsibility is radically different from a responsibility that is assumed in the order of the possible since the latter *qua* possible would make such a responsibility part of an elaborate program and the result of a calculation based on knowledge and know-how. Such a responsibility even begins "to be irresponsible" (Derrida 1992a: 45) in the sense that one is not 'actually' assuming responsibility by acting on 'knowledge' that guarantees a certain course of decision or action. Rather, it is as if one is acting 'foolishly', 'irresponsibly', since one is acting because there are no guarantees of knowledge. This way of thinking about 'responsibility' leads to a problem, if not outright contradiction. It is not clear what responsibility is anymore if "no responsibility could ever be taken without equivocation and with contradiction" (Derrida 1992b: 9). The difficulty and equivocation of the aporia comes from the fact that, *on the one hand*, it looks as if we were measuring responsibility "by the rule of the impossible," that is, "as if doing only what were possible amounted to abandoning the ethical and political realms," and, *on the other hand*, "as if, inversely, in order to take an authentic responsibility it were necessary to limit oneself to impossible, impractical, and inapplicable decisions" (Derrida 1992a: 45).

Yet this notion of 'irresponsible responsibility' makes sense if we remember that were a decision not to undergo the ordeal of undecidability, according to Derrida, there would be no space for responsibility. Undecidability, where knowledge and no-knowledge are effectively both operative, is thus the possibility condition of responsibility. Should a decision come into being through a calculable program and well defined knowledge or reliance on knowledge, this would destroy all sense of responsibility. The decision would have been transformed into a programmable effect of determinate causes for which there can be no moral or political responsibility. Derrida (1992d: 76–77) explains that "the responsibility to think, speak, and act in compliance with this double contradictory imperative—a contradiction that must not be only an apparent or illusory antinomy ... but must be effective and, with experience, through experiment, interminable." In other words: there is no responsibility without an interminable experience of undecidable contradictions and aporias.

We are thus faced with a notion of responsibility that borders on irresponsibility, that is, we are to act with responsibility and with irresponsibility when we are urged to decide in a situation of undecidability. This notion of responsibility "can only exceed (and must exceed) the order of theoretical determination, of knowledge, certainty, judgment, and of statements in the form of 'this is that'" (Derrida 1992a: 81). Conversely, should we seek to reduce responsibility to what is conventionally accepted as the responsibility assumed by an autonomous subject according to knowledge, that is, to what this new sense of responsibility is supposed to exceed in the first place, we would end up giving in to "the so very presentable face of good conscience" to what is supposed to be exceeded, or sought to be exceeded, namely, "error, recklessness, the unthought, and irresponsibility."[4]

Second, the fact that undecidability haunts the decision and that because of this haunting Derrida's notion of responsibility verges on irresponsibility both lead to a certain notion of the subject, a subject who also emerges within the politics of aporia.

The subject of/through the politics of aporia

Generally speaking Derrida rejects the notion of self-conscious, autonomous subject who decides (Derrida 1997b: xi). Therefore, in deciding within the

The aporia of Identity/difference and othering 131

politics of aporia, a would-be deciding subject is not a Cartesian one. Nor is it fully self-present *qua* subject. Indeed, according to Derrida (Derrida in Kearney and Dooley 1999: 66),

> Not only should I not be certain that I made a good decision," retorts Derrida, "but I shouldn't even be certain that I made a decision. ... 'I' never decide, ... 'I' never make a decision in my own name, because as soon as I claim that 'I' have made a decision, you can be sure that is wrong.

The subject's unity and self-determination are not pre-given. They instead are, or, more accurately, claimed to be established through never-ending processes of relating to 'oneself'. The 'never-ending processes of relating', also termed by Derrida as self-repetition, is originary in the sense that it is logically and temporally prior to the 'one' of oneself. The constructed 'oneself' necessarily borrows from socio-historical contexts such as traditions and relations with other subjects who are engaged in similar processes of self-determination. Self-determination is, thus, always a determination that draws on and incorporates what is alien to the self.

The subject's dependence on such processes of repetition introduces *originarily* an otherness which is anterior to the subject's oneself-ness, a process of "irreducibility of an always-already-there" (Derrida 1978: 66). Not only is the subject never the first one to arrive on the scene, so to speak, 'its own' scene of 'self-presence', but the subject also owes its constitution to otherness that preceded it to the scene of 'self-presence'. Derrida (1997b: 299) argues that the other "necessarily invokes and provokes the subject before any genuine questioning can begin." This constitutive otherness continues to reproduce itself within the subject, thereby making the self-determination of the subject a repetition that draws on contexts. And the contexts within which the subject *qua* subject comes to be are themselves constantly changing. This makes repetition never a simple repetition of the same. Rather, every repetition of and within a context involves differentiation of contexts and, therefore, difference from the preceding contexts. Every such repetition is *iterability*. *Iterability* haunts and determines the subject.

Therefore, *speaking of the subject's identity is*, just like in the case of any other identity, *speaking of an iterable play of dissemination that obeys the law of supplementarity with différance as its condition of possibility*. The subject thus comes in and remains with provisional, internally differentiated moments of an incomplete, precarious identity. The movements of *iterability, supplementarity, dissemination* and *différance* thus both proactively and retroactively link together an anterior otherness, which is a past that was never present, to a future that never arrives, and is always deferred. These movements link an open future to an anterior otherness because the latter constantly, but intermittently, renews itself by way of productive iterability, supplementarity and dissemination. The radical alterity of anterior otherness is constitutively linked with the 'promise' of a future. However, because anterior otherness precedes the subject this implies that the promise also precedes the subject and opens the future for the subject. Yet this future is not a horizon of expectations or possibilities (such as utopia or teleology, things which dissemination prohibits and blows up and différance infinitely differentiates and defers). It is a future that is coming but never gets here and becomes never-ending processes of relating now; it is always a promise of a to-come.

Derrida argues that this originary opening of the self to other subjects and to history—to otherness—makes the subject responsive to others in the first place or moment. The subject's responsibility (*qua* responsiveness) is hence inseparable from the debt incurred toward anterior otherness. The originary opening of anterior otherness precedes and accompanies the constitution of the subject, and the latter can only constitute itself in this otherness. As such, the subject has a structure which is one of originary responsiveness or originary responsibility. The subject *qua* subject cannot avoid responding to a constitutively anterior otherness (other subjects and contexts) which precedes it. The subject is always-already-being called upon by anterior otherness.

In sum: A preceding radical alterity, repetition as structural possibility, iterability, and promise of an open future (a to-come future), and the impossible politics of aporia, all combine into a sense of responsibility which is inherent to the subject *qua* subject, who cannot not decide in the terrain of undecidability with an ineluctable subject's responsiveness and responsibility to an anterior otherness and a to-come future (Derrida 1978: 140). Does this imply that this subject can go or is beyond the politics of aporia?

Going beyond the aporiatic politics of identity

The politics of identity *without* identity is a politics of aporia, and any attempt of going beyond it is aporiatic. Yet we do play the politics of identity. This means that in a certain way we do go 'beyond'/'through' it to play the game of identity politics. How? We first need to remember that the politics of aporia is the possibility condition for change since

> aporia is not something negative, not something which in fact paralyses us, but on the contrary it is an ordeal, a test, a crucial moment through which we have to go, even if we are stuck, we have to experience this moment of aporia in order to make a decision, in order to take responsibility, in order to have a future ... the aporia ... is a chance.
> (Derrida 2001: 63)

We thus need to recognize the *chance* that inheres in the politics of aporia, the *chance* that would make continuously possible responsible decisions within a recast form of identity politics, a politics of identity *without* identity. This hence means remaining open to more future arrangements within the promise that autoimmunity and the impossible politics of aporia create and sustain, a promise which is always already originarily pervertible, but not necessarily perverted. And yet one can—or even perhaps cannot not—fall victim to the pressure of an *urgency* to close the argument on/within identity politics in a certain way. However, for such a decision for closure to occur within the terrain of undecidability there has to be an *interruption* (Derrida 2002b: 296). A key question is thus: How to interrupt without eradicating the chance of a future, an open future? How to interrupt without forcing a closure that can only be fatal to the future?

I suggest that we can do so by adopting an ethos of *negotiation* (Derrida 2002b: 13).As already discussed in Chapter 4, the latter occurs when one negotiates between "two incompatible imperatives that appear to be incompatible but are equally imperative;" that is, when "one negotiates by engaging the nonnegotiable in negotiation." Such a negotiation is "without-rest"; it is an "enervating mobility preventing one from ever stopping" and is "a suspension without rest" (Derrida 2002b: 13). This negotiation is different at every moment, from one context to the next, admitting no general rules; it is adjusted "to each moment without, however, the conclusion being a relativism or empiricism" (Derrida 2002b: 17). Negotiation thus can be thought of as "the shuttle ... between two positions" and "the impossibility of establishing oneself anywhere" (Derrida 2002b: 12). Negotiating however "does not prevent us from cutting. One must cut. But one is never sure of the right time, there is always a risk" (Derrida 2002b: 31). In the end, one negotiates with the nonnegotiable "to let the future have a future, to let or make it come, or, in any case, to leave the possibility of the future open" (Derrida and Stiegler 2002: 85).

Negotiating 'identity' thus means that we keep shuttling between the impossible—that is, formulating a closed sense of identity, an identity which is/can be identical to itself—and the aporiatic thinking which by construction cannot not be 'corrupted' and 'haunted' by our desire for closure. It thus seems that if there is any possibility of going beyond the politics of aporia, such a possibility might only come in the form of a never-resting negotiation between an interruption to decide and a future to-come. Going beyond the politics of aporia means then a never-resting, continuous shuttling negotiation between a structural promise of going beyond the aporia and momentarily interrupted and halted, yet always already disrupted, senses of identity.

In the context of the example of 'Euro-Islam', this suggests that Tibi's and Ramadan's attempts in closing 'in' on a Euro-Islam have simultaneously failed and succeeded in thinking a Euro-Islam. The failure consists in the fact they cannot agree among themselves (and with others) on ONE Euro-Islam. They cannot reach closure in their respective discourses on what 'is' Euro-Islam once and for all. Tibi's (2008: 198–99) strategy to build "a compromise between the competing assertions of a European identity and of an Islamic identity ... inspired by the idea of Europe and the historical experience of the Hellenization of Islam in the better days of Islamic civilization" is a never ending process. Not only are 'the idea of Europe' and 'the historical experience' in and of themselves *disseminating* projects which are necessarily *iterated* through repetition and change and always *supplemented* with new ideas from many *traces* of the past and ever fleeting futures yet to come. Not only are 'the universal principles' that Ramadan presents as the immutable foundations of a contextualized Euro-Islam haunted by the *traces* of the past and his expectations of a future yet to come. It is also the case that at the same time this very failure of both is the condition of possibility of thinking/ re-thinking any Euro-Islam. That is, for any such project to be possible the future has to remain necessarily open, non-closed, completely other. Both Tibi and Ramadan would like to turn their respective projects on Euro-Islam into a principle or a set of principles that would then foreclose future projects. That they cannot do so is part of the logic of *without* that drives the politics of aporia that they are engulfed in. It is only in not foreclosing, in not closing 'in' on a Euro-Islam that various continuing projects on Euro-Islam might find their condition of possibility.

Moreover, both Tibi's and Ramadan's projects are interruptions of the without-rest-negotiation. They are strategic moves that interrupt or seek to interrupt the never-resting process of negotiation. In doing so Tibi is engaged in the process of othering. He is, for example, calling for a compromise between what he sees as two identities. Even when he calls on so-called 'Islamic thought' to incorporate "the European values of democracy, laïcité, civil society, pluralism, secular tolerance and individual human rights," he is simultaneously engaged in a process of othering; he is putting this 'Islamic thought' in the place of an 'other' that needs to be changed and incorporated. In short, he is trying to go beyond the othering of Western European Muslims in (and by) Europe by building his arguments and appeals on the process of othering itself. Likewise, in his attempts to radically reform the basis of a principled understanding of Islam, Ramadan cannot escape creating many 'analytical' others that he seeks to learn from and then subsume and go beyond in a sort of Hegelian movement of sublation. Whereas Ramadan is not as rejectionist of extant Islamic/Islamist thought as Tibi is, he nonetheless seeks to doubly negate, to negate the negations of these others in order to reach a 'higher', or more accurately, using his terminology, a more fundamental theorization of the principles of Islamic identity.

On the one hand, this can be interpreted as self-contradiction and inconsistency. However, *on the other hand*, it can also be interpreted as Tibi's and Ramadan's discourses speaking more than both would want to say or recognize. In attempting to go beyond the politics of aporia both Tibi and Ramadan end up being necessarily engaged in a going beyond *without* however going beyond the never-resting negotiation between the possible interruptions and an impossible un-aporiatic Euro-Islam. Tibi's and Ramadan's situations can perhaps be described through similar terms to Derrida's (1978: 110) discussion of the possibility of "*traversing* the philosophical discourse from which it is impossible to uproot oneself totally, to attempt a breakthrough towards what is beyond it, the only chance of reaching it *within language* is by *formally* and *thematically* posing the *problem of the relations between belonging and the breakthrough, the problem of closure."* The *textuality* of Tibi's and Ramadan' texts on Euro-Islam textuality is *at once the closure and non-closure of the text* of Islam in Europe. As put by Derrida (1978: 250),

> one can conceive of the closure of that which is without end. Closure is the circular limit within which the repetition of difference infinitely repeats itself. That is to say, closure is its playing space. This movement is the movement of the world as play.

Paraphrasing Drucilla Cornell, one can say that Euro-Islam, *qua* thinking movement, seeks/should seek to 'take back the future' by letting the future be a future.[5]

6 Autoimmunity of trust *without* trust

Trust has been widely investigated both theoretically and empirically. Whether thought of as the result of a calculation of costs/benefits, a shared identity, or a leap of faith, there always seems to be an *as-if* rhetorical gesture which is ultimately needed to explain how actors move from the base of trust to expectations of trust via suspending judgment on uncertainty and fear of vulnerability to betrayal and exploitation—the actors ultimately act *as-if* they do not fear uncertainty and vulnerability to betrayal. Yet this *as-if* element has remained seriously under-explored. This chapter proposes a way of thinking this '*as-if*' element of trust through a work of deconstruction. The latter shows that the decision to trust occurs in a terrain of structural undecidability with the latter thought of as the possibility condition of trust as well as the subject of trust and a sense of responsibility for this trust. The aporiatic nature of undecidability makes this trust an autoimmune trust which obeys the logic of without which both negates and affirms trust.

Introduction

This chapter considers one specific topic—trust. The *problem* of trust, as much of the literature calls it, has been widely investigated both theoretically and empirically in IR, social sciences, economics, administrative and organizational studies, and philosophy (see, for example: Misztal 1996; Sztompka 1999; Hardin 2002). Trust is usually defined as a subject's willingness to place his/her interests, and sometimes even fate, under the influence or control of others. Trust has also been defined as more or less confidence in systems and institutions. More often than not trust is thought to be the result of predictions based on cost-benefit analysis of actors' interests. "I trust you because your interest encapsulates mine, which is to say that you have an interest in fulfilling my trust," says Hardin (2002: 3). Trust has also been hypothesized to be the product of actors' identities and interests which are socially constructed through social learning processes. Trust has been cast in terms of 'what is right to do', with the would-be trusting believing that the would-be trusted will honor his/her obligation to avoid using his/her freedom of action in a harmful manner to the former. Trust has alternatively been thought of as the result of suspending judgment on uncertainty and fear of betrayal and exploitation and deciding to act on a *leap of faith* of sorts after having exhausted all possible knowledge on actors and their environment. "Trust succeeds where rational prediction alone would fail, because to trust is to live *as if* certain rationally possible futures will not occur," argue Lewis and Weigert (1985: 969). Actors would thus "act *as if* the situation they face was unproblematic" (Möllering 2006: 6; *original emphasis*). As such, this *as-if* element seems to be an essential part of the process of trust. Yet this *as-if* element has surprisingly remained under-explored.

In this chapter I propose a way of thinking about this 'as if' element of trust. I first argue that the trust dilemma emerges due to structural undecidability, and not just to a lack of information, knowledge, and/or fear of vulnerability to exploitation and betrayal. More specifically, I argue that the very condition of undecidability is what creates *both* the urgency for a decision to take the 'as if' leap toward enacting trust *and* the subject (*qua* subject of trust) who assumes responsibility for other participants in the trust process. Such a sense of responsibility goes much beyond and much deeper than any sense of responsibility that, for example, rationalist approaches allow for. Moreover, this kind of trust emerges within the aporiatic politics of undecidability and is a sort of trust *without* trust, obeying *both* the logic of the without (which negates and affirms at the same time) *and* the law of autoimmunity (which, to a certain extent, makes trust immune to itself).

The chapter is organized in five sections. In the first section, I use as an entry point into the proposed conceptualization of the *as-if* element of trust the so-called rationalist (or calculative) approach to the study of trust. I then broaden the discussion by considering the so-called hetero-knowledge approach to trust which posits that trust is a step that we take when we reach the limit of our knowledge. A common thread of these approaches is to think of trust as an 'as-if' leap from the basis of trust to expectation of trust. In the second section, I discuss a few aspects of undecidability relevant to the issue at stake. This paves the way to the third section, where I propose a theorization of the 'as-if' rhetorical gesture. I begin, following Jacques Derrida, with a deconstructive re-thinking of the 'as-if' rhetorical gesture. This leads to the idea that the 'as-if' rhetorical gesture is an event in the sense of 'saying as-if' and as such the 'as-if' gesture is a pervertible promise (in the sense of Derrida). Bringing these elements together paves the way to the fourth section, where I propose that trust based on 'as-if' rhetorical gesture is autoimmune. Because trust *qua as-if* leap is autoimmune this makes the politics of building trust an aporia which obeys the logic of without, a logic that simultaneously negates and affirms. In the last section of the chapter I discuss the ensuing impossible politics of aporia to conclude that building trust within the terrain of structural undecidability is a going beyond the aporiatic politics of undecidability to a 'trust *without* trust'.

Theories of trust

Trust is usually defined as a subject's willingness to place his/her interests, and sometimes even fate, under the influence or control of others, believing that the latter will honor their obligation to avoid using their freedom of action in a harmful manner to the former (Hoffman 2002: 394). Although extant approaches to the problem of trust differ on the feasibility of trust and the degree to which it can be achieved, they all agree that actors who trust one another necessarily face two difficulties—the trustor's lack of certainty about the trustee's intentions and the trustee's room for autonomy. Both elements make the trustor vulnerable to be exploited or betrayed and the would-be trustee susceptible of not gaining the trustor's trust (Luhmann 1979). The trustor's expectations about the trustee's actions, and vice versa, are inherently imperfect and susceptible to revision (Möllering 2006: 8).

Uncertainty and vulnerability are two issues that the literature on trust has particularly explored (see, for example: Wheeler 2008, 2009; Ruzicka and Wheeler 2010). One type of uncertainty which matters most in the context of trust occurs when an actor cannot know the alternative outcomes of a mutual interaction, nor can he/she attribute probabilities to these alternatives. Likewise, one specific kind of vulnerability which is relevant in the context of trust is a sort of an always deferred vulnerability. That is: the trustor knows that he/she could be exploited or betrayed in principle but does not expect to ever become so. The possibility of being harmed by the trustee exists but its actual occurrence is expected to always remain deferred, to never occur. Yet, the actors involved in a relationship of trust do accept the risk of betrayal and exploitation by knowing that trust-related uncertainty and vulnerability are irreducible. Put simply: First, without uncertainty and vulnerability there will not be any need/role for trust. Second, trust occurs only when the actors suspend their concerns with uncertainty and vulnerability: they act *as if* there was no uncertainty and no vulnerability. Therefore, a core element of all conceptualizations of trust is that it is first and foremost a state of favorable expectations regarding other people's actions and intentions. The literature on trust is very rich when it comes to delineating various analytically distinct, if often practically complementary and/or overlapping, bases for producing trust.[1] In the following I focus on the role that the *as-if* element plays in two approaches—the rationalist (or calculative) and *hetero*-knowledge approaches. Although none offers a satisfactory conceptualization/theory of the as-if element, the latter approach provides a point of entry for a thorough exploration.

Rationalist trust

The rationalist approach (e.g., Hardin 2002; Kydd 2006), elaborated in sociology, political science, transaction cost economics, principal-agent theories, and game and signaling theories (and many other areas of social science/theory), argues that trust is the result of predictions based on cost-benefit analysis of actors' interests.[2] The would-be trustor's calculation is done in terms of the would-be trustee's trustworthiness; the more trustworthy the would-be trustee, the more likely trust is to emerge. The likelihood or probability of trust is estimated using available information which, however, is always costly to acquire and remains unavoidably incomplete. Therefore, the potential trustor needs to calculate the value of the sought information before seeking it and probabilistically factor in this price into the cost benefit analysis of whether it is rational to trust.[3]

For example, Hardin (2002) stipulates that a rational choice theory of trust is possible on two grounds: First, there should be incentives for the trusted to fulfill the trust and, second, there should be enough knowledge for the trustor to be able to trust. Hardin (2002: 3) addresses the first issue with his concept of *encapsulated interest* which means "I trust you because your interest encapsulates mine, which is to say that you have an interest in fulfilling my trust." In general, the rational choice approach argues that the actors look for good cognitive and predictive reasons to trust. However, there always is a remainder of uncertainty since the would-be trustee's autonomy and agency always create a potential for exploitation, thereby making the would-be trustor always vulnerable. The would-be trustor cannot give enough rational reasons for bestowing trust on the would-be trustee. Trust becomes a dilemma: On rationalist grounds there are never enough reasons why a trustor may trust a trustee, and since we know that trust occurs there seems that there always is too much trust to rationally account for. The situation is as summarized by Lewis and Weigert, "trust succeeds where rational prediction alone would fail, because to trust is to live *as if* certain rationally possible futures will not occur" (1985: 969; their emphasis), and "trust begins when prediction ends" (1985: 976).

Four issues are worthwhile highlighting concerning the rationalist approach to trust. First, the rationalist approach reaches a terrain of indeterminacy where it cannot prescribe to the actors how to rationally deal with uncertainty and vulnerability, except through an infinite regress of cost-benefit analysis. This however does not alleviate the dilemma but only defers it to create a situation which is neither deterministic nor indeterminate to trust (Hardin 2001: 5). The actors establish trust only by acting *as if* the situation has been resolved.[4]

Second, the rationalist approach assumes an epistemological perspective on trust and posits the subject to be a rational agent who engages in a trust relationship based on calculation contingent on available information. Yet, as argued later in the chapter, raising the question of the subject is crucial to a satisfactory notion of trust. The theorization of the subject proposed in this chapter destroys the taken-for-granted basis for rationalist trust.

Third, most rationalist (and otherwise) approaches argue that feelings of trust betrayal might result from situations of misunderstanding, that is, as a result of miscommunication. That this does happen is not disputable.

However, as explained later, communication or more precisely speech acting in situations of/or leading to trust and otherwise is always already pervertible and susceptible to misfiring. This thus should shift our attention away from an issue of miscommunication to an issue of the condition of possibility of trust. In fact, the misfiring is both the condition of possibility and impossibility of trust.

Fourth, the rationalist approach is silent on the sense of responsibility that always accompanies trust. That the subject of trust and responsibility to trust and for being trusted are important issues which need to be addressed is born by the fact that trust as an experience unfolds for a certain subject, a subject of trust—there is no trust without its subject and vice versa the subject of trust emerges only from within the experience of going through the politics of trust. We thus must inquire: What kind of subject emerges from an experience of trust? What kind of responsibility should the subject of trust bear toward the other? How should we think of this sense of the subject and this sense of responsibility? As explained later in the chapter, I argue that an originary responsibility to otherness and a to-come future and a subject *qua* subject of trust who bears this sense of responsibility concomitantly emerge within and through the undecidable experience of trust.

Hetero-knowledge trust

Hetero-knowledge trust is an approach that seeks to focus on the *as-if* element of trust. This is done through the concept of suspension, which is thought of as a mediator between the bases of trust and the expectations as a manifestation of trust (Möllering 2001: 404, 2006: Chap. 5). The concept of suspension represents an elusive and hard to pin down aspect of trust (Möllering 2001: 414). Figuratively speaking, the transition from the base or good reasons for trust to actual expectations of trust is "imagined as the mental process of leaping—enabled by suspension—across the gorge of the unknowable from the land of interpretation into the land of expectation" (Möllering 2001: 412). Extant literature on trust does not theorize the process through which we reach a point where our interpretations of inescapably incomplete and imperfect knowledge are accepted and our awareness of the unknown, unknowable, unresolved, and irresolvable is suspended (Giddens 1991: 36–42). This suspension makes trust "both more and less than knowledge" (Simmel 1990: 179), even standing "outside the categories of knowledge and ignorance" (Simmel 1950: 318).

A Simmelian-inspired model of trust thus consists of three elements: (1) expectations—the state reached at the end of trust-constructing process, which can be either favorable (trusting) or unfavorable (distrusting); (2) interpretations—making sense of human (and institutional) experiences as bases for trust (that is, having good reasons); (3) suspension—the bracketing of the unknowable and elusive and taking a leap from interpretations to expectations (Möllering 2001: 417). Whereas the concepts of expectations and interpretations are well developed in the literature, suspension needs much more theoretical probing and articulation.

In this pursuit, I argue that the problem of trust is more than just one of deciding whether to trust under a condition of uncertainty and vulnerability rooted in a lack or poor quality of knowledge. I thus propose that trust is a political problem of *deciding whether to trust within a terrain of structural undecidability*. Deciding to take a leap from interpretations to expectations of trust by suspending judgment, that is, acting 'as if' there were no uncertainty about and vulnerability to betrayal, is a decision under a condition of structural undecidability, that is, a condition of not knowing how to decide and what to do. Moreover, although it looks much like a negative condition of decision, undecidability is the possibility condition of, and creates urgency for, the decision to trust, a decision which in itself is the possibility condition of a certain sense of responsibility (Derrida 1999a: 66). The remainder of the chapter explicates this argument.

Undecidability and decision

A common thread of conventional theories of decision is that the decision-maker relies on the available information and makes the 'best' of it according to a set of criteria and constraints. What if, however, all what the decision-maker ends up facing was an oscillation between a set of determined choices, a situation of structural undecidability? Under such conditions, the classical decision maker would remain paralyzed. From Derrida's perspective, actors decide to act not in spite of, but rather because of, undecidability. Actors decide precisely because prior knowledge is insufficient to make possible programmatic or algorithmic action and situations of undecidability demand decision. The decision thus takes the form of an act of invention which cannot be grounded in what precedes it. The act of invention involves an "anxiety-ridden moment of suspense" (Derrida 1989: 955). Note however that this is not a call for ignoring preparation through a gathering and analysis of knowledge and information. Yet, says Derrida (1989: 967),

> the moment of *decision, as such*, always remains a finite moment of urgency and precipitation, since it must not be the consequence or the effect of this theoretical or historical knowledge, of this reflection or this deliberation, since it always marks the interruption of the juridico- or ethico- or politico-cognitive deliberation that precedes it, that must precede it ... Even if time and prudence, the patience of knowledge and the mastery of conditions were hypothetically unlimited, the decision would be structurally finite, however late it came, decision of urgency and precipitation, acting in the night of non-knowledge and non-rule.

The instant of decision is heterogeneous to all (preceding) knowledge. We can thus speak of an aporia that consists of an urgency and that obstructs the horizon of knowledge. This implies that a decision *qua* sovereign and free entails that the decision-maker must be responsible for the decision (Derrida 1997a: 219).

One reason why a decision must remain heterogeneous to knowledge is that the terrain of structural undecidability within which the decision maker decides obeys a logic that transgresses the usual logic of binary oppositions. Conventional theory of decision is underpinned by the necessity of a total separation and delineation of alternatives, allowing no room for overlap or interference between them; a logic of "all or nothing". However, undecidability indicates the impossibility of a definitive separation between inside and outside, and binary opposition in general. Therefore, undecidability functions within certain oppositions that are essential for argumentation, only to undermine these oppositions at the same time by enacting the play of their multiple meanings. This implies that the logic of the play of meanings in undecidability cannot be presented as 'this *and* that' or 'this *or* that.' Derrida (1988: 117) instead argues that the logic of undecidability consists of "'and' and 'or' combinations at the same time; it is a non-binary logic of neither/nor and simultaneously either/or." The logic of undecidability is one of *spectrality* where

> the specter is a paradoxical incorporation, the becoming-body, a certain phenomenal and carnal form of the spirit ... neither soul nor body, and both one and the other. For it is flesh and phenomenality that give to the spirit its spectral apparition, but disappear right away in the apparition, in the very coming of the *revenant* or the return of the spectre.
> (Derrida 1994a: 6)

This means that undecidability does not disappear after the decision is made. The specter and ordeal of the undecidable is not left behind or surpassed. The undecidable haunts through and through every event of decision much like a ghost (Derrida 1989: 965). The decision will always be threatened by the specter of the negated, the neglected, and the unforeseeable (Hägglund 2004: 47). Yet thinking of decision in this way is not a call for decisionism. Rather, deciding under the condition of structural undecidability is an art of the impossible; it is a politics of aporia, a politics of the impossible decision (Bradley 2001: 145).

Is this what happens in the 'as-if' leap from interpretations to expectations, as thought of in the hetero-knowledge approach? Is the *as-if leap* a decision under a condition of structural undecidability? This begs to be explicated. However, should this turn out to be the case, this would mean that thinking of trust *qua* 'as-if' leap amounts to thinking of trust in terms of aporiatic politics. To trust would mean to engage in an art of the impossible, to traverse an aporia. Is such a traversal possible? We thus need to push for a much more thorough understanding of this 'as-if' leap, much more than what extant literature on trust allows for. How are we to understand the work of this *as-if*? What is the logic of this *as-if*? To what extent is this *as-if*, even if portrayed as a 'mere' rhetorical tool, *constitutive* of the social reality of trust that we seek to understand and deal with? I next address these and other aspects of the 'as-if' rhetorical gesture in the sense of Derrida.

The *as-if* gesture

The hetero-knowledge approach argues that trust is the result of suspending judgment on uncertainty and fear of betrayal and exploitation after having exhausted all possible knowledge on actors and their environment. The actors decide to trust *as if* there was no uncertainty and no fear of vulnerability to exploitation. This section explicate the characteristics of the 'as if' gesture by exploring whether it is a constative or performative act, whether it allows and enacts continuity or change through the rhetorical act, whether it is an interpretation of what already existed or is an inaugural retroactive act, and finally whether the 'as if' gesture is an event and in what sense. I conclude that the 'as if' gesture blurs the constative/performative delineation and is their condition of possibility; it is both continuation and change—that is, the 'as if' gesture is iterable; it is an inaugural interpretation; and it is an event *qua* 'saying as-if'. In sum: Rather than just being a 'mere' rhetorical gesture, deploying an 'as if' gesture is enacting an event which creates a certain kind of trust, a trust *without* trust which is autoimmune to itself.

Re-thinking the 'as-if' rhetorical gesture

That the 'as if' rhetorical gesture[5] is a powerful tool used in the formulation of social theory is well recognized across many disciplines of knowledge. Sometimes the gesture takes the form of an explicit rhetorical statement such as "I assume that it is 'as if' ... " Alternatively, we may find the rhetorical deployment using a language of 'ceteris paribus' or 'hypothesis making'. Milton Friedman (1994: 657) explains the importance and force of this gesture *qua* device of theorizing:

> A meaningful scientific hypothesis or theory typically asserts that certain forces are, and other forces are not, important in understanding a particular class of phenomena. It is frequently convenient to present such a hypothesis by stating that the phenomena it is desired to predict behave in the world of observation *as if* they occurred in a hypothetical and highly simplified world containing only the forces that the hypothesis asserts to be important. (*Original emphasis*)

Centuries before Friedman developed what he calls a methodology of economics, Kant had clearly and eloquently deployed the rhetoric of the 'as if' gesture in explicating his philosophy (metaphysics) of morals.[6] The following two excerpts from his *Fundamental Principles of the Metaphysic of Morals* are illustrative:

> Every rational being must so act *as if* he were by his maxims in every case a legislating member in the universal kingdom of ends. The formal principle of these maxims is: 'So act *as if* your maxim were to serve likewise as the universal law (of all rational beings).'
> (Kant 2008: 56; *emphasis added*)

> It seems then *as if* the moral law, that is, the principle of autonomy of the will, were properly speaking only presupposed in the idea of freedom, and *as if* we could not prove its reality and objective necessity independently.
> (Kant 2008: 68; *emphasis added*)

Likewise, the notion of ideal-types developed by Max Weber and followers is another instance of more or less applying the 'as if' gesture to help understand complex social reality with the aid of ideal types *qua* methodological device. As Weber defined it, the ideal type "*is* no 'hypothesis' ... it offers guidance to the construction of hypotheses" and although "it is not a *description* of reality ... it aims to give unambiguous means of expression to such a *description*" (Weber 1949: 90; *original emphasis*). Ideal types work to delineate "what course a given type of human action would take if it were strictly rational, unaffected by errors or emotional factors and if, furthermore, it were completely and unequivocally directed to a single end" (Weber 1964: 96). This implies that an analysis based on ideal types functions *as if* human action were strictly purposive-rationally oriented, undisturbed by error or emotions. Perhaps, for Weber, this is simply a methodological, instrumental reasoning that should facilitate understanding of social reality. However, practice in social science inquiries more often than not ends up losing track of this proviso, thereby conflating what Weber would see a performative use of ideal-type concepts, that is, as methodological means with which to explore empirical questions, with constative use of ideal-types as indeed describing an empirical reality.[7] Is this only an inadequate application of Weber's methodology, or is it perhaps inherent to the very methodology itself, to the very definition of the concept of ideal type in itself? That the delineation of constative/performative is important for Weber's methodology transpires in his attempt to clearly distinguish in logical terms between concepts and judgments (Drysdale 1996: 779–80). As argued down below, such a delineation is problematic and is in fact unsustainable in the case of the *as-if* rhetorical gesture. Nevertheless, it clearly appears that the *seeming* misuse of the device of ideal type is connected with the 'as if' nature of the concept itself.

Therefore, whether one calls the 'as if' gesture a methodology as Friedman does, a powerful linguistic device to promote certain philosophical positions, or more generally a linguistic gesture through which one can simplify the complexity of life into models that are more amenable to conceptualization and theorization, the fact remains that it is rare to come across a satisfactory theorization of this 'as if' gesture. This does not imply that those who deploy the 'as if' gesture in discourse are not aware that the deployment of 'as if' entails acting on a fiction. Vaihinger (1935: 93) indeed argued many years ago that the 'as if' gesture "states that reality as given, the particular, is compared with something whose impossibility and unreality is at the same time admitted." He also explained that the 'as' element in 'as if' defines a relationship between the two things that are contrasted or compared whereas the 'if' goes beyond and "affirms that the condition is an unreal or impossible one" (Vaihinger 1935: 258). For Vaihinger, what makes the 'as if' gesture important is that through it the actors/speakers do effectively act but on the basis of a fiction, that is, people act on a fiction *as if* it were true.

Doesn't this imply that the 'as if' gesture' is more than just providing a basis for acting on a fiction? The fiction deployed in the 'as if' gesture can either be a fiction about the future, or a nostalgia or memory about a fictitious past. In the latter case, one can, for example, see this at work in discourses on a return to the 'golden age' or 'authentic origin', etc. Are these two modes of using the as-if qua fiction the only way for thinking the 'as if' gesture? No says Derrida since "reasoning with the 'as if' is neither a fictionalization of a possible future nor a nostalgic resurrection of a certain past" (Gorkom 2007: 130).

Moreover, Derrida rejects Vaihinger's understanding of the 'as if' gesture as enacting a fiction since for him using the 'as if' gesture is doing something—a saying of 'as if' is a making of something (Derrida 2002a: 210). Thinking that because we are saying 'as if' is tantamount to "abandoning ourselves to the arbitrary, to dream, to imagination, to utopia, to hypothesis" is, for Derrida (2002a: 210), too simplistic. Nor does he accept Kant's deployment of the 'as if' gesture as a way of "putting to work certain types of judgments, for example, the 'reflective judgments' that Kant regularly said operated 'as if' (*als ob*) an understanding contained or comprehended the unity of the variety of empirical laws or '*as if* it were a lucky chance favoring our design'," (Derrida 2002a: 210–11). In fact, Derrida reads in Kant's text more than what Kant allows his text to say, thereby stating that "this 'as if' would itself be something like an agent of deconstructive ferment, since it in some way exceeds and comes close to disqualifying the two orders that are so often distinguished and opposed, the order of nature and the order of freedom" (Derrida 2002a: 211). Derrida (2002a: 211) explains that "in Kantian discourse, the gravity, seriousness, and irreducible necessity of the 'as if' points to nothing less than the finality of nature, that is, a finality whose concept, Kant tells us, is among the most unusual and difficult to pin down. For he says, it is neither a *concept of nature* nor a *concept of freedom*." Not only does a certain 'as if' thus endanger the opposition nature/freedom, the 'as if', according to Kant, also "plays a decisive role in the coherent organization of our experience." The 'as if' gesture thus makes the opposition nature/freedom trembles, as it does to all other oppositions that organize our lives. What is happening here?

Although Kant tries to elevate 'beautiful art' above nature, he comes back and seeks to protect art from 'all constraint of arbitrary rule' by deploying the 'as if' gesture as a way of protecting art 'as if' it were a product of nature (Derrida 2002a: 212–13). The 'as if' as deployed by Kant is expected to come to play in protecting 'beautiful art' from arbitrariness; but how? It does so by creating fuzziness and contamination between beautiful art and mere nature. This means that the 'as if' gesture is not a mere rhetorical gesture without any power. To the contrary, the 'as if' gesture blows up the very delineation that Kant seeks to sharpen and protect by deploying the 'as if' gesture. The deployment of the 'as if' gesture is apparently linked (in the Kantian discourse) to something that happens, an event, without Kant seemingly being aware of it. We need thus, says Derrida (2002a: 213), "to link this 'as if' to the thinking of an event, that is, to the thinking of this thing that *perhaps* happens, that is supposed to *take place*, that is supposed to find its place—and that *would* happen." This move is contrary to the general belief "that, in order, to happen, to take place, an event must interrupt the order of the 'as if', and therefore that its 'place' must be real, effective, concrete enough to belie the whole logic of the 'as if'," (Derrida 2002a: 213). This dichotomy, opposition or hierarchy is shaken and trembles because the very place of the event, where the event takes place, "becomes subject to the modality of an 'as if'," (Derrida 2002a: 213).

How to understand the work of this 'as if' in the sense of Derrida? There seems to be two phases or turns in this process, a phase that I call the 'as' turn and a phase, or, more accurately perhaps, a more or less counter-phase that I call the 'if' turn. In explicating these 'turns' Derrida relies on the notions of performative and event. He (Derrida 2002a: 218) states that

> every performative doubtless produces something; it makes an event come about. But what it *makes* in this way and *makes come about* in this way is not necessarily an *oeuvre*; it must always be authorized by a set of conventions or conventional fictions, of 'as if's' on which an institutional community is founded and to which it agrees.

However, this notion of event is not the one that Derrida would want to have since for him,

> as long as I can produce and determine an event by a performative act guaranteed, like any performative, by conventions, legitimate fictions, and a certain 'as if', then, to be sure, I will not say that nothing happens or comes about, but I will say that what takes place, arrives, happens, or happens *to me* remains still controllable and programmable within a horizon of anticipation or precomprehension, within a *horizon*, period. ... No surprise, thus no event in the strong sense.
> (Derrida 2002a: 233–34)

For Derrida (2002a: 233), an "event takes place only where it does not allow itself to be domesticated by any 'as if', or at least by any 'as if' that can already be read, decoded, or articulated *as such*." It is at this level of Derrida's explication that the 'as' turn becomes more transparent. Indeed, Derrida (2002a: 233) explains that it is in "this small word, the 'as' of the 'as if' as well as the 'as' of the 'as such'—whose authority founds and justifies every ontology as well as every phenomenology, every philosophy as science or knowledge—this small word, 'as'," that "might well be the name of the true problem, not to say the target, of deconstruction." I think what Derrida is saying is that the 'as' of the 'as if' is still preventing the event from being a true event because the 'as' of the 'as if' much like the 'as' of the 'such as' is precisely what defines the foundations of metaphysics and all what deconstruction seeks to make tremble and displace. Hence, the 'as' of the 'as if' still pulls us back to the metaphysics of presence that deconstruction seeks to displace and reconfigure.

Derrida then moves to sever the impact and force of this 'as' on the 'as if' which would allow the event to occur; but how? By going back to what determines an event *qua* event, that is, the experience of the 'perhaps'. Derrida (2002a: 235) explains that:

> The event belongs to a *perhaps* that is in keeping not with the possible but with the impossible. And its force is therefore irreducible to the force or the power of a performative, even if it gives to the performative itself, to what is called the *force* of the performative, its chance and its effectiveness. The force of the event is always stronger than the force of a performative.[8]

This is where the connection with the 'if' phase of the 'as if' becomes more visible; the experience of the *perhaps* has an affinity, a complicity with the 'if' turn of the 'as if' (Derrida 2002a: 235). The thinking of the 'if' turn of the 'as if' is linked to a thinking of the *perhaps* that shatters the horizon.

We thus end up with an 'as if' which is made up of two turns, an 'as' turn and an 'if' turn. The 'as' turn works to keep the 'as if' gesture within the logocentric discourse of the non-eventful performativity. And the 'if' turn pushes the 'as if' toward the force of the perhaps, without an experience of which the event will not be an event as such. Yet, neither the 'as' turn nor the 'if' turn can be a turn without participating in the 'as if'. The two turns necessitate one another while seeking to undermine and eliminate each other's effects on the performative and the event. The 'as' turn works to close off the horizon of the event, whereas the 'if' turn works to shatter and blow up any horizon that might prevent the event from showing itself, from arriving.

In sum: The 'as if' gesture understood in the sense of Derrida is, on the one hand, radically different from the 'as if' of Kant, Weber, Friedman, Vaihinger, and most discourses, while, on the other hand, these conventional readings of the 'as if' are still a 'facet' of the 'as if' in the sense of Derrida. For Derrida (2002b: 354), the 'as if' possesses a sort of possibility which "affects all language and all experience with possible fictionality, phantasmaticity, spectrality." This 'as if', a deconstructed 'as if' for sure, is part of a larger family, a family of "'quasi', 'perhaps', 'spectrality of the *phantasma*," a family the members of which "are the components of another thinking of the virtual, of a virtuality that is no longer organized according to the traditional notion of the possible (*dynamis, potentia, possibilitas*)," says Derrida (2002b: 360). At this point we need to address the following issue: If the 'if' turn of the 'as if' gesture is the possibility condition of the event, how can we speak of this event? Is this an event which is outside the saying, or is it rather the very saying of the event, 'saying the event' itself, 'saying *as-if*'? To explicate this let me first introduce Derrida's notion of 'saying the event'.

The event in 'saying as-if' qua *pervertible promise*

An event, according to Derrida (2007b: 441), is not just something that happens, although this is still true. What is more important is that "an event implies surprise, exposure, the unanticipatable." An event can never be predicted. Nor can we plan for it. Nor can we decide upon it. An event, argues Derrida (2007b: 443), "is that which goes very quickly; there can be an event only when it's not expected, when one can no longer wait for it, when the coming of what happens interrupts the waiting." The event, for Derrida (2007b: 446), is thus "absolutely singular."

Having said this, we are discussing not the notion of 'event' but the notion of 'saying the event', the act of saying the event. What is this 'event' in the phrase 'saying the event'? How do we think of, or determine, the 'saying' in 'saying the event', a saying which is performative, if not more? We indeed are dealing with a statement which "may pretend simply to state, show, and inform, but it actually produces," argues Derrida (2007b: 447). Such a statement is performative through and through, despite being "naturally unsaid, unavowed, and undeclared" as such. Yet this does not change the fact that this kind of 'saying the event' does indeed make 'the event', even if it looks only as a simple saying of the event. As noted by Derrida (2007b: 447), we need to carefully and critically examine "all the mechanisms that hold out the appearance of *saying* the event when they are in fact *making* it, interpreting and producing it."

How should we think of this feature of 'making' in 'saying'? Derrida (2007b: 447–48) explains that there is a difference between a "saying that makes the event while feigning simply to state, describe, and relate it" and a saying that makes the event by first calling our attention to the fact that "event-making is covertly being substituted for event-saying." That we can only see this as "saying the event" is what "overtly presents itself as performative: the modes of speaking that consist not in informing, reporting, relating, describing, or noting" while at the same time effectively "making something happen through speech" (2007b: 447–48). However, the nature of the event as singular and unforeseeable precludes the first type of 'saying' from being a type of 'saying the event' in the first place. Due to these features of the event in 'saying the event', 'saying the event' is not constative, that is, it is no longer knowledge of 'what is'. Nor is it a performative act (in the conventional sense of speech act theory) because "there is no one present, no subject of enunciation to say the event." The event in 'saying the event' defeats both the constative and the performative (Derrida 2007b: 456). Moreover, the event in 'saying the event' is pervertible since the performative which says it also neutralizes it; that is, that this 'saying' "always comes after the event" implies that it misses the event as such and is coterminous with the 'aftermath' of the event, not the singular event itself (Derrida 2007b: 460).

The event in 'saying the event' is still part of language even if it goes beyond both the constative and performative and defeats them both. This, according to Derrida, gives 'saying the event' the structure of a promise. However, the promise that Derrida speaks of is not the promise that conventional speech-act theorists have in mind. Promise for Derrida is not an example of a performative among many others. Rather, any performative and indeed any utterance intrinsically and structurally involves a promise. Derrida (2007b: 458) explains that

> whenever I address the other, when I say to the other 'I'm talking to you,' I'm already in a promise framework. I'm speaking to you means, 'I promise to continue, to go to the end of the sentence; I promise to tell you the truth even if I lie'—and to lie, one must promise to tell the truth. The promise is the basic element of language.

Moreover, Derrida rejects the idea that a promise is always good and cannot be a threat. For Derrida (2007b: 458–59), "a promise must always be haunted by the threat, by its becoming-threat, without which it is not a promise ... For a promise to be possible, it must be haunted or threatened by the possibility of being broken or of being bad." Nor does Derrida adhere to the view that a serious promise can only correspond to a serious intention. He (Derrida 2007b: 459–60) instead holds the view that "pervertibility has to be at the heart of that which is good, of the good promise, for the promise to be what it is ... This threat is not a bad thing; it's its chance. Without the threat, there would be no promise." Because Derrida argues that promise is intrinsic to any utterance, and 'saying the event' is an utterance, this implies that what applies to the Derrida's notion of promise *de facto* applies to the event in 'saying the event'.

Applied to the case of 'saying *as-if*', this discussion implies that the '*as if*' gesture has the structure of a promise, too. More specifically, the 'if' turn of the 'as if' gesture, which is where the event *qua* 'saying *as-if*' occurs, possesses the structure of a promise, and is structurally pervertible. This means that what makes the event through the 'as if' gesture possible also makes it impossible to escape the pervertibility of the event and thus can be thought of as being the condition of impossibility of the event. As discussed in previous chapters, Derrida (2007b: 460) argues that "the impossible must be at the heart of the possible." When this is translated to the event in 'saying *as-if*' we would thus say that the impossibility in the event in 'saying *as-if*' is at the heart of the possibility of the event in 'saying *as-if*'. Derrida (2002b: 235) explains that it is "the thinking of this other mode of the 'if', this more than difficult, im-possible thing, the exceeding of the performative and of the constative/performative opposition."

Back to re-thinking trust

Where does this lead us in terms of thinking trust via the *as-if* leap? We just saw that this 'as if' is made up of two intricately related turns, an 'as' turn and an 'if' turn. The latter is in effect an event in the sense of 'saying *as-if*', which means more accurately, 'saying trust'. This 'saying' trust has the structure of a pervertible promise. Moreover, trust as a 'saying trust' (*qua* pervertible promise) is a decision in the terrain of undecidability. This means that, one the one hand, trust is an impossible decision, or more precisely, trust is a double politics of the impossible, a politics of passing through a path of aporia. Yet, on the other hand, because undecidability within the path of aporia creates urgency for decision, trust is possible—undecidability is the condition of possibility of trust. We thus face a double bind: On the one hand, there is an urgency to trust, and, on the other hand, there is an impossibility haunting this possibility condition of trust. Because, as noted earlier, undecidability calls for a decision which is heterogeneous to prior knowledge and hence consists of an act of invention, trust—the decision to trust by taking an 'as if' leap—is heterogeneous to prior knowledge. However, this heterogeneity is a partial one since the 'as' turn of the 'as if' pulls back the forward movement of the 'if' turn toward pre-existing, contextual, prior knowledge.

Therefore, we can say that the possibility of failure of trust is not only inscribed as a preliminary risk in the condition of the possibility of the success of trust. The possibility of failure *must* continue to mark the event of trust, even when trust succeeds. This pervertibility is the trace of an impossibility that will always haunt trust. As weird as it might sound, we can say that this trust is a *trust without trust*; trust is haunted by the possibility of betrayal in its own self; trust is haunted by non-trust. Yet it is because there is a possibility of trust that trust is/remains haunted by its nemesis. Trust is thus haunted and made possible by the aporiatic politics of the impossible, a double politics of being trust and being without trust, both at the same time. The more one trusts, that is, the more there is trust, the more the possibility of pervertibility becomes stronger. Trust wants to immunize itself to perversion and betrayal; trust wants to minimize the vulnerability to betrayal. Yet this effort to immunize itself against vulnerability to betrayal, this very immunization threatens the condition of possibility of trust *qua* pervertible promise. Threatening the condition of possibility of trust thus threatens the emergence of trust itself. The more trust seeks to immunize itself against its nemesis, that is, vulnerability to betrayal, the more trust weakens and perverts itself. Isn't this a condition of autoimmunity *par excellence*?

Autoimmunity of as-if trust, subject, and responsibility

What does it mean to say that trust is autoimmune? What are some of the important implications of this autoimmunity of trust? How does autoimmunity relate to the aspect of vulnerability to betrayal and exploitation that always threaten trust? Is autoimmunity a 'radicalization' of the notion of vulnerability, a radicalization that makes vulnerability an always-already, originary attribute or aspect of any trust? Trust occurs among the subjects of trust who assume a certain responsibility for this trust. How does a re-thinking of trust as autoimmune trust impact on the notion of subject and related sense of responsibility?

Autoimmunity of trust

As discussed in Chapter 5, rather than being opposed to immunity, autoimmunity, explains Naas (2006: 34), "is a self-destructive 'force'" which emerges from the very gesture of immunization itself. Every entity that seeks to immunize itself ends up, or, more accurately put, begins simultaneously generating autoimmunity, immunity of the self to itself. Autoimmunity is always already originary. An originary desire for an immunized self always already triggers autoimmunity. Therefore, autoimmunity is an originary movement that imprints into the self non-closure to the 'other'. This means that the pair of immunization/auto-immunization is undecidable and originarily haunts the possibility condition of trust.

Earlier, I summarized two important strands of extant literature on trust arguing that trust occurs only when the actors suspend their concerns with uncertainty and vulnerability; that is, the actors act 'as if' there was no uncertainty and no vulnerability. However, from the standpoint for the current section, we see that what is commonly called vulnerability and uncertainty is in fact a *light* characterization of the autoimmune nature of trust. We face a difficult question at this point: When the actors act 'as if' there were no uncertainty and no vulnerability, does this imply that the actors are able to go beyond the autoimmunity of trust? If, as I am arguing, trust is always already autoimmune, how is it that the subjects of this trust can act *as if* there was no autoimmunity? Perhaps, we need to repose the question differently: Wouldn't it make more sense to say that it is the subjectivity of the subject which is recast/reconstructed as accepting the autoimmunity of trust, rather than the subjects 'ignoring' or 'being able to go beyond' the autoimmunity of trust? However, if the subjectivity of the subjects is recast in a different way, does it also imply that the sense of responsibility toward the 'other' is changed or recast? As argued in Chapter 5, the subject who emerges through the ordeal of undecidability and its urgency to decide is a responsible subject. Therefore,

152 *Autoimmunity of trust* without *trust*

the subject emerges from the experience of trust is constitutively marked as a particular subject due to the fact that the experience of undecidability haunts and defines the contours of what follows from it. Derrida argues that the politics of aporia is the enabling condition for the emergence of such a responsibility.

Aporiatic politics of trust without trust

What does this discussion entail for trust *qua* 'as if' leap? First, despite the appearance that taking an 'as if' leap is somewhat 'arbitrary' and a leap into or over an abyss full of many dangers and threats of betrayal and exploitation, as the conventional understanding of trust has it, the issue is not only much more complex. The issue is also not as 'arbitrary' and frightening as it might appear (or, rather, made to appear in extant literature). That the subject of trust emerges with/within trust and that this subject assumes a sense of responsibility that goes much beyond and much deeper than any sense of responsibility that, for example, a rationalist approach would allow for, are in and of themselves far reaching departures from conventional understanding of trust.

Second, the rationalist approach to trust that extant IR (and social theory, more generally) assumes is one source of the difficulty of theorizing trust since presuming a discourse of intention, conscience and goodwill would efface the sense of responsibility that emerges with trust *qua* impossible politics of aporia in the terrain of undecidability. In other words: the over-emphasis that is always put on the fear of vulnerability and uncertainty as obstacles to the emergence of trust in the rationalist approach is due not so much to the 'nature' of trust as to the *rationalist discourse about trust* itself. In contrast, I argue that the very condition of undecidability is what creates both the urgency for a decision to trust as well as the subject (*qua* subject of trust) who assumes responsibility for other participants in the trust process.

Third, trust is an impossible-possible which is not the opposite of the possible. Trust *qua* impossible possible comes with/through a subject, who originarily assumes responsibility for the other. This sense of responsibility originarily reinforces the autoimmunity of trust.

Fourth, the autoimmunity of trust is precisely the condition of possibility of trust since should one be able to completely immunize oneself against betrayal by the other, there will be no undecidability and hence no urgency to trust *qua* aporiatic politics of decision. Otherness for whom the subject assumes an originary responsibility is what precisely always already opens up the possibility for trust.

In sum then, the thinking of trust as 'as if' leap that I am proposing is *not based* on the notion that trust is more or less a calculation through which the subject evaluates the pros and cons (or costs and benefits) of trusting or not trusting, and then decides accordingly. Rather, the thinking of trust that I propose is originarily always already happening. Yet this trust never achieves complete fruition. That is, it remains always already in process under an incessant threat of pervertibility with the latter being the very possibility condition of trust. As such this non-arriving arriving of betrayal originarily inscribes otherness in the subject of trust, thereby making the subject always already responsive as well as responsible to the other as its condition of possibility. Put differently: the condition of autoimmunity originarily always already creates a 'space' where the subject is responsive and responsible to the arriving other *qua* possibility of betrayal. The subject cannot be a subject except as such.

Does this mean that this trust, which is not a calculative trust, is a trust without horizon since it never stops being the product of an originary autoimmunity which always already inscribes the arrival of betrayal *qua* other? Isn't this some sort of oxymoron since trust is precisely, according to conventional wisdom, what creates a horizon of cooperation and thereby lessens the fear of vulnerability and exploitation? Is this trust that I am proposing 'really' a trust after all? Am I not talking about a trust without 'an essence' of trust, a trust *without* trust?

Aporiatic politics of trust

What does 'trust without trust' mean? What is the logic of this without which seems to negate and affirm at the same time? As already discussed in previous chapters, the logic of without is characterized by four main features. First, the logic of without negates without completely negating because it follows the law of iterability, which inscribes change and repetition always. The logic of without thus cannot completely negate the traces of previous meanings. Second, this *without* "marks neither a privation, a lack, nor an absence ... it has the double and ambiguous meaning of what is above in a hierarchy, thus both beyond and more" (Derrida 2008: 158). Third, the logic of without is a sort of a tripartite negation, a negation *without* negation, a *without* which is not a complete without, '*pas sans pas*' (Derrida 1987a: 401). Fourth, the logic of *without* engenders, and is a double politics of the impossible, as one of passing through a path of aporia. We thus end up facing/being stuck into an aporia characterized by undecidability between without and 'not without'. Is it possible to go beyond this aporia?

Drawing on the discussion of impossible-possible in Chapter 5, we can say that the politics of aporia of 'trust *without* trust' is a possibilized impossible—trust does indeed occur. Yet any attempt to go beyond the politics of aporia maintains the very non-closure of the politics of aporia, that is, the politics of trust under the logics of without and autoimmunity remains non-closed and bound to an always arriving trust, a 'to-come' trust. This trust is inherently pervertible, which is the possibility condition of an impossible trust *qua* decision in the terrain of undecidability. What makes this trust very peculiar is that its possibility condition is its very 'weakness' (*qua* always already pervertible promise and autoimmune trust).

Therefore, the 'as if' leap of trust is a pervertible promise which keeps the horizon of this trust in a sort of 'to-come' event, never achieving closure, and never disappearing entirely. The logic of this 'to-come' trust is one of spectrality; it is always already a specter. Whereas the 'as' element of 'as if' pulls us back toward ontology *qua* closure and stable horizon, the 'if' element pushes this limitation away, shatters it and disseminates it into a spectral to-come.

Finally, there are two issues that I have not explicitly addressed in this chapter but nonetheless play a *spectral* role in my analysis. First: Is trust (especially the way I theorize it) only about the willingness to submit to the control of others under conditions of possible betrayal? Put slightly differently: Is trust relevant only when actors decide to trust as if there was no uncertainty? Or, is trust something more general? Isn't trust also a willingness to accept the veracity of what our senses and procedures for enhancing our sense tell us, even though we know that these tools are not always reliable?[9] Don't we trust all the time (or even some of the time) simply because we cannot possibly carry on with our lives otherwise? This issue can be addressed in various ways. I however find it useful to briefly speak to it through a certain reading of Giddens' (1990; 1991) take on trust.

Without engaging into a work of deconstruction of Giddens' thinking apparatus, especially his notion of subjectivity which is to say the least still very much contaminated by the notion of conscious, autonomous, knowledgeable human individual, his approach to trust goes beyond the individual trust by incorporating abstract trust in institutions and systems of expert knowledge. Giddens (1990: 33) argues that "Trust always carries the connotation of reliability in the face of contingent outcomes, whether these concern the actions of individuals or the operation of systems." Giddens (1990: 90) also states that "trust is ... a tacit acceptance of circumstances in which other alternatives are largely foreclosed." As these two quotes illustrate, two elements are crucial to Giddens' approach—*outcome contingency* and *foreclosure of certain alternatives*. My approach generalizes in a certain way these notions, respectively, to undecidability and to what I termed the 'as-if' leap. As such, much of what Giddens discusses in terms of abstract trust (in addition to person-to-person trust) is implicitly addressed in my framework. Whether speaking of personal or abstract trust, trust is always already a trust *without* trust.

Second, it seems that I am perhaps thinking of trust as some sort of 'one-way street' since the argument apparently distinguishes between the trustor and trustee. Isn't it more appropriate to think of trust as a 'two-way street'? Let me make two brief points in this respect. First, I am discussing a certain literature which often distinguishes between trustor and trustee (can I escape the traces of this literature? Very unlikely.) Second, the notion of trust as a decision in the terrain of undecidability is, as argued up above, concomitant with the emergence of a subject who originarily assumes a certain sense of responsibility. Moreover, this subject is not the Cartesian or rational agent.

Rather, and because of the sense of responsibility that emerges from within undecidability, the subject is originarily 'home' to the other toward whom it is originarily responsible and responsive. Can we thus talk about trusting the 'other' when the 'other' originarily haunts the subject of trust? The notion of trust that is suggested in here is always already a 'two-way street'. Or, even more precisely, it is the possibility condition of such a 'two-way street' of speaking of two subjects and of the notion of intersubjectivity for that matter. Subjectivity and a sense of responsibility co-emerge with/within trust with the subject and trust being originarily heteronomous.[10]

7 Re-thinking international constitutional order

The autoimmune politics of binding *without* binding

This chapter presents a deconstruction of Ikenberry's theory of constitutional order via binding institutions. I show how the binding institutions are founded and conserved through an 'arbitrary exercise of power' which takes the form of an originary performative violence. The binding institutions become more or less legitimate as a result of retroactively effacing the originary violence. I also show how the binding institutions are inherently autoimmune to their own logic and rules and that this condition makes the binding of constitutional order a binding *without* binding, that is, a binding which is marred with undecidability and hence an impossible politics of aporia. The latter is however the possibility condition for invention, change, and transformation of the binding institutions beyond mere adjustments and adaptations to new contexts.

Introduction

The question of international/world order has remained an important, some would say almost inescapable, issue in IR theory. Writing about order has become "a *genre* in demand" (Leander 2006: 370). Debates on world order in IR theory are never ending, with each turn bringing to light new aspects and readdressing forever recurring themes. Indeed, many questions that have driven IR theory on international/world order for decades still remain subject to much discussion today.[1] The liberal order led by the US since the end of World War II has been and is still the topic of a large number of studies seeking to explain, rationalize, scrutinize, critique, and otherwise address theoretically and/or empirically the role of the major players in this order, especially the USA, and/or the absence of less visible powers and actors/factors on the world scene.

International institutions are a major component of international order; even hard core realists cannot ignore them completely. Yet students of IR are still divided on the definition and conceptualization of international institutions, how they function, the extent to which they are efficient in achieving their roles, goals, and missions, and the extent to which they are or can be independent of other major international actors such as states and multinational corporations, and so on.[2] A key question that major trends of IR

The autoimmune politics of constitutional order   157

scholarship are still debating is whether and, if yes, how and to what extent international institutions are *binding* on their constituent member actors. Put simply: Can international institutions of international order, such as the UN, bind states, especially major states such as the USA, China, and Russia, to abide by the rules and norms of the institutions? G. John Ikenberry's book *After Victory* (2001) offers a theoretical framework for understanding how *binding institutions of international order* are constructed, function and legitimized.

Specifically, the book addresses the issue of how the victors of hegemonic wars reaping a windfall of power assets get a unique opportunity to construct a new international constitutional order. The victorious power opts neither for domination of, nor for abandoning, the international system to itself,[3] but rather for a durable institutionalized order founded on a set of rules and institutions that bind and commit all member states to a preservation of the status quo (Ikenberry 2001: 4). Weaker states voluntarily confer legitimacy on the order because they feel confident enough that the powerful state will neither dominate them nor abandon them (Ikenberry 2001: 32). The institutions are expected to bind "the leading state when it is initially stronger and the subordinate states later when they are stronger" (Ikenberry 2001: 57). Institutional binding thus means establishing institutional links between the dominant state and weaker states, "thereby limiting its own autonomy and allowing other states to have institutionalized 'voice opportunities' in the decision making of the leading state ... , thereby rendering asymmetric power relations less exploitative and commitment more certain" (Ikenberry 2001: 63).[4]

Ikenberry states that the dominant state needs to be forthcoming about how it exercises its power, not in an arbitrary way, but rather according to institutional rules and procedures. However, the 'arbitrary exercise of power' is in fact constitutive of the constitutional order since the dominant state constructed the rules and procedures in the first place. Moreover, the binding institutions can fall prey to the problem of opportunism which, according to Ikenberry, can only be solved through a mutual conveying of a sense of credible commitment. This means that the binding institutions would need something else to *bind*. For Ikenberry, institutions are nonetheless sticky because the rules and procedures of domination are clearly stipulated and adhered to (Ikenberry 2001: 65). This means that there cannot be any new interpretation of these rules that might be so radical as to undermine the original rules themselves. This implies that not only the states—dominant and dominated—have agreed upon the rules and the procedures but also on the meta-rules and meta-procedures on how to interpret, or more accurately, on how not to re-interpret, these rules and procedures. This leads to an infinite regress. I argue that these tensions within Ikenberry's theory offer a *chance* to extend the theory to unexplored possibilities.

Pursuing this *chance*, I first consider the role of 'arbitrary exercise of power' in the theory. I argue that the binding institutions are founded and conserved through 'an arbitrary exercise of power' which assumes the form of, what

Derrida calls, *an originary performative violence*. The binding becomes (more or less) legitimate as a result of retroactively (more or less) effacing this originary violence. The 'arbitrary exercise of power' is thus essential to Ikenberry's argument and is both its conditions of possibility and impossibility.

Second, I argue that opportunism reflects the fact that the binding institutions are inherently, what Derrida calls, *autoimmune* to their own logic and rules, and this condition makes the institutional binding a binding *without* binding. Therefore, *autoimmunity* with its law of *without* (that is, an undecidable *denegated* negation) haunts the constitutional order through and through. The order is one marred with undecidability and is, hence, an impossible politics of aporia, that is, "an experience of not knowing what path to follow or coming to the point where no path can be found" (Norris 1982: 49). Yet the politics of aporia is the possibility condition for (re-)invention, change and transformation of the binding institutions.

Third, I argue that Ikenberry's role in seeking to explain the historical foundation and evolution or legitimation of binding institutions is of the order of 'saying the event'. Ikenberry's theory is a retroactive performative act that creates the possibility conditions of its own legitimation and validation.

The chapter is organized as follows. The second section first proposes to rethink the concept of binding institutions using Derrida's notions of *performative violence* and *autoimmunity*. The third section then explores the ensuing impossible politics of aporia and sense of responsibility which is heterogeneous to knowledge and calculation. The chapter ends by exploring some lessons of the work of deconstruction.

Binding, performative violence, and autoimmunity

Ikenberry argues that the arbitrary exercise of power is a problem, a solution to which is to institutionalize the exercise of power so that the latter will be more visible, more permanent, and less arbitrary. As such the exercise of power is tamed within the binding institutions. This thus makes it more economical, effective, and lasting for the dominant state and more legitimate in the eyes of the dominated. The binding institutions are thus a restraint on the dominant state's return to power only because power is more fully and effectively, as well as legitimately, exercised within the institutions. However, this '*non-return*' to power is an exercise of power in a more pervasive way; it is entrenched and legitimated very effectively and much less costly. The new arrangement is much more profitable to the dominant state, making its power advantages much more permanent than what a 'naked' exercise of power would provide.

Can we however demarcate an 'arbitrary exercise of power' from such an 'exercise of power within the binding institutions'? My answer to this question is no because the process of constituting the rules and the procedures is in itself an arbitrary exercise of power that has 'forgotten' its originary violence. Indeed, Ikenberry clearly states that hegemonic wars are a unique opportunity for the victorious states to construct a new order through an exercise of power advantage. Therefore, the binding institutions are created, maintained, and work effectively through an inherent arbitrary exercise of power.

Yet can the binding institutions actually emerge and function without the power of the dominant state playing a crucial role in the various processes? Aren't the binding institutions inherently built on the possibility of violence against the weaker members? This much seems to agree more or less with Schweller's (2001: 163) critique, who argues that the hegemon is signaling to potential partners that, at one level, it "does not intend to use its power to settle all matters between them" and, at a second level, that it reserves the right and has the power to do it and might do it if the hegemon feels such a need. Going beyond Schweller's point, I show that the binding institutions are *founded through/with violence, function, and are maintained through/with violence*. To defend this claim I reconsider more carefully the process of *binding*.

Binding in Ikenberry's sense is much more retroactive than proactive. It is perceived and felt as such only *après coup*, only after the institutions have been stabilized and maintained through other means. However, this does not diminish the role of binding in the present and the future. In fact, the *après coup* working of binding institutions is precisely enacted in the present to retroactively determine the conditions of possibility of the present and the future. As such the binding process is a performative deployment of violence at the 'origin'. Yet this 'origin' is not a genuine origin; it instead is a non-originary origin.

The retroactive performative of binding creates the conditions of legitimacy of the binding here and now in the present and potentially for the future. Originary violence is the very source of the binding institutions and the latter become more or less legitimate as a result of retroactively effacing the originary violence. The more successful the effacement process, and thus the more (discursively/interpretatively) violent it is,[5] the more legitimate the binding institutions appear to be. However, the originary violence does not completely disappear. Its specter instead continues to haunt the binding institutions and is reflected in the possibility of arbitrary exercise of power within or beyond the binding institutions; a possibility that Ikenberry fails to completely erase.

Ikenberry's theory thus seems to run into contradiction. *On the one hand*, binding institutions are sought precisely to go beyond and prevent an arbitrary exercise of power by the dominant state, while, *on the other hand*, not only is the very foundation achieved through an exercise of power but so too is the conservation and legitimation of the binding institutions. Does this mean that the dominant state seeks to limit and undermine itself to preserve itself? Not only this, but also the dominant state cannot act otherwise if it wants to found and conserve binding institutions. I think that this is an instance of *autoimmunity*—the binding institutions are autoimmune to their function of binding.

160 *The autoimmune politics of constitutional order*

I develop these arguments first by introducing the notion of originary performative violence in the sense of Derrida and then by proposing a reconfiguration of Ikenberry's concept of binding using this notion. I then explore the possibility of re-thinking the notion of 'binding' beyond the tensions residing in Ikenberry's theory.

Binding through originary performative violence

Because constitutional orders are non-coercive[6] and thus dialogues and communication are important to their founding and maintenance, performative acts play an important role. The moment of foundation is a set of performative acts enacted by the dominant and the dominated states. These *instituting moments* form the frame wherein and through which the set of agreed upon binding rules and institutions would concretize the order by operating "to allocate rights and limit the exercise of power" (Ikenberry 2001: 29) through "shaping, constraining, and connecting mechanisms between states" (Ikenberry 2001: 35). The performative acts take the form of declarations of *mutual commitments*. The performative acts are the *crucial founding moments* of the binding institutions since "the willingness of states to pursue a constitutional settlement will hinge on their ability to convey assurances and commitments" (Ikenberry 1998: 160). Through performative acts the participating states seek to "lock in their commitments and relationships" via various mechanisms (Ikenberry 2001: 41). The acts would be successful if "these mechanisms raise the 'cost of exit' and create 'voice opportunities,' thereby providing mechanisms to mitigate or resolve the conflict" (Ikenberry 2001: 41). The performative acts seek therefore to "specify what it is that states are expected to do and make it difficult and costly for states to do otherwise" (Ikenberry 2001: 42). In sum, the performative acts found an order that functions not according to "the logic of balance" which checks "power with power" but rather according to "the logic of institutional binding" which restrains "power through the establishment of an institutionalized political process supervised by formal-legal authority" (Ikenberry 2001: 43).

I now scrutinize Ikenberry's theory to explore in some depth the role that performativity plays in his concept of binding institutions. An analysis of his text, if pushed far enough, reveals a number of underlying *aporias*. In this pursuit, I begin with a short discussion of a performative act and a number of its important features in the sense of Derrida. This discussion paves the way for an explanation of how performativity simultaneously conserves and legitimates the binding institutions. This occurs through a violent inaugural interpretation of the very conditions of founding the binding institutions via an 'arbitrary exercise of power' by the dominant state. This means that *the process of binding is through and through a violent process* of simultaneously founding and conserving while giving itself a sense of necessity and legitimacy.

When states[7] engage in discourses about founding binding institutions the latter will come into existence through the very same discursive processes. However, no exchange takes place outside a context. The *'after victory'* context wherein the victors get a unique opportunity to construct a new order is particularly important here. How does such a context shape the performative/constative acts of the discursive processes that lead to the founding and legitimation of binding institutions?

Following Chapter 4, we can see the logic of performativity at work in the rules and procedures—contracts—through which the binding institutions are supposed to bind. That these contracts are essentially problematic is due to the fact that

> There is no contract that does not have violence as both an origin ... and an outcome ... The violence that founds or positions *droit* need not be immediately present in the contract ... But without being immediately present, it is replaced ('represented') by the supplement of a substitute. And it is in this ... representativity that originary violence is consigned to oblivion. This amnesic loss of consciousness does not happen by accident. It is the very passage from presence to representation.
>
> (Derrida 1989: 1015)

The inescapable tight relation between foundational violence and conserving violence transpires in Ikenberry's (2001: 55) statement that the dominant state

> enters the postwar period sitting on a declining power base. A binding institutional settlement allows the state to conserve its base by creating rules and institutions that will extend the stream of benefits and advantages into the future.

The rules and institutions are meant to conserve the (potential, if not actual) violent dominance of the leading state. This is also transparent in Ikenberry's response to the question "What makes institutions sticky?" He (2001: 65) writes:

> institutional agreements can embody formal legal or organizational procedures and understandings that strengthen expectations about the orientation of future state behavior.

Whose expectations? These are first and foremost those of the leading state about maintaining and conserving its leading dominant position.

The co-existence of both foundational and conserving violence (as a possibility at least) undoubtedly creates an underlying tension within the binding institutions. Can the leading state and acquiescing states go beyond it? The answer is no because this condition is a reflection of the autoimmune nature of binding institutions.

Autoimmunity of binding qua *promise of commitment*

The problem of founding and conserving binding institutions is, in Ikenberry's theory, one of a promise of mutual commitment. Ikenberry (2001: 61) states that the willingness of the secondary states "to engage in voluntary compliance—will hinge on the ability of the leading state to demonstrate its reliability, commitment, and willingness to forego the arbitrary exercise of power." He (2001: 69) also argues that "states are making a mutual commitment to operate within a given set of institutions and rules."

The problem of commitment is by and large addressed in the IR literature through a rationalist approach which espouses the so-called logic of consequences through a cost/benefit analysis.[8] However, thinking of commitment *qua promise of commitment* is much more relevant for a theory of binding institutions. If the founding of binding institutions essentially occurs through performative acts, then the notion of promise is crucial for addressing the problem because, as discussed in the previous chapters, any performative and indeed any communication intrinsically involves a promise. Promise in the sense of Derrida is not just a performative among others (as in speech act theory). Rather, for him any performative and indeed any utterance intrinsically and structurally involves a promise. Derrida (2007a: 458) explains that

> when I say to the other 'I'm talking to you,' I'm already in a promise framework. I'm speaking to you means, 'I promise to continue, to go to the end of the sentence; I promise to tell you the truth even if I lie'—and to lie, one must promise to tell the truth. The promise is the basic element of language.

Thus, when I say that I commit to you, I am in effect *promising* that I am committing/will commit to you. Moreover, promise is neither good nor bad. Derrida explains that "for a promise to be possible, it must be haunted or threatened by the possibility of being broken or of being bad;" a promise *qua* promise is inherently pervertible (Derrida 2007a: 459–60). However, pervertibility does not annul the repetitive aspect within the promise. A promise implicates in fact a promise continuum (if I can put it in these terms). Derrida uses the example of the vow of marriage to explain such a necessary repeatability—possibility of repetition—within any promise; he (Derrida 2007a: 453) writes:

> The 'yes, I do' that I say when I get married, ... this first, singular, and unique 'yes' must implicate right away my readiness to confirm the 'yes' not only a moment later, but tomorrow, and the day after, and until the end of life. The repetition of the 'yes' must be implicated from the initial moment of the first 'yes'.

This is true both for kept and betrayed promises, as explained by Derrida (1989: 997), because "iterability inscribes the promise as guard in the most irruptive instant of foundation. Thus it inscribes the possibility of repetition at the heart of the originary." This means that any promise is subject to the law of iterability and that both possibilities—repeatability and pervertibility—are

The autoimmune politics of constitutional order 163

constitutive of any promise. This implies that commitment is inherently repeatable and pervertible at the same time, irrespective of any cost–benefit analysis thereof. In fact, Ikenberry (2001: 75, ft 61) more or less recognizes such a simultaneous repeatability and pervertibility in stating that:

> the problem with institutional binding strategies is that they leave states potentially exposed to the opportunistic actions of other states. The leading state, in placing limits on its use of power, *must be confident* that they are not opening themselves to domination or abandonment by the leading state. For self-regarding states to agree to pursue their interests within binding institutions, they *must convey* to each other a credible sense of commitment. They *must be certain* that binding institutions actually do bind. They *must reassure* each other that they will not abandon their mutual restraint and exploit momentary advantages. (*emphasis added*)

Why is Ikenberry using the phrases '*must* be confident', '*must* convey to each other a credible sense of commitment', '*must* be certain that binding institutions actually do bind', '*must* reassure each other' in an almost mechanical repetition? I argue that he is struggling to exorcize the threatening, inherent pervertibility of the binding institutions *qua* promise of commitment. The 'must' that Ikenberry repeats over and over seeks to reinforce the promise. Yet this 'must' is never an 'is' and as such is pervertible. What this 'must' does is to express a need 'to appear as' making the promise. Yet this 'to appear as' does not mute the possibility of pervertibility within the promise and the 'appear as' itself. Likewise, we see Ikenberry struggling against pervertibility when he (2001: 73) admits that

> the greater the postwar power disparities, the more the weaker and secondary states will necessarily worry about domination and abandonment—and, as a result, the greater their incentive to agree to lock themselves into a postwar order that ensures restraint and commitment by the leading state.

Although Ikenberry emphasizes states' 'positive' expectations following a cost/benefit analysis, he cannot completely silence the ineradicable possibility of pervertibility.

The problem of pervertibility of (the promise of) commitment forces Ikenberry to advocate 'increasing returns' to institutions as a way of lessening the impact of a looming threat of pervertibility. The logic of increasing returns takes into consideration the process of path-dependency within this context; yet it nonetheless ignores the important role of iterability. Path-dependency arguments assume a sharp contingent rupture—a critical juncture—that leads to new historical trajectories, proposing that "contingent events set institutional patterns with deterministic properties into motion" (Djelic and Quack

2007: 161). However, this notion of contingent event has remained by and large under-theorized in IR literature.

The notion of contingent event can be thought of in two ways: first, as an event in the sense of Derrida, and, second, as a contaminated event which falls under the law of iterability. As already discussed in previous chapters, an event (for Derrida) is not just something that occurs. More importantly, "an event implies surprise, exposure, the unanticipatable" (Derrida 2007a: 441). An event, argues Derrida (2007a: 443), "is that which goes very quickly; there can be an event only when it's not expected, when one can no longer wait for it, when the coming of what happens interrupts the waiting." In short, an event in the sense of Derrida is singular and cannot be theorized which means that it cannot be discursively deployed to explore the possibility of path-dependency.

In the case of a contaminated event, iterability brings in both conservation and alteration. Iterability thus forces the return to institutions to be simultaneously 'increasing' and 'decreasing'. Put differently: there is no return to institutions without alteration, if only because contexts and actors' interests change. Iterability undermines the determinacy which is posited to occur in 'increased returns' arguments. Thinking of a contingent event in this way would thus defeat the very purpose of path dependency since the latter is meant to explain stability and positive feedback beyond the critical juncture.

The role of the analyst in retrospectively naming a contingent event as such is another dimension to analyzing 'contingent event' that we need to pay attention to. This is of the order of 'saying the event' (discussed in previous chapters). This would mean that all what there is in terms of 'contingent event' in path-dependency arguments is the analyst's 'saying the event'. As we have seen, a 'saying the event' is a statement which "may pretend simply to state, show, and inform, but it actually produces" (Derrida 2007a: 447), even if it looks only as a simple saying of the event. Such a statement is performative through and through, despite being undeclared as such. However, this 'saying' always comes after the event and this implies that it misses the event as such and is coterminous with the 'aftermath' of the event, not the singular event itself. Therefore, the event in 'saying the event' is not constative because it makes the event. Nor is it a performative act because it comes after the event—'saying the event' defeats both the constative and performative (Derrida 2007a: 456). The event in 'saying the event' is thus pervertible.

Therefore, the 'contingent event' would be, according to this interpretation, a retrospective and retroactive declaration, a 'saying the event' by the analyst that there was an event. It is clear that 'saying the event' plays an important role in Ikenberry's (2001: 73, ft 38) statement where he recognizes that "the ability of state leaders to discern the actual character of the postwar power disparities and make judgments about future power trends—even among contemporary elites with modern analytic techniques—is inherently problematic." This however does not prevent him from *declaring* that path-dependency and hence contingent events are key elements to the stickiness of binding institutions. If state leaders and their contemporaries cannot see 'the contingent' event, how do we know that there was such an event? The answer is: through a knowledge of Ikenberry's theory—a 'saying the event'.[9] Ikenberry wants to argue the case for determinacy through 'increased returns' but in seeking to do so he ends up letting indeterminacy leak back into his line of argumentation. It is only through a process of 'saying the event' that he is able to create a sense of coherence in his theory.

These tensions in Ikenberry's theory are due, I suggest, to a condition of *autoimmunity* that inheres within the process of binding. As a binding institution seeks to immunize itself by drawing, so to speak, a defensive wall around itself, the binding inescapably faces a condition of autoimmunity in its attempt to immunize itself. As already discussed, autoimmunity necessarily accompanies any desire for immunity against the other. Thus, in Ikenberry's theory, the process of securing self-certainty or immunization against an arbitrary exercise of power, by the dominant state and against opportunistic behavior by the weaker states through binding institutions, comes originally with and fosters a process of autoimmunity. The latter makes the binding institutions always already liable to the very threats of arbitrary exercise of power and opportunism.

First, the rules of the game are set by the victorious state as a way of preserving its leading and dominant position in the system of states. Yet by the very fact of founding such a constitutional order, this creates the *possibility* of alternative settings emerging from within the binding institutions themselves. This is because the rules of the game are the result of the founding and conserving performative act which falls under the law of iterability. This thus entails both the possibility of continuity and change in the rules, their interpretations and their applications.

This is somewhat reminiscent of the problem that democracy faces wherein the possibility of democratic *alternance* creates the possibility of alternatives *to* democracy.[10] This means that in the case of a constitutional order, the weaker states might behave opportunistically within the rules of the game and represent an alternative to the dominant's choices *as alternance* of voice within the rules of the game. However, the dominant state would seek, without using force or threat thereof, to oppose that which might undermine the very rules of the game that it had founded in the first place. Of course, in order to preserve the constitutional order as such the dominant state would not seek to completely undermine the (its) rules of the game. Likewise, the weaker states do not want to push their luck too far in terms of providing an alternative to the dominant state's choices within the space regulated by the rules of the game. Is this thus another way of saying that both the weaker and the dominant states exercise self-restraint? This indeed seems to be what Ikenberry argues for. Are we therefore arriving at the same conclusion after all this detour through Derrida? The answer is *yes* and *no*. It is *yes* in the sense that Ikenberry is not wrong in arguing for the possibility of self-restraint on the part of both the dominant and weaker states. However, it is *no* in the sense that the possibility of alternatives *to* the binding institutions remains *inherent within* the binding institutions themselves and thus always already threatens the binding institutions from within. Isn't this an instance of autoimmunity?

I argue that it indeed is the case. *On the one hand*, the dominant state wants to legitimize the arrangement by seemingly exercising self-restraint on arbitrary use of its dominant power and by giving 'equal voice' opportunity to the weaker states so as to limit their resorting to opportunistic behavior. The dominant state cannot act otherwise, short of using force or threat thereof. *On the other hand*, in order to create the possibility of binding institutions the dominant state *also* creates the very possibility of the opposite—the possibility of an alternative *to* the rules of the game emerging from within the constitutional order itself. Conversely, while, *on the one hand*, the weaker states adhere to the rules of the game as a way of binding the dominant state in not arbitrarily exercising its power leverage, they would have, *on the other hand*, legitimized into rules of the game what they fear most—an arbitrary exercise of power by the dominant state. Why? It is so because the dominant state founded the very rules of the game in the first place through an unrestrained, arbitrary exercise of power. I therefore argue that *liberty of exercising power* for the dominant state and *voice equality* for the weaker states simultaneously create two inseparable possibilities: *the possibility of reinforcing the bindingness and the possibility of undermining it*. This is an aporia.

The aporia of binding

I suggest that we re-think the 'binding' by affirming its aporia through a logic of without, which negates and affirms at the same time. As discussed in previous chapters, the logic of without is characterized by three main features. First, the logic of without negates without completely negating all the way down due to the law of iterability. Although there is no repetition of meaning without change, it is also true that no change could completely eradiate the trace of previous meanings. Second, he *without* is neither a privation, nor a lack, nor an absence. Third, The logic of without is a sort of a tripartite negation of '*pas sans pas*', which could mean '*without without without*', 'not without not', and '*step without step*'. The logic of *without* thus engenders, and is a double politics of the impossible, as one of passing through an aporia. We are in a situation where Aristotelian logic fails with its laws of non-contradiction and the exclusion of middle.

All what we can say is that *there is binding* but it is a binding which is inherently haunted by its own negation—*binding works by denegating itself*, thereby letting itself always already open to more binding, if always under an act/threat of denegation. Moreover, autoimmunity works to immunize the self against itself *without* becoming fatal; we are instead left with simultaneous immunity and autoimmunity; a continuous co-implication of negation and denegation; an impossible politics of aporiatic autoimmunity. This means that the politics of (founding and conserving) the binding institutions is an impossible politics of aporia.

Impossible politics of aporia

We saw in previous chapters that the politics of aporia consists of passing through a path of aporia, which is an impossible one. This impossible is in the sense of the "more-than-possible, the transgression, the chance, the aleatory, the breach, the rupture, the passage to the limits" (Caputo 1997a: 51). In order to think the impossible we need to 'possibilize' it in a certain way; a possibilization which is not a full possibility but instead "allows itself to be haunted by the specter of its impossibility" (Derrida 2002a: 359).

As also discussed in previous chapters, trace is what enables such a possibilization of the impossible, which is a possibilization *without* turning the impossible into a possible. That is, impossibility penetrates possibility under the form of a trace; a trace that remains after impossibility withdraws from possibility, if we can term it in this way. However, this withdrawal is a withdrawal *without* withdrawal since impossibility was not there to start with, but was rather always already there as a trace. This means that the possible is a possible impossible within which the trace runs. In other words, the impossible is the trace of its impossibility obeying the logic of *without*.

This implies that the impossible aporia of the autoimmune binding institutions is the condition of possibility of binding *without* binding. I suggest that such a way of binding is a decision that assumes a certain sense of responsibility which inheres within the impossible politics of aporia. The possibility condition of such a responsibility is, as Derrida (1992: 41) put it, "a certain *experience and experiment of the possibility of the impossible: the testing of the aporia* from which one may invent the only *possible invention*, the *impossible invention.*"

Decision within undecidability and responsibility

As discussed in Chapter 5, in the politics of aporia we are faced with a well-defined structure of options that are competing with one another and we are unable to decide for any one, while sensing the urgency and necessity of deciding. This is a condition of undecidability. Actors decide to act because of undecidability. The decision takes the form of an act of invention which cannot be grounded in what precedes it. The logic of undecidability is a non-binary logic of neither/nor and simultaneously either/or (Derrida 1981a: 220); it is one of spectrality (Derrida 1994a: 6). This means that undecidability *qua* spectrality does not disappear after the decision is made. The logic of spectrality thus makes the instant of decision heterogeneous to all (preceding) knowledge. The subject has to take responsibility for the decision, a responsibility which is thus heterogeneous to knowledge. In sum, we are faced with a responsibility that verges on irresponsibility when we are urged to decide in a situation of undecidability.

What are some implications of these notions of decision and responsibility for binding institutions? Autoimmunity inherently haunts the binding institutions, which makes the politics of founding and conserving/legitimating the binding institutions an impossible politics of aporia driven by the logic of *without*, a binding *without* binding, a situation of undecidability engendering responsibility which verges on irresponsibility. The notion of responsibility in the sense of Derrida has thus at least two important implications for the question of autoimmune binding institutions. First, it changes our way of thinking of decision as beyond (cost/benefit) calculation and knowledge, and occurring under a situation of urgency marred with undecidability. Second, this notion of responsibility presents a way out of one of the major dilemmas that Ikenberry's theory endures—the problem of opportunistic behavior both by the dominant and by the secondary states. This would mean that instead of founding and conserving the binding institutions on the premise of self-restraint, which is inherently problematic, we need to re-think the notion of binding institutions on premises that pay attention to the impossible politics of binding *without* binding.

Lessons

What sorts of lessons can we draw from this? First, I think that any international order would more or less be built and legitimitated through an originary performative violence and that it would suffer/endure autoimmunity. Nor can any order escape the issue of responsibility that verges on irresponsibility. This means that any order would suffer from the politics of aporia under the logic of *without*—in fact, the very conceptual opposition of 'order/disorder' already suffers and endures from these; it is an autoimmune undecidable.

Yet, and this is the second lesson, such impossible politics of aporia is the possibility condition for invention and change, with the proviso that such an invention and a change obey the logic of *without*. Binding institutions are thus not to be abandoned as mechanisms for founding/conserving international order. Rather, we need to recognize the *chance* that inheres in the politics of aporia, the *chance* that would make possible responsible decisions within a recast form of 'binding institutions'.

This implies that we need to *re-think* both the very notion of 'binding' as well as the *logic* of founding and conserving international order through binding institutions. We would then, perhaps, succeed in pre-empting dichotomous opposition between ethics/responsibility and politics. This is so because we would not only necessarily speak of responsibility (a responsibility which is much more than just a cost/benefit calculation) as inherent to the decisions (through originary performativity) that found and legitimate the order. We would also be able to understand and theorize the dynamic inherent in the binding through the notion of autoimmunity as both a limit on what these institutions can do and as their condition of possibility and chance of transformation. This thereby means remaining open to more future arrangements to come within the structural promise that autoimmunity and the impossible politics of aporia create and sustain.

Third, we need to realize that the process of theorizing itself falls under the logic of undecidability, which entails that there is an urgency to decide, to reach closure in theorizing. Yet one should resist the temptation of closing the argument; seeking closure would be a performative act of violence. That is, the theory should explicate and incorporate the conditions of its own non-closure, of its openness to what is yet to come, to what would disrupt it from within. In theorizing one must continue to assume one's responsibility, all the while knowing that one's decision will always be haunted by the specter of undecidability.

This, I suggest, can be done through Derrida's notion of 'negotiation', that is, the theory should thus be formulated in such a way as to remain engaged in an urgent negotiation between what is negotiable and what is non-negotiable. This, as already discussed in previous chapters, is a negotiation which involves both an urgency to interrupt and an imperative to continue the negotiation. In other words, urgency, undecidability and its entailed responsibility force us to follow an ethos of *negotiation*, which is inseparable from "the concept of the *double bind*," that is, "two incompatible imperatives that appear to be incompatible but are equally imperative" (Derrida 2002a: 13). In short, one negotiates with the non-negotiable "to let the future have a future, to let or make it come, or, in any case, to leave the possibility of the future open," to preempt closure (Derrida and Stiegler 2002: 85).

We must however realize that theorizing 'international order' through such a 'negotiation' will be a treacherous terrain mined with much contradiction. It means that we keep shuttling between the impossible formulation of closed theories of order and the production of aporiatic texts, which by construction cannot not but be 'corrupted' and 'haunted' by our desire for closure. This means, first, that the theorizing 'negotiation' never comes to rest even when it is interrupted, and, second, that the impossible task of reaching theoretical closure spectrally haunts the theoretical frameworks, thus always already insuring/assuring them to remain liable to deconstruction. This means seeking a displacement of conventional ways of theoretical inquiry to affirm, through the work of deconstruction, a work of inquiry via the plays of undecidable infrastructures, such as *iterability, autoimmunity, trace, originary violence, promise, negotiation*, etc., that is, plays that always already open up a *chance* to the future to be a future.

8 The quest for 'illogical' logics of action in IR

This chapter presents a deconstruction of the 'logic of practice' as deployed as a key explanatory notion in social constructivism and other approaches in social theory (and IR theory). I specifically consider the logic of consequences, the logic of appropriation, the logic of habit, the logic of practice, and the logic of communicative action.[1] I find that the presuppositions underpinning these logics of action are *undecidable* and *aporiatic*. I find that the logic of communicative action, which is anchored in the law of performative non-contradiction, is always already accompanied with performative contradiction, and as a result Habermas' presuppositions of criticizable validity claims are always autoimmune and out-of-joint with their claims. The logic of consequences, which is supposed to account for how actors act rationally and responsibly, is found to be one of simultaneous responsibility/irresponsibility and rationality/irrationality. The logic of appropriateness, which is supposed to explain how actors act appropriately, is found to be anchored simultaneously in in-appropriateness and appropriateness. The logic of habit, which is supposed to explain and account for how actors act automatically, ir-reflexively, and repetitively, is found to be both ir-reflexive and reflexive, autoimmune, and out-of-joint with its claimed logic. The logic of practice, which is supposed to be beyond theorization and about "things that one does because they are the 'done thing'," is found to be simultaneously hyper-theorized, if in a negative way, and rhetorically protected through a wager which is a sort of Pascalian wager anchored in an a-theoretical faith.

The 'logic of action'

Systematically explaining and understanding actors' actions are key organizing themes in IR theory.[2] To this end students of IR have introduced a number of logics of action. The notion of 'logic of action' is used as a meta-theoretical explanatory conceptual tool. 'Logic of action' is assumed to possess a set of preconditions, characteristics, and scope that differentiate it from other 'logics'. In this paper I consider five logics of action that are discussed in IR theory (and social theory); these are: the logic of consequences, the logic of appropriation, the logic of practice, the logic of habit, and the logic of communicative action (or argument).

I show that these logics are founded on a theorizing principle that prohibits contradiction between the preconditions of a given logic of action and its performative enactment—that is, a norm of *performative non-contradiction* which is anchored in Aristotle's *law of non-contradiction* of classical logic. Is this a surprise? Apparently it is not since it is in accordance with the widespread belief that we (our theories) must be logically consistent and coherent. Indeed, say, for example, de Mesquita and Morrow (1999: 56, 72), "logical consistency is the first test of a theory because consistency is necessary, though not sufficient, for understanding how international politics works" and "we believe that logical consistency is the gatekeeper for judging theories; a theory that contains logical inconsistencies must be remedied before it can have any empirical content." Likewise, says Zagare (1999: 114),

> There can be *no compromise* here. Without a *logically consistent* theoretical structure to explain them, empirical observations are impossible to evaluate; without a *logically consistent* theoretical structure to constrain them, original and creative theories are of limited utility; and without a *logically consistent* argument to support them, even entirely laudable conclusions, such as Walt's, lose much of their intellectual force. (emphasis added)

What if we were to question this long-held assumption about the necessity of *logical consistency* though? What if we were to raise questions on *this ban* of logical contradictions? In fact, raising these questions is not really that novel. Centuries ago Nietzsche (1967: 280) argued that such attempts to ban contradictions are based on "the belief that we can form concepts, that the concept not only designates the essence of a thing but comprehends it." This however is not acceptable to Nietzsche (1967: 280) because

> "logic (like geometry and arithmetic) applies only to fictitious truths that we have created. Logic is the attempt to understand the actual world by means of a scheme of being posited by ourselves, more correctly: to make it easier to formalize and to compute."

Likewise, echoing Nietzsche's critique, de Man (1979: 124) states that

> the language of identity and of logic asserts itself in the imperative mode and thus recognizes its own activity as the positing of entities. Logic consists of positional speech acts.

He (de Man 1979: 125) also says that

> the text deconstructs the authority of the principle of contradiction by showing that this principle is an act, but when it acts out of this act, it fails to perform the deed to which the text owed its status as act.

More recently, in making his plea for a pragmatic turn in theorizing international politics, Kratochwil (2007: 3) argues that

> traditional logic is indeed a poor philosopher stone for theorizing. Not only do experiments seldom result in clear 'yes' or 'no' answers but the class of 'undecidable' questions, which supposedly cannot exist, is embarrassingly large. Any scientist can attest to this, notwithstanding all attempts of establishing demarcation criteria or specifications of degenerative research programs. A simple yes/no logic also fails to come to terms with the fact that something that is not white need not be black, and this means in practical terms that it provides us with not much guidance for finding out what is the case.

Therefore, according to Nietzsche, de Man, and Kratochwil, and many others, traditional or classical (Aristotelian) logic and its laws of non-contradiction, excluded middle, and consistency are but part of taking positional speech acts in certain epistemological projects that are inherently limited, and have indeed proven to be so.

Drawing on the insights of these and other critics of 'classical logic', I question the implicit and yet dominant reliance on Aristotelian logic in theorizing about politics.[3] More specifically, in this chapter, I question the taken-for-granted ban on performative contradictions in theorizing about the 'logic of action'. Instead of adhering to an Aristotelian notion of contradiction (based on the law of non-contradiction which excludes a simultaneous occurrence of *A* and *non-A*) I take a more general notion of contradiction which is based on Derrida's (1978: 158) remark that contradictions in a more general sense are "nothing other than the relation-to-self of diction as it opposes itself to scription, as it *chases* itself (away) in hunting down what is properly its *trap*—this contradiction is not contingent."[4]

I pursue this task by problematizing the 'logic' of the five logics of action through a work of deconstruction. I thus critique and supplement as well as displace the five logics, without completely rejecting them. I specifically supplement them at the level of the presuppositions—that is, the conditions of possibility and impossibility—of the logics of action with supplements, which, I argue, are threatening to the 'original' logics but yet inescapable.

My approach is to proceed through reading a number of texts that explicate these logics of action. Probing the presuppositions of these texts shows that these logics are marred with tensions, inconsistencies, dilemmas, and contradictions. In doing this I pay particularly attention to how the theme of *performative non-contradiction* is developed, or left out of the discussion even if it is operative in the discourse about this or that logic of action. In the case of the logic of communicative action the issue is addressed upfront through Habermas' 'formal pragmatics' as the framework for communicative action. In the case of the other logics of action a work of careful reading is called for since none of the works that present these logics seem to pay explicit attention to the issue of performative contradiction. Yet, as explained later, this does not imply that they do not presuppose a certain 'theory' or approach to the issue of performative non-contradiction.

The work of deconstruction reveals a constitutive heterogeneity and heteronomy in each of the five logics. However, the work of deconstruction does not call for a rejection of these logics of action. It rather reconfigures them as generalizable in certain ways. The logics of action are found to follow a *quasi-law* of *undecidable aporia*. The latter is a play of signification that continuously displaces through deferral and differentiation whatever presuppositions are posited to undergird the logics, thereby making them *autoimmune* and *out-of-joint* with their supposed respective logic of action.

Specifically, the logic of communicative action, which is anchored in the law of performative non-contradiction, is found to be always already accompanied with performative contradiction. That is, Habermas' presuppositions—criticizable validity claims of truth validity, normative rightness, and sincerity or truthfulness—of communicative action geared toward mutual understanding is found to be always *out-of-joint*, thereby making the logic of communicative action an *autoimmune* logic. The logic of consequences is found to be an *autoimmune* logic of *responsibility* which always already contaminated by *irresponsibility*. The logic of appropriateness is found to be an *autoimmune* logic which always already affirms *appropriateness* with *inappropriateness*. The logic of habit is found to be an *autoimmune* logic which is *out-of-joint*. The logic of practice, which is supposed to be beyond theorization and about "things that one does because they are the 'done thing'," (Bourdieu 1990: 18) is found to be simultaneously hyper-theorized, if in a negative way, and rhetorically protected through a wager which is a sort of Pascalian wager anchored in an a-theoretical faith. I present a discussion of each of the five logics in the next sections and then end the chapter with some thoughts about the implications of this way of thinking about the logic of action for a re-thinking of IR theory.

Logic of communicative action (argument)

Risse deploys Habermas' theory of communicative action to propose and conceptualize the logic of arguing in IR based on "processes of argumentation, deliberation, and persuasion," which "constitute a distinct mode of social interaction to be differentiated from both strategic bargaining—the realm of rational choice—and rule-guided behavior—the realm of sociological institutionalism" (Risse 2000: 1–2). These meta-theoretical approaches, argues Risse (2000: 3), should be thought of as ideal-types, each having its own logic of action according to its own rationality toward the goals of action. Risse admits however that "we should not exaggerate the differences among metatheoretical orientations" since "one single metatheoretical orientation probably will not capture" the complexity of action, which means that we should be concerned more with "how far one can push one logic of action to account for observable practices and which logic dominates a given situation"(Risse 2000: 3). More emphatically, he explains that:

> We often act both strategically and discursively—that is, we use arguments to convince somebody else that our demands are justified—and by doing so we follow norms enabling our interaction in the first place (language rules, for example). As a result, the empirical question to be asked is not whether actors behave strategically or in an argumentative mode, but which mode captures more of the action in a given situation.
>
> (Risse 2000: 18)

Risse's approach is a straightforward deployment of Habermas' theory of communicative action, which is an attempt to identify the necessary preconditions of communication geared toward mutual understanding and consensual agreement.[5]

Habermas develops his theory of communicative action by using a methodology of *rational reconstruction*. He specifically formulates a theory of *formal pragmatics* that seeks to uncover the formal necessary conditions (embedded in language) for any communication to take place in any language. *Formal pragmatics*, explains Maeve (2001: 3),

> aims at a systematic reconstruction of the intuitive linguistic knowledge of competent subjects, the intuitive 'rule consciousness' that a competent speaker has of her own language. It aims to explicate pre-theoretical knowledge of a general sort as opposed to the competencies of particular individuals and groups. It thus calls to mind the unavoidable presuppositions that guide linguistic exchanges between speakers and hearers in everyday processes of communication in any language.

In formulating his theory Habermas draws on speech-act theory[6] to conclude that, in seeking mutual understanding through communication, the actor

> must raise at least three validity claims with his utterance, namely: 1. That the statement made is true ... ; 2. That the speech act is right with respect to the existing normative context ... ; and 3. That the manifest intention of the speaker is meant as it is expressed
>
> (Habermas 1984: 99)

Communicative action consists of discourses that test these three validity claims. Habermas differentiates between communicative and strategic actions since, for him, the latter are "interactions in which at least one of the participants wants with his speech act to produce perlocutionary effects on his opposite number" (Habermas 1984: 295).[7]

Habermas (1984: 99) views the above three validity claims as necessary preconditions that participants in a discourse should uphold short of which they would fall into *performative contradiction,* that is, they would state certain claims and in doing so they would undermine those very same claims by performatively upholding or claiming the opposite. For example, recognizing the possibility of lies in using a language implies that we are inherently assuming that one should, or is expected to, be sincere in using language. Put differently: every discourse has built in it some inherently necessary conditions that anyone who is involved in communication must presuppose, short of which they would fall into performative contradiction. Habermas (1990: 80) explains that

> a performative contradiction occurs when a constative speech act $k(p)$ rests on noncontingent presuppositions whose propositional content contradicts the asserted proposition p.

This is different from the notion of Aristotelian (classical logic) contradiction which is usually claimed to arise when a proposition A and its opposite *non-A* are simultaneously asserted as true. Put differently: Habermas argues that "the communicative use of language harbors an immanent obligation to justify validity claims, if need be", and "a performative contradiction occurs when the claims that one makes on a locutionary level deny the very possibility of such a justification" (Jay 1992: 266).

Habermas calls his explorations of and extensions to Austin's and Searle's theory of speech-acts *formal pragmatics,* which he distinguishes from other theories of meaning by focusing on how "the meanings of linguistic expressions ... contribute to speech acts that satisfy the validity claims of truth, truthfulness, and normative rightness," that is, the focus is on the "formal properties of speech situations in general" (Habermas 2001: 31). He explains that "obviously in performing speech acts we also performatively produce the conditions that make possible the utterance of sentences in the first place" (Habermas 2001: 73). There is thus simultaneously a communication about states of affairs and a sort of meta-communication about and enactment of the possibility conditions of the meaning of these states of affairs. Habermas' formal pragmatics seeks to account for this simultaneity by reconstructing "the rule system that a competent speaker must know if she is able to fulfill this postulate" (Habermas 2001: 74).

Habermas refers to these necessary conditions as a *counter-factual ideal speech situation* wherein there is a fundamental symmetry among the participants in the discourse. These conditions are such that, says Benhabib (1996: 70), all participants have "the same chances to initiate speech acts, to question, to interrogate, and to open debate," "the right to question the assigned topics of the conversation," and "the right to initiate reflexive arguments about the very rules of the discourse procedure and the way in which they are applied and carried out."

The *idealizing presuppositions* are however not in the sense of Kant. Rather, they are thought to constitute a formalization of presuppositions that are always already operative in everyday communicative action and "are unavoidable in the sense that they belong to the very meaning of what it is to take part in argumentation" (Maeve 2001: 5). This means that they are "typically counterfactual and will not as a rule be satisfied more than approximately" (Maeve 2001: 5). Yet they are also meant to be context transcending since they "refer to the *conduct* or practice of all forms of argumentation" (Maeve 2001: 5). Habermas is thus advocating a sort of general argumentation which, according to Pedersen (2008: 471), can be schematically represented as "1. CTA, 2. CTA only if ISS, 3. therefore the ISS exists" where CTA stands for communication oriented toward agreement, and ISS stands for ideal speech situation. This means, says Pedersen (2008: 471), that "we have to make certain anticipations in order to understand the practice in question, and that these anticipations are of a context-transcending kind."

Habermas elaborated his theory of communicative action through the methodology of *rational reconstruction* of the communicative competencies of participants in actual social practices. Rather than being based on the methodology of nomological hypotheses testing, Habermas' approach seeks to *"systematically reconstruct the intuitive knowledge of competent subjects"* (Habermas 1979: 9). It thus seeks to explicate meaning through "rational reconstruction of generative structures underlying the production of symbolic formations" (Habermas 1979: 13). Rational reconstruction is concerned with "domains of pretheoretical *knowledge*," that is, "proven intuitive foreknowledge" (Habermas 1979: 14). This implies that "reconstructive understanding refers only to symbolic objects characterized as well formed by competent subjects themselves" (Habermas 1979: 14). More specifically, rational reconstruction seeks to formulate "species competences" that "can be compared with general theories" (Habermas 2001: 14). As a result, "reconstructive procedure ... transforms a practically mastered pretheoretical knowledge (know-how) of competent subjects into an objective and explicit knowledge (know-that) to an extent sufficient sense" (Habermas 2001: 15).

How do we arrive at this intuitive or pre-theoretical knowledge? Habermas explains that we can bring it to consciousness "through the choice of suitable examples and counterexamples, through contrast and similarity relations, through translation, paraphrase, and so on—that is, through a well-thought-out maeutic method of interrogation" (Habermas 2001: 19). How do we conclude that such assertions about context-transcendental conceptual structure through transcendental investigation are acceptable? Habermas explains that although it is always hypothetical, "as long as the assertion of its necessity and universality has not been refuted, we term *transcendental* the conceptual structure recurring in all coherent experiences" (2001: 21–22). This means that this context-transcending knowledge is no *a priori* one. Rather, transcendental investigation is to be understood as "a reconstruction of general and unavoidable presuppositions of experiences that can lay claim to objectivity" (Habermas 2001: 24).

Therefore, Habermas' formulation of formal pragmatics through a *methodology of rational reconstruction* is, as summed up by Pedersen (2008: 458), "an attempt to establish an epistemological position that makes strong theoretical demands." The goal in rational reconstruction, explains Pedersen (2008: 466–67), is

> to reconstruct the deep structures that are considered the preconditions for all utterances as they appear on the surface. This reconstruction aims at uncovering universal competences in competent language users. What is to be uncovered is a pre-theoretical competence, a competence of which the actor is not reflexively conscious.

To sum up: The logic of argument is anchored in communicative action, and the latter is based on three elements. First, Habermas uses *rational reconstruction as a methodology* to reconstruct systematically pre-theoretical intuitive knowledge of competent subjects.[8] Second, this intuitive knowledge is formulated as a *formal pragmatics*. The latter is a theorization of the deep structures—*truth validity, normative rightness, and sincerity or truthfulness*—beneath all utterances; structures that constitute unavoidable preconditions of communication geared toward mutual understanding and consensus. Third, formal pragmatics is based on the law of *performative non-contradiction* which entails that a constative speech act rests on non-contingent presuppositions and that the latter should not contradict the assertive propositions of the former. Performative contradiction occurs "when what is said is undercut by how it is said" (Jay 1992: 266).[9]

What to make of these three features of the 'logic of argument'? Let me begin with the dimension of performative contradiction. This notion is a cornerstone of Habermas' edifice in his endeavor of re-thinking social theory through the methodology of rational reconstruction. As summarized by Pedersen (2009: 389), Habermas seeks in his three major research projects—a *theory of communicative action, discourse ethics,* and *deliberative democracy*—to rationally reconstruct strong idealizations as necessary preconditions of the respective practices. These strong idealizations, such as the ideal speech situation of formal pragmatics, play the role of counterfactual fictions. The latter define what can be termed as normative boundaries without being transcendental *à la* Kant. The counterfactual fictions thus play a role of 'as if' they were transcendental. That is, as put by Power (1995–96: 1013),

> At the level of this 'as if' logic, it is necessary to read the universalist claims of Habermas' theory of communication in terms of a metaphorical movement from the local to the universal, a movement that is never complete and that approaches universality only as a limitation of the local. Hence, the universality of ideal speech is not simply posited by Habermas, but rather 'unfolds' as an internal condition of the local that points beyond itself only 'problematically' in Kant's sense.

178 The quest for 'illogical' logics of action in IR

What Habermas seeks to do is thus to preserve a sort of "transcendental" Kant's sense of regulative idea without its Kantian transcendentalism (Power 1993: 39). This implies that we cannot grasp the meaning of whatever is presented as an 'as if' independently of what is being practically characterized (Power 1993: 41). Therefore, the general competences that Habermas speaks about in his communicative theory are to be understood 'as if' they were operative rules (Power 1993: 41). That is, Habermas presents these competences *as if* they were general, *as if* they were pre-theoretical. That the element of 'as-if' is the *nerve* of Habermas' whole edifice is evidenced in Habermas' (1996a: 1518) own recognition that

> when Power analyzes the concept of 'counterfactual presuppositions,' or more generally the 'vocabulary of the "as if,"' he puts his finger on the nerve of my entire theoretical undertaking. There is still much work to be done in this area.

Moreover, the following statement is illustrative of how Habermas deploys the 'as if' gesture:

> to *idealize forms of communication*, that is, to think of processes of communication *as if* they took place under idealized conditions, is not *per se* absurd.
>
> (Habermas 2001c: 55)

What to make of this 'as if' that plays such a crucial role in Habermas' methodology of rational reconstruction? I propose, as explained and developed in Chapter 6, to follow Derrida's insights in this respect.

As discussed in Chapter 6, the rhetorical 'as if' is made up of two intricately co-implicated turns, an 'as' turn and an 'if' turn. The 'if' turn is effectively an event of 'saying *as-if*'. This 'saying' has the structure of a pervertible promise. Moreover, this 'saying' (*qua* pervertible promise) is a decision in the terrain of undecidability. Undecidability occurs when we are faced with a well determined and defined set of options and we are not able to decide which way to decide under a condition of urgency and necessity to decide. This means that the decision is an impossible decision, or, more accurately, it is a double politics of the impossible, a politics of passing through a path of aporia. Yet because undecidability creates urgency for decision, the 'saying' is possible—undecidability is the condition of possibility of this 'saying'.

We hence face a double bind in Habermas' discourse on the 'as-if transcendental' preconditions of communicative action. *On the one hand*, there is an urgency to seek such transcendental competences, and, *on the other hand*, there is an impossibility haunting this precondition of communicative action. Because undecidability calls for a decision which is heterogeneous to prior knowledge and thus consists of an act of invention, communicative action—the decision to communicatively act in the sense of Habermas, that is, to communicatively act based on 'as if' transcendental preconditions—is heterogeneous to prior knowledge. Yet, this heterogeneity can only be a partial one since the 'as' turn of the 'as if transcendental' gesture pulls back the forward movement of the 'if' turn toward pre-existing knowledge (see Chapter 6).

In theorizing about the preconditions of communicative action Habermas focuses on the 'if' turn and does not pay *explicit* attention to the 'as' turn which is always already co-implicated with the 'if' turn. However, the 'as turn' is operational in the methodology of rational reconstruction which is inescapably contaminated by its context. Not only does Habermas draw on a vast amount of literature in making his case for rational reconstruction and communicative action. He also argues that rational reconstruction "transforms a practically mastered pretheoretical knowledge (know-how) of competent subjects into an objective and explicit knowledge (know-that) to an extent sufficient sense" (Habermas 2001: 15). In other words, Habermas posits a dichotomy between practically mastered pre-theoretical knowledge and 'as if' transcendental unavoidable presuppositions. Rational reconstruction is then claimed to bridge or transform pre-existing 'know-how' knowledge into an objective and explicit 'know that' knowledge.

Habermas thus seeks to bridge the 'as turn' (encapsulated in what he calls 'know how') with the 'if turn' (encapsulated in what he calls the 'know that') of the 'as if' gesture that says 'as if transcendental' presuppositions. This, *on the one hand*, is superfluous or redundant because the two turns are always already co-implicated and inseparable. While, *on the other hand*, it is impossible since the two turns cannot be thought of as separate 'sides' of a bridge. Habermas thinks he can do this through his notion of philosopher *qua* 'stand-in and interpreter', or in Habermas' words,[10]

> philosophy while advised to withdraw from the problematic roles of usher and judge, can and ought to retain its claim to reason, provided it is content to play the more modest roles of stand-in and interpreter.
> (Habermas 1992: 4)

That is, the philosopher can reflexively detach him/herself from and/or detect the pre-theoretical 'know-how' to see it as such and hence turn it into a theoretical 'know-that'.

Therefore, we can say that the impossibility of transcendental preconditions is not only inscribed as a preliminary Kantian contamination in these 'as-if' transcendental preconditions. This pervertibility is the trace of an impossibility that will always haunt Habermas' transcendental-like preconditions. We can say that these preconditions are transcending *without* being transcendental. The preconditions are haunted by the possibility of self-negating themselves, that is, they are haunted by non-transcendental preconditions. Yet it is because there is a possibility of transcendental preconditions that they remain haunted by their nemesis. Transcendental preconditions are thus haunted and made possible by the aporiatic politics of the impossible, a politics of transcending without being transcendental. In other words, the more one speaks of these preconditions *as if* they were transcendental, the more the possibility of pervertibility of their transcendental character becomes stronger, that is, contaminating them with a non-transcendental. This is quite an *aporia*.

Seeking to protect the quasi-transcendental character of the preconditions from this aporia, Habermas posits the law of performative non-contradiction, that is, if a constative speech act rests on non-contingent presuppositions, then the latter should not contradict the assertive proposition of the former. The goal of this law[11] is thus to immunize the act of saying 'as if' from performative contradiction, thereby precluding and preempting self-perversion. Yet this effort to immunize speech situations from self-contradiction, this very immunization, threatens the condition of possibility of the saying *qua* 'as-if'.

Put differently: Is it possible to prevent the 'as if' operation from contaminating the law of performative non-contradiction? Doesn't the *quasi-law* of 'as if' always already pervert the *law* of performative non-contradiction the moment we say 'as if'? Doesn't the law of performative non-contradiction become a *quasi-law* where the performative becomes an *as-if performative* which is contaminated and perverted with the constative? Likewise: Doesn't the non-contradiction become an *as-if non-contradiction* which is contaminated and perverted with contradiction? The more the *law* of non-contradiction seeks to protect a clear demarcation of the quasi-transcendental precondition from the constative and thus immunize the former from the latter, the more the quasi-transcendental preconditions lose their *quasi-ness* and thus the more they fall toward the abyss of Kantian transcendentalism, which Habermas struggles to reject irrevocably. And as a consequence, the more Habermas' discourse falls under the law of performative self-contradiction. In sum: Habermas rejects Kantian transcendentalism and then necessarily falls toward it the moment he seeks to avoid performative contradiction by imposing a law of performative non-contradiction. Habermas' theory wants to prohibit performative contradiction and, in doing so, cannot not practice it in its immunizing discourse[12]—*this is autoimmunity par excellence*.

What about the 'formal' in Habermas' formal pragmatics? Formal pragmatics seeks to reconstruct the presuppositions of everyday processes of communication. It seeks—*qua* theory—to produce (or, in Habermas' words, to reconstruct) the inevitable, quasi-transcendental presuppositions of communicative action. Habermas (2001b: 13–14) explains that

> In accordance with formal pragmatics, the rational structure of action oriented toward reaching understanding is reflected in the presuppositions that actors *must* make if they are to engage in this practice at all. The necessity of this '*must*' has a Wittgensteinian rather than Kantian sense. That is, it does not have the transcendental sense of universal, necessary, and noumenal condition of possible experience, but has the

grammatical sense of an 'inevitability' stemming from the conceptual connections of a system of learned—but for us inescapable—rule-governed behavior.

The 'formal' remains always provisional and never 'sufficiently' 'formal' since it cannot escape being contaminated and determined by traces of 'non-formal' meaning from natural languages that we cannot escape. Habermas (2001b: 13–14) explains that

> after the pragmatic deflation of the Kantian approach, 'transcendental analysis' means the search for presumably universal, but only *de facto* inescapable conditions that must be met for certain fundamental practices or achievements.

The above 'presumably universal' is, given the previous discussion, to be understood in the sense of the 'as if universal'. However, isn't the combination of 'presumably universal', 'only de facto inescapable', and 'must' some sort of a contradiction, or, more accurately, some sort of performative contradiction? It is clear that Habermas is struggling not to fall into the Kantian trap of transcendentalism. In this pursuit, Habermas raises 'experience', that is, experience *qua* 'must', into a final arbiter. Formal pragmatics is an effort to 'reconstruct', that is, theorize, this unavoidable 'experience' of 'must'; a 'must' that recurs so often in Habermas' discourse in an almost mechanical way as the following statements illustrate:

> We know at least intuitively that certain of these presuppositions cannot be fulfilled under normal empirical restrictions, yet we *must* nevertheless assume that these idealizing presuppositions are *sufficiently* fulfilled.
> (Habermas 2001c: 55–56)

> It must be shown for each of these conditions of a so-called ideal speech situation (through the demonstration of performative self-contradictions) that they belong to the *unavoidable* presuppositions of argumentation
> (Habermas 2001c: 56).

> Anyone who *seriously* engages in argumentation must indeed presuppose that the conditions of an 'ideal speech situation' alluded to are *sufficiently* realized.
> (Habermas 2001c: 57).

Moreover, Habermas (2001c: 55) characterizes these presuppositions as being actually efficacious counterfactuals:

> In performing an act of communication, we can assume in a self-reflexive fashion that a pragmatic precondition of this communication is fulfilled

even though this assumption may not be objectively correct; when our communication does not actually fulfill the assumed condition, we have acted under a *counterfactual presupposition*.

He (Habermas 2001b: 35) also writes that

> these unavoidable presuppositions of argumentative practice, no matter how counterfactual, are by no means mere constructs. Rather, they are *actually efficacious* in the behavior of the participants themselves.

Therefore, ultimately it is the 'de facto' characteristic of these presuppositions that determines their actual efficacy. Habermas (2001b: 13) also admits that

> the transformation of Kant's 'ideas' of pure reason into 'idealizing' presuppositions of communicative action raises difficulties especially for understanding the factual role of performatively presupposed counterfactual assumptions.

The fact of mutual understanding, if it happens, is hence sustained with performatively presupposed counterfacts and fictions, or, as put by Power (1995–96: 1010),

> material practices are constituted paradoxically by certain fictions that provide the conditions of possibility of their operations and of their manner of making facts visible.

The constitution 'by certain fictions' is however at the level of the performative, that is, those who engage in communicative action performatively, non-intentionally, presuppose these assumptions. To put it in another way: the presuppositions are enacted *de facto* at the level of the formal pragmatic aspect of the performative, not the linguistic content of the performative. And this is why Habermas argues that one would fall into a performative contradiction in rejecting these assumptions. The very constitution of any non-self-contradicting performative is thus anchored in these assumptions and that the latter are 'experienced' *de facto*, unconsciously and unintentionally, at the level of 'know-how' not at the level of 'know-that', in any communicative act that does not fall into performative contradiction.

Habermas is therefore speaking of a certain 'experience' which seems to be different from his sense of (communicative) experience.[13] It is an 'experience' which occurs in the absence of any intentionality of the speaker (and hearer). We can even say that it is an 'experience' without any knowledge of it; it is an 'experience' which is un-known, unnoticed, and unregistered within communicative action (that is, communicative experience *qua* understanding (Habermas 1979: 9)). It is an 'experience' which is not experienced *qua present experience* by those engaged in the communicative action. The participants in the communicative action do not know that they are experiencing this 'experience' of performatively not-contradicting the presuppositions (of validity claims) as the condition of possibility of the success of their communicative action. It is thus a sort of ghost-like 'experience' since the latter 'enables' the participants in a successful communicative action without them having any immediate, non-mediated registration of this spectral 'experience'. This 'experience', which is what Habermas terms as a 'know-how', is turned into a 'know-that' through the methodology of rational reconstruction. It is thus experienced without being experienced in the Habermas' sense of the term of communicative experience *qua* present understanding. And it is through this ghostly experience that the presuppositions are, according to Habermas, de facto operative.

Moreover, this 'un-experienced experience', 'experience without experience', seems to be more primordial than the experience of communicative action, not in a chronological sense but rather in a constitutive sense *qua* precondition of communicative experience. We thus have two types of experience: the experience of communicative action which is a present, intentionality-driven, conscious (communicative) experience *qua* present understanding, and a more primordial and constitutive 'experience', which is 'absent', not registered and not intentionality driven, with the inescapable fact that this second *un-experienced* experience being the precondition of the *experienced* experience. Therefore, we have a sort of generalized 'experience' as the condition of possibility of the experience of communicative action in the sense of a 'must' and 'counterfactual ideal speech situation' that Habermas speaks of.

As repeatedly explained by Habermas, this 'must' and this 'ideal' are not in the sense of a Kantian (regulative) idea. Yet the *un-experienced* experience would not 'be' without the *experienced* experience of the communicative action. It is only through the performance of communicative action that the presuppositions are effective *qua* preconditions. That is: *on the one hand*, Habermas strongly asserts that there cannot be a communicative action—a not performatively contradicting action—without these presuppositions. *On the other hand*, these presuppositions cannot be efficacious outside the very communicative action itself. It is *as if* communicative action lifts itself from its bootstraps.

Therefore, the fictions and counterfactuals are to be understood in the sense of 'as if'. Can we then say that the idealizing presuppositions *qua* counterfactuals are 'as if' they were efficacious? However, this would mean that they are not fictitious in the usual sense of the term. Given the earlier discussion of 'as if', this implies that the idealizing presuppositions are simultaneously fictitious and not fictitious. Put differently: the idealizing presuppositions are a sort of an idealization *without* idealization—idealization is not pure but is rather contaminated by non-idealizations. Formal pragmatics is therefore not as pure as Habermas claims it to be. The dichotomy that Habermas draws between formal and non-formal pragmatics is undecidable.[14]

This however does not imply that Habermas' theory is to be rejected; *to the contrary* we *must* keep walking with Habermas to try to traverse his aporiatic path of idealizing presuppositions, despite Habermas' best efforts to reach a certain closure at the level of formal pragmatics of criticizable idealizing presuppositions (validity claims).[15]

To put it in another way: Habermas' communicative action is an experience, a present experience, which essentially and necessarily depends on a sufficient realization of counterfactual presuppositions of formal pragmatics. However, as discussed above, this communicative experience, that is, experienced experience, is constituted through an un-experienced experience, which thus is a sort of vanishing experience, obeying a spectral logic of ghosts. This vanishing, un-experienced experience is thus an experience of trace, a vanishing trace, which appears as vanishing. The condition of possibility of the experience of communicative action is thus a vanishing trace, which operates through vanishing.

Therefore, the constitutive fiction that Habermas speaks of as being the inescapable presupposition of communicative action is a trace that appears by effacing itself and thus can never be or become present. If this is the case, wouldn't this make rational reconstruction, that is, the operation through which we arrive at the presuppositions of formal pragmatics a quest for 'something' that is never present but rather always already vanishing and self-effacing?

Habermas rejects Kant's transcendentalism and opts for formal pragmatics to reconstruct the preconditions—*qua* pre-theoretical presuppositions—of communicative action geared towards understanding. These presuppositions are necessary counterfactuals and idealizing conditions. Only those "who *seriously* engage in argumentation must indeed presuppose that the conditions of an 'ideal speech situation' alluded to are *sufficiently* realized," writes Habermas (2001c: 57). The non-serious are discounted. As such the conditions of the ideal speech situation are sufficiently realized, that is, the situation is 'under control' at the level of presuppositions. Under these *serious* conditions, there isn't much room for play, except as distortion. Under these conditions, the experience of communicative action is sufficiently idealized and as such it is sufficiently restricted; that is, we have a *restricted economy* of communicative action where seriousness prevails and where play has no place.

However, the condition of possibility of this restricted economy is a vanishing trace which can never be present. It is hence impossible to close this restricted economy of communicative action because the presuppositions *qua* vanishing trace, which make it possible to control this restricted economy and thus make it into a closed economy, can never be pinned down. This means that, *on the one hand*, Habermas' presuppositions function to make communicative action a closed economy. Yet, *on the other hand*, these presuppositions *qua* trace are never present but rather always already self-effacing and because of this they simultaneously undercut the closure of the communication economy. This is an aporia. *Communicative action constitutively depends on an aporia and rational reconstruction is aporiatic.*

Having said this, Habermas does speak of rational *re*-construction, not construction, of the presuppositions of communicative action.[16] Is he getting access to, that is, is he *present*-ing, *re*-represent-ing the trace? Because the vanishing trace is never present it means that Habermas is *supplementing* the trace, or, more accurately, the place of the vanishing trace in the discourse on presuppositions. Through an operation of *supplementation* Habermas is adding 'something' to the trace without however replacing the trace because there is no presence of the trace to be replaced to start with.

What enables Habermas to do so? And what is this 'something' that Habermas is adding qua *supplement*? What enables Habermas to act *supplementarily* is the *citationality*—ability/capacity to be cited in different contexts—of the trace.[17] And the 'something' that he seems to be adding to the trace is the inherent possibility of transformation that necessarily accompanies *citationality*, that is, *iterability*—the ability to be iterated with simultaneous repetition and transformation—of a trace. This implies that not only is what Habermas calls a presupposition (presupposed criticizable validity claims) never quite the same, identical to itself, but it also falls under a law of repetition. That is, presuppositions are repeated while being transformed—they are iterable. Therefore, not only are the validity claims 'criticizable' and 'fallible', they are also and, more importantly, *out-of-joint* with themselves, differing, deferred, and, more generally, *différantial*. This would make rational reconstruction a combination of the operations of *différance* and *supplementarity* with the 're' in *re*construction made possible through the operations of *iterability* and *citationality* of the presuppositions *qua vanishing self-effacing trace*.

In sum, the logic of communication action (and Risse's logic of argument by extension) is anchored in three dimensions—rational reconstruction, formal pragmatics, and the law of performative non-contradiction. Risse and like-minded IR scholars desire to turn these into an explanatory logic of action. However, the above discussion shows that this is an impossible possible task—the discourse of the logic of communicative action cannot be a restricted economy of explanation. First, Habermas' law of performative non-contradiction, which is meant to be a guarantee of successful communicative action geared toward mutual understanding and the methodology of rational reconstruction, is autoimmune—it is always already accompanied with performative contradiction. Second, the condition of possibility of such a restricted economy, if it were to exist, will be a vanishing trace which can never be present (and can never be 'presentated'), thereby making it impossible to restrict the economy of explanation. The methodology of rational reconstruction produces an aporiatic economy of explanation, that is, an aporiatic logic of action *qua* explanatory framework. Third, rational reconstruction is a combination of the operations of *différance* and *supplementarity* and as a result the presuppositions—criticizable validity claims—are an always *out-of-joint*, vanishing trace.

Logics of consequences and appropriation

The logic of consequences is based on the notion that actors engage in action based on strategic decision-making processes through which they calculate the costs and benefits of alternative courses of action given prior preferences and taking into account whatever information they have on each other's preferences. The logic is thus teleological and rationalist. Rational choice approaches in IR theory are direct applications of these ideas. As put by March and Olson (1989: 950),

> Those who see actions as driven by expectations of consequences imagine that human actors choose among alternatives by evaluating their likely consequences for personal or collective objectives, conscious that other actors are doing likewise.

The logic of appropriateness is based on the notion that actors are driven by a sense of appropriateness which is linked to their sense of identity. Action is norm and rule regulated, that is, as put by March and Olson (1989: 951),

> Human actors are imagined to follow rules that associate particular identities to particular situations, approaching individual opportunities for action by assessing similarities between current identities and choice dilemmas and more general concepts of self and situations. Action involves evoking an identity or role and matching the obligations of that identity or role to a specific situation. The pursuit of purpose is associated with identities more than with interests, and with the selection of rules more than with individual rational expectation.

Instead of being tied to interests and calculations of costs and benefits, action is based on what is cognitively speaking appropriate for a particular conception of self and on what is ethically virtuous (March and Olson 1989: 951).

March and Olsen recognize that the delineation of the two logics is not as sharp as it sounds. They note that "action generally cannot be explained exclusively in terms of a logic of either consequences or appropriateness" since "actors are constituted both by their interests, by which they evaluate their expected consequences, and by the rules embedded in their identities and political institutions. They calculate consequences and follow rules," (March and Olson 1998: 952). Yet they nonetheless argue that "the two logics are sufficiently distinct to be viewed as separate explanatory devices" (March and Olson 1989: 953–54).

In his critique of March and Olsen, Goldmann (2005: 36–37) suggests three ways of interpreting the two logics, (1) as "*perspectives* from which politics may be seen—contrasting views about what is the essence of politics, contending approaches to the study of politics, or the like," (2) as "*theories* about politics—propositions about what politics is like and why," and (3) as "*ideal types* with which actually existing politics may be compared." He however notes that there is much ambiguity and confusion on what these logics are or stand for, stating that "the logics are ascribed both to scholars and to actors. In the former case they are generalizations about opposing perspectives among analysts. In the latter case they are theories about the way in which actors think and argue" (Goldmann 2005: 38).

Goldmann (2005: 38) argues nevertheless that the logics "must be separable from each other when applied to the same object. We must be able to determine whether a particular piece of research represents one 'side' or the other 'side.' It must be possible to assess the separate contribution of each factor in the explanation of action." Why? Because he seems to accept that these logics are "ideal types," which by definition (*qua* Weber) "must be mutually excluding" (Goldmann 2005: 38). Yet he finds it hard to settle down on this issue and indeed questions such a clear separation of the two logics. A way out that Goldmann suggests is to separate the "methodological question of the construction of concepts" from the "the empirical question of what influences actors." He (Goldmann 2005: 38–39) thus states that "if they turn out to be interrelated in an empirical sense ... this is not a problem but a finding."

What to make of this verdict? Most students of IR would more or less agree with Goldmann on the mutual exclusivity of the two logics. That much is evidenced by the multitude of published works that seek to theoretically and empirically make a stronger case for one or the other logic. Most would also agree with Goldmann on more or less attributing the position of adjudication to the 'empirical side' of the issue. Why do scholars continue to advocate one or the other of the two logics, *as if* we did not know very well that these are theoretical constructs, that is, *ideal-types*, which can be more or less useful as methodological tools to theorize about social reality and as such cannot simply be 'representing' social reality? Thinking of these two logics as ideal-types falls well within the methodology of rational reconstruction of the ideal speech situation that Habermas uses to reconstruct the formal pragmatics of communicative action. For Habermas, as explained up above, the ideal speech situation is a counter-factual conceptual tool in the sense that it is their absence or contradicting them that needs justification rather than their operation. Are the logics of consequences and appropriation also counter-factual conceptual tools (*qua* ideal-types)?

That these logics are deployed counter-factually has to do with the fact that we treat them *as if* they were not theoretical constructs—ideal types—deployed for the sake of analysis, especially in doing empirical research. However, knowing very well that they are ideal types, even the most objectivist/positivist social scientist would not expect to find them empirically operational in such a 'pure' form. If one were to use the language of statistical hypothesis testing, one could say that this researcher's interest is in rejecting a null hypothesis which stipulates that 'the logics are *not* empirically operational'. This would counterfactually indicate that the logics are perhaps more or less operational. Yet, isn't this possibility already implied in the 'as if' treatment of these logics? Doesn't the 'as if' imply that the logics are *perhaps* operational *and perhaps* not? A *perhaps* that neither negates nor affirms them, but rather, at the same time, both negates and affirms the possibility that the logics are operational.

Moreover, performative non-contradiction in the specific case of Habermas' theory of communicative action entails that a constative speech-act rests on non-contingent presuppositions and that the latter should not contradict the assertive proposition of the former. Applied to the logic of consequences performative non-contradiction would imply that the core (foundational) assumptions of the logic should not be contradicted by the claims made in the logic. The latter is about choosing among a set of alternatives depending on their consequences, *ceteris paribus*. However, what often goes unnoticed is that the actor is presumed to act simultaneously upon knowledge about consequences and non-knowledge, with the latter rhetorically encapsulated in the *ceteris paribus* clause, which is a necessary component of the logic of consequences. The clause of *ceteris paribus* is nothing but an 'as-if' representation of social reality, which implies that the actor is not solely driven by expectations of consequences but rather by an ambiguous combination of expectations of consequences and an 'as if' condition that 'covers up' the non-knowledge implied by the *ceteris paribus* clause.

However, by definition of the logic of consequences, a responsible actor is one who acts upon expected consequences. It would then be irresponsible (or, if you will, irrational) to act with no knowledge on expected consequences, or more broadly put, non-knowledge. Put in Habermas' Jargon, the logic of consequences suffers from a necessarily constitutive performative contradiction. Because of the non-contingent presupposition of *ceteris paribus* clause in the logic, the actor *cannot not act simultaneously responsibly and irresponsibly*. Put differently: the actor can act rationally and responsibly according to consequences if, and only if, the actor irrationally and irresponsibility relies on non-knowledge *qua* a *ceteris paribus* clause. This is quite *aporiatic*.

How does the logic of appropriateness fare on the dimension of performative non-contradiction? According to this logic actors choose an appropriate course of action based on their sense of identity and by matching obligations that ensue for their sense of identity to a specific situation (March and Olsen 1989: 23). This means, as explained by Sending (2002: 452), that "*the appropriateness of an action cannot be established apart from or prior to the constitutive rules that define the normative space (understood as what is appropriate) of the particular political community.*" Actors should thus comply with the constitutive rules that define the normative space of their particular political community if they want to act appropriately. Consistency between the constitutive rules and the sense of identity is necessary for acting appropriately. Because rules and identity are necessarily interpreted to be meaningful, this means that the actors must interpret their sense of identity and the constitutive rules in a consistent way. What are the *ex ante* criteria, if they exist, for such a consistency of the two interpretations to happen? And what are the conditions of possibility for this consistency? Does it mean that actors need to engage in self-regulation or mutual regulation to create and maintain such a consistency in interpreting the constitutive rules and their sense of identity? This would imply that certain regulative-like rules are the conditions of possibility of the 'right' interpretation of constitutive rules.

What is the meaning of this modifier 'right'? It cannot mean 'appropriate' because it constitutes and defines what is 'appropriate'. Does it thus mean that some 'in-appropriate', 'other-than appropriate', is the condition of possibility of the 'appropriate'? Actors hence 'inappropriately' regulate their interpretations of the constitutive rules of the normative space of their political community and their sense of identity to be able to act 'appropriately'. What does it mean to regulate in an inappropriate way? It perhaps means to de-regulate in a certain way. It also perhaps means to create inconsistency in a certain way. Isn't this a performative contradiction *par excellence*? In order for the actors to act appropriately they *cannot not* enact a performative contradiction between the *conditions of possibility for acting* appropriately and *acting* appropriately; they act in-appropriately to create consistency between interpretations of the constitutive rules and interpretations of their sense of identity.[18] This seems to accord with Wittgenstein's (1953: PI201) statement that

> no course of action could be determined by a rule, because every course of action can be made out to accord with the rule. ... if everything can be made out to accord with the rule, then it can also be made out to conflict with it.

Paraphrasing Wittgenstein we can say: every course of action can be made out to be appropriate. And if everything can be made out to be appropriate, then it can also be made out to be inappropriate. And so there would be neither appropriateness nor in-appropriateness. And I would add: they will be both appropriateness and inappropriateness, always already if there is anyone of the two.

In sum, most students of IR recognize that the two logics of consequences and appropriateness are theoretical constructs. Yet many treat them *as if* they are not, that is, using them counterfactually in the sense of trying to reject the null hypothesis which says that 'the logics are *not* empirically operational'. Because there is no smoking-gun type test of this null hypothesis, the position which is always ultimately taken *ad infinitum* is that the logics are perhaps operational and perhaps not. The two logics are thus inherently much more ambiguous than their respective proponents suggest. Moreover, both logics are aporiatic. The logic of consequences suffers from a necessarily constitutive performative contradiction because of its non-contingent presupposition of *ceteris paribus* clause. The actor *cannot not act at the same time responsibly and irresponsibly*. Likewise, the logic of appropriateness also suffers from performative contradiction. In order for the actors to act appropriately they *cannot not* enact a performative contradiction between the *conditions of possibility for acting* appropriately and *acting* appropriately; they act in-appropriately to be able to act appropriately. *Both logics are autoimmune logics.*

Logic of practice

The notion of practice has of late come to dominate social theory.[19] Yet, as put by Turner (1994: 2), "the concept is deeply elusive. What are 'practices'? What is being referred to, for example, by Wittgenstein's phrase 'the inherited background against which I distinguish between true and false'? What are 'tacit pictures of the world'?" These are few of the questions that drive the discourse about practice in social theory. Answers to these questions in social sciences and theory form a very rich and diverse spectrum of approaches and even schools.[20]

The notion of practice is by and large meant to signify that our explicit interpretations and understandings are secondary to what we do *qua* practices. That is, practice is used "to identify the locus of this background understanding or competence that makes it possible to follow rules, obey norms, and articulate and grasp meanings" (Rouse 2006: 5503). This does not imply however that practice is dissociated from the background conditions of its enactment. To the contrary, as put by Taylor (1985: 33–34),

> the vocabulary of a given social dimension is grounded in the shape of social practice in this dimension; that is, the vocabulary would not make sense, could not be applied sensibly, where this range of practices did not prevail. And yet this range of practices could not exist without the prevalence of this or some related vocabulary.

Practice theorists usually see in practice no more than performances that enact the practice, that is, the ongoing performative reproduction of the practice. However, as astutely noted by Rouse (2006: 505),

> these performances cannot be properly characterized or understood apart from their belonging to or participation within a practice sustained over time by the interaction of multiple practitioners and/or performances.

One key aspect of the debates on the role and characteristics of practice is the relationship to language or vocabulary articulation. *On the one hand*, many theorists argue that "what unites the disparate performances of a practice is their linguistically-expressible background, which amounts to the practitioners' shared but unarticulated understanding of their performances" (Rouse 2006: 515). *On the other hand*, there is the notion of *tacit* knowledge, that is, "a level of competence or performance prior to, and perhaps even inaccessible to verbal articulation ... what can be shown but not said, or competently enacted only when freed from verbal mediation" (Rouse 2006: 515).[21]

This creates a dilemma for the social theorist/scientist. *On the one hand*, we cannot grasp the logic of practice except through conceptual constructs which, argues Bourdieu (1990: 11), more or less objectify practice and its logic through instruments such as "genealogies, diagrams, synoptic tables, maps ... transcription in writing." Yet, *on the other hand*, any attempt to articulate the logic of practice is tantamount to destroying it as such. We therefore are faced with "the practical contradictions of scientific analysis of a practical logic," retorts Bourdieu (1990: 11). This, using Habermas' jargon, is nothing but performative contradiction. Bourdieu (1990: 12) explains that:

> if practices had as their principle the generative principle which has to be constructed in order to account for them, that is, a set of independent and coherent axioms, then the practices produced according to perfectly conscious generative rules would be stripped of everything that defines them distinctively as practices, that is, the uncertainty and 'fuzziness' resulting from the fact that they have as their principle not a set of conscious, constant rules, but practical schemes, opaque to their possessors, varying according to the logic of the situation, the almost invariably partial viewpoint which it imposes, etc.

Practices are nothing but their very performativity, that is, says Bourdieu (1990: 18), practices are

> things that one does because they are the 'done thing', 'the right thing to do', ... they may have, strictly speaking, neither meaning nor function, other than the function implied in their very existence, and the meaning objectively inscribed in the logic of actions or words that are done or said in order to 'do or say something'.

Bourdieu (1990: 86) thus argues that "practice has a logic which is not that of the logician." He (1990: 19) indeed draws a direct opposition "between logical logic, armed with all the accumulated instruments of objectification, and the universally pre-logical logic of practice." What are some key features of this *pre-logical logic* of practice, in addition to escaping the purview of the formal logic of the logicians? Four such features stand out clearly in this respect:

1. *The logic of practice is not logic in the sense of Aristotelian logic.* Not only the logic of practice escapes any attempt to formalize it through any axiomatic, it also defies the rigor or constancy of logical logic for the sake of economical simplicity and successful polysemy. This implies that scientific analysis (as we usually think of it) cannot operationalize the logic of practice. Yet the logic of practice is based on a system of objectively coherent generative and organizing schemes. The latter function in the practical state as an often imprecise but systematic principle of selection (Bourdieu 1990: 86, 91, 92, 102).

2. *The logic of practice is always temporal*, unfolding in time and cannot be separated from the flow of time. This means that the logic of practice inherently possesses the property of irreversibility and is directional. Yet the logic of practice can only be grasped by de-temporalizing it (Bourdieu 1990: 81, 92, 98).
3. *The logic of practice cannot be theoretically apprehended and does not operate through concepts.* Analysts' attempts to do so end up missing everything that makes the temporal reality of practice in process (Bourdieu 1990: 81, 100).
4. *The logic of practice makes practice totally present in the present.* In doing so it excludes attention to itself (Bourdieu 1990: 92).

Although Bourdieu's logic of practice seems to be a stand-alone notion, especially given the numerous explications and qualifications that Bourdieu deploys to clarify it, its meanings, operations and implications cannot be satisfactorily grasped separately from the concept of *habitus*. Bourdieu characterizes the habitus as that which gives "disproportionate weight to early experiences," (Bourdieu 1990: 54). The habitus consists of

> systems of durable, transposable dispositions, structured structures predisposed to function as structuring structures, that is, as principles which generate and organize practices and representations that can be objectively adapted to their outcomes without presupposing a conscious aiming at ends or an express mastery of the operations necessary in order to attain them.
> (Bourdieu 1990: 53)

He explains that the habitus is a "a product of history" and that it

> produces individual and collective practices—more history—in accordance with the schemes generated by history. It ensures the active presence of past experiences, which, deposited in each organism in the form of schemes of perception, thought and action, tend to guarantee the 'correctness' of practices and their constancy over time, more reliably than all formal rules and explicit norms
> (Bourdieu 1990: 54)

Bourdieu describes the habitus as "the principle of the continuity and regularity", that is, as a "system of dispositions" which is

> a present past that tends to perpetuate itself into the future by reactivation in similarly structured practices, an internal law through the law of external necessities, irreducible to immediate constraints.
> (Bourdieu 1990: 54)

At the same time Bourdieu (1990: 54) describes the habitus as the principle "of the regulated transformations" that neither "extrinsic, instantaneous determinisms" nor "purely internal but equally instantaneous determination of spontaneist subjectivism" can explain. The habitus is thus both the principle of continuity and transformation. This means that the habitus, *qua* "acquired system of generative schemes," "makes possible the free production of all the thoughts, perceptions and actions inherent in the particular conditions of its production—and only those" (Bourdieu 1990: 55). This thus constitutes an "infinite yet strictly limited generative capacity", which can be understood, argues Bourdieu (1990: 55), only if we transcend oppositions such as "determinism and freedom, conditioning and creativity, consciousness and the unconscious, or the individual and society."

Therefore, the *habitus* acts "as a system of cognitive and motivating structures", that is, as "a world of already realized ends—procedures to follow, paths to take—and of objects endowed with a 'permanent teleological character'" (Bourdieu 1990: 53). However, this teleology is not in the usual sense of the term. Rather, explains Bourdieu (1990: 55), the teleological "limits are set by the historically and socially situated conditions" of the productions of the habitus and by "the conditioned and conditional freedom" that the habitus provides. This means that what occurs as event "is as remote from creation of unpredictable novelty as it is from simple mechanical reproduction of the original conditioning" (Bourdieu 1990: 55). What Bourdieu is dealing with here is, of course, nothing but the usual structure vs. agency problematique as usually posed in social theory. He (Bourdieu 1990: 55) thus suggests that the ways through which the generative capacities of the habitus operate are such that the generated practices "cannot be described either as the autonomous development of a unique and always self-identical essence, or as a continuous creation of novelty." Why?

Bourdieu's answer is that the genesis of practice is the result of "the necessary yet unpredictable confrontation between the *habitus* and an event" with the proviso that such an event "can exercise a pertinent incitement on the *habitus* only if the latter snatches it from the contingency of the accidental and constitutes it as a problem by applying to it the very principles of its solution" (Bourdieu 1990: 55). In other words, an event would not count as such if the habitus does not make it as such—the habitus defines the horizon of possible events, the horizon of what counts as "'reasonable', 'commonsense', behaviors (and only these)" (Bourdieu 1990: 55–56). This implies that what counts as practices in the present "cannot be deduced either from the present conditions which may seem to have provoked them or from the past conditions which have produced the *habitus*, the durable principle of their production" (Bourdieu 1990: 56).

How do we then account for practices? Bourdieu (1990: 56) explains that it can only be done "by relating the social conditions in which the *habitus* that generated them was constituted, to the social conditions in which it is implemented." This means that practices are not fully driven by the external determinations of the immediate present. It rather means that such a relative autonomy of the present practices is the result of a combination of the immediate present conditions and "the *habitus*" *qua* "embodied history, internalized as a second nature and so forgotten in history", *qua* "active presence of the whole past" (Bourdieu 1990: 56). Does this mean that practice is not autonomous if we take into account the habitus? The answer is no, if however in a strongly nuanced way. As summed up by Bourdieu (1990: 56), the autonomy of practice

> is that of the past, enacted and acting, which, functioning as accumulated capital, produces history on the basis of history and so ensures the permanence in change that makes the individual agent a world within the world. The *habitus* is a spontaneity without consciousness or will, opposed as much to the mechanical necessity of things without history ... as it is to the reflexive freedom of subjects 'without inertia'.

The habitus thus acts so as to enable

> practices to be objectively harmonized without any calculation or conscious reference to a norm and mutually adjusted in the absence of any direct interaction or ... explicit coordination.
> (Bourdieu 1990: 58–59)

And in the face of crises and critical challenges that might disrupt the operation of the habitus, the latter protects itself

> through the systematic 'choices' it makes among the places, events, and people that might be frequented ... by providing itself with a milieu to which it is as pre-adapted as possible, that is, a relatively constant universe of situations tending to reinforce its dispositions by offering the market most favorable to its products.
> (Bourdieu 1990: 61)

We are faced here with what Bourdieu terms as "the most paradoxical property of the *habitus* ... the paradox of the information needed in order to avoid information," that is, the habitus purges "information by rejecting information capable of calling into question its accumulated information, if exposed to it accidentally or by force, and especially by avoiding exposure to such information" (Bourdieu 1990: 60–61). This means that the habitus produces filtered and sanctioned strategies that enable "agents to cope with unforeseen and constantly changing situations," all the while creating the appearance that these strategies are "determined by the future" (Bourdieu 1990: 61). This however does not always work, especially when, as explained by Bourdieu (1990: 62),

> the sense of the probable future is belied and when dispositions ill-adjusted to the objective chances because of a hysteresis effect ... are negatively

sanctioned because the environment they actually encounter is too different from the one to which they are objectively adjusted.

The habitus remains operational only when "the conditions in which the *habitus* functions have remained identical, or similar, to the conditions in which it was constituted" (Bourdieu 1990: 62). However, this does not mean that the habitus is rigid; rather the habitus 'self-servingly' (for the lack of a better word) "adjusts itself to a probable future which it anticipates and helps to bring about because it reads it directly in the present of the presumed world, the only one it can ever know" (Bourdieu 1990: 64).

According to Bourdieu, we cannot speak of the logic of practice (or practice *tout court*) without the habitus. Can we, for instance, say that the habitus is a structure and the logic of practice is a corresponding logic of agency? The answer is *simultaneously* a very *light* yes and a very *light* no. *On the one hand*, as it transpires from the above numerous statements by Bourdieu, the habitus is much more than just a structure, although it does possess some features of structuring. *On the other hand*, the habitus is not an agent in the sense that agency is given in the literature on structure/agent or objectivist/subjectivist opposition approaches.

Bourdieu's elaboration of the notion of logic of practice (and practice) is more or less an extension of his formulation of how to think beyond the opposition objective/subjective. He argues that the logic of practice cannot be apprehended theoretically in its 'logic' as such without turning it into something else, into a logician's logic. Is this possible though? Isn't Bourdieu in his refusal to theorize the logic of practice engaging nonetheless in a sort of theorizing? Isn't Bourdieu by seeking to avoid falling into performative contradiction at the same time engaging into another sort of performative, a performative that *does* through *saying it* what it does not want to do? That is, Bourdieu does through saying what he says he should not do and as such the saying negates itself by claiming to avoid negating itself, the saying undermines itself in striving not to undermine itself. Isn't this also a sort of performative contradiction? In other words: can Bourdieu not contaminate the logic of practice (with 'some' theory) by saying that he is not theorizing about it? Bourdieu desires to avoid—theorizing—speaking about a theory of the logic of practice. Yet isn't he already too late? Hasn't he already spoken of the logic of practice at the very moment he is saying that we cannot apprehend it theoretically? Isn't he engaged in a sort of rational reconstruction via a *negativae* of sorts?

Via *negativae*, as already introduced in previous chapters, is a general mode of thinking and speaking wherein we speak of what the 'thing' cannot be or is not; negative theology is a classic example of this mode of speaking. The claims that this mode makes by negating them are everything that the thing in itself cannot be. The thing in itself is thus a pure transcendental, extra-linguistic, and cannot be appropriated through any discourse or language. This leads to major conceptual, logical, and linguistic difficulties since "every claim to the 'things themselves' is a claim within and by means of the resources of certain semi-systems, linguistic and otherwise, situated within the framework of a complex set of contextual presuppositions" that can never be saturated (Caputo 1997a: 17). This makes the via *negativae* mode fall prey to the logic of the double bind of *negation/denegation*. *On the one hand*, negating the 'thing' under consideration, and, *on the other hand*, simultaneously negating everything else except the 'thing' under consideration, that is, denegating.

Bourdieu does not theorize the logic of practice and yet discusses it *as if* from a theoretical distance, *as if* by putting a *theoretical space* between '*his thinking* about the logic of practice' *and* 'the *logic of practice*'. Bourdieu does not discuss this *theoretical space*. He does however desire to delineate the boundaries of this space, that is, the boundaries of theorizing the logic of practice, boundaries that seek to protect the logic of practice from becoming the logic of the logicians. He therefore does not want to contaminate the 'substance' of the logic of practice; he only speaks of the discernable 'contours' of the logic of practice *as done in practice in the present*.

Bourdieu argues that the moment we try to move beyond the logic of practice *qua* present, that is, to speak (*ex ante* or *ex post*) of the logic of practice, outside the practice, it is not a logic of practice anymore—the logic of practice is present presence, or would not be a logic of practice anymore. The 'is' of the logic of practice can only be as 'presence'. Yet Bourdieu speaks of the logic of practice outside/after/before practice, outside its presence; what is he speaking about? Is he not speaking formally about the logic of practice in the absence of the 'can only be present logic of practice', that is, formally in the absence of any 'content' or 'substance' of the logic of practice that he refuses to theorize? Can we not say that Bourdieu's via *negativae* discourse about the logic of practice is a rational reconstruction of the conditions of possibility of practice geared toward keeping the practice as, and only as, a present presence?

Using via *negativae* discourse in making the case of a logic of practice that cannot be theorized without turning it into a logical logic (of the logicians) that has nothing to do with practice, Bourdieu, by the same token and in a much stronger way, does what he struggles not to do, that is, he theorizes the logic of practice into a sort of hyper-theory of practice. In other words: Bourdieu insists in calling it the logic of practice and yet he endeavors to argue that it is a logic *without* logic. This *without* thus engenders a double politics of passing through an aporia, that is, "the very impossibility of … deciding when exactly we are without or 'not without'" (Bradley 2001: 143–44). The logic of practice is thus a logic 'without and not without' logic.

Yet despite such undecidability in the logic of practice Bourdieu insists on advocating it and deploying it, why? Bourdieu seems to take a wager on this logic of practice, a wager that cannot be theorized or for that matter rationalized. It is a wager which is quite reminiscent of Blaise Pascal's wager, the task of which, according to Rescher's (1985: 19–21) interpretation, is to show that belief is rationally warranted—in the specifically prudential (not evidential!) mode of rational warrant ... the Wager argument is aimed at *motivating* belief rather than at *demonstrating* its validity—at inaugurating faith where it is lacking rather than consolidating it where it exists.

Let's be clear: Bourdieu does not explicitly take a wager. However, his continuous insistence, careful qualification, and detailed elaboration have the effects of a wager. Bourdieu's rhetoric is much like Pascal's in presenting

> the Wager as an argument to address the doubter in such a way that neutralizes the passions that interfere with conversion. ... The visibly pragmatic argument of the Wager is in fact part of a greater epistemic argument
> (Velchik 2009: 6–7)

In other words, Bourdieu is struggling with an epistemic argument; he is trying to make an epistemic argument without objectifying the logic of practice and thus using it. How are we thus to understand all the qualifications and justifications that Bourdieu engages into? I propose that Bourdieu is taking a wager and this tacit wager is anchored in a certain *faith*, not a religious faith, but nevertheless a *faith* of sorts. It is not a faith in/for anything; it is not a faith with any content. Rather, it is a call for a faith without faith in any dogmatism or anything else. It is, as put by Caputo (1997a: 61), "to believe without quite knowing in what it is believed'." Yet, this faith without faith is not faithlessness either since it is indeed presumed to anchor Bourdieu's wager-based rhetoric (for a 'logic of practice') that he deploys to speak of it. Bourdieu's tacit faith is a *faith without* and *not without* faith. Bourdieu has a certain faith in an un-theorizable, should-not-be-theorized, 'logic of action', which is undecidable and is a 'without and not without' logic, and all his arguments if taken together amount to defending why we would wager on such a faith.[22]

Logic of habit

In our daily lives, our actions are not always driven by cost/benefit calculations, norms, or the enactment of certain practices. In fact, says Hopf and like-minded scholars of social theory, much of what we do is done habitually—unintentionally, unconsciously, involuntarily, and even effortlessly (Hopf 2010: 3). That is: a large part of our actions are driven by a logic of habit which produces "both the awareness, and unawareness, of much of reality" (Hopf 2010: 3). In discussing various types of orientation of social action, Weber introduces traditional behavior and ingrained habituation as one of four orientations;[23] he says (1968: 24–25):

> Strictly traditional behavior ... lies very close to the borderline of what can justifiably be called meaningfully oriented action ... it is very often a

matter of almost automatic reaction to habitual stimuli which guide behavior in a course which has been repeatedly followed. The great bulk of all everyday action to which people have become habitually accustomed approaches this type. Hence, its place in a systematic classification is not merely that of a limiting case.

The logic of habit operates through a sort of automatism to eliminate "rationality, agency, and uncertainty" (Hopf 2010: 6). That habits are ubiquitous does not make them less ambiguous though. Indeed, habits, says Hopf (2010: 3), simultaneously "imply actions by giving us ready-made responses to the world that we execute without thinking" and "prevent other behavior by short-circuiting any need to think about what we are doing." Using a much stronger language, Hopf asserts that "what is perceived as reality is already pre-cooked in our heads" (2010: 3), and that "social structures of habit not only may account for what we perceive and do, but also for what we do not perceive or do" (2010: 4).

Many years ago John Dewey (1930: 175–76) explicitly stated that "the more numerous our habits the wider the field of possible observation and foretelling. The more flexible they are, the more refined is perception in its discrimination and the more delicate the presentation evoked by imagination." Dewey (1930: 66–67) went further to suggest that "habit is an ability, an art, formed through past experience." The kind of habits, argued Dewey (1930: 66–67), determines whether it plays the role of a constraint or limitation that is nothing but a "repetition of past acts adopted to past conditions" or becomes the sources of "new emergencies."

Habits have multiple origins; they "may be learned through instrumental cost–benefit calculations or through socialization to some normative standard. They may also be acquired through mere imitation of what does, and does not, go on in the world around us" (Hopf 2010: 4). Cognitive need, social structural reinforcement and urgency due to time constraints all feedback positively to sustain existing habits (Hopf 2010: 4). Yet habits are not immune to changes, even when they are very durable and promoters of status quo. We thus find it "instrumentally rational to break habits if the cost of following them becomes too high" and we recognize it as such. We also break habits when we are "convinced that they are normatively unacceptable," or when after enough "conscious deliberation" we decide to override them for some reason or another (Hopf 2010: 5). Moreover, argues Hodgson (2004: 653),

> reasons and beliefs themselves depend upon habits of thought. Habits act as filters of experience and the foundations of intuition and interpretation ... Even rational optimisation, if and when possible, must involve rules. In turn ... rules have to become ingrained in habits in order to be deployed by agents. ... rational choices themselves are always and necessarily reliant on prior habits.

Habits are believed to have their own logic which is quite peculiar. Hopf (2010: 8) claims that "the logic of habit ... denies agency to actors who are acting habitually;" yet he also asserts that "habits are necessary for agency." He is thus arguing that habits seem to play the role of a condition of possibility of reflective agency since, were it "not for much of our daily lives being ordered automatically, without reflection, we could not feasibly be reflective agents in other domains" (Hopf 2010: 8). That is: habits provide a taken-for-granted background that constrains what is imaginable without negating the possibility of reflective agency (Hopf 2010: 9). If habits are such that they 'constrain', does this imply that they are 'agents' on their own, or perhaps structures?[24]

John Dewey suggests that habits have what he terms as "positive agencies." How to think of such an 'agency' that seems to restrict 'agency' as we usually think of it? Dewey (1922: 42) explains that "the essence of habit is an acquired predisposition to ways or modes of response." William James (1893: 143) thought that "habit is thus the enormous fly-wheel of society, its most precious conservative agent." Thorstein Veblen (1898: 390) also wrote of habit as "a coherent structure of propensities" which can be realized in unfolding activity. Veblen (1898: 188) argued that "man mentally digests the content of habits under whose guidance he acts, and appreciates the trend of these habits and propensities."

This discussion of habits can be roughly speaking summed up in four main points. First, habits are ambiguous and not as clear cut as Hopf seems to suggest. Second, even if habits constitute a background which is more or less taken for granted, this background not only possesses 'agency' in a certain way but this 'agency' can be negative in the sense of limitation as well as positive in the sense of creativity. Third, habits are latent in the sense that, as explained by Hodgson (2004: 652), "if we acquire a habit we do not necessarily use it all the time. It is a propensity to behave in a particular way in a particular class of situations." Fourth, habits are enacted in moments of some sort of actors' performativity without self-reflexivity preceding or accompanying the enactment. Taken together these four features raise a number of questions.

If habits are latent backgrounds, how do we theorize about them? Only after the fact, that is, the fact that we, analysts or actors in moments of *ex-post* reflexivity and observation, categorize some act as habit. Isn't this a sort of rational reconstruction since at the moment that a habit is enacted it is not perceived as such but rather done without much thinking about it? And if habits are recognized as such only through an *ex-post* rational reconstruction, this is a reconstruction of what? Plausibly it is a reconstruction of features that make it a habit, that is, according to the above discussion, features like automatism of sorts that eliminates "rationality, agency, and uncertainty" from the act at the very moment it is enacted. However, Dewey and others do attribute to habit a certain 'agency' *qua* propensity to behave in a certain way. We can thus (perhaps) say that this 'agency' is the condition of possibility of actors' agency as we usually speak of it and that we can assert this through a methodology of (*ex-post*) rational reconstruction.

And if habits are instances of a non-reflexive performativity, what are the conditions of felicity or failure of such a performativity (that is, if we adhere to Austin's and Searle's version of speech-act theory)? It appears, according to Hopf and others, conditions such as non-reflexivity, cognitive needs, social structural reinforcement, and urgency to act due to time constraints allow habits to be efficacious conditions. Doesn't this mean that actors who enact habits should not fall into performative contradiction in the sense that they should not realize that these are 'habits' (which are a sort of automatism as defined by Hopf and the others)? Put differently: it will be a performative contradiction to act from habit while simultaneously realizing that one is acting from habit—that is, one cannot act reflexively from 'habit'. Should that occur, one would effectively be acting reflexively in a certain way (such as, for example, via instrumental rationality) which is anything but acting from 'habit', as defined by Hopf and others. This would mean that for habits to be as such they should abide by the law of performative non-contradiction. This means that *we* cannot *think* of habits (in an *ex-post* way) except as being based on the law of performative non-contradiction. The law of performative non-contradiction thus seems to be a condition of possibility of 'habits'.

Having said this, what is this 'agency'—habit *qua* 'agency'—that Dewey and others speak of? This is an ir-reflexive, ir-rational, and *automatic* 'agency'. The person acts automatically (out of habit, unconsciously) and thus he/she repeats something from the past. By acting out of habit the person is acting in an 'automatic' way. *Automatos* comes from Greek and means 'acting of one's will' with *matos* meaning 'willing'. This means that a person who is acting out of habit is *willingly* acting to repeat habits from the past. *On the one hand*, the person is acting ir-reflexively and unconsciously (out of habit as usually understood), and, *on the other hand*, the person is 'acting of one's will' (that is, automatically) to repeat past habits. Isn't this a performative contradiction? Indeed, the condition of possibility of acting out of habit is automatism which we usually use to mean it to be 'ir-reflexive'. Yet 'automatos' means 'acting of one's will'. Therefore: the person is *thought* to act ir-reflexively, out of habit, and in doing so the person is *thought* to 'act of one's will', that is, automatically. Isn't then the *argument* for 'habit' (as presented by Hopf and the others) indeed an *argument* for an 'ir-reflexive reflexivity' or, perhaps, an 'ir-reflexive willingness' to act? A performative contradiction *par excellence*! In sum: it seems that we cannot think of habits except as based on the law of performative non-contradiction but at the same time this very conceptualization is a performative self-contradiction which makes *'acting out of habit' an ir-reflexive reflexivity*. Acting out of habit is an *undecidable performative contradiction/non-contradiction*.

Moreover, acting automatically out of habits implies that one is reiterating some acts from the past. That is, these acts can be transported, translated, or transposed from context to context. Does this mean that they are a-contextual, some sort of universal or a-historical, infinitely malleable since there is potentially a countless number of contexts? It will be far-fetched to believe that our acts can be of this kind. However, this means then they are more or less changed from context to context—they are at the same time repeated and transformed. Because there is no limit to the variety of contexts that we are faced with, it implies that acting out-of-habit is always iterable—*iterability is a constitutive feature of habits.*

We can even say that habits are operations of traces and supplementarity at work. *On the one hand*, what gets reenacted is but traces and not 'actual' acts from the past since it will be impossible to efface the effects of context on human acts, that is, to replicate exactly an act from the past. *On the other hand*, for such traces of past acts to be meaningful in a current context, they must be supplemented with other meanings, a sort of contextual adaptation. Therefore, what an actor who acts out of habits does is to supplement traces of past acts with addenda that add 'something' (such as new meanings or reinterpretation of meanings) to the traces without replacing them. This makes *habits* the results of *a combination of the operations of trace, iterability and supplementarity.*

However, a trace is never fully present but rather always self-effacing. This means that habits—*qua* reenacted traces—are never fully present. In other words, the moment a person begins to act out of habit, that is, reenacting a trace of some act from the past, not only is it not a trace anymore, that is, the element of trace effaces itself from the act. It is also the case that the present act is an act of invention. Put differently: acting out of habit means simultaneously repeating some act from the past to efface it and inventing some new act. This implies that a *person who acts out of habit simultaneously undermines the habit*—acting out of habit is self-perverting. Acting out of habit is supposed to protect or at least preserve this habit from any change but ends up precisely erasing the habit—enacting of the habit and erasing are concurrent. Isn't this a case of autoimmunity? The logic of habit is an *autoimmune* logic and thus acting out of habit is always *out-of-joint*.

The undecidability and autoimmunity of logics of action

All five logics of action are found to be undecidable and autoimmune. The logic of communicative action, which is anchored in the law of performative non-contradiction, is always already accompanied with performative contradiction, and as a result Habermas' presuppositions of criticizable validity claims are always autoimmune and out-of-joint with their claims. The logic of consequences, which is supposed to account for how actors act rationally and responsibly, is found to be one of simultaneous responsibility and irresponsibility, and rationality and irrationality. The logic of appropriateness, which is supposed to explain how actors act appropriately, is found to be anchored simultaneously in in-appropriateness and appropriateness. The logic of habit, which is supposed to explain and account for how actors act automatically, ir-reflexively, and repetitively, is found to be ir-reflexive and reflexive-based, autoimmune and out-of-joint. The logic of practice, which is supposed to be beyond theorization, is found to be simultaneously hyper-theorized, if in a negative way, and rhetorically protected through a wager, a sort of Pascalian wager anchored in an a-theoretical faith, a faith which is 'without and not without' faith.

All five logics are aporiatic and these inherent aporias cannot be resolved. These aporias are fissures in the discourse which regulated argumentative economies seek to resolve in order to preserve some theoretical consistency. These aporias are much more than antinomies because

> The aporia must be endured as interminable in order for experience to take place ... the deconstructive aporia is perhaps best formulated by showing how the conditions for the possibility of something also prove to be the conditions for its impossibility.
>
> (Norris 1982: 49)

This means that the politics of aporia is the possibility condition for (re-)invention, change and transformation. We thus need to recognize the *chance* that inheres in the politics of aporia, the *chance* that would make continuously possible responsible decisions within a recast form of 'logic of action', a politics of logic *without* logic, a paradoxical politics of an illogical logic of action. This thereby means remaining open to more future arrangements within the promise that autoimmunity and the impossible politics of aporia create and sustain; a promise which is always already originarily pervertible, but not necessarily perverted. And yet one can—or even perhaps cannot not—fall victim to the pressure of an *urgency* to close the argument on the 'logic of action' in a certain way. However, for such a decision for closure to occur within the terrain of undecidability there has to be an *interruption* (Derrida 2002b: 296). How can we however interrupt without eradicating the chance of a future, an open future? How to interrupt without forcing a closure that can only be fatal to the future? It thus seems that if there is any possibility of going beyond the politics of aporia of the various 'logics of action', such a possibility might only come in the form of a never-resting negotiation between an interruption to decide and a future to-come. Going beyond the politics of aporia means then a never-resting, continuous shuttling negotiation between a structural promise of going beyond the aporia and momentarily interrupted and halted, yet always already disrupted, senses of 'logic of action'.

9 Concluding *without* a conclusion

I am at the point in the book where I must—I am supposed to—conclude[1] my works of deconstruction of various theories of IR and draw implications for IR theory and beyond. Right here I face the first difficulty: Can I conclude without falling in the very traps that the work of deconstruction divulges and makes visible? Can I conclude the works of deconstruction? Isn't the work of deconstruction infinite? Must not the work of deconstruction remain unfinished, always already, by definition, by construction, by practice, and, some would even say, ethically? Moreover, have I reached any 'conclusion'— as usually understood—in any of the chapters, that is, conclusions that I can perhaps attempt to summarize in here? Isn't any attempt to summarize but an attempt to stop more or less arbitrarily the restless shuttling negotiation of the works of deconstruction? Can I escape the restless negotiation without violence to my very text, my very attempt to re-think IR in other ways? Isn't such an attempt a performative contradiction *par excellence*? Why do— must—I fear falling into performative contradiction anyway? Can I escape a seemingly unstoppable logic of practicing performative contradiction? And in raising these questions, am I not being ungrateful to the reader after all these chapters and hundreds of pages by not providing a summary of the 'gist' of the arguments of the book?

Much like the norm of writing books these days which dictates that an author must provide an introduction to the book, there is a norm or at least an expectation that one must provide a conclusion. Much like the preface of the book is both a chance and a threat to the future of the book, to the possibility that the book might be read, so too the conclusion is a threat and chance to the possibility that the book might be read in its entirety. Reading the introduction and/or the conclusion of a book before or instead of the in-between chapters is indeed quite common a practice. Any author would readily argue that such a reading misses the 'gist' of the book, the core of the book, even if one gets more or less the arguments (if in a summary form) of the book. What about a book which claims to be about *showing* deconstruction at work? One of the declared goals of this book is 'to show the *experience* of deconstruction at work'—to *live* the experience of deconstruction by following the textual weaving of the writing itself, the rhetorical narrating of the works of deconstruction. How can one summarize this? When engaging in an experience of deconstruction, the text is not just a medium—it is more importantly the 'flesh' and 'bone' of deconstruction at work.

I must therefore submit that because the work of deconstruction is always an interminable experience, the only type of conclusion that one can conclude with is, cannot not be, but a concluding *without* a conclusion, a concluding that obeys the logic of without. I must also submit that such a way of concluding *without* a conclusion is a 'saying concluding', a saying that seeks to do what it says, which is to interrupt the process of restless negotiation between the negotiable, that is, the finite number of words and phrases that I can possibly write in this book, and the interminable experience of deconstruction which incessantly calls for more deconstruction. This is an impossible task that I am putting myself to. Perhaps I can address it by possibilizing it in a certain way, by making it into an impossible possible, a possible which necessarily remains haunted by a trace of impossibility. I am thus facing a double bind.

On the one hand, I feel the urge and quite frankly the 'external' pressure (actual or to come) to try to summarize—harvest—the fruits of the eight chapters of the book.

On the other hand, I hear, and I am haunted by, the irresistible call of deconstruction for more deconstruction—a call for deconstructing this conclusion of the book.

This leads to an extremely difficult question. That is: What would a deconstruction of this conclusion amount to as I am writing it (this conclusion)?

I think that my only way out, which is an impossible passage through the aporia of the double bind, is to continue experiencing deconstruction even in this last phase of the book. This is no easy task because this 'last' experience of deconstruction (in this book) must be two simultaneous experiences—one experience is to deconstruct my very 'harvest', and, the other experience is to deconstruct this very deconstruction of the 'harvest'. How can I do this? How can I live these two experiences, together? Yet, isn't this what I promised to do in Chapter 1 of the book? Is my promise already perverted? I am not sure that it is not, at least not yet.

Perhaps, I must deconstruct the 'harvest' of my book by reading Arfi reading Arfi as a sort of deconstruction as self-inheritance. This is a paraphrasing of Samir Haddad's (2006) title "Reading Derrida Reading Derrida: Deconstruction as Self-Inheritance." In this essay, Haddad (2006: 505) argues that

> Derrida inherits from himself through self-citation. In citing himself while at the same time modifying his citation, Derrida sets into motion a deconstruction of his own text that he does not seem to anticipate. It is this movement of deconstruction that enables Derrida's text to live on. Derrida inherits from himself through self-citation.

I should perhaps try to follow Derrida by engaging in self-citing—that is, from the chapters where I carry on the deconstruction of IR theory—and then in citing myself modify the citations so as to set into motion a deconstruction of my own text, a deconstruction that I should not be able to anticipate. Only in this way would my works of deconstruction explicated in the various chapters of the book be enabled to live on, that is, to be harvested as living-on, as *survivant*.

Yet, isn't this a truism, at least at the level of practice? In other words, it is without doubt that writing a conclusion that harvests—or, more accurately, seeks to harvest—the fruits of the book is a self-citation, a self-inheritance through self-citation. This means that any conclusion of a book is almost always a self-inheritance, by default. However, not every self-inheritance is a deconstruction. Is it not? Didn't I argue throughout the book that every repetition is always already a transformation, that is, every repetition, including summaries, falls under the law of iterability? However, because a summary, a 'harvesting', is also a saying 'in other words' it is also at the same a supplementation; it falls under the law of supplementarity. Moreover, the saying 'in other words' also opens the door for and falls under the law of dissemination, which opens a snag in the 'summary' and blows up any horizon of meaning, if without completely eradicating the latter. This thus makes—cannot not make—the 'in other words' a movement of différance which differs from the 'main' text (or chapters) and defers the closing in or closure of the summary—a harvest—of the book in the conclusion.[2]

This raises the question: Is the conclusion part of the book or is it a 'new book' which is emerging from behind the 'borders' of the book already written? This implies that writing a conclusion that seeks to 'harvest' the fruits of the book is an undermining of the closed book *par excellence*.

How can one avoid this (assuming for the moment that one wants/must want to avoid this)? Perhaps, by being faithful to the book and not letting one's writing take threatening 'tangents' at the end of the book. However, it is at this point that one must be careful so as not to fall back into a position of metaphysics of presence, that is, by trying to replicate exactly what was said in the chapters of the book in a succinct way, which easily verges on reification. In other words, one should be careful to remain faithful to the work of deconstruction launched in the various chapters, but how? I think that one can do this by continuing the work of deconstruction through a harvesting *qua* living-on, *survivre*. But what is this 'living-on' [survivre]?

The structure of a text is, according to Derrida (1985: 122), a "*surviving* structure."[3] The law or logic of this survival is however not one of 'either/or'. Rather, it is one than admits Aristotelian impossibilities such as defying the laws of identity, non-contradiction, and the excluded middle; that is, a text that "neither lives nor dies; it lives *on*. And it 'starts' only with living on" (Derrida 2004: 82–83). This implies for Derrida (2007c: 24) that "We are all survivors who have been granted a temporary reprieve [*en sursis*]." However, the meaning of Derrida's notion of survival "*is not to be added on* to living and dying." Rather, survival, in the sense of Derrida (2007c: 26), "is originary: life *is* living on, life *is* survival [la vie *est* survie]." Derrida (2007c: 26) explains that:

> "All the concepts that have helped me in my work, and notably that of the trace or of the spectral, were related to this 'surviving' as a structural and rigorously originary dimension. It is not derived from either living or dying. No more than what I call 'originary mourning', that is, a mourning that does not wait for the so-called 'actual' death."

He (Derrida 2007c: 51–52) also says that:

> Survival is an originary concept that constitutes the very structure of what we call existence, *Dasein*, if you will. We are structurally survivors, marked by this structure of the trace and of the testament. But, having said that, I would not want to encourage an interpretation that situates surviving on the side of death and the past rather than life and the future. No, deconstruction is always on the side of the *yes*, on the side of the affirmation of life. Everything I say—at least from *'Pas'* (in *Parages*) on—about survival as a complication of the opposition life/death proceeds in me from an unconditional affirmation of life. This surviving life beyond life, life more than life, and my discourse is not a discourse of death, but, on the contrary, the affirmation of a living being who prefers living and thus surviving to death, because survival is not simply that which remains but the most intense life possible.

What to make of this notion of the text as structure of survival when one re-thinks the practice of writing a conclusion at the end of a book (a book that proposes to re-think IR theory)? How does it affect one's writing? Or, perhaps, more accurately, how does it affect the very process of 'harvesting' at the end of the book?

According to Haddad (2006), the act or practice of self-citing or self-inheritance of an author, which is what writing a conclusion is, is an instance of autoimmunity. Is this a problem? No, since as explained by Haddad (2006: 506), it is "precisely in being autoimmune that this act of self-citation allows the Derridean text to survive, living on beyond the control of its author." I thus perhaps must make my act of self-citation in the conclusion an autoimmune one. And hence my works of deconstruction can survive and live on beyond my control, that is, my attempt to 'harvest' the works of deconstruction, and hence halt the movement of deconstruction in them.

This leads to the following question: How can I engage in self-inheritance?[4] According to Derrida (1994: 16), an inheritance is always necessarily *heterogeneous*, that is, inheritance must be marked by a difference without opposition, by "a 'disparate' and a quasi-juxtaposition without dialectic." Derrida (1994: 16) explains that:

> An inheritance is never gathered together, it is never one with itself. Its presumed unity, if there is one, can only consist in the *injunction to reaffirm in choosing*. 'One must' means *one must* filter, sift, criticize, one must

sort out several different possibles that inhabit the same injunction. And inhabit it in a contradictory fashion around a secret. If the readability of a legacy were given, natural, transparent, univocal, if it did not call for and at the same time defy interpretation, we would never have anything to inherit from it. ... One always inherits from a secret—which says 'read me, will you ever be able to do so?' The critical choice called for by any reaffirmation of the inheritance is also, like memory itself, the condition of finitude. ... The injunction itself (it always says 'choose and decide from among what you inherit') can only be one by dividing itself, tearing itself apart, differing/deferring itself, by speaking at the same time several times—and in several voices.

How does this affect, or what does it imply for, my ruminations concerning my impossible possible conclusion? One way to answer this question is by paraphrasing Derrida as follows:

Writing a conclusion qua self-inheritance will never be a conclusion that is gathered together. My conclusion will never be one with itself. The presumed unity of my conclusion, if I could ever write one, can only consist in the injunction to reaffirm in choosing, that is, my writing, my 'saying in conclusion' will be but an injunction to reaffirm in choosing from what I have already written in the previous chapters. This means that I will have to filter, sift, criticize what I have already written in previous chapters; that I will have to sort out several different possibles that inhabit the same injunctions that I have already explicated in the previous chapters. Such an injunction to reaffirm will be a translation, a translation inhabited in a contradictory fashion around a secret; that is, as if I were looking for a secret that I somehow missed or could not reach in my previous chapters. That is: as if I were looking for a secret which says read me in your conclusion, will you ever be able to show me in your conclusion? Why is it so? Simply because if the readability of my legacy were given, natural, transparent, univocal, if it did not call for and at the same time defy interpretation, I would never have anything to inherit from it, that is, in trying to 'harvest' my fruits in a conclusion. Yet such an injunction through affirmation, such a hunting of a secret which seems to have hidden itself in the chapters, which always say 'choose and decide from among what you inherit' from the previous chapters, can only be one and happen by dividing itself, tearing itself apart, differing/deferring itself, by speaking at the same time several times—and in several voices, that is, by being a différantial movement, différance.

And this is where autoimmunity kicks in through the movement of différance that self-inheritance, that is, writing a conclusion, cannot escape *qua* text. By seeking to filter and distill the conclusion from the book, by seeking to 'harvest' the fruits of the book, I would end up "betraying the heritage *in the name of* the heritage" (Derrida 2005c: 89). This is reminiscent of what Haddad says in commenting on Derrida's re-reading himself, in citing from his *Politics of Friendship* in developing his *The Reason of the Strongest*. Haddad (2006: 512) writes that:

> It is not simply that Derrida wrote one text, and now writes another that incorporates and extends the first, confining it to the past. In the writing of the second text, more specifically in this citation in the second text, Derrida does not just change the name. For I want to argue that in this act of citation the first text is transformed in a fundamental way—*Politics of Friendship* no longer stays the same in appearing as it does in 'The Reason of the Strongest'. ... it is in the interjection that Derrida makes—'I could have in fact said "autoimmune" force'—that this transformation occurs.

Therefore, according to Haddad (2006: 516), "Derrida thus inherits from himself ... and this event of self-inheritance produces an event of deconstruction." How? Haddad (2006: 516) explains that "any act of citation involves a certain suspension of defences, since the boundaries marking the limits of the text cited are ignored so as to lift out the passage in question," that is, citation is transgressive, and "this particular act of citation involved an insertion and suggested modification of the original text," which "compounds the already violating nature of the act."

Therefore, in writing a conclusion one engages an operation of self-deconstruction through autoimmune self-inheritance. This implies that the author *qua* author is compromised, since, as explained by Derrida (2005c: 45), autoimmunity "consists not only in committing suicide but in compromising *sui-* or *self-*referentiality, the *self* or *sui* of suicide itself." This leads to what Haddad (2006: 517) describes as "when the self is acting according to a process of autoimmunity, there is perhaps no longer a stable self that can be seen to be putting itself to death, and suicide starts to lose its meaning."

Therefore, in seeking to continue the work of deconstruction through the conclusion *qua* autoimmune self-inheritance, I am not seeking to commit suicide since the latter is not meaningful anymore due to autoimmunity. Not only (as already pointed out in the introductory chapter) is an author never truly sovereign in his/her writing. Sovereignty, as explained by Derrida (2005c: 101), "is always in the process of positing itself by refuting itself, by denying or disavowing itself; it is always in the process of autoimmunizing itself."

This is what I think my conclusion can be. In other words, I do not see the need or the necessity, or, more accurately, I find it a dauntingly impossible task, to write a conclusion that seeks to harvest the fruits of the book in a conventional way. This is not a 'conventional book' and how can I thus write a 'conventional' conclusion for it.[5] Does this imply that I am breaking the promises that I made in the introductory chapter?

On the one hand, some readers might say yes indeed. I would not disagree *too much* with them, if in a certain way however. Why? First, I presented this book as a re-thinking of IR theory, as *theories* and as *process of writing* these theories. Whereas I addressed these two aspects more or less in the various chapters, I remained silent on how to conclude the chapters, that is, on what is a conclusion of a process of work deconstruction. This is an issue which is rarely addressed in IR theory or social theory/science in general. And this is for a good reason since, as discussed in the introductory chapter, closure is of the 'essence' of a 'good', 'consistent' and 'productive' theorizing. One issue that has struck me always in reading Derrida is that it is very rare (in fact, I can't remember a contrary instance) where Derrida wrote a conclusion for anyone of his works, that is, a conclusion in the conventional sense of the term that summarize the 'gist' of the writing. *Et pour cause*! How can one write a conclusion in the conventional way and remain faithful to the injunction of deconstruction, that is, not to fall back into the metaphysics of presence (of the written book)?

Second, as discussed up above, writing a conclusion is inescapably an operation of autoimmune self-inheritance. However, isn't this always already the future of any written book? That is: this book will inescapably fall under multiple operations of deconstruction—in fact, *qua* self-deconstruction—whenever it is read by other readers, and as a matter of fact, even by me!

Third, I promised in the introductory chapter that my writing will be a work of deconstruction 'at work' (so to speak) through and through, an experience of deconstruction at work. As such I could not let my writing fall into the trap of attempting a closure through a 'harvesting' of the fruits of the book. This is a promise that I hope I have kept.

Fourth, throughout the chapters of the book I spent much time speaking of the conditions of possibility and impossibilities of the various texts that I read. I also included a discussion of the condition of possibility and impossibility of writing a book that seeks to re-think IR theory via works of deconstruction. Likewise, this conclusion is in fact an exploration of the conditions of possibility and impossibility of writing a conclusion for such a book.

And *this is my other hand*, that is, I disagree with readers that might claim that I have not kept my promises.

Perhaps, some readers might now say: fine, but what is in here for IR theory, even after it is re-thought through works of deconstruction? In Chapter 1, I wrote "I thus read to re-affirm the possibility of other readings, readings that keep the possibility of futural readings always already open." Is there a better way for doing this than not writing a conventional conclusion at all? Indeed, the only writing that can truly avoid the threat of closure is the one that is not written at all. I do this strategically so as to let "My text deconstructs itself through itself by ineluctably putting into practice the various aporias that inhere not only in the theories that I critique but also in the conceptual, logical, rhetorical strategies and 'pseudo-concepts' that I rely on in trying to make the cases that I claim to be making" (quoted from Chapter 1). In other words: I want to show how the work of deconstruction reaffirms the need for concluding a book *without* providing a conventional conclusion but instead by displacing the meaning and role of a conclusion and then grafting it with new meanings and roles that are not really meanings and roles in the usual sense of these terms. In short: I want to write a pseudo-conclusion. Let me put in another way: In all my works of deconstructing IR theories (texts) I endeavored to bring forth the aporias that inhere within these theories (texts) without seeking to lift or resolve these aporias. I instead claimed that these aporias are the chances for IR theory to have a future. In this conclusion I hope to have shown that re-thinking IR theory through works of deconstruction also shows that the conclusion of such an effort *qua* book is deconstructible and can only be a pseudo-conclusion, a concluding *without* a conclusion. And I promise (one again) that this falls well within the claim made in Chapter 1 that

> I suggest a rethinking of the process of theorizing which does not seek closure through resolving these aporias but rather structurally makes non-closure as the condition of possibility of theorizing itself.

A concluding *without* a conclusion is what, I think, structurally keeps the non-closure of the theorizing process. In this book, which I endeavored to keep structurally unfinished, I hope that I more or less (sometimes more than less and sometimes less than more) experience what Derrida describes in the following three statements:

> The suspension of negotiation I am talking about, on the contrary, is a suspension that cannot be theoretical; theory is not possible, or rather, theoretism is not possible.
>
> (Derrida 2002: 13)

> One can conceive of the closure of that which is without end. Closure is the circular limit within which the repetition of difference infinitely repeats itself. That is to say, closure is its playing space. This movement is the movement of the world as play.
>
> (Derrida 1978: 250)

> Negotiation operates in the very place of threat, where one must [*il faut*] with vigilance venture as far as possible into what appears threatening and at the same time maintain a minimum of security—and also an internal security not to be carried away by this threat. This, too, is negotiation.
>
> (Derrida 2002: 16–17)

With this I hereby conclude *without* a conclusion what I hope will have remained a book *qua* experience in *negotiation* with a re-thinking of IR theory through works of deconstruction.

Notes

1 Re-thinking via deconstruction *qua* affirmation

1 Unfortunately, this continues to be misunderstood as meaning that text is all what (Derrida thinks) there is (that is, texts in the usual meaning of the term such as this text that I am writing using my computer).
2 His two books 'Glas' and 'Circumfessions' speak miles to an absence of genre as we usually speak of it, yet without completely annihilating the possibility of a completely radical genre.
3 All of these authors have also published other works that draw on Derrida's (and others') thinking in addressing various IR issues.
4 Campbell's previous work *'Writing Security'* also draws on Derrida and others in re-thinking US foreign policy and the notion/practice of national identity.
5 This does not imply that Derrida is not liable to critique and in fact many have indeed done that, even his friendliest friends (e.g., Jean Luc Nancy and others). Yet the richness of his thinking is far from having been seriously tapped into by the students of IR theory.
6 Although I am using these labels I would not be able to define or even give examples of such works. In fact, most scholars of IR who are labeled in this way do not believe in these labels. Rather, it is their opponents or others in general who call them as such; deconstructing the genealogies of these should prove a very interesting work.
7 This point will be explicated later on in the book though the logic of *parergonality*.
8 As put by Derrida in *Of Grammatology* (1974: 49): metaphysics of presence is 'the exigent, powerful, systematic, and irrepressible desire' that anything can be being-present to itself, self-presented, self-authenticated; it is a belief in a fixed presence beyond the reach of play of language and historical conditions in general such as positing an essence.
9 As put by Derrida, "One could call play the absence of the transcendental signified as limitlessness of play, that is to say as the destruction of ontotheology and the metaphysics of presence" (Derrida 1974: 50). See also Heidegger (2007: 432).
10 This 'must' is not to be understood in a normative sense but rather as a *constitutive* necessity, or if you will as an 'empirical' necessity.
11 In Hart's terms (1989: 67–68), "To deconstruct a discourse is to show, by reference to its own assumptions, that it depends upon prior differences which prevent that discourse from being totalised. This dependence does not lead to an infinite regress, however, for at a certain level these differences can be thematised under the rubric of trace, différance or archi-écriture – words which name a mode of difference which is transcendental yet incapable of forming a firm ground."
12 Diction is defined in the Oxford English Dictionary as "1. the choice and use of words and phrases in speech or writing; 2. the style of enunciation in speaking or

singing." Building on Derrida's comment on 'contradiction', 'diction', and 'scription', one can say that efforts to get rid of 'contradictions' in a text (such as a theory) is indeed trying to get rid of the very efforts to assert a self-identity of the text (or theory); in other words: there is no self-identity to a text without the movement of self-contradiction (the problematique of the identity is discussed more thoroughly in Chapter 5).

13 It in fact is an aporia; that is, I find myself on an aporiatic path: all what I wrote up to this point is through and through impregnated with Derrida's thinking and work, even when not acknowledged as such. Using a very Derrida-like phrase I would say that Derrida's thinking is through and through a constitutive outside of this book, since the very first pages of this chapter. And yet I must interrupt and declare my 'strategy' of dealing with Derrida due to a certain exigency of a certain style of writing, a writing style that has become more or less conventional in IR academic literature.

2 'Testimonial faith' in/about IR philosophy of science

1 Methodology is not about methods but rather about the logic of concepts formation. For a brief overview of concept formation see: Sartori (1970; 1991) and Bevir and Kedar (2008).
2 See, for a recent illustration of the debates, the exchanges between Monteiro et al. (2009), on the one hand, and Bohman (2009), Chernoff (2009), Jackson (2009), Kurki (2009), and Mercado (2009), on the other.
3 It is remarkable that neither the word 'faith' nor the phrase 'leap of faith' are mentioned in the index of the book despite of the fact that they provide a crucial anchor of Jackson's notion and pragmatics of wagers (as he clearly stipulates it). In a footnote (ft. 5, 236) Jackson adds the following qualification: "Or—as Nick Onuf (1989, 46), a little less poetically, puts it—a 'psychocultural penchant'." Whereas this looks on the face of it as different, I do not think that it is; speaking of penchant or faith does not change the beyond explanation nature of what Jackson wants to alert us to.
4 Fisch (2008: 608–9) explains that we must "distinguish between two very different, if related, twentieth century philosophical turns toward language." A first turn "represents a decidedly modernist redirecting of philosophical attention from an outward focus on the perennial problems of philosophy (such as the problem of evil, the mind-body problem, the nature of the good, etc.) toward a reflexive, inward focusing on the normative vocabulary of philosophical discourse itself (asking, rather, what we can coherently mean by using the term 'evil' and 'good,' indeed, what it means to mean anything at all; or how to understand and analyze utterances about what is better than what, and, indeed, what it means to understand and analyze any utterance at all)," and a second turn "undertook a systematic reflection on the very role of language in mind, thought, knowledge and practice."
5 The first task of deconstruction is "a systematic elucidation of contradictions, paradoxes, inconsistencies, and aporias constitutive of conceptuality, argumentation, and the discursiveness of philosophy" (Gasché 1986: 135). The contradictions, aporias, and inconsistencies that deconstruction operates on are fissures in the discourse which a regulated (conceptual) economy seeks to avoid in order the preserve the ethico-theoretical consistency and decision basis that seem to orient the discourse (Gasché 1986: 136). What the operation of deconstruction attempts to do therefore is to provide an account for these contradictions by 'grounding' them in ungrounded 'infrastructures' (Gasché 1986: 142).
6 I might be accused of 'eclectic or selective' reading. In a certain way this is true. However, in deconstruction every reading cannot be otherwise, and yet every

reading is always already contaminated and contextualized by non-selected texts and contexts. Every text is weaved into a textuality (ies) that cannot be totalized.
7 Destinerrance stands for "a fatal possibility of erring by not reaching a predefined temporal goal in terms of wandering away from predefined spatial goal" and as such remains "connected to *différance*, that is, to a temporality of differing and deferring, without present or presence, without ascertainable origin or goal" (Miller 2006: 893–94).
8 Derrida 1988: 62. Iterability will be more thoroughly discussed in Chapter 5.
9 I am only introducing 'supplementarity' very briefly in this chapter, that is, just enough to serve the purpose of the work of deconstruction in this chapter. I will address it more thoroughly in Chapter 5 where I deconstruct 'identity'.
10 Jackson also clearly demarcates faith from science and thus he is much in line with Weber's thinking on the issue.
11 Examples of undecidable terms are: *pharmakon* which means and functions both as poison and remedy, *supplement* which means and functions both as addition and replacement, and *différance* which means and functions as difference and deferral, spacing and temporization.
12 Pascal (2002: 44) introduced his notion of wager as follows: "Let us then examine this point, and say, 'God is, or He is not.' But to which side shall we incline? Reason can decide nothing here. There is an infinite chaos which separated us. A game is being played at the extremity of this infinite distance where heads or tails will turn up. What will you wager? According to reason, you can do neither the one thing nor the other; according to reason, you can defend neither of the propositions. Do not, then, reprove for error those who have made a choice; for you know nothing about it. 'No, but I blame them for having made, not this choice, but a choice; for again both he who chooses heads and he who chooses tails are equally at fault, they are both in the wrong. The true course is not to wager at all.' Yes; but you must wager. It is not optional. You are embarked. Which will you choose then? Let us see. Since you must choose, let us see which interests you least. You have two things to lose, the true and the good; and two things to stake, your reason and your will, your knowledge and your happiness; and your nature has two things to shun, error and misery. Your reason is no more shocked in choosing one rather than the other, since you must of necessity choose. This is one point settled. But your happiness? Let us weigh the gain and the loss in wagering that God is. Let us estimate these two chances. If you gain, you gain all; if you lose, you lose nothing. Wager, then, without hesitation that He is."
13 This is illustrated in Jackson's statement that "Certainly the passion with which partisan advocates of one or another methodology insist on the ultimate rectitude of their preferred way of producing knowledge often reminds one of doctrinal disputes, as does the way in which such advocates not infrequently mistake the forceful pronouncement of their most basic presuppositions for arguments that might warrant those presuppositions—or for arguments that anyone other than those who already believe the proffered doctrine would find at all compelling" (Jackson 2010: 189).
14 James (1979: 20). I read Jackson and James together because of Jackson's declared faith in his analyticism. It would be interesting to also conjointly read other works by, say, John Dewey, Charles Pierce, Richard Rorty, whom Jackson cites in his book.
15 Rorty (1999: 155) charges William James of "getting off on the wrong foot" when, in making his case for *The Will to Believe*, "James accepts exactly what he should reject: the idea that the mind is divided neatly down the middle into intellect and passion, and the idea that possible topics of discussion are divided neatly into the cognitive and non-cognitive." Rorty (1999: 160–61) declares that "the kind of religious faith which seems to me to lie behind the attractions of both utilitarianism

and pragmatism is, instead, a faith in the future possibilities of moral humans, a faith which is hard to distinguish from love for, and hope for, the human community." He (1999: 161) then adds, "What is distinctive about this state is that it ... carries us beyond the imagination of the present age of the world." Isn't this in some ways what Jackson would have called for had he not stopped short by just advocating a 'faith' in the wagers without pursuing further toward the implications of what it means to call for such a 'faith'? Perhaps.
16 John Dewey (1947), another key father of American pragmatism, opted for a different perspective on faith. He endeavored to articulate a secular alternative to traditional religions in his book *Common Faith*.
17 I go back to these pseudo-notions in the following chapters to explore them in more depth, as needed.
18 Demiurge—joining together *demos* (people) and *ergos* (worker)—is in Platonism what shaped the material world.
19 The logic of denegation is *"neither* both negation and affirmation *nor* either negation or affirmation," but is rather both a *'neither this nor that'* and *'both this and that'* logic (Taylor 1992: 175).

3 *Khôra* as the condition of possibility of the ontological *without* ontology

1 I have already introduced in the previous chapter, if briefly only, the logic of without. As discussed later, this logic is expressed in Derrida's phrases *'pas sans pas'* and *'sans sans sans'*, which can be translated as 'without without without', 'not without not', 'without not without', and 'step without step' (Derrida 1986b; 1987a,b).
2 Bhaskar does not completely reject his previous work since, as summarized by Patomäki, "in *Dialectic* (or *Plato Etc*.) there is no systematic reassessment of earlier concepts and arguments but rather an indication that dialectical CR [Critical Realism] is simply a new and fully consistent layer added on top of the foundation of CR (i.e. *Realist Theory* and *Naturalism*)." (Patomäki 2010: 62, ft. 11).
3 My task is in some ways similar to Patomäki who states that "the point is not to replace CR with another philosophical position, or to launch an overall attack against the arguments of Realist Theory and Naturalism, but to show important ambiguities and limitations of CR and indicate a non-sectarian and future-oriented way forward," (Patomäki 2010: 62). Although I sense the importance of his critique, I do not think that he is going far enough away from the 'Bhaskarian' spirit or path since he seeks to re-place all Bhaskarian adoptions of 'science' with more contemporary ones. I think that this is overdue but yet still doesn't go far enough to raise the questions that I pose in this chapter, questions that, for example, some physicists are raising nowadays (see for example: d'Espagnat 2006).
4 For an interesting study on the early history of the concept 'ontology', see: Mora (1963).
5 I think it worthwhile mentioning Patomäki's recent work in which he quite persuasively uses a Bhaskarian scheme (so to speak) to refute Bhaskar's lack of attention to contemporary science, thereby shaking the ground beneath Bhaskar's approach to the possibility of naturalism in social sciences by raising fatal questions about Bhaskar's intransitives (Patomäki 2010).
6 Ontological monovalence is based on the premise that "any instance of real negation can be analyzed in purely positive terms" (Bhaskar 1993:7).
7 As pointed out by Patomäki, who is by no means an enemy of Critical Realism (CR), "many of those students who become interested in CR do not apply CR ideas to doing better substantive research but, rather, are content to iterate Bhaskar's criticisms of positivist and post-positivist approaches, in spite of contrary advice," and that "to a significant degree, the foundational, texts of CR—*Realist Theory and Naturalism*—have Indeed, been beyond philosophical and scientific

criticism within the critical realist camp." It is remarkable that Patomäki is presenting one of the strongest 'internal' critique of Bhaskar's Critical Realism in this article (Patomäki 2010: 60–61). This is to be contrasted with his 2002 book which falls more squarely within more conventional readings of Critical Realism (although one should mention that Patomäki does bring in elements from Habermasian and Foucauldian thinkings in an attempt to go beyond a few of Bhaskarian strictures).

8 Yet Derrida's dealings with the discourse of negative theology goes far beyond than a mere illustrative purpose. As put by Caputo, "Derrida finds in negative theology a unique and irreducible idiom for answering the call by which we are all addressed, whether our discursive inclinations are theological, antitheological, or a/theological (or something else). For we are all—this is Derrida's wager—dreaming of the wholly other that will come knocking on our door (like Elijah), and taking language by surprise, will tie our tongue and strike us dumb (almost), filling us with passion. That is why, with the passage of the years, Derrida's relationship with negative theology became more and more affirmative and more and more linked by the impossible. The difference is that in negative theology the *tout autre* always goes under the name of God, and that which calls forth speech is called 'God,' whereas for Derrida every other is wholly other (*tout autre est tout autre*)" (Caputo 1997: 3–4).

9 St. Augustine states that "God is wise without wisdom;" God is "good without goodness;" God is "powerful without power."

10 Although I have already introduced *khôra* in the previous chapter, I continue the discussion herein by detailing some of its 'features'.

11 Bhaskar's book '*From East to West*' addresses the topic of God and related metaphysical issues. I think that this work deserves more than just a mention in a footnote. Indeed, in this work Bhaskar engages Bhaskar against Bhaskar for another more or less different Bhaskar; thus making a call for a work of deconstruction (Bhaskar 2000). To put it very briefly and somewhat inescapably hastily and violently: Without pretending to be able to explain herein the full play of logic, grammar, rhetoric, and concepts that Bhaskar is struggling to clarify, it seems to me that he is stuck within a hyper-essentiality mode of speaking of man and God and he is, at the same time, seeking to go beyond it (see, for example, p. x and p. 47). Yet Bhaskar (p. ix) had nonetheless already retreated and circumscribed his task by declaring upfront in this book that "the essential thesis of this book is that man is essentially God (and therefore also essentially one, but also essentially unique); and that, as such, he is essentially free and already en-lightened, a freedom and enlightenment which is overlain by extraneous, heteronomous determinations which (a) occlude and (b) qualify this essential fact. To reclaim and realize his essential freedom, man has to shed both the illusion that he is not essentially Godlike and free and the constraining heteronomous determinations (constituting an objective world of illusion, duality and alienation) which that illusion grounds. To become free or realize his freedom man must thus shed both the illusions that he is not (essentially) and that he is (already, only and completely) free!" I think that Bhaskar is trying to reach closure too soon too fast and thereby falling back into the metaphysics of presence (or absence for that matter). It seems that in this book Bhaskar is a hyper-Hegelian, more Hegelian than Hegel or any of his disciples. I think that ultimately many of these tensions in Bhaskar's thinking, as it has often been the case, are in part related to the fact that he has not developed a philosophy or theory of 'sign', 'language', and semiotics' (ironically, despite his opposition to what he terms as 'linguistic fallacy', (2000: 25, 26)). As put by Nellhaus, "the critical realist philosophy of Roy Bhaskar has not provided an adequate account of signs. Indeed, in two of his recent books (1993; 1994) Bhaskar devotes merely a diagram and two pages of sketchy text toward analyzing the sign

structure, even though without signs, meanings are literally unthinkable. The undertheorization of signs results in theoretical and political difficulties. For example, the exact ontological status of signs and meanings is unclear, which casts a shadow over Bhaskar's larger ontological framework, especially since he holds that society is concept-dependent" (Nellhaus 1998: 1). Moreover, Bhaskar makes 'categorial realism' (2000: 33–39) an indispensable element of Transcendental Dialectic Critical Realism. Yet he never engaged in a sustained analysis/deconstruction of the very concept of 'category', or, more precisely, 'the category of category' or 'categoriality'. In this respect Bhaskar remains very Aristotelian in his approach to language, despite the fact that his philosophy is a sustained practice of continuous linguistic/categorial bifurcation upon bifurcation, even when augmented with borrowings from East Asian languages/systems of belief and thoughts (for a deconstruction of 'categoriality' see: Derrida 1982: 175–205).
12 I explain this notion of 'saying the ... ' later in the book when I discuss it in the context of 'saying the event' in the next chapter.
13 Note that I have already considered more or less this issue from the perspective of the philosophy of science in the previous chapter.
14 However, even if one were to accept such a view, it does not diminish the importance of the question on the logic of such an approach. That is: this chapter can be understood as proposing another logic, a logic different from customarily adopted Aristotelian or even Hegelian logics. It would, for example, be worthwhile pursuing Patomäki's exploration to new possibilities that an adoption of quantum logic (more than just quantum physics as a science) would open up for/against/beyond Critical Realism. Such a venture (drawing, for example, on Plotnitsky's work in this regard) would go far in emphasizing the issues that I raise in this chapter, and the book more generally (Plotnitsky 1993; 1994).
15 Although Jackson refuses to call it a 'framework', the vocabulary that he develops is indeed an *enframing* of what he believes is ordinarily tacit in the conduct of IR inquiry.
16 This means that *différance* is a differing and a deferral relationship between 'terms' which turns these 'terms' into a concatenation of presence and absence. Each term contains within itself both the mark of a past element and the mark of the relation with a future element.

4 Rethinking the 'agent-structure' problematique

1 The issue has also been the subject of long-lasting debates in practically all disciplines of social science, philosophy, and humanities.
2 As argued much later on in this chapter, I think that Wight's frame (or *parergon*) makes him see dualism almost everywhere in the literature (*ergon*) that he critiques, thus falling under the logic of *parergonality*.
3 See Walker (1993) on this issue as applied to IR.
4 Obviously, Wight cannot use an ontological argument to *ground* these "basic" building blocks of his ontology. As already discussed in the previous chapter, Bhaskar in his 1993 book introduces the notion of "absenting absence" or radical negativity as the ground for his previous ontological model that Wight is still adhering to.
5 This notion of play of differences is "no longer simply a concept, but rather the possibility of conceptuality, of a conceptual process and system in general." *Différance*—qua systematic play of differences without positive elements that 'differ'— is the condition of possibility for the formation of concepts, conceptuality, and conceptual systems in general. Derrida explains that "this does not mean that the *différance* that produces differences is somehow before them, in a simple and unmodified—in-different—present. *Différance* is the non-full, non-simple, structured and differentiating origin of differences." (Derrida 1982: 11)

6 Wight had earlier written in the book, without much explanation, "the self, or agent" and "the notion of self refers to an individual's sense of identity, personality, and perception of the social world." Is the 'self' the same as the 'agent'? Is the 'self' the same as 'identity'? Although these might be minor issues for Wight and thus he did not explicate them, they are important questions that do speak to the heart of Wight's problem of ontological prioritizing. See Chapter 5 where I deconstruct the notion of identity.
7 I prefer to speak of sovereign subject rather than of freedom of subjectivity as Wight does (following Spivak). Of course the two are not strictly separable; yet there are important differences between them.
8 In discussing the space of infrastructures, Gasché (1986: 180) notes that "because it is situated beyond the common opposition of structures and genesis, the space of infrastructures, as the space of structurality in general," and "lies beyond the opposition of system and fragment, whole and part, infinity and the finite."
9 For an interesting discussion of agency in IR classical realism and social-constructivism, see Barkin (2010: 100–17). Barkin's critique is very insightful but unfortunately declares agency to be untheorizable within the confines of classical realism and social-constructivism.
10 Note that Barkin points to this important element of contingency in raising the problem of theorizing agency but stops short of pursuing it further as an entry point for theorizing agency.
11 Note that Austin duly noted the ambiguity of the distinction between performative and constative in his Harvard lectures.
12 I will discuss the notion of 'saying the event' more thoroughly as I deploy it in Chapter VI when deconstructing the 'as-if' rhetorical gesture of trust.
13 I am using quotations marks around 'meta-theory' to alert the reader that the usual meaning of meta-theory is not to be taken for granted and is in fact deconstructible through, for example, the logic of parergonality as discussed in Chapter 3.
14 The inverted marks around 'co-constitution' signify that I am not dealing with the notion of co-constitution as usually understood in IR literature. Rather, it is a co-constitution in the infrastructural space of undecidables.

5 Identity/difference and othering

1 I use quotations around the term 'empirical' to emphasize the point that due to the logic of parergonality a theory/empirical demarcation is deconstructible, and hence cannot be sustained in the usual way.
2 While I remain at the level of generalities on this complex issue, there is much variation and diversity of how West European governments deal with the issue of 'Islam in Western Europe'. Addressing such issues would take the chapter far away from its main line of analysis though.
3 I use 'forward' and 'backward' in quotes to signify non-linearity.
4 The sense of responsibility that I am proposing in this chapter is roughly speaking not in contradiction with Williams' (2005) notion. However, his notions of responsibility and decision do not go far enough in identifying the key roles of undecidability and aporiatic politics. In contrast, the ideas on responsibility and decision that I pursue in this chapter, following Derrida, constitute cornerstones of works by Campbell (1998) on nationalism and responsibility, Zehfuss (2007) on war, memory and responsibility, and Bulley (2010) on ethical foreign policy and responsibility. These authors and I are all seeking to go beyond impasses that IR literature suffers from due to self-imposed limitations. I think that which we are seeking to go beyond in our (and many others') quest is nicely summarized by the following quote from Zehfuss' (2007: 264) book:

Thus we would perhaps rather bypass our responsibility to decide and instead rely on knowledge. Knowledge incurs our trust, and it nicely takes away the agonizing: if we know what is right, we may embark on this course of action in good conscience. This, however, means that in fact we act irresponsibly; we give ourselves over to the illusion that responsibility has been taken care of when we have actually shied away from the very question. The point is that there is no knowledge that may make just or responsible for the blowing-up of civilians abroad, for example in order to protect other civilians.

5 It will be very interesting to draw some policy and institutional implications of this perspective on Euro-Islam, a task that I can only defer to future work.

6 Autoimmunity of trust *without* trust

1 Some of these can be categorized as process-based, characteristic-based, and institutional-based trust, cognition-based and affect-based trust, or calculus-based, knowledge-based and identification-based trust (Misztal 1996; Seligman 1997; Hoffman 2005; Möllering 2006).
2 This approach dominates most, but not all, studies of trust in IR literature (see: Kydd 2006; Hoffman 2005).
3 This leads to the economic paradox of information: that is, you need to estimate the price of information to assess the latter's value, but the price of information cannot be known before the information is known.
4 It is not hard to show how other approaches to trust (such as those based on institutionalism and thin social-constructivism) also end up relying implicitly, if not explicitly, on assuming an as-if leap as the final step to take toward trust.
5 On the one hand, I am using the term 'gesture' in a very broad sense, that is, as a discursive gesture, which is more than just 'rhetorical' (in the usual sense of the term rhetoric). On the other hand, the chapter is indeed a deconstruction of such usual understanding and deployment of 'rhetorical gesture' by showing how even 'casual' and 'discounting' usage is in fact much more constitutive of our actions and decisions such as to trust. I thank Nick Onuf for alerting me to the risk that 'calling the as-if performative act a gesture' might diminish the force of my argument.
6 See Onuf's (1998: 95–98) discussion of the 'as-if' rhetoric in Kant's texts.
7 See Chapter 2 for a deconstruction of the ideal type.
8 Derrida's use of the word 'force' is quite unusual and needs to be understood as follows:

> "The word *force* is indeed very obscure. Force is the common but always different possibility of the 'movement' of 'life', of 'desire', of impulses, of as many metonymies as you like. *Force* is basically a very common name for designating that for which we do not have a clearly expressible concept in a given philosophical code. In philosophy, the value of force has always been in representing what resisted conceptual analysis. Hence the risk. However, what gives me a kind of confidence (perhaps too much confidence) in the word *force* is a truly Nietzschean axiomatic: force is always a 'difference of force'. Force is differential, there is not a substance of force. When one says that force is differential, what one is really saying is that force is not something. It is not a substance, it is not something that is stabilizable. Which would fall under phenomena. So when I name *force* I am thinking of a differentiality, which thus, as differentiality, is also immediately trace or writing, a network of marks, and marks that are codable, like any marks, in iterability, and at the same time inscribe and erase themselves or inscribe and can erase themselves.

What is 'proper' to any mark is the power to erase itself. If a mark has a structure such that – as I often say – *it succeeds only* by erasing itself, it succeeds only by erasing itself. Or it occurs through an erasing ... erasing itself. At that moment force is itself also a weakness. It is a manner of not appearing. When one says force is a weakness and that sometimes, well, there is more force in weakness or that weakness is revealed to be stronger than force, at that moment one is engaged in a discourse on force that no longer has the coherence of classical logic and is no longer reliable. And in fact this is what I am always referring to, at least vaguely, when I say *force*; force is not power, finally. It is not something; force is always inscribed in a space where a ruse (not a subjective ruse but a ruse of structure) is possible, making the weakest strongest."

(Derrida 2002b:35)

9 I thank Nick Onuf for raising this issue.
10 This brief discussion has some similarities and points of contacts with Odysseos' (2007) argument on the subject of coexistence which draws on a Heidegger's thinking. There are however some important differences which I cannot dwell on in here without going far afield.

7 Re-thinking international constitutional order

1 See, for illustrative purpose, the symposium published in Cooperation and Conflict, 2006, 41 (4). The literature cited therein is quite comprehensive.
2 For some illustrative literature on these issues, see Chorev and Babb (2009); Weiss (2009); Duffield (2007); Onuf (2002); Koremenos *et al.* (2001); Johnston (2001); March and Olsen (1998); Keohane (1988).
3 Whenever I am referring to Ikenberry's argument I use his notion of 'power', without implying that I espouse or reject it. This chapter is much more a deconstruction of the role of 'exercise of power' in the theory of constitutional order than a deconstruction of 'power' as such. I use a certain concept of 'violence' to deconstruct the binding institutions as conceptualized in Ikenberry's theory. Doing so is however not meant to convey that 'power' and 'violence' are/are not interchangeable. Only a deconstruction of a specific deployment of 'power' in a situation can help shed light on such an issue. Nor do I think it necessary to theorize 'power' before I can deconstruct a 'certain exercise of power' as deployed in a 'situation'.
4 Schweller (2001: ft 14, 168–169.) succinctly notes that "Although Ikenberry does not make this point, what distinguishes constitutional systems from the alternatives is not the property of systemic binding but rather the institutionalized and purposive nature of constitutional-type binding strategies. International systems of all varieties, from the most imperially integrated to the most fragmented clusters of multiple independencies, essentially bind together in some way discrete political entities. This is because, to be labeled a system of any kind, the constitutive parts must be more or less interconnected so as to form a whole. History records a wide range of international systems. How these distinct patterns of relations among states have functioned to produce order and stability has varied according to the unique set (or lack thereof) of institutions, assumptions, and codes of conduct by which the groups of political entities have attempted to regulate the systems that have bound them together."
5 As put by Derrida (1978: 147–48), "Violence appears with *articulation* ... every historical language carries within it an irreducible conceptual moment, and therefore a certain violence."
6 "Coercive" is used in the sense that Ikenberry uses it.

7 I do not mean to reify states; this is just a shorthand notation for the actors speaking in the name of the state and the likes.
8 See next chapter for a deconstruction of this logic.
9 Likewise, an analysis of the other factors that Ikenberry uses to argue his case for institutional stickiness can also be shown to be a 'saying the event'.
10 As put by Derrida (2005: 30–31), "the great question of modern representative and parliamentary democracy, but perhaps of all democracy, is, in the logic of the turn, of the other turn, of the other time and therefore of the other, of the *alter* in general, that the *alternative to* democracy can always be *represented* as a democratic alternance."

8 The quest for 'illogical' logics of action in IR

1 This list is not meant to be exhaustive, yet it does include the five most used logics of action in IR theory.
2 Although there is definitely a connection with 'action theory' as developed in social theory (and more specifically sociology) I am specifically focusing on the 'logic of action'.
3 For a recent suggestion on how to go beyond the strictures of Aristotelian logic, see Arfi (2010c).
4 All emphasized (italicized) texts within quotes are original, except when stated otherwise.
5 An agreement that is achieved communicatively is, according to Habermas (1984: 266), one that "cannot be imposed by either party, whether instrumentally through intervention in the situation directly, or strategically through influencing the decisions of opponents."
6 Although Habermas draws on speech-act theory, he goes beyond it to differentiate between perlocutionary acts "as a special class of strategic interactions in which illocutions are employed as means in a teleological context of action" and illocutionary acts as communicative actions understood as "those linguistically mediated interactions in which all participants pursue illocutionary aims, and only illocutionary aims, with their mediating acts of communication" (Habermas 1984: 293–95). As summarized by Maeve (2001: 7), "from the speech act theory of Austin and Searle, Habermas takes over the emphasis on utterances rather than sentences as the central unit of analysis. He also associates himself with their move beyond the traditional narrow focus on assertoric and descriptive modes of language use to include—potentially on an equal footing—other ways of using language, such as acts of promising, requesting, warning or disclosing."
7 More generally, Habermas suggests a typology of social action based on four concepts: teleological (expanded to strategic) action, normatively regulated action, dramaturgical action, and communicative action. Likewise, "Habermas divides communicative utterances into three broad categories according to the explicit claims they raise: constative speech acts, which are connected in the first instance with truth claims (assertions are the paradigm here), regulative speech acts, which raise claims to normative rightness (promises and requests are paradigms here), and expressive speech acts, which are connected with claims to truthfulness (disclosures and avowals are paradigms here)" (Maeve 2001: 4).
8 "Communicative competence" of actors, explains Habermas (2001: 29), is "the ability of a speaker oriented to mutual understanding to embed a well-formed sentence in relations to reality."
9 Comparing Habermas and Foucault, Jay (1992: 268) notes that "the challenge Foucault presents to the cogency of performative contradiction thus arises from his positing of the exemplary character of a literary language that is wholly exterior to the intentionality of a speaking subject. If in this use of language there is no

meaningful actor responsible for the speech acts whose locutionary and illocutionary responsible dimensions can be consistent or contradictory, then it makes little sense to employ performative criteria to judge the value of arguments or to characterize social tensions."
10 See Chapter 7 for a related critique of the role of analyst in theorizing about path dependence.
11 It is a law that Habermas has never stopped trying to enforce in his debates with others, for, as put by Jay (1992: 262), "There can, in fact, be few more withering rebukes in his vocabulary than the charge of 'performative contradiction,' which he uses again and again to challenge the validity of his opponents' positions."
12 Lacanians and Žižek might say that when Habermas makes 'performative non-contradiction' into a law he creates the unconscious desire to violate it, and he hence succumbs to it with much *jouissance*.
13 This discussion is generally speaking inspired by Derrida's notion of 'experience'. For a nice and comprehensive, as well as insightful, discussion of Derrida's take on 'experience' see: Direk (1998).
14 See, in this respect, Lenoble's (1995–96) similar critique of Habermas.
15 See Lenoble (1995–96) for a similar discussion of the undecidability of the criticizable validity claims.
16 In his critique of Habermas, Thomassen notes that "Habermas' reconstruction of the necessary presuppositions ... is a construction rather than a neutral reconstruction" (2008: 41). Although I more or less sense what Thomassen means, I do think that the two can be delineated in this way—that is, every construction is inescapably also a reconstruction, even if only partially so (see the discussion of rethinking in the introductory chapter).
17 Citationality, in the sense of Derrida (1988), means that whatever is cited cannot be tied to a subject's intention.
18 Nicholas Onuf rejects the distinction between regulative and constitutive rules as false, arguing instead that all social rules are simultaneously constitutive and regulative (Onuf 1989: 50–52, 61–65; 1998: 173). Would this conflation lift the performative contradiction? It would but only at the price of also nullifying the constructivist concept of logic of appropriateness, since this logic is based on a delineation of regulative from constitutive rules.
19 Practice theory seeks to transcend oppositions such as subject vs. object, observer vs. observed, action vs. perception; oppositions that have been a durable and pervasive in the history of social theory (Bourdieu 1990; Giddens 1984).
20 This has led Rouse (2006: 500) to retort that "perhaps the ubiquity of practice talk merely reflects current intellectual fashion with no substantial conceptual significance, or worse, an underlying theoretical confusion assimilating incompatible conceptions of social life under a superficially common term." Likewise, this has led Turner (1994: 116) to argue that "the idea of 'practice' and its cognates has this odd kind of promissory utility. They promise that they can be turned into something more precise. But the value of the concepts is destroyed when they are pushed in the direction of meeting their promise."
21 Practice theorists influenced by the thinking of Heidegger, Gadamer, Dilthey, and the hermeneutical tradition argue that "the process of interpreting social practices never ends" since anyone engaged in interpretation "brings to it further unarticulated presuppositions, whose articulation would invoke still further background, and so on" (Rouse 2006: 516–17). Put differently: assuming a 'tacit' background of knowledge of sorts is an infinite regress.
22 A note in passing: Much of this analysis can also be applied to Kratochwil's call for a pragmatic turn to theorizing which he succinctly summarizes in the following statement: "I argue for a pragmatic turn in theorizing not in the hope of having now found a new foundation after the failure of the epistemological project, but

with the understanding that such a turn represents a good bet in pursuing our research while remaining attentive to the importance of meta-theoretical issues that arise in its course" (Kratochwil 2007:1).
23 Weber (1968:24–25) writes: "(1) instrumentally rational (*zweckrational*), that is, determined by expectations as to the behavior of objects in the environment and of other human beings; these expectations are used as 'conditions' or 'means' for the attainment of the actor's own rationally pursued and calculated ends; (2) value-rational (*wertrational*), that is, determined by a conscious belief in the value for its own sake of some ethical, aesthetic, religious, or other form of behavior, independently of its prospects of success; (3) affectual (especially emotional), that is, determined by the actor's specific affects and feeling states; (4) traditional, that is, determined by ingrained habituation."
24 It is not farfetched to think of 'habits' in terms of 'habitus'. However, the literature on either one does not suggest such a connection. Nor does the extant literature seem to believe it useful to think of habits as structure. Yet, all three concepts are obviously more or less connected, conceptually and more so in practice.

Concluding *without* a conclusion

1 According to the Oxford English Dictionary 'conclude' comes from Middle English with the sense of "convince". It specifically comes from Latin *concludere*, that is, from *con* "completely" and *claudere* "to shut". A few contemporary meanings of 'to conclude' are to bring (something) to an end, come to an end, arrive at a judgment or opinion by reasoning, say in conclusion, decide to do something.
2 A conclusion seeking to 'harvest' the fruits of the book in a succinct form is thus necessarily a *translation* at the 'end' of the book, that is, a conclusion is *self-translation*. Such a translation is what Jakobson (2000: 261) called "*Intralingual* translation or *rewording*," which "is an interpretation of verbal signs by means of other signs of the same language." However, a deconstructed notion of translation is no translation in the usual sense of the term, that is, as transport or restitution of meaning since the latter is deconstructed and becomes an effect of *différance* and other motifs that deconstruction deploys. This implies that translation is "*im-possible*, if one understands it as the transport of a signified, identical to itself, from one language to another." This implies that 'harvesting' the fruits of the book in a conclusion form is *impossible*. Yet at the same time "translation becomes a necessity *for all*" simply because there is no transcendental signified or meaning, no universal 'language'. Translation obeys a regime of being simultaneously imposed and being interdicted (Crépon 2006: 309). This is expressed by Derrida (2001: 178) as: "As a matter of fact, I don't believe that anything can ever be untranslatable—or, moreover, translatable." In other words, translation seems to follow an unintelligible and contradictory axiom which postulates that "nothing is translatable; nothing is untranslatable" (Derrida 2001: 178). Derrida calls this an *economy of in-between-ness*, that is, as he (Derrida 2001: 178–79) explains,

> "a certain *economy* that relates the translatable to the untranslatable, not as the same to the other, but as same to same or other to other. Here 'economy' signifies two things, *property* and *quantity: on the one hand,* what concerns the law of *property (oikonomia, the law-nomos* of the *oikos,* of what is proper, appropriate to itself, at home—and translation is always an attempt at appropriation that aims to transport home, in its language, in the most appropriate way possible, in the most relevant way possible, the most proper meaning of the original text, even if this is the proper meaning of a figure, metaphor, metonymy, catachresis, or undecidable impropriety) and, *on the other hand,* a law of

quantity—when one speaks of economy, one always speaks of calculable quantity."

This implies that writing a conclusion is both an impossible and possible task. Paraphrasing Derrida (2007a: 212), one could perhaps say that a conclusion is a place where 'the pure unstranslatable and the pure translatable pass one into the other'.

3 If I were to pursue a discussion of conclusion *qua* translation, I would mention that in explaining this structure *qua surviving* of the text, Derrida (2004: 82–83) writes,

> "A text lives only if it lives on, and it lives *on* only if it is at *once* translatable *and* untranslatable ... Totally translatable, it disappears as a text, as writing, as a body of language. Totally untranslatable, even within what is believed to be one language, it dies immediately. Thus triumphant translation is neither the life nor the death of the text, only or already its living *on*."

4 I am sure that the reader has already noticed the oxymoron nature of this self-inheritance; that is, I 'survive' my own death as the author of this book to then inherit from my book. This logic is of the same order of the role of the gaze in Lacanian theory where the subject witnesses its own birth via a 'gaze'. As put by Žižek (2003: 64), "it is as if we are observing the 'primordial scene' from behind our eyes, *as if* we are not immediately identified with our look but stand somewhere 'behind' it." In my case, the subject inherits from itself through the structure of survival.

5 In fact, I would want to argue that ANY conclusion can never be 'conventional' for all the reasons that I discussed in this chapter.

Bibliography

Allen, Christopher. 2004. Endemically European or a European Epidemic? Islamophobia in a Post 9/11 Europe. In: *Islam & the West: Post 9/11*, edited by Ron Geaves, Theodore Gabriel, Yvonne Haddad, and Jane Idleman Smith. Aldershot: Ashgate.

Almond, Ian. 1999. Negative Theology, Derrida and the Critique of Presence: A Poststructuralist Reading of Meister Eckhart. *Heythrop Journal* XL: 150–65,

Amin, Ash. 2004. Multi-ethnicity and the Idea of Europe. *Theory, Culture & Society* 21(2): 1–24

Archer, Margaret. 1995. *Realist Social Theory: the Morphogenetic Approach*. Cambridge: Cambridge University Press.

Arfi, Badredine. 2010a. Auto-Immunity of Trust *without* Trust. *Journal of International Political Theory* 6 (2) (October): 188–216.

———2010b. Rethinking International Constitutional Order: The Auto-immune Politics of Binding *without* Binding. *Millennium: Journal of International Studies* 39(2) (December): 299–321

———2010c. *Linguistic Fuzzy Logic Methods in Social Sciences*. New York: Springer-Verlag.

Barkin, J. Samuel. 2010. *Realist Constructivism: Rethinking International Relations Theory*. New York: Cambridge University Press.

Barton, John Cyril. 2003. Iterability and the Order-Word Plateau: 'A Politics of the Performative' in Derrida and Deleuze/Guattari. *Critical Horizons* 4 (2): 227–64.

Benhabib, Seyla. (ed.). 1996. *Democracy and Difference: Contesting the Boundaries of the Political*. Princeton, NJ: Princeton University Press.

Berman, Paul. 2007. Who's Afraid of Tariq Ramadan. *The New Republic* 236 (17) June 4.

Bevir, Mark and Asaf Kedar. 2008. Concept Formation in Political Science: An Anti-Naturalist Critique of Qualitative Methodology. *Perspectives on Politics* 6 (3): 503–17.

Bhabha, Homi. 1994. *The Location of Culture*. New York: Routledge.

Bhaskar, Roy. 1978. *A Realist Theory of Science*. Sussex: Harvester.

———1979. *The Possibility of Naturalism*. Sussex: Harvester.

———1986. *Scientific Realism and Human Emancipation*. London: Verso.

———1993. *Dialectic: The Pulse of Freedom*. London: Verso.

———2000. *From East to West: Odyssey of a Soul*. New York: Routledge.

Bohman, James. 2009. What Is to Be Done? The Science Question in International Relations. *International Theory* 1 (3): 488–98

Bourdieu, Pierre. 1990. *The Logic of Practice*. Sanford, CA: Stanford University Press.

Bowen, John R. 2004. Beyond Migration: Islam as a Transnational Public Space. *Journal of Ethnic and Migration Studies* 30 (5): 879–94.

Bradley, Arthur. 2001. Without Negative Theology: Deconstruction and the Politics of Negative Theology. *Heythrop Journal* XLII: 133–47.
——2002. Thinking the Outside: Foucault, Derrida and Negative Theology. *Textual Practice* 16(1): 57–74.
Brown, Malcolm D. 2006. Comparative Analysis of Mainstream Discourses, Media Narratives and Representations of Islam in Britain and France Prior to 9/11. *Journal of Muslim Minority Affairs* 26 (3): 297–312.
Brubaker, Rogers and Frederick Cooper. 2000. Beyond "Identity". *Theory and Society* 29: 1–47.
Bulley, Dan. 2009. *Ethics as Foreign Policy: Britain, the EU and the Other*. London: Routledge.
——2010. The Politics of Ethical Foreign Policy: A Responsibility to Protect Whom?. *European Journal of International Relations* XX (X): 1–21.
Buruma, Ian. 2007. Tariq Ramadan Has an Identity Issue. *New York Times* February 4
Butler, Judith. 1995. "For a Careful Reading." In: *Feminist Contentions: A Philosophical Exchange*, edited by Seyla Benhabib, Judith Butler, Drucilla Cornell, Nancy Fraser, 127–44. London: Routledge.
Campbell, David. 1998. *National Deconstruction: Violence, Identity, and Justice in Bosnia*. Minneapolis, MN: University of Minnesota Press.
Caputo, John D. 1997a. *The Prayers and Tears of Jacques Derrida: Religion without Religion*. Bloomington, IN: Indiana University Press.
——1997b. *Deconstruction in a Nutshell: A Conversation with Jacques Derrida*. New York: Fordham University Press.
——2003. Without Sovereignty, Without Being: Unconditionality, The Coming God and Derrida's Democracy To Come. *Journal for Cultural and Religious Theory* 4 (3): 9–26.
Carlbom, Aje. 2006. An Empty Signifier: The Blue-and-Yellow Islam of Sweden. *Journal of Muslim Minority Affairs* 26 (2): 245–61.
Chernoff, Fred. 2009. Defending Foundations for International Relations Theory. *International Theory* 1 (3): 466–77.
Chia, Robert. 1994. The Concept of Decision: A Deconstructive Analysis. *Journal of Management Studies* 31 (6): 781–806.
Chorev, Nitsan and Sarah Babb. 2009. The Crisis of Neoliberalism and the Future of International Institutions: A Comparison of the IMF and the WTO. *Theory and Society* 38: 459–84
Chu, Henry. 2009. Islamic Scholar Tariq Ramadan Defends his Views. *LA Times* September 22.
Cohen, E. 2004. My Self as an Other: On Autoimmunity and 'Other' Paradoxes. *Journal of Medical Ethics, Medical Humanities* 30: 7–11.
Connolly, William. 1991. *Identity/Difference: Democratic Negotiations of Political Paradox*. Ithaca, NY: Cornell University Press.
Coole, Diana. 2005. Rethinking Agency: A Phenomenological Approach to Embodiment and Agentic Capacities. *Political Studies* 53: 124–42.
Crépon, Marc. 2006. Deconstruction and Translation. The Passage into Philosophy. *Research in Phenomenology* 36: 299–313.
Culler, Jonathan. 2000. Philosophy and Literature: The Fortunes of the Performative. *Poetics Today* 21 (3): 502–19.
d'Espagnat, Bernard. 2006. *On Physics and Philosophy*. Princeton, NJ: Princeton University Press.

De Man, Paul. 1979. *Allegories of Reading: Figural Language in Rousseau, Nietzsche, Rilke, and Proust*. New Haven, CT: Yale University Press.
de Mesquita, Bruce Bueno and James D. Morrow. 1999. Sorting through the Wealth of Notions. *International Security* 24 (2): 56–73.
Delanty, Gerard. 2002. Models of European Identity: Reconciling Universalism and Particularism. *Perspectives on European Politics and Society* 3 (3):345–59.
Derrida, Jacques. 1973. *Speech and Phenomena*. Evanston, IL: Northwestern University Press.
——1974. *Of Grammatology*. Baltimore, MD: The Johns Hopkins University Press.
——1978. *Writing and Difference*. Chicago, IL: University of Chicago Press.
——1981a. *Positions*. Chicago, IL: The University of Chicago Press.
——1981b. *Dissemination*. Chicago, IL: University of Chicago Press.
——1982. *Margins of Philosophy*. Chicago, IL: University of Chicago Press.
——1986a. Declarations of Independence. *New Political Science* 7 (1): 7 – 15.
——1986b. *Parages*. Paris: Éditions de Galilée.
——1987a. *The Post Card: From Socrates to Freud and Beyond*. Chicago, IL: The University of Chicago Press.
——1987b. *The Truth in Painting*. Chicago, IL: Chicago University Press.
——1988. *Limited Inc*. Evanston, IL: Northwestern University Press.
——1989. Force of Law: The 'Mystical Foundation of Authority'. *Cardozo Law Review* 11: 919–1045.
——1992a. "How to Avoid Speaking: Denials." In: *Derrida and Negative Theology*, edited by Harold Coward and Toby Fosbay. Albany, NY: SUNY Press.
——1992b. "Passions: 'An Oblique Offering'." In: *Derrida: A Critical Reader*, edited by David Wood, 5–35. Cambridge: Blackwell.
——1992c. *Given Time: I. Counterfeit Money*. Chicago, IL: The University of Chicago Press.
——1992d. *The Other Heading: Reflections on Today's Europe*. Bloomington, IN: Indiana University Press.
——1993. *Aporias*. Stanford, CA: Stanford University Press.
——1994a. *Specters of Marx: The State of the Debt, the Work of Mourning, & the New International*. New York: Routledge.
——1994b. *Demeure, Fiction and Testimony*. Stanford, CA: Stanford University Press.
——1995a. Archive Fever: A Freudian Impression. *Diacritics* 25 (2): 9–63.
——1995b. *On the Name*. Stanford, CA: Stanford University Press.
——1997a. *Adieu to Emmanuel Levinas*. Stanford, CA: Stanford University Press.
——1997b. *The Politics of Friendship*. New York: Verso.
——1998. *Monolingualism of the Other or the Prosthesis of Origin*. Stanford, CA: Stanford University Press.
——1999a. Hospitality, Justice and Responsibility. In: *Questioning Ethics: Contemporary Debates in Philosophy*, edited by Richard Kearney and Mark Dooley, 65–83. New York: Routledge.
——1999b. Marx & Sons. In: *Ghostly Demarcations: A Symposium on Jacques Derrida's Specters of Marx*, edited by Michael Sprinker, 213–69. New York: Verso.
——2000. *Of Hospitality*. Stanford, CA: Stanford University Press.
——2001a. To Forgive: The Unforgivable and the Imprescriptible. In: *Questioning God*, edited by John D. Caputo, Mark Dooley, and Michael J. Scanlon, 21–51. Bloomington: Indiana University Press.

——2001b. *Deconstruction Engaged*. Urbana-Champaign, IL: University of Illinois Press.
——2001. What Is a 'Relevant' Translation? *Critical Inquiry* 27 (2): 174–200.
——2002a. *Without Alibi*. Stanford, CA: Stanford University Press.
——2002b. *Negotiations: Interventions and Interviews, 1971–2001*. Stanford, CA: Stanford University Press.
——2002c. Faith and Knowledge: The Two Sources of 'Religion' at the Limits of Reason Alone. In: *Acts of Religion*, edited by Gil Anijadar, 42–101. New York: Routledge.
——2003a. Autoimmunity: Real and Symbolic Suicide. In: *Philosophy in a Time of Terror*, edited by Giovanna Borradori, 85–136. Chicago, IL: University of Chicago Press.
——2003b. The "World" of the Enlightenment to Come (Exception, Calculation, Sovereignty). *Research in Phenomenology* 33: 9–52.
——2005a. Poetics and Politics of Witnessing. In: *Sovereignties in Question: The Poetics of Paul Celan*, edited by Jacques Derrida, Outi Pasanen, Thomas Dutoit, 65–96. New York: Fordham University Press.
——2005b. *On Cosmopolitanism and Forgiveness*. New York: Routledge.
——2005c. *Rogues*. Stanford, CA: Stanford University Press.
——2007a. *Psyche: Inventions of the Other. Volume I*. Stanford, CA: Stanford University Press.
——2007b. A Certain Impossible Possibility of Saying the Event. *Critical Inquiry* 33 (Winter): 441–61.
——2007c. *Learning to Live Finally. The Last Interview*. Hoboken, NJ: Melville House Publishing.
——2008. *Psyche: Inventions of the Other, Vol. II*. Stanford, CA: Stanford University Press.
Derrida, Jacques and Maurizio Ferraris. 2001. *A Taste for the Secret*. Cambridge: Polity Press.
Derrida, Jacques and Bernard Stiegler. 2002. *Echographies of Television*. Oxford: Polity Press.
Derrida, Jacques and Elisabeth Roudinesco. 2004. *For What Tomorrow ... A Dialogue*. Stanford, CA: Stanford University Press.
Dessler, David. 1989. What's at Stake in the Agent-Structure Debate? *International Organization* 43 (3): 442–73.
Dewey, John. 1922. *Human Nature and Conduct: An Introduction to Social Psychology* (1st ed.). New York: Holt.
——1930. *Human Nature and Conduct*. New York: Modem Library.
——1947. *A Common Faith*. New Haven, CT: Yale University Press.
Direk, Zeynep. 1998. *The Renovation of the Notion of Experience in Derrida's Philosophy*. Ph.D. Dissertation, The University of Memphis, United States.
Djelic, Marie-Laure and Sigrid Quack. 2007. Overcoming Path Dependency: Path Generation in Open Systems. *Theory and Society* 36 (2): 161–86.
Doty, Roxanne L. 1997. Aporia: A Critical Exploration of the Agent-Structure Problematique in International Relations Theory. *European Journal of International Relations* 3 (3): 365–92.
Drysdale, John. 1996. How Are Social-Scientific Concepts Formed? A Reconstruction of Max Weber's Theory of Concept Formation. *Sociological Theory* 14 (1): 71–88.
Duffield, John. 2007. What Are International Institutions? *International Studies Review* 9: 1–22.

Edkins, Jenny. 1999. *Poststructuralism & International Relations: Bringing the Political Back In*. Boulder, CO: Lynne Rienner Publishers.

Emirbayer, Mustafa and Ann Mische. 1998. What Is Agency? *American Journal of Sociology* 103 (4): 962–1023.

Fisch, Menachem. 2008. Taking the Linguistic Turn Seriously. *The European Legacy* 13 (5): 605–22.

Foucault, Michel. 1977. Nietzsche, Genealogy, History. In: *Language, Counter-Memory, Practice: Selected Essays and Interviews*, edited by D. F. Bouchard. Ithaca, NY: Cornell University Press.

Friedman, Milton. 1994. The Methodology of Positive Economics. In: *Readings in the Philosophy of Social Science*, edited by Michael Martin and Lee C. McIntyre, 647–60. Cambridge, MA: The MIT Press.

Gasché, Rodolphe. 1986. *The Tain of the Mirror: Derrida and the Philosophy of Reflection*. Cambridge, MA: Harvard University Press.

Giddens, Anthony. 1976. *New Rules of Sociological Method*. London: Hutchinson.

——1984. *The Constitution of Society*. Berkeley, CA: University of California Press.

——1990. *The Consequences of Modernity*. Stanford, CA: Stanford University Press.

——1991. *Modernity and Self-identity*. Cambridge: Polity Press.

Goldmann, Kjell. 2005. Appropriateness and Consequences: The Logic of Neo-Institutionalism. G*overnance: An International Journal of Policy, Administration, and Institutions* 18 (1): 35–52.

Gorkom, Joris Van. 2007. What If? On Respect, Secret, and Spectre. *Mosaic* 40 (2): 117–32.

Grillo, Ralph. 2007. An Excess of Alterity? Debating Difference in a Multicultural Society. *Ethnic and Racial Studies* 30 (6): 979–98.

Habermas, Jürgen. 1979. *Communication and the Evolution of Society*. London: Heinemann.

——1983. Interpretive Social Science vs. Hermeneuticism. In: *Social Science as Moral Inquiry*, edited by Norma Haan, Robert N. Bellah, P. Rabinow, and William M. Sullivan, 251–69. New York: Columbia University Press.

——1984. *The Theory of Communicative Action. Volume One: Reason and the Rationalization of Society*. Cambridge: Polity Press.

——1990. *Moral Consciousness and Communicative Action*. Cambridge, MA: The MIT Press.

——1992. *Moral Consciousness and Communicative Action*. Cambridge, MA: The MIT Press.

——1996a. Reply to Symposium Participants. *Cardozo Law Review* 17 (4&5): 1477–1557.

——1996b. *Between Facts and Norms: Contributions to a Discourse Theory of Law and Democracy*. Cambridge, MA: The MIT Press.

——2001. *On the Pragmatics of Social Interaction: Preliminary Studies in the Theory of Communicative Action*. Cambridge, MA: The MIT Press.

——2001b. From Kant's Ideas of Pure Reason to the 'Idealizing' Presuppositions of Communicative Action: Reflections on the Detranscendentalized 'Use of Reason'. In: *Pluralism and the Pragmatic Turn: The Transformation of Critical Theory*, edited by William Rehg and James Bohman, 11–39. Cambridge, MA: The MIT Press.

——2001c. *Justification and Application: Remarks on Discourse Ethics*. Cambridge, MA: The MIT Press.

——2008. *Between Naturalism and Religion*. Malden, MA: Polity Press.

Haddad, Samir. 2006. Reading Derrida Reading Derrida: Deconstruction as Self-Inheritance. *International Journal of Philosophical Studies* 14 (4): 505–20.

Haddad, Yvonne Yazbeck and Tyler Golson. 2007. Overhauling Islam: Representation, Construction, and Cooption of 'Moderate Islam' in Western Europe. *Journal of Church and State* 49 (3): 487–515.
Hägglund, Martin. 2004. The Necessity of Discrimination: Disjoining Derrida and Levinas. *Diacritics* 34 (1): 40–71.
Hardin, Russell. 2001. Conceptions and Explanations of Trust. In: *Trust in Society*, edited by K. S. Cook, 3–39. New York: Russell Sage Foundation.
——2002. *Trust and Trustworthiness*. New York: Russell Sage Foundation.
Hart, Kevin. 1989. *The Trespass of the Sign: Deconstruction, Theology and Philosophy*. Cambridge: Cambridge University Press.
Harvey, Irene E. 1986. *Derrida and the Economy of Différance*. Bloomington, IN: Indiana University Press.
——1989. Derrida, Kant, and the Performance of Parergonality. In: *Derrida and Deconstruction*, edited by Hugh J. Silverman, 59–76. New York: Routledge.
Heidegger, Martin. 2007. The End of Philosophy and the Task for Thinking. In: *Martin Heidegger. Basic Writings from Being and Time (1927) to The Task of Thinking (1964)*, edited by David Farrell Krell. New York: Routledge.
Hodgson, Geoffrey M. 2004. Reclaiming Habit for Institutional Economics. *Journal of Economic Psychology* 25: 651–60
Hoffman, Aaron. M. 2002. A Conceptualization of Trust in International Relations. *European Journal of International Relations* 8 (3): 375–401.
——2005. *Building Trust: Overcoming Suspicion in International Conflict*. Albany, NY: State University of New York Press.
Hopf, Ted. 2010. The logic of habit in International Relations. *European journal of International Relations* XX (X): 1–23
Horwitz, Noah. 2002. Derrida and the Aporia of the Political, or the Theologico-Political Dimension of Deconstruction. *Research in Phenomenology* 32 (1): 156–76.
Howarth, David. 2000. *Discourse*. Buckingham: Open University Press.
Ikenberry, G. John. 1998. Constitutional Politics in International Relations. *European Journal of International Relations* 4 (2): 147–77.
——2001. *After Victory: Institutions, Strategic Restraint, and the Rebuilding of Order after Major Wars*. Princeton, NJ: Princeton University Press.
Jackson, Patrick Thaddeus. 2009. A Faulty Solution to a False(ly Characterized) Problem: A Comment on Monteiro and Ruby. *International Theory* 1 (3): 455–65.
——2010. *The Conduct of Inquiry in International Relations: Philosophy of Science and Its Implications for the Study of World Politics*. New York: Routledge.
Jakobson, Roman. 2000. On linguistic Aspects of Translation. In: *The Translation Studies Reader 2000*, edited by Lawrence Venuti, 113–18. New York: Routledge.
James, William. 1979. *The Will to Believe and Other Essays in Popular Philosophy*. Cambridge, MA: Harvard University Press.
James, Williams. 1893. *Writings 1878–1899: Psychology, Briefer Course*. New York: Holt.
Jay, Martin. 1992. The Debate over Performative Contradiction: Habermas versus the Poststructuralists. In: *Philosophical Interventions in the Unfinished Project of Enlightenment*, edited by Axel Honneth, Thomas McCarthy, Claus Offe, and Albrecht Wellmer, 261–79. Cambridge, MA: The MIT Press.
Johnston, Alastair Iain. 2001. Treating International Institutions as Social Environments. *International Studies Quarterly* 45: 487–515.
Kant, Immanuel. 2008. *Fundamental Principles of the Metaphysics of Morals*. New York: Casimo Inc.

Karic, Enes. 2002. Is 'Euro-Islam' a Myth, Challenge or a Real Opportunity for Muslims and Europe? *Journal of Muslim Minority Affairs* 22 (2): 435–42.
Kastoryano, Riva. 2003. France, Germany and Islam: Negotiating Identities. *Immigrants & Minorities* 22 (2&3): 280–97.
Kearney, Richard and Mark Dooley. 1999. Hospitality, Justice and Responsibility: A Dialogue with Jacques Derrida. In: *Questioning Ethics: Contemporary Debates in Philosophy*, edited by Richard Kearney and Mark Dooley, 65–83. New York: Routledge.
Kearney, Richard. 1984. *Dialogue with Contemporary Continental Thinkers*. Manchester: Manchester University Press.
Keohane, Robert O. 1988. International Institutions: Two Approaches. *International Studies Quarterly* 32: 379–96.
Koopmans, Ruud, Paul Statham, Marco Giugni, and Florence Passy. 2005. *Contested Citizenship: Immigration and Cultural Diversity in Europe*. Minneapolis, MN: University of Minnesota Press.
Koremenos, Barbara, Charles Lipson, and Duncan Snidal. 2001. The Rational Design of International Institutions. *International Organization* 55: 761–99.
Korteweg, Anna and Gökçe Yurdakul. 2009. Islam, Gender, and Immigrant Integration: Boundary Drawing in Discourses on Honour Killing in the Netherlands and Germany. *Ethnic and Racial Studies* 32 (2): 218–38.
Kratochwil, Friedrich. 2007. Of False Promises and Good Bets: A Plea for a Pragmatic Approach to Theory Building (the Tartu Lecture). *Journal of International Relations and Development* 10: 1–15.
Kurki, Milja. 2009. The Politics of the Philosophy of Science. *International Theory* 1 (3): 440–54.
Kydd, Andrew. 2006. *Trust and Mistrust in International Relations*. Princeton, NJ: Princeton University Press.
Laclau, Ernesto. 1990. *New Reflections on the Revolution of Our Time*. New York: Verso.
Layder, Derek. 1985. Beyond Empiricism? The Promise of Realism. *Philosophy of the Social Sciences* 15 (3): 255–74.
Leander, Anna. 2006. Paradigms as a Hindrance to Understanding World Politics. *Cooperation and Conflict* 41 (4): 370–76.
Lenoble, Jacques. 1995–96. Law and Undecidability: A New Vision of the Proceduralization of Law. *Cardozo Law Review* 17: 935–1004.
Lévi-Strauss, Claude. 1968. *Structural Anthropology. Volume One*. Harmondsworth: Penguin.
——1994. *The Raw and the Cooked*. London: Pimlico.
Lewis, J. D. and A. Weigert. 1985. Trust as a Social Reality. *Social Forces* 63 (4): 967–85.
Loyal, Steven and Barry Barnes. 2001. "Agency" as a Red Herring in Social Theory. *Philosophy of the Social Sciences* 31 (4): 507–24.
Luhmann, Niklas. 1979. *Trust and Power: Two Works by Niklas Luhmann*. Chichester: Wiley.
Maeve, Cooke. 2001. Meaning and Truth in Habermas's Pragmatics. *European Journal of Philosophy* 9 (1): 1–23.
March James G. 1988. *Decisions and Organizations*. Oxford: Blackwell.
March, James G. and Johan P. Olsen. 1989. *Rediscovering Institutions*. New York: Free Press.
——1995. *Democratic Governance*. New York: Free Press.
——1998. The Institutional Dynamics of International Political Orders. *International Organization* 52 (4): 943–69.

Mercado, Raymond. 2009. Keep Muddling Through? *International Theory* 1 (3): 478–87.
Milem, Bruce. 2007. Four Theories of Negative Theology. *Heythrop Journal* XLVIII: 187–204.
Miller, J. Hillis. 2001. *Speech Acts in Literature*. Stanford, CA: Stanford University Press.
——2006. Derrida's Destinerrance. *MLN* 121: 893–910.
Minister, Stephen. 2007. Derrida's Inhospitable Desert of the Messianic: Religion within the Limits of Justice Alone. *Heythrop Journal* XLVIII: 227–42.
Misztal, B. A. 1996. *Trust in Modern Societies*. Cambridge: Polity Press.
Möllering, Guido. 2001. The Nature of Trust: From Georg Simmel to a Theory of Expectation, Interpretation and Suspension. *Sociology* 35 (2): 403–20
——2006. *Trust: Reason, Routine, Reflexivity*. New York: Elsevier Press.
Monteiro, Nuno P. and Keven G. Ruby. 2009a. IR and the False Promise of Philosophical Foundations. *International Theory* 1(1): 15–48.
——2009b. The Promise of Foundational Prudence: A Response to our Critics. *International Theory* 1(3): 499–512.
Mora, José F. 1963. On the Early History of 'Ontology'. *Philosophy and Phenomenological Research* 24 (1): 36–47.
Morin, Marie-Eve. 2007. The Self, the Other, and the Many: Derrida On Testimony. *Mosaic* 40 (2): 165–78.
Mouffe, Chantal. 1994. For a Politics of Nomadic Identity. In: *Travellers' Tales: Narratives of Home and Displacement*, edited by George Robertson et al., 105–13. New York: Routledge.
Naas, Michael. 2006. "One Nation ... Indivisible": Jacques Derrida on the Autoimmunity of Democracy and the Sovereignty of God. *Research in Phenomenology* 36:16–44.
Nellhaus, Tobin. 1998. Signs, Social Ontology, and Critical Realism. *Journal for the Theory of Social Behaviour* 28: 1–24.
Nietzsche, Friedrich. 1967. *The Will to Power*. New York: Random House.
Norris, Christopher. 1982. *Deconstruction: Theory and Practice*. London: Methuen.
Oakes, Guy. 1988. *Weber and Rickert: Concept Formation in the Cultural Sciences*. Cambridge, MA: The MIT Press.
Odysseos, Louiza. 2007. *The Subject of Coexistence: Otherness in International Relations*. Madison, MN: University of Minnesota Press.
Onuf, Nicholas Greenwood. 1989. *World of Our Making: Rules and Rule in Social Theory and International Relations*. Columbia, SC: University of South Carolina Press.
——1998. *The Republican Legacy in International Thought*. New York: Cambridge University Press.
——2002. Institutions, Intentions and International Relations. *Review of International Studies* 28: 211–28.
Otterbeck, Jonas. 2005. What is Reasonable to Demand? Islam in Swedish Textbooks. Journal of *Ethnic and Migration Studies* 31 (4): 795–812.
Pascal, Blaise. 2002. *Pensées*. Grand Rapids, MI: Christian Classics Ethereal Library. http://www.ccel.org/ccel/pascal/pensees.html.
Patomäki, Heikki and Colin Wight. 2000. After Postpositivism? The Promises of Critical Realism. *International Studies Quarterly* 44 (2): 213–37.
Patomäki, Heikki. 2002. *After International Relations: Critical Realism and the (re) Construction of World Politics*. New York: Routledge.
——2010. After Critical Realism? The Relevance of Contemporary Science. *Journal of Critical Realism* 9 (1): 59–88.

Pedersen, Jørgen. 2008. Habermas' Method: Rational Reconstruction. *Philosophy of the Social Sciences* 38 (4): 457–85.
——2009. Habermas and the Political Sciences: The Relationship between Theory and Practice. *Philosophy of the Social Sciences* 39 (3): 381–407.
Plotnitsky, Arkady. 1993. *Reconfigurations: Critical Theory and General Economy*. Gainesville, FL: University Press of Florida.
——1994. *Complementarity: Anti-Epistemology after Bohr and Derrida*. Durham, NC: Duke University Press.
Poole, Elizabeth. 2002. *Reporting Islam: Media Representations of British Muslims*. London: I. B. Taurus.
Power, Michael K. 1993. Habermas and Transcendental Arguments: A Reappraisal. *Philosophy of the Social Sciences* 23 (1): 26–49.
——1995–96. Habermas and the Counterfactual Imagination. *Cardozo Law Review* 17: 1005–25.
Ramadan, Tariq. 1999. *To Be a European Muslim*. Leicester: The Islamic Foundation.
——2004. *Western Muslims and the Future of Islam*. New York: Oxford University Press.
——2006. Muslims, the Pope and European Identity. *NPQ* Fall: 14–18.
——2007. Islam Today: The Need to Explore Its Complexities. *Nieman Reports* Summer: 23–25.
——2009. *Radical Reform: Islamic Ethics and Liberation*. New York: Oxford University Press.
Rescher, Nicholas. 1985. *Pascal's Wager: A Study of Practical Reasoning in Philosophical Theology*. Notre Dame, IN: University of Notre Dame Press.
Rickert, Heinrich. 1986. *The Limits of Concept Formation in Natural Science: A Logical Introduction to the Historical Sciences*. New York: Cambridge University Press.
Risse, Thomas. 2000. "Let's Argue!": Communicative Action in World Politics. *International Organization* 54 (1): 1–39.
Rorty, Richard.1999. *Philosophy and Social Hope*. New York: Penguin Books.
Rouse, Joseph. 2006. Practice Theory. In: *Handbook of the Philosophy of Science. Volume 15: Philosophy of Anthropology and Sociology*, edited by Stephen Turner and Mark Risjord, 499–540. New York: Elsevier.
Ruzicka, Jan and Nicholas J. Wheeler. 2010. The Puzzle of Trusting Relationships in the Nuclear Non-Proliferation Treaty. *International Affairs* 86 (1): 69–85.
Ryba, Thomas. 1997. Derrida, Negative Theology and the Trespass of the Sign. *Religion* 27: 107–15.
Saint-Blancat, Chantal and Ottavia Schmidt di Friedberg. 2005. Why are Mosques a Problem? Local Politics and Fear of Islam in Northern Italy. *Journal of Ethnic and Migration Studies* 31 (6): 1083–1104.
Sartori, Giovanni. 1970. Concept Misformation in Comparative Politics. *The American Political Science Review* LXIV (December): 1033–53.
——1991. Comparing and Miscomparing. *Journal of Theoretical Politics* 3(3): 243–57.
Saussure, Ferdinand de. 1974. *Course in General Linguistics*, trans. Roy Harris. Chicago, IL: Open Court Classics.
Saussure, Ferdinand de. 1986. *Course in General Linguistics*. Chicago: Open Court Publishing.
Schweller, Randall L. 2001. The Problem of International Order Revisited. *International Security* 26 (1): 161–86.

Seligman, Adam B. 1997. *The Problem of Trust*. Princeton, NJ: Princeton University Press.
Sending, Ole Jacob. 2002. Constitution, Choice and Change: Problems with the 'Logic of Appropriateness' and its Use in Constructivist Theory. *European Journal of International Relations* 8 (4): 443–70.
Simmel, G. 1950. *The Sociology of Georg Simmel*. New York: Free Press.
—— 1990. *The Philosophy of Money*. 2nd ed. London: Routledge.
Soysal, Yasemin Nuhoğlu. 1997. Changing Parameters of Citizenship and Claims-making: Organized Islam in European Public Spheres. *Theory and Society* 26: 509–27.
Staten, Henry. 1984. *Wittgenstein and Derrida*. Lincoln, NB: University of Nebraska Press.
Sztompka, Peotr. 1999. *Trust: A Sociological Theory*. Cambridge: Cambridge University Press.
Taylor, Charles. 1985. *Philosophy and the Human Sciences: Philosophical Papers 2*. Cambridge: Cambridge University Press.
Taylor, Mark C. 1992. nO nOt nO. In: *Derrida and Negative Theology*, edited by Harold Coward and Toby Foshay, 167–98. Albany, NY: SUNY Press.
Thomassen, Lasse. 2008. *Deconstructing Habermas*. New York: Routledge.
Tibi, Bassam. 2008. *Political Islam, World Politics and Europe: Democratic Peace and Euro-Islam vs Global Jihad*. New York: Routledge.
Turner, Stephen. 1994. *The Social Theory of Practices*. Chicago: University of Chicago Press.
Vaihinger, Hans. 1935. *The Philosophy of 'As If.'* Trans. C. K. Ogden. New York: Barnes and Noble.
Veblen, T. B. 1898. Why is Economics not an Evolutionary Science? *Quarterly Journal of Economics*, 12 (3): 373–97.
Velchik, Michael. 2009. Pascal's Wager is a Lie: An Epistemic Interpretation of the Ultimate Pragmatic Argument. *Aporia* 19 (2): 1–9.
Volpi, Frédéric. 2007. Constructing the 'Ummah' in European Security: Between Exit, Voice and Loyalty. *Government and Opposition* 42 (3): 451–70.
Walker, R. B. J. 1993. *Inside/Outside: International Relations as Political Theory*. New York: Cambridge University Press.
Ware, Owen. 2004. Dialectic of the Past/Disjuncture of the Future: Derrida and Benjamin on the Concept of Messianism. *JCRT* 5 (2): 99–114.
—— 2006. Universality and Historicity: On the Sources of Religion. *Research in Phenomenology* 36: 238–54.
Weber, Max. 1946. Science as a Vocation. In: *From Max Weber: Essays in Sociology*, edited by H.H. Gerth and C. Wright Mills, 129–158. New York: Oxford University Press
Weber, Max. 1949. *The Methodology of the Social Sciences*. Glencore, IL: The Free Press.
—— 1964. *The Theory of Social and Economic Organization*. London: The Free Press.
—— 1968. Basic Sociological Terms. In: *Economy and Society*, translated by G. Roth and C. Wittich. Berkeley: University of California Press.
Weiss, Thomas G. 2009. Toward a Third Generation of International Institutions: Obama's UN Policy. *The Washington Quarterly* 32 (3): 141–62.
Wendt, Alexander E. 1987. The Agent-Structure Problem in International Relations Theory. International Organization 41 (3): 335–70.
Wendt, Alexander. 1999. *Social Theory of International Politics*. New York: Cambridge University Press.

Wheeler, Nicholas J. 2008. 'To Put Oneself into the Other Fellow's Place': John Herz, the Security Dilemma and the Nuclear Age. *International Relations* 22 (4): 493–509.
——2009. Beyond Waltz's Nuclear World: More Trust May be Better. *International Relations* 23 (3): 428–45.
Wight, Colin. 2006. *Agents, Structures and International Relations: Politics as Ontology.* New York: Cambridge University Press.
Williams, Michael C. 2005. *The Realist Tradition and the Limits of International Relations.* New York: Cambridge University Press.
Wittgenstein, Ludwig. 1953. *Philosophical Investigations.* Oxford: Blackwell.
Zagare, Frank C. 1999. All Mortis, No Rigor. *International Security* 24 (2): 107–14.
Zehfuss, Maja. 2002. *Constructivism in International Relations: The Politics of Reality.* New York: Cambridge University Press.
——2007. *Wounds of Memory: The Politics of War in Germany.* Cambridge: Cambridge University Press.
Zemni, Sami. 2002. Islam, European Identity and the Limits of Multiculturalism. In: *Religious Freedom and the Neutrality of the State: The Position of the European Union,* edited by W. A. R. Shadid and P. S. Van Koningsveld. Leuven: Peeters.
Žižek, Slavoj. 1997. *The Abyss of Freedom.* Ann Arbor, MI: The University of Michigan Press.
——2003. *Tarrying with the Negative: Kant, Hegel and the Critique of Ideology.* Durham, NC: Duke University Press.

Index

Not all author citations are listed in the index; readers requiring a complete list of cited authors and works should consult the reference section. Derrida's work is discussed throughout, and mentions of him are not fully itemized in the index.

9/11, legacy 105–6

absence 116
absenting absence 57
Absolute 64
acting, contingency of 84
After Victory 157ff
after victory context 160–61
agency 72–73; conditional 91–95; as contingency 84–85; of habit 199–200; positive 199; re-thinking 81–95; registration of 85; as sovereignty 84–85; tripartite notion 81, 82; unconditional event 85–90; as unconditional event of agency 94; Wight's notion 81–84
agent-structure problem 71–73, 95–101
Almond, Ian 57
Amin, Ash 107, 113
amnesia 4–5
analyticism 42
anterior otherness 131–32
aporia 17–18, 132; of binding 166–68; conditional/unconditional 72; impossible politics 167; politics of 127–28
arbitrary exercise of power 157–58
arche 37
Archer, Margaret 82
as-if element 137, 143–51, 152–53, 154
as-if gesture 143–48, 178
as if logic 177, 178
autogenesis 63, 64

autoimmunity 3, 83, 87–90, 124–27, 128, 164–65; binding and performative violence 158–66; binding institutions 158, 159; logics of action 201–2; suicide 208; of trust 151–52

Barkin, J. Samuel 97
Barnes, Barry 84
behavior, traditional 197–98
belongingness 113
Benhabib, Seyla 175
Bhabha, Homi 34
Bhaskar, Roy 55, 56–57, 63, 73, 74, 81–82, 84
binding: *aporia* of 166–68; performative violence and autoimmunity 158–66; as promise of mutual commitment 161–66; retroactive 159; through originary performative violence 160–61
binding institutions 157–58, 168–69
book, structure and layout 19–24
borrowings 4
Bourdieu, Pierre 173, 191–97
Bradley, Arthur 49, 59, 60, 196
Brubaker, Rogers 103, 112
Bulley, Dan 14
Butler, Judith 84

Campbell, David 13–14
Caputo, John D. 52, 53, 58, 60, 62, 87, 89, 128, 167, 196
ceteris paribus clause 187
change 1; and repetition 119, 120–21
Christian Neoplatonism 62

citationality 185
closure 5–7, 16, 135, 210
co-constitution 97
commitment 161–66
communication: iterability 120; polysemy 35
communicative action, restricted economy of 184, 185
concluding 203–4
conclusion: possibility of writing 209–10; role in book 205
conclusions, deconstructibility 6–7
'concrete' research 64, 69
conditional agency 91–95
conditional/unconditional aporia 72
conditions of possibility and impossibility 4–5, 72
conjoined identity 118
Connolly, William 102, 113, 124–25
consensus, about science 30
conservation 94
constative/performative dichotomy 5, 91
contamination 37, 86–87, 90
context-transcending knowledge 176
contingency 84–85
contingent event 163–64
contradiction 172, 175, 177
contradictory coherence 80
Coole, Diana 84
Cooper, Frederick 103, 112
Cornell, Drucilla 135
cost-benefit analysis 136
counter-factual ideal speech situation 175
counterfactual presupposition 182
counterfactuals 177, 181, 183, 184
critical realism 42, 56–57, 63, 65–66
criticism, openness to 30
Culler, Jonathan 91

Dasein 206
De Man, Paul 171
debates, proliferation 29
decisions: in publishing 9–10; and undecidability 141–43; within undecidability and responsibility 167–68
deconstruction: as infinite 203–5; process of 4, 75–76
deferral 78
denegation 58–59, 166
Dessler, David 71, 73
destinerrance 35
determinacy 164–65

deviant 79
Dewey, John 198–99
Dialectic 55
Dialectic Critical Realism 57
dialectical critical naturalism 57
différance 68, 69, 78, 81, 114–17, 128, 131
difference: defining 103; identity and undecidability 112–14 *see also* identity/difference
differentiation 36, 115
dissemination 2, 35–36, 37, 41, 121–22, 128, 131, 134
diversity, methodological and theological 43
Doty, Roxanne L. 96

Edkins, Jenny 12–13
either-or logic 56
encapsulated interest 139
enframing 65–69
epistemic fallacy 56
ergon 68–69, 101
Euro-Islam 104–7, 108, 114, 133–35
European identity 106–7
event 85–87, 146–47; contingent 163–64; saying the event 94, 148–50, 164–65
event-making 94
exclusion 123
experience 182–83
external relations 73–74

faith 41; experience of 52–53; James' view 45–46; manifestation 50; pseudo-notions 29; rationality and irrationality 43; testimonial 41–53; use and connotations of term 45
faith/knowledge delineation 45–46
fallacy 56
fictions 177, 184
formal pragmatics 175, 180–83
Foucault, Michel 112
framework of conception 2
framing 5
Friedman, Milton 143

Gasché, Rodolphe 17, 41, 79, 124, 126
general infrastructural space 41
Giddens, Anthony 73, 74, 84, 140, 154
God 59–60
Goldmann, Kjell 186–87
Golson, Tyler 105, 106
Grillo, Ralph 104
grounding 18

Habermas, Jürgen 173ff, 201
habits 197–201
habituation 197–98
habitus 192–95
Haddad, Samir 204, 206, 208
Haddad, Yvonne Yazbeck 105, 106
Hardin, Russell 136, 139
Harvey, Irene E. 66–67, 68, 69, 100
hauntology 72, 87, 88
hegemony 158–59
hetero-knowledge theory 137, 140–41, 143
Hodgson, Geoffrey M. 198, 199
Hopf, Ted 197, 198–200
Horwitz, Noah 18
hospitality 86–87
Howarth, David 76, 77, 78
hybridity 34–35, 41
hyper-essentiality 62
hypo-essentiality 62

ideal types 8–9, 30–31, 187; contamination 34; defining 32, 33; functions 32–33; hybridity 34–35; as ideas 33–34; as-if gesture 144; as imaginary constructs 33–35; iteration of 37; and linguistic turn 31–41; of methodologies 42–43; as signifying concepts 36
idealizing presuppositions 175–76
ideas 33–34
identity 10–11; beyond politics of 132–35; conjoined 118; difference and undecidability 112–14; European 106–7; Muslim/Islamic 105; negotiation 133–34; 'out-of-joint-ness' 118–24; as play of dissemination 121–22; as play of iterability 119–21; as play of supplementarity 122–24; as trace 117
identity/difference: autoimmunity 124–27; beyond *aporia* of othering 127–32; beyond politics of identity 132–35; *différance* 114–17; Muslims in Western Europe 104–7; othering 124–27; 'out-of-joint-ness' 118–24; overview 102–4; Ramadan, Tariq 109–12; Tibi, Bassam 107–9, 110–11
Ikenberry, G. John 157ff
immanent readings 3
immunity/autoimmunity 127–32 *see also* autoimmunity
impossible possible 89–90
inauguration 92–94
indivisible sovereignty 87

infrastructural space 72
inheritance 206–9
institutional binding 157–58
institutions: iterability 164; stickiness 161, 164
integration, Muslims in Western Europe 110–11
internal relations 74
International Relations: divisions 2; politics of 14–15
international/world order, overview 156
interpretations of interpretation 31–32
interruption 133, 202
intransitive objects 56, 63
intuitive knowledge 176
ipseity 88
IR theory, re-thinking 3–4
irrationality: of faith 43; of reality 40–41
irresponsibility 129–30
iterability 36, 41, 91–92, 93–94, 119–21, 128, 131; of habit 201; institutions 164; logic of without 166; of promises 162–63; of traces 185
iteration 134; of ideal type 37; in (re-)thinking 1

Jackson, Patrick T. 26ff, 65, 66–69
James, William 44–46, 199
Jay, Martin 175, 177

Kant, Immanuel 143–46, 178
khôra 48–50; as condition of possibility of the ontological 63–64; ontological as 55; pseudo-determinations of 61–62; as receptacle 61–63
know-how 176, 179, 182
know-that 176, 179, 182
knowledge: context-transcending 176; intuitive 176; tacit 190
knowledge/faith delineation 45–48
Kratochwil, Friedrich 172

Laclau, Ernesto 118, 129
language 2–3, 15–17; polysemy 35; role of 75; theory of 76–77, 115
law of performative non-contradiction 180, 185, 187
Layder, Derek 56
leaps of faith 27, 31, 41, 44, 53
lessons, binding institutions 168–69
Lévi-Strauss, Claude 76–77
Lewis, J.D. 137, 139
linguistic model of structure 73
linguistic turn 2; and ideal types 31–41

literature, structure in 73–76
logic of appropriateness 173, 186–90, 201
logic of communication action 173–86, 201
logic of consequences 186–90, 201
logic of habit 173, 197–202
logic of practice 170–73, 190–97, 202
logic of without 49, 55, 57–61, 63, 128, 153, 166; *khôra* 62
logics of action: autoimmunity 201–2; undecidability 201–2
logocentrism 16
Loyal, Steven 84

Maeve, Cooke 174, 176
March, James G. 186
marks 77–78
marriage, as promise of mutual commitment 162
meaning differentiation 36
meaning, play of 35
messianicity 50
meta-narrative 4
metaphor 78–79
metaphysics of presence 16
methodologies, ideal types 42–43
Milem, Bruce 58
Miller, J. Hillis 91, 92, 93, 119
mind-world dualism 27, 42
mind-world monism 27, 42
minimal remainder 78
Möllering, Guido 137, 140
Morin, Marie-Eve 51
Mouffe, Chantal 118
multiculturalism 104
Muslims, in Western Europe 104–7
mutual commitment 161–66

Naas, Michael 87–89, 151
necessity 47
negation 58–59
negation/denegation 59
negative discourse 58
negative theology 57–61; *khôra* 62
negativity 57
negotiation 9, 94–95, 133–34, 210
neo-realism 15
neopositivism 42
Nietzsche, Friedrich 171
non-being 57, 63
non-closure 115
non-originarity 115
non-plenitude 36

Norris, Christopher 18, 48, 202
not speaking 58–59
now 11

Oakes, Guy 38–39
objectivity 38, 40
objects, transitive and intransitive 56
Olson, Johann, P. 186
ontological fallacy 56
ontologism, overview 54
ontology: need for 54; primacy 83
Onuf, Nicholas Greenwood 73
originary performative violence 158
originary performativity 85
othering 108, 124–27, 134; beyond *aporia* 127–32
'out-of-joint-ness' 118–24

paleonymics 18–19
parergon 66–69, 101
parergon/ergon distinction 68–69
parergonality 69; agent-structure problem and social theory 98–101
Pascal's Wager 43–44, 196–97, 202
passion 44–45
path-dependency 164–65
pathological 79
Patomäki, Heikki 64, 65–66
Pedersen, Jørgen 176, 177
performative 146; and event 85–86
performative contradiction 175, 177, 191
performative non-contradiction 172, 200
performative violence, binding and autoimmunity 158–66
performativity 5, 47, 85, 91–93
pervertibility: of promises 162–63; of trust 150
phenomenalism 27, 42
philosophical ontology 64–65
philosophy, position of 65
planes of social activity 74
Plato 48, 61–62
play 79, 80, 81, 115–16, 118
pluralism 29
'plus d'être' 60
politics of *aporia* 127–28; impossible 167; inherent chance 202; responsibility 128–30; and subject 130–32
polysemy 35
positive agency 199
positive ontology *see* ontologism
possibility 47, 52
possibilization 90

power, arbitrary exercise of 157–58
Power, Michael K. 177–78, 182
practice, concept of 190–93
pre-logical logic of practice 191–92
preconditions 179–80
premises, and presuppositions 30
presence 116
preservation 119
presuppositions 4, 30, 55
primordial supplementation 36, 122–23
process-based theorizing 83
promise of mutual commitment 161–66
promises 162–63
pseudo-concepts 3, 5, 11, 41, 55
pseudo-determinations, of *khôra* 61–62
public criticism 30
publication, limits and expectations 7–10
pure signifiers 77
purity, deprivation of 90
putting to rest 28–29

Ramadan, Tariq 109–12, 114, 133–35
rational reconstruction 176–77, 185, 187
rationalist theory 138–40, 151
rationality: of faith 43; of reality 40
re-grafting, signs 78
re-thinking 1, 3–4, 6
reactions, expectations of 7
reality: as 'out there' 56; rationality and irrationality 40–41
reason 47
reflexivity 42, 200
regime of truth 72
registration, of agency 85
relation of spectrality 85
relativism, Weber's rejection of 38–39
religion 46
repeatability, of promises 162–63
repetition, and change 119, 120–21
Rescher, Nicholas 43
research, enframing 65–69
responsibility: and decision 167–68; politics of *aporia* 128–30
restricted economy, of communicative action 184, 185
retroactive performativity 85
revealability, and revelation 48
revelation/revealability 48, 49–50
Rickert, Heinrich 39
right 189
Risse, Thomas 173–74
Rouse, Joseph 190

Russell Paradox 39
Ryba, Thomas 58

Saussure, Ferdinand de 11, 76–77, 115
saying the event 148–50, 164–65
'saying the non-being' 64
saying trust 150–51
Schweller, Randall A. 159
science 27–30
scientific claims, public criticism 30
Scott Appleby, R. 109
secrecy 51–52
self 83
self-citing 204–5, 206
self-contradiction 7
self-deconstruction 5
self-determination 131
self-inheritance 206–9
self-presence 131
self-referentiality 75
self-repetition 131
Sending, Ole Jacob 187
Sharia 110
signification 123
signifiers 77
signifying concepts 36
signs 76–78
Simmel, Georg 140
simulacra 52
snags 35, 121
social cube 74
social theory: and agent-structure problem 98–101; necessity of ontology 54–55
sovereign subject 83–84
sovereignty 84–85, 87–90, 208
spectrality 40, 41, 85, 87, 142
speech-act theory 92, 174
Spivak, Gyatri 81
St. Augustine 49, 59
structuralism 76–77, 79–80
'structuralist' moment 80
structurality 79–81
structure: in IR literature 73–76; of texts 205–6; through deconstruction 76–81
subject, politics of *aporia* 130–32
sublation 119
suicide 208
supplementarity 36, 37, 41, 122–24, 128, 131, 201
supplementation 122–23, 134, 185
supplements 4

survival 205–6
suspension 140–41

tacit knowledge 190
Taylor, Charles 190
telos 37
temptation of knowledge 47
testimonial faith 41–53
testimony 29, 51
texts: deconstruction 103–4; structure of 205–6
theology, negative 57–61
theories 1–2, 8
theorizing, re-thinking 6
theory of communicative action 174–75, 187
theory of language, Saussure 76–77, 115
Tibi, Bassam 107–9, 110–12, 114, 133–35
Timaeus 48, 61–62
time 10–11
total solution 28
totalization 79
traces 11, 35, 41, 77–78, 80, 81, 90, 116–17, 119, 124, 134, 167; of habit 201; iterability of 185
traditional behavior 197–98
transcendental analysis 181
transfactualism 27, 42
transitive objects 56
translation 15–16
tripartite notion of agency 81, 82
trust 148–50; autoimmunity 151–52; hetero-knowledge theory 137, 140–41, 143; as-if element 137, 143–51, 152–53, 154; as-if gesture 143–48; overview 136–37; possibility of failure 150; rationalist theory 138–40, 151; saying trust 150–51; theories of 138–41; and uncertainty 138; undecidability and decision 141–43; and vulnerability 138, 139; without trust 153–55
Turner, Stephen 190

un-experienced experience 183
uncertainty, and trust 138
unconditional, contamination of 86–87
unconditional event 85–90
undecidability 37, 39–40, 53, 72, 75, 83, 89, 103, 127, 128; and decision 141–43, 167–68; identity and difference 112–14; logics of action 201–2
urgency 95

Vaihinger, Hans 145
value-judgements 36
value relevance 38–39, 40, 42
Veblen, Thorstein 199
Velchik, Michael 43
via negativae 195–96
violence 37, 93–94; originary performative 160–61
vulnerability, and trust 138, 139

wager-based miraculous science 41–53
wagers 27–28, 42–44, 65, 69 *see also* Pascal's Wager
Walker, R.B. 55
Waltz, Kenneth 15, 79
Ware, Owen 48, 50, 118
Weber, Max 144, 197–98; as inspiration 29–31 *see also* ideal types
Weigert, A. 137, 139
Wendt, Alexander 55, 71, 73
Wight, Colin 55, 64, 65, 71, 73–75, 81–84, 95–97, 98–101
Wittgenstein, Ludwig 189
working hypothesis 45
Wright, Colin 55ff
writing 5; as deconstruction 19; difficulty of 15; expectations of 203–4; motivation for 24–25

'you have to believe me' 50–51

Zagare, Frank C. 170–73
Zehfuss, Maja 13
Zemni, Sami 104
Žižek, Slavoj 221, 223

For Product Safety Concerns and Information please contact our EU
representative GPSR@taylorandfrancis.com
Taylor & Francis Verlag GmbH, Kaufingerstraße 24, 80331 München, Germany

www.ingramcontent.com/pod-product-compliance
Lightning Source LLC
Chambersburg PA
CBHW070600300426
44113CB00010B/1336